Checking on the Progression of Ideas

(Chapter 2)

✔ Does my thesis statement accurately reflect the content of my paper? If not, what changes should I make? Delete or redo stray material? Alter the thesis statement?

✔ Have I included all information that will help the reader grasp my meaning?

✔ Does my writing flow logically and smoothly from one point to the next?

Strengthening Paragraph Structure and Development

(Chapter 8)

✔ Does each paragraph have only one central idea?

✔ Is the idea stated in a topic sentence or clearly implied?

✔ Does the topic sentence help to develop the thesis statement?

✔ Do the sentences within each paragraph advance the topic sentence?

✔ Is each paragraph appropriately organized?

✔ Is the relationship between successive sentences clear?

✔ Does each paragraph contain enough supporting detail?

✔ Is each paragraph clearly and smoothly related to those that precede and follow it?

Clarifying Sentences and Words

(Chapters 9 and 10)

✔ Are my sentences clearly and effectively constructed?

✔ Have I varied the pattern and length of my sentences?

✔ Do I know the meanings of the words I use?

✔ Do I explain meanings my reader may not know?

✔ Have I used the appropriate tone and level of diction?

✔ Does/would figurative language enhance my style?

✔ Have I avoided wordiness, euphemisms, clichés, and mixed metaphors?

Correcting Misuse of English

(Handbook)

✔ Have I inspected my writing for the types of errors listed in the revision symbols on the back endpapers?

STRATEGIES FOR SUCCESSFUL WRITING

James A. Reinking
Andrew W. Hart

Ferris State College

PRENTICE-HALL, Englewood Cliffs, New Jersey 07632

Library of Congress Cataloging-in-Publication Data

REINKING, JAMES A.
  Strategies for successful writing.

  Includes index.
  1. English language—Rhetoric. 2. English language—
Grammar—1940-   I. HART, ANDREW W., 1921-
II. Title.
PE1408.R426 1986   808'.042   85-19218
ISBN 0-13-851460-7

Editorial/production supervision: Virginia Rubens
Interior design: Levavi & Levavi
Manufacturing buyer: Harry P. Baisley

ISBN 0-13-851460-7   01

ACKNOWLEDGMENTS

R. T. Allen, "The Porcupine," from *Children, Wives, and Other Wildlife* by Robert Thomas Allen. Copyright ©
  1970 by Robert Thomas Allen. N.Y.: Doubleday, 1970.
Bonnie Angelo, "Those Good Ole Boys," *Time*, Sept. 27, 1976, p. 47.
Maya Angelou, "Grandmother's Encounters," in *I Know Why the Caged Bird Sings* (New York: Random House,
  1969), p. 26.
"Antigen," *Encyclopaedia Britannica*, 1974, I, 417.
Carl Becker, *Freedom and Responsibility in the American Way of Life* (N.Y.: Vintage-Knopf, 1945).
Eric Berne, *A Layman's Guide to Psychiatry and Psychoanalysis*, © 1947, 1957, 1968 by Eric Berne. Reprinted by
  permission of Simon & Schuster, Inc.
Bruno Bettelheim, "Joey: A 'Mechanical Boy,'" *Scientific American* March 1959, p. 122.

(*Acknowledgments continue on page 488, which constitutes an extension of the copyright page.*)

For Scott

Contents

Part II: WRITING STRATEGIES

Part IV: SPECIAL TYPES OF WRITING

Part III: BUILDING BLOCKS

Part V: HANDBOOK

Preface

Strategies For Successful Writing is a comprehensive rhetoric–handbook that offers ample material for a full year of freshman composition. Instructors teaching a one-term course can make selections from chapters 1–10 and from whatever types of specialized writing suit the needs of their students. Our approach is traditional but is tempered by an awareness of recent thinking about the writing process. The process, however, does not become its own objective, overwhelming and intimidating students.

Because we strongly believe that a composition textbook should be written to the student, we have aimed for a style that is informal without being condescending, conversational yet clear and concise. We believe that our style invites students into the book, lessens their apprehensions about writing, and provides a model for their own prose.

The text follows a logical whole-to-parts sequence comprising five parts. The opening section provides an overview of basic writing considerations. The next three focus on the different writing patterns, the elements—paragraphs, sentences, words—that make up compositions, and specialized kinds of writing. The final section is a comprehensive handbook. Each part offers a variety of exercises that reinforce points in our discussion and expand assignment options.

Part I, "The Basics," includes two chapters. Chapter 1, "Writing: A First Look," introduces students to the purposes of writing, the qualities of good writing, and audience awareness. Chapter 2 looks at the composing process. After preliminary remarks on understanding the assignment, we explore several strategies for focusing on a suitable topic as well as several ways of generating support for it. Next, we look at the requirements of a good thesis statement and then at organizing information by means of an informal outline. Finally, we discuss writing the first draft and then revising it, posing several sets of questions that serve as revision guidelines. To make the different stages more concrete, an unfolding case history gradually evolves into the first draft and final version of a student paper. Marginal notes highlight key features of the finished product.

The five chapters in Part II, "Writing Strategies," feature the different modes, or patterns, for developing papers. We discuss every pattern clearly and completely, to enhance students' understanding and facilitate their writing efforts. The patterns are presented as natural ways of thinking and therefore as effective ways of organizing writing. Except for argument, which rates a separate chapter, patterns are paired according to function, an approach that helps students grasp their utility and importance. Chapter 3 focuses on exploring time, space, and events by means of narration and description, Chapter 4 on showing relationships through classification and comparison, Chapter 5 on explaining how and why through process analysis and cause and effect, and Chapter 6 on achieving clarity with illustration and definition. Chapter 7 shows how to convince others through argument. Instructors who favor different pairings or another sequence will find it easy to mix and match patterns as they choose.

The discussion in each chapter follows a similar approach. We first explore the key elements of each pattern and then provide concise but thorough writing guidelines. The discussion concludes with a handy revision checklist, which highlights main points for students to remember. Two complete essays, one student and one professional, follow the discussion of each pattern. The student essays represent realistic, achievable goals and spur confidence, while the professional ones broaden students' understanding by displaying a wide range of styles, tones, and subject matter. The questions that follow each essay reinforce the general principles of good writing as well as the key points we make in our discussions. For some instructors these essays will make a separate reader unnecessary. Each chapter ends with fifteen writing suggestions.

In Part III, "Building Blocks," we shift from full-length essays to the elements that make them up. Chapter 8, "Paragraphs," first discusses the function and positioning of the topic sentence; then the characteristics of effective paragraphs—unity, organization, coherence, and adequate development; and finally introductory, transitional, and concluding paragraphs. Throughout this chapter, as elsewhere, carefully chosen examples and exercises form an integral part of the instruction.

In Chapter 9, "Effective Sentences," we briefly review sentence parts and then move to various strategies for writing effective sentences. Here we consider word order in independent clauses, coordinating and subordinating ideas, positioning modifiers to create loose, periodic, and interrupted sentences, and the use of parallelism, verb voice, and fragments. The concluding section, "Beyond the Single Sentence," offers practical advice on crafting and arranging sentences so they work together harmoniously.

Chapter 10, "Diction, Tone, Style," deals with words and the effect they create. After an opening caveat on the importance of selecting words with the right meaning, we distinguish between abstract and concrete words as well as between specific and general terms. This part also includes a discussion of the dictionary and thesaurus. The next part, on rhetorical effect, explains levels of diction and tone as well as how to use them. The third part, "Special Stylistic Techniques," covers various types of figurative language and irony. The final part focuses on recognizing and avoiding wordiness, euphemisms, clichés, and mixed metaphors.

Part IV, "Special Types of Writing," concentrates on four specialized types of college and on-the-job writing. Chapter 11, "The Essay Examination," offers useful advice on studying for exams, assessing test questions, and writing exams. To help students write properly focused and developed responses, we analyze three answers (two poor, one good) to the same exam question. For reinforcement, we include exercises that require students to analyze a good answer and judge two responses to a question.

Chapter 12, "Writing About Literature," uses Stephen Crane's "The Bride Comes to Yellow Sky" as a springboard for its discussions. The chapter focuses on plot, narrator and point of view, character, setting, symbols, irony, language, and theme—the elements students will most likely be asked to deal with. For each element, we first present basic features and then offer writing guidelines. The chapter ends with general tips for writing about literature and a sample paper that analyzes a character in "The Bride."

Chapter 13, "The Library Research Paper," is a thorough and practical guide to writing the research paper. Our presentation includes seven stages: learning about the library, choosing a topic, assembling a working bibliography, taking notes, organizing and outlining, acknowledging and handling sources properly, and writing the paper. In response to reviewer suggestions, we have given special emphasis to recognizing and avoiding plagiarism, introducing quotations, and documenting source material. The documentation style described in Chapter 13 is the 1984 MLA system. Instructors who prefer to have students use footnotes or endnotes will find this system discussed in the appendix. As in Chapter 2, a progressive case history gradually evolves into a first draft and final version of a student paper: "Robots in Industry: A Boon for Everyone." Marginal notes on the final version indicate changes made during revision. Our detailed treatment should make supplemental handouts or a separate research paper guide unnecessary.

Chapter 14, "Business Letters and Résumés," speaks to a practical reality by reminding students that the value of writing extends beyond the English classroom. We begin by pointing out the features of successful letter language, then discuss the parts of the business letter and preparations for mailing. The final part explains and illustrates letters of inquiry, order letters, complaint letters, job application letters, and personal data sheets. The example letters address a variety of situations—requesting information for a classroom project, ordering household appliances, asking that a faulty order be replaced, finding a job—that suggest the utility of these kinds of writing.

Part V is a comprehensive handbook that consists of six parts: "Sentence

Elements," "Sentence Errors," "Punctuation and Mechanics," "Spelling," "Glossary of Word Usage," and "Glossary of Grammatical Terms." Explanations skirt unneeded grammatical terminology and are reinforced by exercises in the first three parts. The spelling unit presents four useful spelling rules and an extensive list of commonly misspelled words. The glossary of word usage offers similarly comprehensive coverage of troublesome usages. The glossary of grammatical terms includes brief definitions of terms discussed in detail earlier in the handbook, together with page numbers directing users to the expanded discussions. Instructors can use the handbook either as a reference guide or as a basis for class discussion.

Our instructor's manual, *Strategies for Successful Teaching,* provides answers to all the discussion questions and, where appropriate, to the exercises. In addition, for those instructors charting their approach or refining their direction, Professor Roxanne Cullen has helped us prepare a smorgasbord of possible approaches to teaching freshman composition, including such options as teacher-centered and student-centered classrooms, peer editing, and workshop writing. In addition, she discusses various ways of assessing writing, provides a selected bibliography of books and articles which may interest composition teachers, and offers useful suggestions for teaching each part of the text.

Like other textbook writers, we are indebted to many people. Our colleagues at Ferris State College and elsewhere assisted us in numerous ways: criticizing portions of the manuscript, testing approaches and exercises in their classrooms, suggesting examples to include, and helping with library research. They include Sandy Balkema, Arthur Bennett, Mary Braun, Ann Breitenwischer, John Caserta, Ada Lou Carson, Roxanne Cullen, Paul Devlin, Joe Dugas, Hugh Griffith, Don Hanzek, Fred Howting, Marvin Mengeling, Elaine Nienhouse, and Elliott Smith. We are also grateful to the many reviewers, too numerous to mention, whose penetrating comments on each draft helped a manuscript gradually evolve into a book. Many thanks also to Maurine Lewis and our friends at Prentice-Hall, whose editorial expertise and congenial guidance were vital to this project: Phil Miller, Joyce Perkins, and Virginia Rubens. We would be remiss if we didn't mention our typists, particularly Emma Crystal, Coleen Hunsanger, Becky Jacobs, Karen Rynearson, and Sally Walton, who were ever helpful in meeting deadlines. Finally, we'd like to thank Paul Hart for his generous help with cartoons, and St. Martin's Press for allowing us to incorporate material from our textbook *Writing for Career-Education Students* into this book.

J.A.R.
A.W.H.

STRATEGIES
FOR
SUCCESSFUL
WRITING

CHAPTER ONE

Writing

A FIRST LOOK

Why write? Hasn't the tempest of technology swept all of us into a brave new electronic world? Aren't its telephones, portable cassette recorders, and computer networks—all the magical devices of our new electronic estate—fast dooming ordinary writing? Not long ago, some people thought and said so, but events haven't supported those predictions. Although electronic devices have made some writing unnecessary, the written word flourishes both on campus and in the world of work. Furthermore, there's every evidence that writing will become even more important in the future.

Writing offers very real advantages to both writers and readers:

1. It provides a permanent record of thoughts, actions, and decisions.
2. It makes communications more precise and effective.
3. It saves the reader's time; we absorb information more swiftly when we read it than when we hear it.

Many people will expect you to write for them. College instructors ask you to write reports, term papers, and essay exams. Job hunting usually requires you to write application letters. And once you're hired, writing will probably figure in your duties. Science, engineering, business, and law certainly require frequent writing, but so do other occupations. If you work as a police officer, you'll be expected to file a report on every accident and crime you investigate. Similarly, if your field is public health, reporting on the inspections you have carried out and the tests you have performed will be an important part of your duties. And if you're an elementary school teacher, you'll need to maintain records of your students' progress. The ability to write will earn you better grades, help you get the job you want, and speed your advancement afterwards.

THE PURPOSES OF WRITING

Whenever you write, you need some clear purpose to guide both you and your reader. If you don't know why you're writing, neither will your reader. Fulfilling an assignment doesn't qualify as a real writing purpose, although it may well be what sends you to your desk. Faced with a close deadline for a term paper or an on-the-job report, you may tell yourself, "I'm doing this because I have to." To have an authentic purpose, however, you must be able to answer this question: What do I want this piece of writing to do for my reader and myself? Here are four common *general writing purposes,* two or more of which often join forces in a single piece:

1. To Inform.   Presenting information is one of the most common writing purposes. The boating enthusiast who tells landlubber classmates how to handle a skiff plays the role of teacher, as does the researcher who summarizes the results of an investigation for co-workers. Some professional writers carve careers out of writing articles and books that fill gaps in the public's knowledge. These writers investigate timely topics, become short-term experts, and pass along their findings in an easily understood form. Instructors often ask you to write exams and papers so that they can gauge your academic progress. The information you provide shows them how well you have mastered the course material.

2. To Persuade.   You probably have strong views on many issues, and your feelings may sometimes impel you to try swaying the reader. In a letter to your fellow townspeople, you might attack a proposal to establish a nearby chemical waste dump. Or alarmed by a sharp jump in state unemployment, you might write to your state senator and argue for a new job-training program.

3. To Express Yourself.   Creative writing includes personal essays, fiction, plays, and poetry, as well as journals and diaries. But self-expression has a place in other kinds of writing too. Almost everything you write provides the opportunity to display your personality and mastery of words and to enliven your prose with vivid images and fresh turns of phrase.

4. To Entertain.   Some writing is meant just to entertain; other writing couples entertainment with a more serious purpose. A light-hearted approach to dull or difficult material can help your reader to absorb it. Satire lets you expose the shortcomings of individuals, ideas, and institutions by poking fun at them. An intention to entertain can add savor to many kinds of written messages.

Besides having one or more *general purposes,* each writing project has its own *specific purpose.* For instance, you may argue the advantages of owning a solar home, explain why some people join religious cults, express your feelings about conformity, or satirize a presidential candidate's views.

Having a specific purpose helps you make decisions at every stage of the writing process. It helps you define your audience, since the needs and interests of your readers govern what you say and how you say it. Moreover, it helps you to select the right details, to organize your material effectively, and to avoid going off in directions that won't interest your reader.

The following example from *Newsweek* magazine has a clear, specific purpose.

The Costs of Going 55
CHARLES A. LAVE

The campaign to educate us about the benefits of the 55-mph limit has been strident and persistent. Somehow this new wonder drug, the 55 limit, is supposed to cure our national energy problem, save lives and cause us all to pursue a more virtuous existence. But wonder drugs often have unfortunate side effects, and this one is no exception. I want to focus your attention on some of these undesirable side effects.

The major cost associated with the 55-mph limit is an enormous chunk of wasted travel time. Specifically, it costs about 102 man-years of extra travel time to save one life. In contrast to this considerable cost, the energy savings associated with the 55-mph limit are so trivial that we could get about the same conservation effect by simply assuring that everyone kept his tires properly inflated. (Consider the whimsical implications of this fact: imagine an elite sidewalk Pressure Patrol, armed with air gauges, ticketing cars for low pressure.)

There is another way of evaluating the costly side effects of the 55-mph wonder drug: the value of time. The principle is simple: time is money, and studies have shown that commuters are willing to pay up to 42 percent of an hour's wage to save an hour of travel time. Thus, when transportation analysts measure the benefits of new subway systems, like BART or METRO, they count up the number of travel hours that would be saved by the transit improvement, and then multiply by the value of time to compute a dollar measure of the benefits. The same principle can also be used to assign a dollar cost to the extra travel time caused by slowing down traffic. When we do this we find that the 55-mph limit causes enough of a traffic slowdown to waste about $6 billion worth of travel time per year.

The National Highway Traffic Safety Administration says we save about 4,500 lives per year because of the 55-mph limit. Hence, it costs about $1.3 million per life saved. Is this a bargain, or are there other social policies that might save more lives for less money? Well, it has been estimated that placing a smoke detector in every home in the U.S. would save about as many lives in total as the 55-mph limit, and would cost only $50,000 to $80,000 per life saved; or more kidney-dialysis machines could save lives for only about $30,000 per life; or additional mobile cardiac-care units cost only about $2,000 per life saved; and there are even a great number of highway improvements that can be made, through reducing roadside hazards, which cost only about $20,000 to $100,000 per life saved. At a cost of $1.3 million per saved life, the 55-mph limit is hardly a bargain.

For a more humane way of calculating the cost of the 55-mph limit, we might compare the 2,710 million extra travel hours (from lower travel speeds) to the reduction in fatalities. This shows that it costs 102 man-years of wasted time to save one life. Yes, that means 102 years of extra time riding around in your automobile in order to save one life. Now, I confess to some trouble keeping up with the latest theological notions as to the nature of hell, but 102 years traveling in an automobile fits my personal notion of that place rather closely. . . .

At the outset, the author hints at his purpose by using a title that suggests a negative aspect of the 55-mph speed limit: cost. The last sentence of the first paragraph states the purpose explicitly. The remaining paragraphs show the costs of obeying the speed limit and suggest less costly ways of reducing highway deaths and saving energy. Everything Lave has written relates to his purpose.

Now examine the next paragraph, which does *not* have a firmly fixed specific purpose.

Community is a sea in which people swim unconsciously, like fish. We fail to recognize our neighbors as fellow humans, and they show the same lack of fellow-feelings for us. A complete lack of concern for one another is evident in today's complex society. What is community? Is it a plant? A building? A place? A state of being? Knowing what it is, we can see if such a place exists. To know community, one must realize who he or she is. Identity of a person is the first step in establishing a community.

This writer can't decide what aspect of community to tackle. The opening sentence suggests an attempt at a definition, but the next two veer onto the shortcomings of the modern community. Notice also how aimlessly the thoughts drift. The vague leadoff sentence asserts "Community is a sea . . . ," but the later question "What is community?" negates this opening. Furthermore, if community is a plant, a building, or a place, why must we realize who we are in order to know it? This contradictory and illogical paragraph reveals a writer groping for a purpose.

The paragraph, however, isn't a wasted effort. These initial musings offer several possibilities. By zeroing in on and developing the first sentence, the writer might show some very interesting similarities between community and a sea. By pursuing the idea in the second and third sentences, he might show the callous nature of modern society. The last two sentences might lead to a statement on the relationship between individual and community. A specific purpose can sometimes emerge from preliminary jottings.

THE QUALITIES OF GOOD WRITING

Three qualities—freshness, a sense of style, and effective organization—help to ensure that a piece of prose will meet your reader's expectations.

1. Freshness.   Fresh writing either relates something new or handles old ideas in a new way. Genuinely original ideas and information are scarce commodities, but you can find new meaning in old materials and relate old material to an unexpected topic. Keep the expression of your ideas credible, however; far-fetched notions spawn skepticism.

2. Sense of Style.   Readers don't expect you to write with the stylistic flair of Erma Bombeck or Art Buchwald. Indeed, such writing would impair the neutral tone needed in certain kinds of writing—technical reports and legal documents, for example. Readers *do,* nevertheless, expect you to write in a style that conveys your message clearly. And if you strengthen your style with vigorous, forceful words, readers will absorb your points with even greater interest. The chapters ahead show you how to use language in ways that are in keeping with your own views and personality. Chapters 9 and 10, in particular, will help you develop a sense of style in your writing, as will the many readings throughout the book.

3. Effective Organization.   A paper should have a beginning, a middle, and an end; that is, an introduction, a body, and a conclusion. The introduction sparks interest and acquaints the reader with what's to come. The body, organized in a clear and effective fashion, delivers the main message. The conclusion ends the discussion so the reader feels satisfied rather than suddenly cut off. Organizational patterns, or strategies of development, are the subject of Part II. Pages 169–175 discuss introductions and conclusions.

Freshness, style, and organization are weighted differently in different kinds of writing. An employer who asks you to write a contract proposal for paving a city's streets will probably attach less importance to freshness than to clear writing and careful organization. On the other hand, freshness is paramount if you're describing an autumn forest scene. You will learn more about these qualities throughout this book.

THE AUDIENCE FOR YOUR WRITING

Everything you write is aimed at some audience—a person or group of people you want to reach. The ultimate purpose of all writing is to have an effect on a reader (even if that reader is you), and therefore purpose and audience are closely linked. Our earlier discussion makes this point clear by indicating that purpose can be to inform *someone* of something, to persuade *someone* to believe or do something, to express feelings or insights to *someone*, or to entertain *someone*. Any of these objectives requires that you *know* that someone, the audience for your writing.

Writing operates on a delayed-action fuse, detonating its ideas in the readers' minds at another time and place. Sometimes problems follow. In face-to-face conversations, you can observe your listener's reactions from moment to moment, and whenever you note signs of hostility, boredom, or puzzlement, you can alter your tone, offer some examples, or ask a question. You can also use gestures and facial expressions to emphasize what you're saying. When you write, however, the words on the page carry your message. Once written work has left your hands, it's on its own. You can't call it back to clear up a misunderstanding or satisfy a disgruntled reader.

Establishing rapport with your audience is easy when the writing is aimed at your friends or someone else you know a great deal about. You can judge the likely response to what you say. Often, though, your writing will be directed to people you know only casually or not at all: employers, customers, fellow townsfolk, and the like. In such situations, you'll need to assess your audience before starting to write.

A good way to size up your readers is to develop an audience profile. This profile will emerge gradually as you answer the following questions:

1. What is the educational level, age, social class, and economic status of the audience I want to reach?
2. Why will this audience read my writing? To gain information? Learn my views on a controversial issue? Enjoy my creative flair? Be entertained?
3. What attitudes, needs, and expectations do they have?

4. How are they likely to respond to what I say? Can I expect them to be neutral? Opposed? Friendly?
5. How much do they know about my topic? (Your answer here will help you gauge whether you're saying too little or too much.)
6. What kind of language will communicate with them most effectively? (See "Level of Diction" section in Chapter 10.)

As this profile suggests, an audience may be general or specialized. College writing assignments often ask you to envision a general reader—one who is intelligent but lacking specialized knowledge of your topic, receptive but unwilling to put up with boring or trite material. At other times, you'll be asked to write for a specialized audience—one with some expertise in your topic. Clearly, this difference will affect what you say to each audience and how you say it.

Let's see how audience can shape a paper. Suppose you are writing an explanation of how to take a certain type of X-ray. If your audience is a group of general readers who have never had an X-ray, you might note at the outset that taking one is much like taking an ordinary photograph. Then you might explain the basic process, including the positioning of the patient and the equipment, comment on the safety and reliability of the procedure, and note how much time it takes. You probably would use few technical terms. If, however, you were writing for radiology students, you might emphasize exposure factors, film size, and required views. This audience would understand technical terms and want a detailed explanation of the procedure. You could speak to these readers as colleagues who appreciate precise information.

Audience shapes all types of writing in similar fashion, even your personal writing. Assume you've recently become engaged, and to share your news you write two letters: one to your clergyman, the other to your best friend back home. You can imagine the differences in details, language, and general tone of each letter. Further, think how inappropriate it would be if you inadvertently sent the letter intended for one to the other. Clearly, different readers call for different approaches.

EXERCISE

The three excerpts below deal with the same subject—antigens—but each explanation is geared to a different audience. Read the passages carefully; then answer the following questions:

1. What audience does each author address? How do you know?
2. Identify ways in which each author appeals to a specific audience.

1.   The human body is quick to recognize foreign chemicals that enter it. "Foes" must be attacked or otherwise got rid of. The most common of these foes are chemical materials from viruses, bacteria, and other microscopic organisms. Such chemicals, when recognized by the body, are called *antigens*. To combat them, the body produces its own chemicals, protein molecules called *antibodies*. Each kind of antigen causes the production of a specific kind of antibody. Antibodies appear in the body fluids such as blood and lymph and in the body's cells.

L.D. Hamilton, "Antibodies and Antigens,"
The New Book of Knowledge

2.   [An] *Antigen* [is a] foreign substance that, when introduced into the body, is capable of inducing the formation of antibodies and of reacting specifically in a detectable manner with the induced antibodies. For each antigen there is a specific antibody, the physical and chemical structure of which is produced in response to the physical and chemical structure of the antigen. Antigens comprise virtually all proteins that are foreign to the host, including those contained in bacteria, viruses, protozoa, helminths, foods, snake venoms, egg white, serum components, red blood cells, and other cells and tissues of various species, including man. Polysaccharides and lipids may also act as antigens when coupled to proteins.

"Antigen," *Encyclopaedia Britannica*

3.   The substance which stimulates the body to produce antibodies is designated *antigen* (antibody stimulator). . . .

Most complete antigens are protein molecules containing aromatic amino acids, and are large in molecular weight and size. However, it has been demonstrated that other macromolecules, such as pure polysaccharides, polynucleotides, and lipids, may serve as complete antigens.

However, certain other materials, incapable of stimulating antibody formation by themselves can, in association with a protein or other carrier, stimulate antibody formation and are the antigenic determinants. These determinants are referred to as *incomplete antigens* or *haptens* and they are able to react with antibodies which were produced by the determinant-protein complex.

However, before an antigen can stimulate the production of antibodies, it must be soluble in the body fluids, must reach certain tissues in an unaltered form, and must be, in general, foreign to the body tissues. Protein taken by mouth loses its specific foreign-protein characteristics when digested in the alimentary tract. It reaches the tissues of the body as amino acids or other altered digested products of protein. Consequently, it no longer meets the requirements for antigenic behavior.

Orville Wyss and Curtis Eklund,
Microorganisms and Man

Just as you would not dial a telephone number at random and then expect to carry on a meaningful conversation, so you should not expect to communicate effectively without a specific audience in mind.

Several times in this chapter we've referred to your audience, the final target of your writing. But it's also important that your writing please you, too—that it satisfy your sense of what good writing is and what the writing task requires. You are, after all, your own first reader.

CHAPTER TWO

The Writing Process

Many students believe that good essays are dashed off in a burst of inspiration by "born writers." Students themselves often boast that they cranked out their topnotch papers in an hour or so of spare time. Perhaps. But for most of us, writing is primarily a skill we can learn and a process we can master, though natural ability and even "inspiration" may sometimes help.

Although successful writers can often describe the way they go about their work, writing is a flexible process. No one order guarantees success, and no one approach works for every writer. Some writers establish a firm purpose and draft a detailed plan for carrying it out at the start of every project. Others begin with a tentative purpose or plan and discover their final direction as they write. As a project proceeds, the writer is likely to leapfrog backward and forward one or more times rather than to proceed in an orderly, straightforward sequence. Part way through a first draft, for instance, a writer may think of a new point to present, then pause and jot down the details needed to develop it. Similarly, part of the conclusion may come to mind as the writer is gathering the necessary details for supporting a key idea.

Regardless of how it unfolds, the writing process consists of the following stages. Advancing through each stage will guide you if you have no plan or if you've run into snags with your approach. Once you're familiar with them, you can combine or rearrange them to suit your needs.

> Understanding the assignment
> Zeroing in on a topic
> Gathering support
> Developing a thesis statement
> Organizing the information
> Writing the first draft
> Revising the essay

UNDERSTANDING THE ASSIGNMENT

Different instructors adopt different approaches in making writing assignments. Some instructors provide a specific topic, some favor a choice among several topics, and some allow free choice. Some assignments dictate the length and format of the essay; others leave those choices up to you. Whatever the case, be sure you understand the assignment before you go any further.

Think of it this way. If your employer asked you to report on how working conditions in your office should be improved and you turned in a report on how workers' fringe benefits could be improved, would you expect your employer's approval? Following directions is crucial in any writing project. If you have any questions about the assignment, ask your instructor to clear them up then and there. Don't be timid: it's much better to ask than to receive a low grade for failing to follow directions.

ZEROING IN ON A TOPIC

A subject is a broad area for discussion: sports, college life, popular culture, and the like. A topic is one small segment of a subject; for example, the 1919 World Series, Nirvana College's academic probation policy, the demise of discos. To create an effective essay, you need a topic narrow enough to develop fully and interestingly within the length limitation. You can treat a narrow topic in depth instead of stringing out a series of boring generalities about too general an issue.

GENERAL GUIDELINES

If you choose your own topic, pick one that you know something about or can learn enough about in the time available. Avoid old, chewed-over chestnuts like arguments about the use of marijuana, abortion, or open visitation in college dormitories. With few exceptions, papers on these topics rehash the same old points. For example, nearly every case for legalizing marijuana contends that it's no more harmful than alcohol, quotes an expert who maintains that it's not addictive, and argues that blocking legalization does not prevent use. Such familiar arguments won't spark your reader's interest.

To enliven any topic, bring to it your own perspective, your perceptions and thoughts, directed as always toward a particular audience. Aim for originality by giving the material your own special slant.

STRATEGIES FOR FINDING A TOPIC

Whenever your instructor assigns a general subject, you'll need to stake out a limited topic suitable for your paper. If you're lucky, the right one might come to mind immediately. More often, though, you'll need to resort to some special strategy for finding a topic. Here are five proven strategies from which to choose.

Tapping Your Personal Resources.   Personal experience furnishes a rich storehouse of writing material. Over the years, you've packed your mind with a host of memories: family gatherings, school activities, movies, concerts, plays, parties, TV programs, dates, discussions, arguments, and so on. Maybe you've even recorded the more memorable happenings in a diary. All these experiences create beliefs or feelings or expose you to facts that provide suitable writing topics. Suppose you've been asked to write on some aspect of education. Recalling the difficulties you had last term in registering for a full slate of courses, you might choose to write about revamped registration procedures. Or if you're a hopeless TV addict who must find a narrow topic in the broad subject of advertising, why not put your observations to work by analyzing TV advertising techniques?

Anything you've read in magazines or journals, newspapers, novels, short stories, or textbooks can also trigger a topic in your mind. O. Henry's short story "The Last Leaf," in which a character almost dies of pneumonia, might suggest a paper on some miracle drug or a bout of illness you had. An article reviewing the career of a well-known politician might lead to thoughts of a friend's experience in running for the student council. Possibilities crowd our lives, waiting for us to recognize and seize them.

Select five of the subjects listed below. Tapping your personal resources, name one topic suggested by each. For each topic, list three questions that some reading would help you answer.   **EXERCISE**

1. Life on a city street
2. A particular field of work
3. Some branch of the federal bureaucracy
4. Concern for some aspect of the environment
5. Parents
6. Saving money
7. A best-selling book
8. Some aspect of nature
9. Marriage
10. Contemporary forms of dancing
11. The energy crisis
12. Fashions in clothing
13. Trendiness
14. Human rights

15. Home ownership
16. Schools in your town
17. Leisure activities
18. The two-income family

19. Public transportation
20. Childhood fears
21. A new scientific discovery
22. A religious experience

Sorting Out a Subject.   All of us sort things. We do it whenever we tackle the laundry, clear away a sinkful of dishes, or tidy up a basement or garage. Let's see how we might handle a cluttered basement. To start off, we'd probably sort the contents according to type: books in one spot, clothing in a second, toys in a third. That done, chances are we'd do still more sorting, separating children's books from adults' and stuffed animals from games. As we looked over and handled the different items, long-buried, bittersweet memories might start flooding from our subconscious. Memories of an uncle, now dead, who sent this old adventure novel . . . of our parents' pride when they saw their child had learned to ride that now battered bicycle . . . of the dance that marked the debut of the evening gown over there.

Sorting out a subject follows a similar scenario. First, we break our broad subject into categories and subcategories, then allow our minds to rove over the different items and see what topics we can turn up. The chart on page 17 shows what one student found when she explored the general topic of public transportation.

As you'll discover for yourself, some subjects yield more topics than others; some, no topics at all.

EXERCISE   **Select two of the following subjects; then subdivide those two into five topics.**

Advertising	Popular music
Dwellings	Social classes
Fashions	The space program
Magazines	Sports
Movies	Television programs
Occupations	Vacations

Asking Questions.   Often, working your way through the following set of basic questions will lead you to a manageable topic.

1. Can I define my subject?
2. Does it break into categories?

Land			Water		Air	
Buses	Taxis	Trains	Sea-going	Lake, River	Airplanes	Helicopters
County bus services for the handicapped	Rights of passengers	The Orient Express, the Twentieth Century Limited	The Titanic		Air traffic controllers' strike	Air taxis
Bus tours	Preventing crimes against drivers	Monorails	Luxury liners		Overbooking flights	Cargo
Jitney buses		Preventing subway crimes	Theme cruises		Making air travel safer	
Problem of smoking on buses		Guardian Angels	Modern sea pirates		Coping with hijacking	
Improving bus terminals		Amtrak	Traveling by freighter		Causes and prevention of jet lag	
Designing buses to accommodate the handicapped		Japan's high-speed trains	The impact of overseas flights on ship travel		Development of the Concorde	
		Deterioration of railroad trackbeds			Noise pollution around airports	

3. If so, what comparisons can I make among these categories?
4. If my subject is divided into parts, how do they work together?
5. Does my subject have uses? What are they?
6. What are some examples of my subject?
7. What are the causes or origins of my subject?
8. What impact has my subject had?

Let's convert these general questions into specific questions about telescopes, a broad general subject:

1. What is a telescope?
2. What are the different kinds of telescopes?
3. How are they alike? How do they differ?
4. What are the parts of each kind of telescope, and how do they work together?
5. What are telescopes used for?
6. What are some well-known telescopes?
7. Who invented the telescope?
8. What impact have telescopes had on human life and knowledge?

Each of these questions offers a starting point for a suitably focused essay. Question 3 might launch a paper comparing reflecting and refracting telescopes; question 8 might be answered in a paper about the planning and construction of the 200-inch reflecting telescope at California's Mount Palomar observatory.

EXERCISE   **Convert the general questions into specific questions about two of the following subjects; then suggest two essay topics for each of your two subjects.**

Astrology	Games	Shopping malls
Books	Microorganisms	Stars
Colleges	Plays	Television
Emotions	Religion	Warships

Free Writing.   The free-writing strategy snares your thoughts as they race through your mind, yielding a set of sentences that you then look over for writing ideas. To start things off, turn your pen loose and write for about five minutes on your general subject. Put down everything that comes into your head, without worrying about the accuracy of your grammar, spelling, or punctuation. What you produce is for your eyes alone. If the thought flow becomes blocked, write "I'm stuck, I'm stuck . . ." until your brain and your hand come up with something else. When your writing time is up, go through your sentences one by one and extract whatever material appears to be the kernel of a topic. If you draw a blank, write for another five minutes and look again.

The following example shows the product of one free-writing session. Jim's instructor had assigned a two- or three-page paper on some aspect of sports; and since Jim had been a member of his high-school tennis team, his thoughts naturally channeled themselves toward this sport.

> Sports. If that's my subject, I'd better do something on tennis. I've played enough of it. But what can I say that would be interesting? It's very popular, lots of people watch it on TV. Maybe I could write about the major tennis tournaments. I'm stuck. I'm stuck. Maybe court surfaces. That sounds dull. I'm stuck. Well, what about tennis equipment, clothing, scoring? Maybe my reader is thinking about taking up the game. What do I like about tennis? The strategy, playing the net, when to use a topspin or a backspin stroke, different serves. I'm stuck. I'm stuck. Maybe I could suggest how to play a better game of singles. I used to be number one. I can still remember Coach harping on those three Cs, conditioning, concentration, consistency. I'm stuck. I'm stuck. Then there's the matter of special shots like lobs, volleys, and overheads. But that stuff is for the pros.

This example suggests at least three papers. For the beginning player, Jim could focus on equipment and scoring. For the intermediate player, he might write on conditioning, concentration, and consistency; for the advanced player, on special shots.

Brainstorming.   Brainstorming, a close cousin of free writing, captures fleeting ideas in words, fragments, and sometimes sentences, rather than in a series of sentences. Brainstorming garners ideas faster than the other strategies do. But unless you move immediately to the next stage of writing, you may lose track of what some of your fragmentary jottings mean.

To illustrate how free writing and brainstorming compare, we've converted our free-writing example into the following list, which typifies the results of brainstorming.

Popularity of tennis	Playing the net
Major tournaments	Topspin
Court surfaces	Backspin
Equipment	Different serves
Clothing	Conditioning
Scoring	Concentration
Doubles strategy	Consistency
Singles strategy	Special shots—lobs, drop volleys, overheads

EXERCISE   **Return to the five subjects you selected for the exercise on page 15. Free write or brainstorm for five minutes on each one; then choose a topic suitable for a two- or three-page essay. State your topic, intended audience, and purpose.**

Narrowing a familiar subject may yield not only a topic, but also the main divisions for a paper on it. Jim's free-writing session uncovered several possible tennis topics as well as a way of approaching each: by focusing on lobs, drop volleys, and overheads when writing about special shots, for example. Ordinarily, though, the main divisions will emerge only after the writer has gathered material to develop the topic.

CASE HISTORY   Now that you're familiar with some narrowing strategies, let's see how one student handles an actual writing situation. George's composition class has been reading and talking about the growing influence of the conservation movement. His instructor asks him to write a two- or three-page paper on a topic of his choice, related to this general subject. To begin, he first lists two major categories of his general subject: conserving natural resources and protecting endangered animals. Next, he thinks over what he has touched on in class as well as what he already knows. His first category yields such topics as combating acid rain, developing efficient solar heating systems, and protecting beaches against oil spills. The second category yields these topics: banning whale hunting, captive breeding of endangered animal species, and controlling poaching in Africa. Because he has recently seen an interesting TV program on captive breeding, he decides to pursue that topic. (*To be continued in the next section.*)

GATHERING SUPPORT

Once you've decided on a topic, you'll need to find things to say about it. This supporting material can include several sorts of information: facts, ideas, examples, observations, sensory impressions, memories, and the like. Without the proper backup, papers lack force, vividness, and interest. They may confuse or mislead readers.

STRATEGIES FOR GATHERING SUPPORT

If you are writing on a familiar topic, much of your supporting material may come from your own head. Brainstorming is the best way to retrieve it. With unfamiliar topics, brainstorming won't work. Instead, you'll have to do some background reading. Whatever the topic, familiar or unfamiliar, talking with friends, parents, neighbors, or people knowledgeable about the topic can also produce useful ideas.

Brainstorming.   Brainstorming a topic, like brainstorming a subject, yields a set of words, fragments, and occasionally sentences that will furnish ideas for the paper. Assume that Jim, the student who explored the subject of tennis, wants to show how conditioning, concentration, and consistent play can improve one's game. His brainstorming list might look like this:

> always keep ball in play
> don't try foolish shots
> place ball so opponent runs
> stay in good condition yourself
> running
> jogging
> skipping rope
> keeps you on your toes
> keep your mind only on the game
> personal distractions
> courtside distractions
> temper distractions
> don't continually drive ball with power
> two-on-one drill
> lob ball over opponent's head
> return a down-the-line passing shot
> don't try spectacular overheads
> chance for opponent to make mistake
> game of percentages
> games are lost, not won

You can see how some thoughts have led to others. For example, the first jotting, "always keep ball in play," leads naturally to the next one, "don't try foolish shots." "Place ball so opponent runs" leads to "stay in good condition yourself," which in turn leads to the notations of ways to stay in condition, and so forth.

Don't worry if your brainstorming notes look chaotic and if some seem irrelevant. Sometimes the most unlikely material turns out to be the freshest and most interesting. As you organize and write your paper, you'll probably combine, modify, and omit some of the notes, as well as add others.

Prepare a brainstorming sheet of supporting details for one of the topics you developed for the exercise on page 20.   **EXERCISE**

Reading.   When you have to grapple with an unfamiliar topic, look to the library for material to develop it. Before starting your trek there, however, turn to Chapter 13 and read what we say under the headings "The Card Catalog," "Computerized Card Catalogs," and "Periodical Indexes." These sections discuss the tools you'll need to unearth promising information, and will also acquaint you with two publications that list subject headings you can check. Once you're at the library, obtain your subject headings and then start tracking down your sources. As you look through each book or article, jot down any information that looks useful. These jottings may take the form of direct quotations, or you may rewrite the material in your own words.

Whenever you use someone else's ideas in your paper, you must give proper credit to your source. This rule applies both to direct quotations and to material you have rephrased. Failure to observe it constitutes plagiarism; that is, literary theft, a serious offense that can result in failure in your course or even expulsion from school. Unless you're doing a library research paper, your instructor will probably require only that you mention the speaker's or writer's name and identify the publication in which the material appeared. (See Chapter 13, "Handling Quotations" and "Avoiding Plagiarism.")

Talking with Others.   You can expand the pool of ideas gained through brainstorming or reading by drawing upon the knowledge of the people around you. Imagine you're writing a paper about a taxpayers' revolt that's gathering steam in your state. After going to the library and checking the leading state newspapers, you find that most of the discontent centers on property taxes. You then decide to supplement what you've read by asking questions about the tax situation in your town.

Your parents and neighbors tell you that property taxes have jumped 50 percent in the last two years. The local tax assessor tells you that assessed valuations have risen sharply and that state law requires property taxes to keep pace. She also notes that this situation is causing some people living on fixed incomes to lose their homes. A city council member explains that part of the added revenue is being used to repair badly deteriorating city streets, to build a new library wing, and to buy more fire-fighting equipment. The rest is going to the schools. School officials tell you they're using their extra funds to offer more vocational courses and to expand the program for learning-disabled students. As you can see, asking questions can broaden your perspective and provide information that will help you to write a more worthwhile paper.

CASE
HISTORY
(*continued*)

Because the topic that interests George—the captive breeding of endangered animal species—is unfamiliar, he turns to the library. Before starting the actual search, he draws up a list of subject headings to guide his investigation:

Animals, treatment of
Rare animals

Wildlife, conservation of
Wildlife, preservation of
Zoo animals
Zoo breeding of animals

The card catalog shows the first and third subject headings but only one book on his topic. When he checks the *Readers' Guide,* however, he finds several articles with promising titles listed under "Rare Animals." Skimming the first two, he finds that they cover more facets of his topic than he can handle adequately in two or three pages, so he decides to narrow his topic even further and discuss only the requirements for successful captive breeding. *(To be continued in the next section.)*

DEVELOPING A THESIS STATEMENT

A thesis statement sets forth the main idea of a piece of writing, usually in one sentence. The thesis statement points you in a specific direction, helping you to stay on track and out of tempting byways. In addition, it tells your reader what to expect.

Thesis statements can emerge at several points along the way to a first draft or even after the first draft has been written. If an instructor gives you a controversial topic on which you hold a strong opinion, the statement may just pop into your head right away. If you go through the process of narrowing to a topic you know very well, a statement may develop as your focus narrows. Ordinarily, though, the thesis statement must wait until you've amassed and examined your supporting information.

As you examine, search for the central point in your support and for the key points that back it up. Then use these to develop your thesis statement. Casting the central idea in question form may help you to uncover backup ideas and write a thesis statement. For example:

Central point:	Robots face an uncertain future in American industry.
Question:	What are some of the drawbacks to using robots in American industry?
Thesis statement:	The expense of producing robots, the lack of qualified personnel to service them, and the moral problems of replacing workers with them—all cloud the future of robots in American industry.

The thesis statement stems from the specifics the student unearthed while answering the question.

REQUIREMENTS OF
A GOOD THESIS STATEMENT

Unless intended for a lengthy paper, a thesis statement *focuses on just one central point or issue*. Suppose you prepare the following thesis statement for a two- or three-page paper:

> Centerville College should reexamine its policies on aid to students, open admissions, and vocational programs.

This sprawling statement would commit you to grapple with three separate issues. At best, you could hope to make only a few general remarks about each one. In contrast, the following thesis statement would do nicely for a brief paper:

> Because of falling enrollments and the rising demand among high-school graduates for job-related training, Centerville College should expand its vocational offerings.

It shows that the writer will focus on *two facets of one issue*.

A good thesis statement also *tailors the scope of the issue to the length of the paper*. Two or three pages would yield only a smattering of poorly supported general statements on the thesis "Many incoming college freshmen face crucial adjustment problems." Pared down to "Free time is a responsibility that challenges many college freshmen," the idea could probably be developed adequately.

Finally, a good thesis statement accurately *forecasts the content of the paper and sometimes the organization as well*. Assertions built on fuzzy, catchall words like *fascinating, bad, meaningful,* or *interesting,* or statements like "My paper is about . . ." tell neither writer nor reader what's going on. To illustrate:

> New York is a fascinating city.

> My paper is about no-fault divorce.

These examples raise a host of questions. Why does the writer find New York fascinating? Because of its skyscrapers? Its night life? Its theaters? Its restaurants? Its museums? Its shops? Its inhabitants? And what about no-fault divorce? Will the writer attack it, defend it, trace its history, suggest ways of improving it? To find out, we must journey through the paper, hoping to find our way without a road-map sentence.

Now look at the rewritten versions of those faulty thesis statements:

> I love New York because of its many theaters and museums.

Compared to traditional divorce, no-fault divorce is less expensive, promotes fairer settlements, and reflects a more realistic view of the causes for marital breakdown.

These statements tell the reader not only what points the writer will make but also the order they will follow.

IMPLIED THESIS STATEMENTS

Not all papers have an explicit thesis statement. Narratives and descriptions, for example, often merely support some point that emerges from the events and details. Furthermore, professional writers sometimes imply their thesis rather than state it directly. Nonetheless, a core idea underlies and controls all effective writing.

CHANGING YOUR THESIS STATEMENT

Once you have set down a thesis statement, don't think of it as engraved on marble. Before your paper is in final form, you may need to change the thesis statement several times. If you draft it during the narrowing stage, you might reshape it to reflect what you uncovered while gathering your support. Or you might amend it after writing the first draft, having discarded some ideas, built up others, and drawn together what remains, so that things begin to fit together.

Tentative or final, formulated early or late, the thesis statement serves as a beacon, keeping your purpose firmly in the spotlight.

As George reads and takes notes, he finds that the problems encountered in captive breeding fall into two categories: social and physical. Since the two categories seem equally important, he arbitrarily elects to discuss social problems first. After a little thought, he comes up with this thesis statement:

CASE HISTORY *(continued)*

Captive breeding of endangered animals is complicated by the special social and physical requirements of individual species. *(To be continued in the next section.)*

---

1. **Write a thesis statement for the sheet of supporting details that you developed for the exercise on page 21.**

EXERCISE

2. **Explain why each of the following does or does not qualify as an effective thesis statement for a two- or three-page essay.**

   A. My paper discusses the problem of employee absenteeism in American industry.
   B. Living on a small island offers three advantages: isolation from city problems, the opportunity to know your neighbors, and the chance to go fishing whenever you want.

C. Although I don't know much about running a college, I know that Acme College is not run well.
D. Expanding our nation's armaments increases the chance of nuclear war and imposes an unneeded tax burden on the American taxpayer.
E. Many people, motivated by the desire to begin a new and more virtuous life, have abandoned the established modes of life and set up communities based on utopian ideals.
F. Vacationing in Britain is a nice way to spend a summer.
G. Extending Middletown's intracity transit system will save consumers money, reduce pollution, and increase city revenues.
H. Most cable TV companies provide subscribers with several specialized-program channels.

ORGANIZING THE INFORMATION

If you have ever listened to a rambling speaker spill out ideas in no particular order, you probably found it hard to pay attention to the speech, let alone make sense of it. So, too, with disorganized writing. A garbled listing of ideas serves no one; an orderly presentation highlights your ideas and helps communication succeed.

The topic you select determines the approach you take. In narrating a personal experience, such as a mishap-riddled vacation, you'd probably trace the events in the order they occurred. Similarly, in describing a process, say caulking a bathtub, you'd take the reader step by step through the whole procedure. To describe a hillside view near your home, you might work from left to right. Or you could first paint a word picture of some striking central feature and then fan out in either direction. Other topics dictate other patterns: for example, to show comparison and contrast, discuss causes and effects, and break things into categories. Part II describes the basic organizational approaches in detail.

You can best organize long pieces of writing, such as library research papers, by following a formal outline (see Chapter 13, "Organizing and Outlining.") For shorter papers, however, a simple, informal system of *flexible notes* provides a suitable writing plan.

THE FLEXIBLE NOTES SYSTEM

To create a set of flexible notes, write each of your key points at the top of a separate sheet of paper. If you have a thesis statement, refer to it for your key points. Next, list under each heading the supporting details that go with it. Drop any details that don't fit and expand any points that need more support. When your sheets are finished, arrange them in the order you expect to use in your essay. The completed notes for the tennis paper might look like this:

Conditioning
stay in good condition yourself
running
jogging
skipping rope
keeps you on your toes
two-on-one drill
lob ball over opponent's head
return a down-the-line passing shot

Concentration
keep your mind only on the game
overcome distractions: personal, courtside, temper

Consistency
always keep ball in play
don't try foolish shots
placc ball so opponent runs
don't continually drive ball with power
don't try spectacular overheads
chance for opponent to make mistake
game of percentages
games are lost, not won

Since conditioning, concentration, and consistency are simultaneous concerns, this listing arranges them according to their probable importance, in a progression from least to most important.

Now you're ready to draft a plan showing how many paragraphs you'll have in each part of the essay and what each paragraph will cover. Sometimes the number of details will suggest one paragraph; other times you'll need a paragraph block—two or more paragraphs. Here's a plan for the tennis essay.

Conditioning
stay in good condition yourself
running
jogging
skipping rope   } Off-the-court conditioning
keeps you on your toes
two-on-one drill
lob ball over opponent's head   } On-the-court conditioning
return a down-the-line passing shot

Concentration
keep your mind only on the game
overcome distractions: personal, courtside, temper

Consistency
always keep ball in play
don't try foolish shots
place ball so opponent runs ⎫
don't continually drive ball with power ⎬ Placing shots
don't try spectacular overheads ⎭
chance for opponent to make mistake ⎫
game of percentages ⎬ Playing
games are lost, not won ⎭ percentages

These groupings suggest two paragraphs about conditioning, one about concentration, and two about consistency.

EXERCISE   **Organize into flexible notes the supporting details that you prepared for the exercise on page 21. Arrange your note pages in a logical sequence and draft a plan showing the number and content of the paragraphs in each section.**

CASE
HISTORY
(*continued*)

George has no difficulty preparing the flexible notes for his paper on captive breeding. Working from his thesis statement, he first draws up a list of supporting details for each category of problems. Then he arranges them as mentioned in the thesis statement and drafts his paragraph-by-paragraph plan. This is the result:

Social Problems   Three-paragraph
                                        block

Mating problems ⎫
Need to separate felines until ready to ⎬ Paragraph on
    mate   mating problems
Same for pandas and pygmy hippo- ⎭
    potami

Male-female compatibility problems ⎫ Paragraph on
Choosiness of great apes ⎬ compatibility
Problem with male orangutan ⎭ problems

Infant care problems ⎫
Mishandling of babies by golden mar- ⎪ Paragraph on
    mosets ⎬ infant-care
Reason: captive-raised marmosets ig- ⎪ problems
    norant of infant care ⎪
Similar problems with gorillas ⎭

Physical Problems	Two-paragraph block	CASE HISTORY *(continued)*
Dietary problems Deaths of improperly nourished primate infants Solution: dietary fortifiers	Paragraph on dietary problems	
Breeding problems Case of breeding hooved and horned animals Difficulties with polar bears Mother's need for seclusion after cubs born Solution to problem: artificial ice caves	Paragraph on breeding problems	

(To be continued in the next section.)

WRITING THE FIRST DRAFT

Now on to the first draft of your essay. The writing should go rather quickly. After all, you have a topic you're qualified to write about, a thesis statement that indicates your purpose, enough support to develop it, and a written plan to follow.

But sometimes you may have trouble getting started. When you sit down to write, the words won't come, and all you can do is doodle or stare at the blank page. Perhaps the introduction is the problem. Many writers are terrified by the thought of the opening paragraph. They want to get off to a good start but simply can't figure out how to begin. If this happens to you, skip the introduction for the time being. Once you have your main points on paper, an effective opening will come more easily.

Here are some general suggestions for writing a first draft.

1. Stack your thesis statement, flexible notes, and written plan in front of you. They will start you thinking.
2. Skip every other line (double-space) and leave wide margins. Then you'll have room to revise later.
3. Write quickly; capture the drift of your thoughts. Concentrate on content and organization. Get your main points and supporting details on paper in the right sequence. *Don't* spend a lot of time correcting grammatical or punctuation errors, improving your language, or making the writing flow smoothly. You might lose your train of thought and end up doodling or staring again.
4. Take breaks at logical dividing points; for example, when you finish discussing a key point. Before you start to write again, scan what you've written.

Now for some specific suggestions that will help you with the actual writing:

1. Rewrite your thesis statement at the top of your first page to break the ice and build momentum.
2. Write your first paragraph, introducing your essay and stating your thesis. If you get stuck here, move on to the rest of the paper.
3. Follow your plan as you write. Begin with your first main point and work on each section in turn.
4. Look over the supporting details listed under the first heading in your flexible notes. Write a topic sentence stating the central idea of the paragraph.
5. Turn the details into sentences; use one or more sentences to explain each one. Add other related details, facts, or examples if they occur to you.
6. When you move from one paragraph to the next, try to provide a transitional word or sentence that connects the two.

EXERCISE   **Using the plan you prepared for the exercise on page 28, write the first draft of an essay.**

CASE HISTORY *(continued)*   After George prepares his writing plan, he uses it, along with his thesis statement and the notes taken in the library, to write the first draft shown here.

Captive Breeding in Zoos

This paper is about captive breeding. Today, humans hinder nature's species right to survive. Man is making it hard for over one hundred species of animals to continue to exist. But captive breeding in the worlds zoos may be just what the doctor ordered. This rescue attempt is a complex and difficult undertaking. Captive breeding of endangered species is complicated by the special social and physical requirements of individual species.

There are many social problems that have to be solved for the successful reproduction of endangered species in zoos. Mating is one of the most important of these problems. One propagation "must" for many felines, pandas, and pygmy hippopotami is the complete separation of sexes until they're "ready." Leland Stowe says that cheetahs almost never get together unless they can't see or smell each other ahead of time. When females exhibit a certain behavior, they bring on the male.

Male-female compatibility is a social problem. Great apes seem to be as particular as people in choosing mates. Stowe tells about an orangutan that turned a cold shoulder on the females in the National Zoo located in Washington, D.C. Then they shipped him to a zoo in Colorado. There, he took up with one of the females. The curator of the zoo, William Zanten, says he's "been siring offspring ever since."

Social factors hurt care of infant primates. Sheldon Campbell talks about this in *Smithsonian* magazine. He writes about the problems of breeding golden marmosets. These are monkeys that live in Brazil. The scientists found that captive-born parents neglected their young. Sometimes they even killed them. The problem was due to the fact that the marmosets had no experience living in a family situation. They didn't know what to do. Emily Hahn writes about gorillas in *The New Yorker*. She says that those raised by humans make poor mothers. Those raised by dutiful mothers make good parents.

The second important stumbling block to successful captive breeding is physical problems. Ignorance of dietary needs can be bad. Stowe talks about the captive breeding of gorillas and says that when this breeding was first getting started, infants exhibited a very high mortality rate. Then the babies were given iron and meat protein, the latter rich in Vitamin B-12. They were sprinkled on bananas, and the bananas were fed to the babies. The survival rate markedly improved.

Animals can be bred more easily if they are in an environment that duplicates that animal's natural habitat. Hooved and horned animals are an easy job because of the similarity in terrain and climate of their natural habitats to zoo habitats. Polar bears are a lot tougher. Mothers want to be let alone until their cubs are up and about. Because of this fact, the bears often kill their babies. Stowe says they solved this problem by building replicas of artic ice caves. The mothers and cubs are left alone until they emerge from the cave. John Perry, Director of the National Zoo, said this:

> The world is our zoo—a zoo that must be well-managed, its resources carefully husbanded, for these are the only resources it can ever have. We have appointed ourselves the keepers of this zoo, but we cannot live outside its gates. We are of it. Our lives are inextricably intertwined with the lives of all that live within. Their fate will be ours.

Our endangered species can survive only by nature's implacable test—sustained births by second and third generations. It will take decades to reach such a verdict of success. Thus we can see that captive breeding is beset by many problems. (*To be continued in the next section.*)

REVISING THE ESSAY

Actually, you have done a great deal of revision even before you start to revise your first draft. True, most of the revising occurs at this stage. But earlier changes might include altering the approach to your topic, replacing some support, modifying your thesis statement, or rearranging the order of your flexible notes. One stage of the writing process often triggers a reevaluation of another. Good writers continually look for shortcomings in the appropriateness, support, logic, and organization of their ideas.

"NOW THAT WE'VE BOILED YOUR PAPER DOWN TO THE RELEVANT MATERIAL, I THINK YOU'RE READY TO RE-WRITE."

Reprinted by permission of Richard N. Bibler.

Revising isn't easy. You need to bridle your ego and fear and become your own first critical reader. Set aside natural feelings of accomplishment ("After all, I've put a great deal of thought into this") and dread ("Actually, I'm afraid of what I'll find if I look too closely"). Remember, if you fail to view your work critically, your readers will do it for you.

After you've completed the first draft, set it aside for at least a half day, longer if time permits. This interval will put distance between you and your writing and sharpen your critical eye. When you return to the draft, read it out loud. Hearing it will help you catch errors such as missing words, excessive repetition, clumsy sentences, and sentence fragments.

One reading is not enough. Read your essay at least four times, once for each of these reasons:

To check on the progression of ideas
To strengthen paragraph structure and development
To clarify sentences and words
To correct misuse of English

In addition, read for any errors that occur frequently in your writing. Later chapters discuss paragraphs, sentences, and words in detail, and the handbook sections, "Sentence Errors" and "Spelling," offer assistance with usage and spelling problems. Check them for more information about the points introduced here.

CHECKING ON THE PROGRESSION OF IDEAS

Read first to verify the accuracy of your thesis statement. Have you delivered what you promised? If not, you'll either have to chop, redo stray parts, or alter your thesis. Then make certain you've said all that you meant to say. Fill in any gaps in thought or places where a reader might need more information. Make sure that your writing flows logically and smoothly. Clarify connections among ideas so that a reader will have no difficulty moving from one point to the next.

If you sense flaws in the organization of your essay, list each of its major and supporting points. Then check this outline for logic and completeness. Add new points, rearrange existing parts, or rewrite weak sections as necessary.

STRENGTHENING PARAGRAPH STRUCTURE AND DEVELOPMENT

Now examine your paragraphs one by one. Pose these basic questions about each paragraph, and correct any shortcomings you find:

1. Does the paragraph have one, and only one, central idea?
2. Does the central idea help to develop the thesis statement?
3. Does each statement within the paragraph help to develop the central idea?
4. Does the paragraph follow an appropriate pattern of organization?
5. Is the relationship between successive sentences clear?
6. Does the paragraph contain enough supporting detail?

7. Is each paragraph clearly and smoothly related to those that precede and follow it?

Your answers to these questions will probably trigger changes. Some paragraphs may be stripped down or deleted, others beefed up, still others repositioned.

CLARIFYING SENTENCES AND WORDS

Examine all your words and sentences for clarity, using the questions below as touchstones:

1. Is each sentence clearly and logically constructed?
2. Do I know the meanings of the words I use?
3. Do I explain the meanings of terms my reader may not know?
4. Is my writing wordy?
5. Have I carelessly omitted any words?

CORRECTING MISUSE OF ENGLISH

Using the "Sentence Errors" section of the handbook, inspect your writing for mistakes in English. As you revise, look especially for problems that have given you trouble in the past.

If you spell poorly, check for spelling errors by slowly reading your essay backward, from the last word to the first. You can then concentrate only on the spelling of individual words, and content will not interfere. Check your dictionary or the list of commonly misspelled words in the "Spelling" section of the handbook if you're uncertain about a spelling. Finally, keep a list of problem words, so that you can be on the lookout for them.

WRITING THE INTRODUCTION AND CONCLUSION

If you've put off writing your introduction, do it now. Generally, short papers begin with a single paragraph that includes the thesis statement. Sometimes the statement needs to be rephrased so that it meshes smoothly with the rest of your paragraph. The introduction acquaints the reader with you and your topic; it should clearly signal your intention as well as spark the reader's interest. Pages 169–172 discuss and illustrate effective introductions.

The conclusion wraps up your discussion. Generally a single paragraph in short papers, a good ending summarizes or supports the paper's main idea. Pages 172–175 discuss and illustrate effective conclusions.

SELECTING A TITLE

All essays require titles. Unless a good title unexpectedly surfaces while you are writing, wait until you finish the paper before choosing one. Since the reader must see the connection between what the title promises and what the essay delivers, a good title is both accurate and specific. To title the essay on captive breeding "Captive Breeding: A Look at the Process" would be misleading, for the paper doesn't spell out the steps of a process. A specific title suggests the essay's focus rather than just its topic. For example, "Captive Breeding: Difficult but Necessary" is clearer and more precise than simply "Captive Breeding." The essay highlights difficulties, not the technique as a whole.

To spark your reader's interest, you might try your hand at a clever or catchy title, but don't get so carried away with creativity that you forget to relate the title to the paper's content. Here are some examples of common and clever titles:

Common: "Handling a Hangover"

Clever: "The Mourning After"

Common: "Buying Your Home with Other People's Money"

Clever: "Home Free"

Use a clever title only if its wit or humor doesn't clash with the overall purpose and tone of the paper.

Revise the first draft you prepared for the exercise on page 30 and give it a suitable title.

EXERCISE

After letting the first draft of the essay on captive breeding sit for a couple of days, George revises it carefully according to the guidelines in this chapter. The end result, with its thesis statement and topic sentences emphasized, begins on page 36.

CASE HISTORY *(concluded)*

Captive Breeding: Difficult But Necessary

Today, as in the past, humans encroach on the basic right of nature's species to survive. Through ignorance, oversight, and technological developments, we are threatening the survival of over one hundred animal species. Until their environments can be safeguarded against harmful human intrusion, the last chance for the threatened species may depend upon captive breeding in zoos. But this rescue attempt is a complex and difficult undertaking. In particular, each species presents social and physical problems that must be solved for breeding to succeed.

Among the social problems that complicate successful reproduction, mating problems loom especially large. For instance, the male and female of many feline species must be kept completely separated until both animals are ready to mate. Leland Stowe, writing in National Wildlife magazine, notes that cheetahs almost never mate unless kept where the one cannot see or smell the other. Once the female shows signs of receptivity, a male is placed in her cage, and mating then occurs. Pandas and pygmy hippopotami show the same behavior.

A related social problem with certain species is male-female compatibility. Great apes, for instance, seem to be as particular as human beings in choosing mates. Stowe relates an amusing case of a male orangutan that totally spurned the females in the Washington, D.C. National Zoo. Shipped to a zoo in Colorado, he succumbed to the charms of a new face and has, according to curator William Zanten, "been siring offspring ever since."

    Social factors can also imperil proper care of infant primates. In a Smithsonian magazine article, Sheldon Campbell talks about the problems scientists encountered in trying to breed golden marmosets, a species of Brazilian monkey. Early attempts failed because the captive-born parents neglected and sometimes accidentally killed their babies. Observation showed that the problem occurred because the marmosets had no experience living in a family situation—they simply didn't know how to handle their offspring. Gorillas reared by humans may also make poor mothers, reports Emily Hahn in The New Yorker. On the other hand, those reared by dutiful mothers are usually good parents themselves.

    Physical problems rival social problems as stumbling blocks to successful captive breeding. Ignorance of a species' dietary needs, for instance, can have disastrous consequences. Early in the captive breeding of gorillas, infants exhibited a very high mortality rate, Stowe notes. Then meat protein and iron, the former rich in Vitamin B-12, were sprinkled on bananas and fed to the babies. As a result, the survival rate markedly improved.

    An environment that duplicates a species' natural habitat favors easy propagation. Hooved and horned animals present few breeding problems because the zoo habitats are similar in terrain and climate to their natural habitats. Polar bears, on the other

Margin annotations:

Topic sentence, with link to preceding paragraph

Specific details: problems with marmosets

Mention of other species with rearing problems

Linking device

Transition sentence: signals switch to discussing physical problems

Topic sentence, with link to transition sentence

Specific details: problems with gorillas

Linking device

Topic sentence

Linking device

hand, present difficult problems. Unless the mothers have complete privacy until the cubs can get around, they often kill the babies. To prevent this from happening, Stowe says, zoos now construct replicas of arctic ice caves and leave mothers and cubs completely alone until the new family emerges from the cave.

In his book The World's A Zoo John Perry, director of the National Zoo, has spoken of the need to save our endangered species.

Conclusion: quotation plus statement reinforcing idea that captive breeding presents difficulties

> The world is our zoo—a zoo that must be kept well-managed, its resources carefully husbanded, for these are the only resources it can ever have. We have appointed ourselves the keepers of this zoo, but we cannot live outside its gates. We are of it. Our lives are inextricably intertwined with the lives of all that live within. Their fate will be ours.

The difficulty, unfortunately, is as great as the urgency of this problem. Only sustained births by second- and third-generation captive animals can ensure the survival of our endangered species. And it will take decades to achieve the necessary success.

The marginal notes identify some of the elements that help make this paper effective. The most important point, however, is that the paper is successful because the writer followed an appropriate sequence in arriving at an effective topic, gathering the proper support, developing a thesis statement, organizing the information, and writing and revising the first draft.

Starting with the title and proceeding paragraph by paragraph, compare the first and final versions of the paper on captive breeding. Note the changes and how they have improved the essay.   EXERCISE

CHAPTER THREE

Exploring Time, Space, and Events

NARRATION AND DESCRIPTION

NARRATION

Clicking off the evening news and padding toward bed, Heloise suddenly glimpsed, out of the corner of her eye, a shadow stretching across the living room floor from under the drawn curtains.

"Wh–who's there?"

No response.

Edging backward toward the phone, her eyes riveted on the shadow, she stammered, "I–I don't have any money."

Still no answer.

Reaching the phone, she gripped the receiver and started to lift it from its cradle. Just then. . . .

Just now you've read the start of a *narrative*. A narrative relates a series of events. The events may be real—as in histories, biographies, travel accounts, and newspaper stories—or imaginary, as in short stories, novels, and plays. The narrative urge stirs in all of us, and like everyone else, you have responded almost from the time you first began to talk. In your younger years you probably swapped many stories with your friends, recounting an exciting visit to a circus or amusement park or enjoying a blow-by-blow account of the episode that got a classmate expelled from school. Today you may share with a friend the odd happening in your biology laboratory or listen to your spouse complaining about a hard day at school or work.

PURPOSE

A narrative, like any other kind of writing, makes a point or has a purpose. The point can be summed up in one or two sentences or left unstated, but it always shapes the writing of an effective narrative.

One narrative purpose is simply to tell what happened or to establish an interesting or useful fact. The reporter who chronicles a heated city council meeting, an airplane hijacking, or a lively congressional committee hearing usually wants only to set facts before the public. Progress reports and the minutes of meetings also represent information-only narratives.

Most narratives, however, go beyond merely reciting events. Writers of history, biography, and autobiography generally attempt to show the motives that lie behind the events and lives they portray.

Narratives of personal experience, too, offer lessons and insights. In the following extract, the conclusion of a narrative about an encounter with a would-be mugger, the writer offers a personal observation on self-respect:

> I kept my self-respect, even at the cost of dirtying my fists with violence, and I feel that I understand the Irish and the Cypriots, the Israelis and the Palestinians, all those who seem to us to fight senseless wars for senseless reasons, better than before. For what respect does one keep for oneself if one isn't in the last resort ready to fight and say, "You punk!"?
>
> Harry Fairlie, "A Victim Fights Back"

ACTION

Action plays a central role in any narrative. Other writing often only suggests action, leaving readers to imagine it for themselves:

> A hundred thousand people were killed by the atomic bomb, and these six were among the survivors. They still wonder why they lived when so many others died. Each of them counts many small items of chance or volition—a step taken in time, a decision to go indoors, catching one streetcar instead of the next—that spared him. And now each knows that in the act of survival he lived a dozen lives and saw more death than he ever thought he would see. At the time, none of them knew anything.
>
> John Hersey, *Hiroshima*

This passage may *suggest* a great deal of action—the flash of an exploding bomb, the collapse of buildings, screaming people fleeing the scorching devastation—but *it does not present the action*. Narration, however, re-creates action:

> When I pulled the trigger I did not hear the bang or feel the kick—one never does when a shot goes home—but I heard the devilish roar of glee that went up from the crowd. In that instant, in too short a time, one would have thought, even for the bullet to get there, a mysterious, terrible change had come over the elephant. He neither stirred nor fell, but every line of his body had altered. He looked suddenly stricken, shrunken, immensely old, as though the frightful impact of the bullet had paralyzed him without knocking him down. At last, after what seemed a long time—it might have been five seconds, I dare say—he sagged

flabbily to his knees. His mouth slobbered. An enormous senility seemed to have settled upon him. One could have imagined him thousands of years old. I fired again into the same spot. At the second shot he did not collapse but climbed with desperate slowness to his feet and stood weakly upright, with legs sagging and head drooping. I fired a third time. That was the shot that did for him. You could see the agony of it jolt his whole body and knock the last remnant of strength from his legs. But in falling he seemed for a moment to rise, for as his hind legs collapsed beneath him he seemed to tower upward like a huge rock toppling, his trunk reaching skywards like a tree. He trumpeted, for the first and only time. And then down he came, his belly towards me, with a crash that seemed to shake the ground even where I lay.

George Orwell, "Shooting an Elephant"

Orwell's account offers a stark, vivid replay of the slaying. Nothing significant is left for the reader to infer.

POINT OF VIEW

The narrative writer may adopt either of two points of view—first person or third person. In first-person narration, one of the cast of characters tells what happened, whereas a third-person narrator stays completely out of the story. Personal narratives and autobiographies are written in the first person, as are many travel accounts and works of fiction. Biographies, histories, and news stories use the third person, as do some travel accounts and many works of fiction.

Personal pronouns identify the writer's point of view. In first-person narration, the storyteller is identified by pronouns such as *I, me, mine, we,* and *ours.* With the third person, the narrator remains unmentioned, and the various characters are identified by nouns and such pronouns as *he, she, him,* and *her.* These two paragraphs illustrate the difference.

FIRST-PERSON NARRATION

We would go to the well and wash in the ice-cold, clear water, grease our legs with equally cold stiff Vaseline, then tiptoe into the house. We wiped the dust from our toes and settled down for schoolwork, cornbread, clabbered milk, prayers and bed, always in that order. Momma was famous for pulling the quilts off after we had fallen asleep to examine our feet. If they weren't clean enough for her, she took the switch . . . and woke up the offender with a few aptly placed burning reminders.

Maya Angelou, "Grandmother's Encounters"

As this example shows, first-person narrators may refer to other characters in the narrative by using nouns and third-person pronouns.

THIRD-PERSON NARRATION

In the depths of the great city walk the assorted minute creatures who do not suspect the fate that hangs over them. A young woman sweeps happily from store to store, pushing a baby carriage along. Businessmen stride purposefully into their office buildings. A young black sulks down the sidewalks of his tenement, and an old woman tugs her shopping basket across a busy thoroughfare. The old woman is not happy; she has seen better days. Days of parks and fountains, of roses and grass, still stir in her memory. Reaching the other side, she stops and strains her neck upward, past the doorways, past the rows and rows of mirror glass, until her eyes rest on the brilliant blue sky so far away. She looks intently at the sky for a few minutes, noting every cloud that rolls past. And the jet plane. She follows the plane with her deep-socketed eyes and for some unexplainable reason suspects danger. She brings her gaze back to earth and walks away as the jet releases a large cloud of brownish-yellow gas. The gas hangs ominously in the air for a while, as if wanting to give humankind just a few more seconds. Then the cloud slowly descends to the surface, dissipating as it goes. By the time it reaches the glittering megalopolis, it is a colorless, odorless blanket of death.

Richard Latta

EXERCISE   **Identify the point of view in each of the following excerpts.**

1.   The bus screeched to a stop, and Pat stepped out of it and onto the sidewalk. Night enveloped the city, and a slight drizzle fell around her as she made her way to Al's office. Turning the corner, she stepped into the dark entryway. The receptionist had gone home, so she proceeded directly to the office. She knocked on the door and entered. Al, standing behind his desk and looking out the window, turned toward her with a startled look on his face.

Jennifer Webber

2.   It had really begun back in the Charlestown Prison, when Bimbi first made me feel envy of his store of knowledge. Bimbi had always taken charge of any conversation he was in, and I had tried to emulate him. But every book I picked up had few sentences which didn't contain anywhere from one to nearly all of the words that might as well have been in Chinese. When I just skipped those words, of course, I really ended up with little idea of what the book said. So I had come to the Norfolk Prison Colony still going through only book-reading motions. Pretty soon, I would have quit even these motions, unless I had received the motivation that I did.

Malcolm X, *The Autobiography of Malcolm X*

DIALOGUE

Dialogue, or conversation, animates many narratives. Good dialogue livens the action and involves the reader more closely in the events. Written conversation, however, does not duplicate the way we actually talk. In speaking with friends, we repeat ourselves, throw in irrelevant comments, use slang, lose our train of thought, and overuse expressions like "you know," "uh," and "well." Dialogue that duplicated real talk would sink any narrative.

Good dialogue creates the impression of real conversation without copying it exactly. It uses simple words and short sentences, and it doesn't bog down in the excessive repetition of such phrases as "he said" and "she replied." If the conversation unfolds in a clear sequence, the reader can easily identify the speaker. To heighten the illusion of reality, the writer may use an occasional sentence fragment, slang expression, pause, and the like, as the following passage shows.

> Mom was waiting for me when I entered the house.
> "Your friends. They've been talking to you again. Trying to persuade you to change your mind about going into baseball. Honey, I wish you'd listen to them. You're a terrific ballplayer. Just look at all the trophies and awards you've. . . ." She paused. "Joe's mother called me this morning and asked if you were playing in the game on Saturday. Davey, I wish you would. You haven't played for two weeks. Please. I want you to. For me. It would be so good for you to go and—and do what you've always. . . ."
> "O.K., Mom, I'll play. But remember, just for you."
>
> Diane Pickett

Note the mother's use of the slang expression "terrific" and of sentence fragments like "your friends" and "for me" as well as the shift in her train of thought and the repetition of "and." All of this lends an air of reality to the mother's talk.

WRITING A NARRATIVE

Most narratives you write for your composition class will stem from personal experience and will therefore use the first person. Make sure that the experience you pick illustrates some point. A paper that tracks the minute-by-minute course of an appendicitis attack may meander along to little purpose. But if that same information is shaped by your purpose of illustrating a point—say, that it's unwise to ignore signs of oncoming illness—the attack can be a worthwhile topic.

Any narrative inevitably includes many separate events, enough to swamp your narrative boat if you tried to pack them all in. Here are but some of the events that might form part of the chronology of an appendicitis attack:

Awakened	Entered building	Walked to cafeteria
Showered	Greeted fellow	Ate lunch
Experienced acute	employees	Returned to work
but passing pain	Began morning's	Began afternoon's
in abdomen	work	work
Dressed	Felt nauseated	Collapsed at work
Ate breakfast	Met with boss	station
Opened garage	Took coffee break	Was rushed to
door	Visited bathroom	hospital
Started car	Experienced more	Underwent
Drove to work	prolonged pain in	diagnostic tests
Parked in employee	abdomen	Had emergency
lot		operation

To make the narrative effective, single out the key events, those that bear directly on your purpose, and build the narrative around them. The attacks of pain and nausea certainly qualify, as do the collapse and what follows it. A smoothly flowing narrative will also include some secondary events, but these require only sketchy treatment.

Use the opening of your paper to set the stage. Tell when and where the action takes place and supply any necessary background information, using explanation, action, or both. If you state your point openly, do it here or in your conclusion. The body of the narrative propels the action forward. Often, it features one or more conflicts involving two people or two clashing impulses in one person's head. The body of the narrative usually ends at some turning point, with matters about to be resolved. The conclusion ties up any loose ends and settles any conflicts. Action ceases, and the outcome allows the reader to grasp your point if it is left unstated.

To avoid stranding your reader, use time signals whenever the development of the action might be unclear. Words, phrases, and clauses like *now, next, finally, after an hour,* and *when I returned* help the reader keep pace with the events. Don't get carried away, though; a paper loaded with signals makes the sequence more important than the events themselves.

REVISION CHECKLIST

Thinking about these questions will help you revise your narrative.

- ✔ Have I made the point (stated or unstated) that I set out to make?
- ✔ Have I included all the key events that relate to my purpose? Given each the appropriate emphasis? Used time indicators where needed?
- ✔ Have I chosen the appropriate point of view?
- ✔ If I used dialogue, does it ring true?

EXAMPLE ESSAYS OF NARRATION

The Beach Bum
GAIL BARTLETT

STUDENT
WRITING

If I remember right, Pete Miller was his name. I can't remember for sure,   1
for it happened a long time ago. I met him that summer on the beach of Sanford
Lake. I was lying on my extra-large towel, letting the scorching sun slowly soak
the water droplets off my body, when some clumsy fool flopped by and flipped
sand all over me. Jerking up, an angry glare on my face, I was ready to scream
at the clod when my mouth opened wide in surprise. This fox was tall with jet-
black hair and sky-blue eyes. The summer sun had tanned his body to a golden
brown which made me envious as I compared it to my own vague coloring. It was
clearly evident that he had spent most of his summer on this beach. Immediately
my anger evaporated, and a smile came to my face. In a flirting tone I joked,
"Hey, Bud, watch where you're kicking that sand."

He grinned back and said, "Come on out in the water, and I'll help you wash   2
it off, unless, of course, you want it left on. I can see you've already discovered it
helps for a deep tan. Ha!"

I decided I had nothing to lose and hopped off my towel. As we raced to   3
the water, I could feel him glancing at me, and I knew at once that he had intentionally tripped in the sand only to get my attention. This pleased me but made
me even more self-conscious than usual. Not many guys noticed me, and I never
was quite sure how to act.

For the rest of the afternoon, we swam in the warm water. Never before   4
would I have wasted a good tanning sun like that day's to play in the water, but
for some reason I felt this day was different. He must have been all alone, for I
didn't meet any of his friends. It was only the two of us, and I was very grateful,
for I knew I would not be so much at ease if there were others around. To my
amazement, he asked me out for the next night to go to a bonfire he and his bud-
dies were having farther down on the beach. I accepted hesitantly, as I had dated
only a few times before.

With great pains I tried to decide what I should wear. Wanting to impress   5
him, I didn't wear my usual jeans and grubby sweatshirt. Instead I chose my new
plaid slacks and halter top, which were not at all comfortable. While nervously
waiting for him, I dabbed on a little extra perfume and a few extra swishes of
blusher. The door bell rang, and instantaneously I was on my feet and at the door.
The introduction to my parents wasn't exactly what I would describe as smooth,
and I certainly was not at ease.

We arrived at the fire about 9:00 P.M., and already twenty of his friends   6
had gathered. They were just beginning to pass the beer, and when he handed
me one I accepted for fear of disappointing him if I said no. It was not normal
for me to drink, and I didn't feel myself at all. I became afraid of what his friends
would think of me. They were laughing and telling jokes, but not wanting to say
something that would embarrass him I sat silent. When asked a question by his

closest friend, I could only shake my head in answer. The first hour went by quickly, for my date stayed by my side and tried in vain to include me in the conversation. I could not force myself to act normally. It was as though I were being rated, and I wanted a high score so badly I would not allow my true personality to show through for fear of not fitting in and being rejected. I felt as if I were going to suffocate. It was hard for me to hold back my laughter as the jokes grew increasingly funny. Only a timid giggle would I let escape my lips. My date became discouraged—I now can see why—but at that time the reason puzzled me. He left me to talk to a girl on the other side of the fire who was casually telling a joke. She spoke freely and with the confidence I wished I had. He enjoyed her easiness of manner, and so did many of the others. I could tell this by the way they were attracted to her side of the fire. Everyone was having a jolly time, and there I sat, suppressing myself in my fear. Finally the guy I had wanted so much to impress returned and asked in a cold tone, "Are you about ready to go?"

7   I answered with disappointment, "I am, if you are."

8   We slowly trudged to the car, making trite comments along the way. On the way home I wanted so badly to tell him that usually I was not so quiet and shy. I wanted to tell him how much fun I really could be and that I had acted as I had only because I was afraid he or his friends would think me odd or different in some way. But instead of saying all this, I only sat in a quiet closet, drawing myself farther into the corner with every mile.

9   As I climbed into bed I was angry with myself and vowed that I would never be that way again. I would force myself to be natural no matter what anyone thought. It seemed for certain that I would never be given another chance with this fox. Two weeks passed without my seeing or hearing a word from him. Every day I sat and daydreamed of what could have happened that night had I been myself and a little more at ease. Things could have worked out so nicely for me.

10   Two weeks later, after I had given up all hope, I answered the ringing phone one night with a bored hello. Lo and behold, it was the beach bum! My nerves shook and my eyes watered as I told him I would be happy to go to a skating party with him that weekend. Hanging up the phone, I released an exultant scream and ran to my room to think in quiet. This time I was not going to wear anything but my usual jeans, and I would act the way I felt if it killed me.

11   Through my upstairs bedroom window, I watched him slowly advance to the door, and I could feel that this was going to be the night I wanted so badly. We left the house, and I glanced quickly over at him with a confident smile as we strolled down the sidewalk. The skating rink was crowded, and I recognized most of the people there as his friends whom I had met before. I was surprised at how much friendlier they were to me than at our previous meeting. It was all because I wore a smile and not only listened to them talk but also offered a few quips of my own. When one of the guys skated up beside me and put his arm around me, I didn't look at the floor and shy away as I had done before but returned his warmness by putting my arm around him. My date seemed to enjoy my company and stayed near me the whole evening, glancing at me every now and then in disbelief that I could be the girl he had taken out two weeks before. We laughed and joked the night away, and things went much more smoothly than the last time.

While returning to my home he said, "I had a wonderful time tonight and would like to see you again sometime. You're really a lot more fun than I thought you were. Why were you so quiet at the bonfire?"   12

Slyly I answered, "Oh, was I quiet that night?" With a grin and a look from the corner of his eye, he squeezed my hand. To myself I thought, "How much better it is to be yourself and act the way you feel rather than to try to please others." It had seemed such a hard ordeal to get the others to like and accept me in the beginning, but now I realized that it hadn't been their fault at all—only mine.   13

---

1. Identify the point of view of the narrative.
2. List the words, phrases, and clauses that serve as time signals. What has the writer accomplished by using them?
3. This narrative spans about two weeks. At what points has the writer omitted events? Why?
4. What sentence states the point of the narrative? Why is it positioned where it is?

DISCUSSION QUESTIONS

The Perfect Picture*
JAMES ALEXANDER THOM

PROFESSIONAL WRITING

It was early in the spring about 15 years ago—a day of pale sunlight and trees just beginning to bud. I was a young police reporter, driving to a scene I didn't want to see. A man, the police-dispatcher's broadcast said, had accidentally backed his pickup truck over his baby granddaughter in the driveway of the family home. It was a fatality.   1

As I parked among police cars and TV news cruisers, I saw a stocky, white haired man in cotton work clothes standing near a pickup. Cameras were trained on him, and reporters were sticking microphones in his face. Looking totally bewildered, he was trying to answer their questions. Mostly he was only moving his lips, blinking and choking up.   2

After a while the reporters gave up on him and followed the police into the small white house. I can still see in my mind's eye that devastated old man looking down at the place in the driveway where the child had been. Beside the house was a freshly spaded flower bed, and nearby a pile of dark, rich earth.   3

"I was just backing up there to spread that good dirt," he said to me, though I had not asked him anything. "I didn't even know she was outdoors." He stretched his hand toward the flower bed, then let it flop to his side. He lapsed back into his thoughts, and I, like a good reporter, went into the house to find someone who could provide a recent photo of the toddler.   4

A few minutes later, with all the details in my notebook and a three-by-five   5

*FROM *Reader's Digest*, August 1976, pp. 113–14. Copyright © by The Reader's Digest Association, Inc. Reprinted with permission.

studio portrait of the cherubic child tucked in my jacket pocket, I went toward the kitchen where the police had said the body was.

6   I had brought a camera in with me—the big, bulky Speed Graphic which used to be the newspaper reporter's trademark. Everybody had drifted back out of the house together—family, police, reporters and photographers. Entering the kitchen, I came upon this scene:

7   On a Formica-topped table, backlighted by a frilly curtained window, lay the tiny body, wrapped in a clean white sheet. Somehow the grandfather had managed to stay away from the crowd. He was sitting on a chair beside the table, in profile to me and unaware of my presence, looking uncomprehendingly at the swaddled corpse.

8   The house was very quiet. A clock ticked. As I watched, the grandfather slowly leaned forward, curved his arms like parentheses around the head and feet of the little form, then pressed his face to the shroud and remained motionless.

9   In that hushed moment I recognized the makings of a prize-winning news photograph. I appraised the light, adjusted the lens setting and distance, locked a bulb in the flashgun, raised the camera and composed the scene in the viewfinder.

10   Every element of the picture was perfect: the grandfather in his plain work clothes, his white hair backlighted by sunshine, the child's form wrapped in the sheet, the atmosphere of the simple home suggested by black iron trivets and World's Fair souvenir plates on the walls flanking the window. Outside, the police could be seen inspecting the fatal rear wheel of the pickup while the child's mother and father leaned in each other's arms.

11   I don't know how many seconds I stood there, unable to snap that shutter. I was keenly aware of the powerful story-telling value that photo would have, and my professional conscience told me to take it. Yet I couldn't make my hand fire that flashbulb and intrude on the poor man's island of grief.

12   At length I lowered the camera and crept away, shaken with doubt about my suitability for the journalistic profession. Of course I never told the city editor or any fellow reporters about that missed opportunity for a perfect news picture.

13   Every day on the newscasts and in the papers, we see pictures of people in extreme conditions of grief and despair. Human suffering has become a spectator sport. And sometimes, as I'm watching news film, I remember that day.

14   I still feel right about what I did.

DISCUSSION QUESTIONS

1. Thom notes in his opening paragraph that he is "driving to a scene I didn't want to see." How does this statement help explain what happens later?
2. Identify the introduction, body, and conclusion of the narrative. Where does the climax occur?
3. Paragraph 10 contains numerous descriptive details. What bearing do these details have on Thom's decision?
4. Like most narratives, this one has a conflict. What is it? When do we become aware of it?

5. The narrative includes an indirect statement of its point. What is the point? Where is it found?

6. Do you think that Thom made the right decision? Why or why not?

---

1. **Narrate an experience which required you to make a difficult choice between two different courses of action. Provide background material that helps illustrate the difficulty you had making your choice.**

2. **Clichés often make statements that offer shrewd insights into human affairs. An effective narrative frequently has this same purpose. Write a personal narrative that illustrates the point made by one of these clichés or another that your instructor approves. You can restate the point directly in your own words or leave it unstated, but it must be clearly evident to a reader. Select your key events and arrange them in an appropriate order. As you write, use time indicators to guide your reader through your narrative.**

    a. A first impression may turn out to be misleading.
    b. A harsh exterior sometimes masks a soft heart.
    c. We get too soon old and too late smart.
    d. The best things in life are free.
    e. Behind every cloud is a silver lining.
    f. Poverty can be the greatest form of wealth.
    g. The longest way around is sometimes the shortest way home.
    h. A little learning is a dangerous thing.
    i. What you don't know can sometimes hurt you.
    j. The road to hell is paved with good intentions.
    k. Pride goes before a fall.
    l. Hemingway was right (or wrong) when he defined courage as "grace under pressure."
    m. Little strokes fell great oaks.
    n. The early bird gets the worm.
    o. Pennywise, pound foolish.

DESCRIPTION

The sound of sizzling hot dogs, cooking on a grease-spattered grill, gave way to the whirling buzz of a cotton-candy machine. Fascinated, we watched as the white cardboard cone was slowly transformed into a pink, fluffy cloud. Despite its Fiberglas appearance, the sticky puffs melted on my tongue into sweet sugar. Soon our faces and hands were gummed with goo.

You are there. Seeing, hearing, touching, tasting. This is one writer's *description* of a small segment of a county fair. Effective description creates sharply etched word pictures of objects, persons, scenes, events, or situations. Sensory impressions—reflecting sight, sound, taste, smell, and touch—form the backbone of descriptive writing. Often these sensory observations build toward one dominant impression that the writer wants to evoke.

The human mind is not merely a logical thinking machine. Because of our emotional makeup, we react with shock to the photo of a battered and bloody victim of child abuse. We feel stirrings of nostalgia upon hearing some song from our early childhood. We smile with satisfaction when quenching our summer thirst with tart sips from a tall, frosted glass of lemonade or from something with a bit more zing. Responses like these, as much as the ability to think rationally, help define the human makeup.

PURPOSE

Although description rarely occurs in pure form, it often enriches other writing. In this role, it appears everywhere: in histories and biographies, fiction and poetry, journalism and advertising. Occasionally, it even glints amidst the staid prose of technical writing. Creating images and mood is sometimes the sole end of description, as when a poet paints a word canvas of a flower-strewn meadow or a boggy, fog-shrouded moor. But description also helps us to understand or persuades us to act. A historian may juxtapose the pomp and splendor of the Versailles court with the wretched squalor of a Paris slum to help show why the French Revolution came about. And all of us have experienced the persuasive power of advertising's descriptive enticements.

Description will provide effective backup for the writing you do in your composition classes, helping you to drive home your points with force and vividness.

SENSORY IMPRESSIONS

Precise sensory impressions, the heartbeat of descriptive writing, begin with close physical or mental observation. If you can reexamine your subject, do it. If not, concentrate on your memory of it; then capture its features with appropriate words. When you can't find the right words, try a comparison. Ask yourself what your subject (or part of it) might be likened to. Does it smell like a rotten egg? A ripe cantaloupe? Burning rubber? Does it sound like a high sigh? A soft rustle? To come across, the comparison must be accurate and familiar. If the reader has never smelled a rotten egg, the point is lost.

Here is a passage marked by particularly vivid sight impressions.

> After our meal we went for a stroll across the plateau. The day was already drawing to a close as we sat down upon a ledge of rock near the lip of the western

precipice. From where we sat, as though perched high upon a cloud, we looked out into a gigantic void. Far below, the stream we had crossed that afternoon was a pencil-thin trickle of silver barely visible in the gloaming. Across it, on the other side, the red hills rose one upon another in gentle folds, fading into the distance where the purple thumblike mountains of Adua and Yeha stretched against the sky like a twisting serpent. As we sat, the sun sank fast, and the heavens in the western sky began to glow. It was a coppery fire at first, the orange streaked with aquamarine; but rapidly the firmament expanded into an explosion of red and orange that burst across the sky sending tongues of flame through the feathery clouds to the very limits of the heavens. When the flames had reached their zenith, a great quantity of storks came flying from the south. They circled above us once, their slender bodies sleek and black against the orange sky. Then, gathering together, they flew off into the setting sun, leaving us alone in peace to contemplate. One of the monks who sat with us, hushed by the intensity of the moment, muttered a prayer. The sun died beyond the hills; and the fire withdrew.

Robert Dick-Read, *Sanamu: Adventures*
in Search of African Art

At first, the western sky glows with a "coppery fire," which then expands into "an explosion of red and orange" that sends "tongues of flame" heavenward and then withdraws as the sun disappears. Comparisons strengthen the visual impression: the "pencil-thin" stream, the "thumblike" mountains stretching across the sky "like a twisting serpent." The familiar pencil, thumb, and serpent help us to visualize the unfamiliar landscape.

The next passage focuses on taste:

My own special chef's salad is a taste bud's delight. The cool moistness of fresh lettuce, the plump cherry tomatoes that squirt their tart juices against the palate, the hard-boiled egg slices garnished with paprika, and the bland, buttery avocados offer a soothing contrast to the fiery Mexican peppers that burn their way down the throat, the mouth-puckering saltiness of anchovies, and the intense bitterness of black Greek olives. Assorted garnishes add their own special zest: sugar-cured ham slivers, crisp, smoke-flavored bacon bits, pungent garlic salt, and crunchy herbed croutons. Sharp blue cheese dressing tops everything, adding its final piquancy to the assorted taste sensations.

Rick Price

As we read this passage, we can almost taste the tart juices of the tomatoes, the fieriness of the peppers, the bitterness of the olives, and the sharp piquancy of the dressing.

Most descriptions blend several sense impressions, rather than focusing on just one. In the following excerpt, Mark Twain, reminiscing about his uncle's farm, includes all five senses in his description. As you read it, note where Twain's impressions are especially effective.

As I have said, I spent some part of every year at the farm until I was twelve or thirteen years old. The life which I led there with my cousins was full of charm, and so is the memory of it yet. I can call back the solemn twilight and mystery of the deep woods, the earthy smells, the faint odors of the wild flowers, the sheen of rain-washed foliage, the rattling clatter of drops when the wind shook the trees, the far-off hammering of woodpeckers and the muffled drumming of wood pheasants in the remoteness of the forest, the snapshot glimpses of disturbed wild creatures scurrying through the grass—I can call it all back and make it as real as it ever was, and as blessed. I can call back the prairie, and its loneliness and peace, and a vast hawk hanging motionless in the sky, with his wings spread wide and the blue of the vault showing through the fringe of their end feathers. I can see the woods in their autumn dress, the oaks purple, the hickories washed with gold, the maples and the sumachs luminous with crimson fires, and I can hear the rustle made by the fallen leaves as we plowed through them. I can see the blue clusters of wild grapes hanging among the foliage of the saplings, and I remember the taste of them and the smell. I know how the wild blackberries looked, and how they tasted, and the same with the pawpaws, the hazelnuts, and the persimmons; and I can feel the thumping rain, upon my head, of hickory nuts and walnuts when we were out in the frosty dawn to scramble for them with the pigs, and the gusts of wind loosed them and sent them down. I know the stain of blackberries, and how pretty it is, and I know the stain of walnut hulls, and how little it minds soap and water, also what grudged experience it had of either of them. I know the taste of maple sap, and when to gather it, and how to arrange the troughs and the delivery tubes, and how to boil down the juice, and how to hook the sugar after it is made, also how much better hooked sugar tastes than any that is honestly come by, let bigots say what they will.

Mark Twain, *Autobiography*

EXERCISE   **Spend some time in an environment such as one of the following. Concentrate on one sense at a time. Begin by observing what you see; then jot down the precise impressions you receive. Now do the same for impressions of touch, taste, smell, and sound.**

1. The woods in the early morning
2. A city intersection
3. A restaurant or cafeteria
4. A scenic spot under a full moon
5. A storm
6. A pool or other recreation area
7. A crowded classroom or hallway
8. A grocery store
9. A park or playground
10. A holiday gathering

DOMINANT IMPRESSION

Skillful writers select and express sensory perceptions with an eye toward creating a *dominant impression*, one that will emerge from the description as a whole. A verbal picture of a storm about to strike, for example, might be crafted to evoke feelings of fear by describing sinister masses of slaty clouds, cannon salvos of thunder, blinding lightning flashes, and viciously swirling wind-caught dust.

The following paragraph establishes a sense of security as the dominant impression:

> A marvellous stillness pervaded the world, and the stars together with the serenity of their rays seemed to shed upon the earth the assurance of everlasting security. The young moon recurved, and shining low in the west, was like a slender shaving thrown up from a bar of gold, and the Arabian Sea, smooth and cool to the eye like a sheet of ice, extended its perfect level to the perfect circle of a dark horizon. The propeller turned without a check, as though its beat had been part of the scheme of a safe universe; and on each side of the *Patna* two folds of water, permanent and sombre on the unwrinkled shimmer, enclosed within their straight and diverging ridges a few white swirls of foam bursting in a low hiss, a few wavelets, a few ripples, a few undulations that, left behind, agitated the surface of the sea for an instant after the passage of the ship, subsided splashing gently, calmed down at last into the circular stillness of water and sky with the black speck of the moving hull remaining everlastingly in its centre.
>
> Joseph Conrad, *Lord Jim*

The first sentence directly identifies the impression, "security," to which the "stillness" and the "serenity" contribute. Other details also do their part: the "smooth" sea, the "perfect circle" of the horizon, the "safe universe," the quick calming of the water, and the moving hull "everlastingly" in the center of water and sky.

EXERCISE

Select one of the following topics and write a paragraph that evokes a particular dominant impression. Omit any details that run counter to your aim.

1. A multi-alarm fire
2. A repair facility (automobile, appliance, and so on)
3. A laboratory
4. Some aspect of summer in a particular place
5. A religious service
6. A doctor's or dentist's office
7. A dark street

8. A parade or other celebration
9. Some landmark on your college campus
10. A municipal night court or small-claims court

VANTAGE POINT

You may write a description from either a fixed or a moving vantage point. A fixed observer remains in one place and reports only what can be perceived from there. Here is how Marilyn Kluger describes the Thanksgiving morning sounds she remembers hearing from her bed as a child:

> On the last Thursday in November, I could stay in bed only until the night chill left the house, hearing first the clash of the heavy grates in the huge black iron range, with its flowery scrolls and nickled decorations, as Mother shook down the ashes. Then, in their proper sequence, came the sounds of the fire being made—the rustle of newspaper, the snap of kindling, the rush of smoke up the chimney when Mother opened the damper, slid the regulator wide open, and struck a match to the kerosene-soaked corncobs that started a quick hot fire. I listened for the bang of the cast-iron lid dropping back into place and for the tick of the stovepipes as fierce flames sent up their heat, then the sound of the lid being lifted again as Mother fed more dry wood and lumps of coal to the greedy new fire. The duties of the kitchen on Thanksgiving were a thousand-fold, and I could tell that Mother was bustling about with a quicker step than usual.
>
> Marilyn Kluger, "A Time of Plenty"

A moving observer views things from a number of positions, signaling changes in location with phrases such as "moving through the turnstile" and "as I walked around the corner." Below, H. L. Mencken takes us with him as he observes from a moving express train.

> On a Winter day some years ago, coming out of Pittsburgh on one of the expresses of the Pennsylvania Railroad, I rolled eastward for an hour through the coal and steel towns of Westmoreland county. It was familiar ground; boy and man, I had been through it often before. But somehow I had never quite sensed its appalling desolation. Here was the very heart of industrial America, the center of its most lucrative and characteristic activity, the boast and pride of the richest and grandest nation ever seen on earth—and here was a scene so dreadfully hideous, so intolerably bleak and forlorn that it reduced the whole aspiration of man to a macabre and depressing joke. Here was wealth beyond computation, almost beyond imagination—and here were human habitations so abominable that they would have disgraced a race of alley cats.
>
> I am not speaking of mere filth. One expects steel towns to be dirty. What I allude to is the unbroken and agonizing ugliness, the sheer revolting mon-

strousness, of every house in sight. From East Liberty to Greensburg, a distance of twenty-five miles, there was not one in sight from the train that did not insult and lacerate the eye. Some were so bad, and they were among the most pretentious—churches, stores, warehouses, and the like—that they were downright startling; one blinked before them as one blinks before a man with his face shot away. A few linger in memory, horrible even there: a crazy little church just west of Jeannette, set like a dormer-window on the side of a bare, leprous hill; the headquarters of the Veterans of Foreign Wars at another forlorn town, a steel stadium like a huge rat-trap somewhere further down the line. But most of all I recall the general effect—of hideousness without a break. There was not a single decent house within eyerange from the Pittsburgh suburbs to the Greensburg yards. There was not one that was not misshapen, and there was not one that was not shabby.

H. L. Mencken, "The Libido for the Ugly"

The phrase "on one of the expresses of the Pennsylvania Railroad" signals that Mencken will be a moving observer, and "From East Liberty to Greensburg" pinpoints the extent of his journey. "West of Jeannette," "another forlorn town," and "somewhere further down the line" specify the positions from which he views the church, the headquarters of the veterans' organization, and the stadium.

Whether you adopt a fixed or moving vantage point, be sure to report only what would be apparent to someone actually on the scene. If you start describing how a mountain looks from a balcony, don't suddenly leap to the description of a flower on the mountainside; the flower would not be visible from your vantage point.

EXERCISE

1. **Writing as a fixed observer, describe in a paragraph your impressions of one of the following. Be sure to indicate your vantage point.**

   a. A post office lobby two weeks before Christmas
   b. The scene following a traffic accident
   c. A classroom when the bell rings
   d. A campus lounge
   e. An office
   f. The entrance to some building

2. **Writing as a moving observer, describe in a paragraph or two your impressions as you do one of the following things. Clearly signal your movements to the reader.**

   a. Walk from one class to another
   b. Shop in a grocery store
   c. Walk from your home to the corner
   d. Cross a long bridge

e. Water-ski
f. Go through a ticket line and enter a theater, auditorium, or sports arena.

SELECTION OF DETAILS

Effective description stems as much from exclusion as inclusion. Never try to be a camera. Doing that shows your reader only that you can see, not write. Instead, select details deliberately to help build the impression you intend to create. Good description evolves not from a realistic portrayal of the entire subject, but rather from discriminating choices that point toward a frame of mind, a mood, an impression. Read the following description of nighttime skiing.

> The glowing orb of the moon, shedding its pale, silvery radiance on the ski slope, seemed to cast a spell. Crystal iridescence of powdered snow twinkled in the night. Shadows cast by the skiers appeared as mysterious silhouettes darting in and out among snow-covered trees. The gentle breeze combing through the branches created a luring musical chant which drifted into my head, taking control. Delicate snowflakes danced by, kissed me on the face, and seemed to beckon me up the hill.
>
> Sue Mutch

The writer of this paragraph evokes a sense of enchantment by taking note of the "pale, silvery radiance" of the moon, the "crystal iridescence" of the snow, the "mysterious silhouettes" of the skiers darting among the trees, and the "luring musical chant" of the wind. She ignores such details as the boisterous snatches of conversation among the skiers, the crunch of ski poles digging into the snow, and the creaking towline moving to the top of the slope. Mentioning these things would detract from the desired sense of enchantment.

ARRANGEMENT OF DETAILS

A random listing of details would garble any description. Some pattern is needed for the reader to absorb impressions in an order that fulfills your purpose. Some version of spatial arrangement usually works well. You could systematically progress from bottom to top, top to bottom, left to right or vice versa, front to back or vice versa, or the like. You could describe Saturday afternoon at the football game by starting with the jammed parking lot, moving into the bustling stadium, and finally zooming in on the sights, sounds, and smells of the playing field. Or if you wanted to highlight the surroundings rather than the central event, the order could be reversed. Going another route, you might start with some striking central feature and then branch out to the things around it. You could capture the center of a mall by first describing an ornate fountain illuminated with flashing, multicolored lights, then shifting to the flickering reflection of these lights on the skylights above, the glinting coins in the fountain pool, and the store fronts on either side.

Sometimes a description follows a time sequence. A writer might, for example, portray the changes in a woodland setting as winter gives way to spring and spring, in turn, yields to summer.

WRITING A DESCRIPTION

Before you start to write, establish a firm sense of purpose. What impression do you want to emerge? What sensory details will help create it?

Effective description stems from accurate, fresh observations translated into words. We've all tolerated writers who tell us that raindrops "pitter patter," clouds are "fleecy white," and the sun is "a ball of fire." This worn-out writing does nothing to deepen our perception of the rain, the clouds, or the sun. Don't be satisfied with stale language.

By contrast, read how one student describes her auditory impressions of the kitchen at breakfast time:

> Sure signs of a new day are the sounds in the kitchen as breakfast is prepared. The high sigh of the gas just before it whooshes into flame and settles into a whispering hum blends with the gurgling of the water for the morning coffee. Soon the gloop, gloop, gloop of the coffee sets up a perky beat. Then in mingles the crackle of creamy butter on a hot skillet and the shush of an egg as it meets this fiery foe. Ribbons of bacon start to sizzle in the spitting grease. The soft rustle of plastic as bread is removed from its wrapper floats on the air and seems to form part of the atmosphere. The can opener whirs, and the orange juice concentrate drops with a splat into the blender, which whizzes together the orange cylinder and splashed-in water. For minutes after the blender stops, tiny effervescing bubbles fizz.
>
> Kim Burson Swiger

You are there in the kitchen, hearing the sounds this writer has carefully selected and freshly described for you.

Here is a general guide for the framework of your paper. Set the backdrop and establish your vantage point in the opening paragraph. Use each middle paragraph to develop one of the main features, and arrange them in an appropriate order. End by pulling the impressions together in some way, perhaps by supplying a type of perspective.

REVISION CHECKLIST

Ask yourself these questions as you revise your description.

✔ Have I conveyed how my topic looks, sounds, feels, tastes, or smells? Would comparisons or more precise descriptive terms help me to share my perceptions with the reader?

✔ Have I evoked one dominant impression? Can I strengthen this impression by adding certain selected details? By eliminating details that detract from the impression?

✔ Have I used an appropriate vantage point? If the observer is moving, have I signaled changes in location? Have I included only details that would be visible to the observer?

✔ Have I arranged my details in an order appropriate to the topic?

EXAMPLE ESSAYS OF DESCRIPTION

STUDENT WRITING

The Big One
REBECCA MUTCH

1   With a final crack of a bat and a lofting fly ball, baseball ended for the year. The last swirl of water gurgling down the drain of the community pool marked the end of its season. These closings marked the beginning of another event, the county fair. This season I was elected to take my little brother on a ride—"the big one," in his words.

2   Once again I found myself in the familiar grass lot bordering the fairground. The fair itself was completely surrounded by a fence. No one could see what was inside. The only clues were carried in the wind. Muffled echoes of carnies hawking their games, excited squeals of children, and blaring carnival tunes, frequently punctuated by sharp, crackling static, blended with the tantalizing fragrance of popcorn, the spicy aroma of pizza, and the sweet molasses smell of caramel corn.

3   As we entered the main gate and handed our tickets to the men whose baskets already overflowed with torn stubs, my eyes immediately confirmed what my ears and nose had already reported. In one step we had gone from a semiquiet and relaxed world into an ever-revolving one. Dazzling lights, blinking out of control, seemed to flirt with anyone and everyone. Children, their white T-shirts covered with splotches of chocolate and mustard, dashed ahead of their parents and returned shortly, screaming about the giant bear that waited ahead. The distant shuffling crowds appeared as moving shadows, their features blurred.

4   The little tug on my sleeves reminded me of that big ride that waited ahead. The path up the midway, packed with a cushion of sawdust, was strewn with empty popcorn boxes, scraps of papers, and crumpled cigarette packages.

Game booths and food huts, their pennants whipping and snapping in the   5
wind, dotted the path on both sides and formed two long serpent-like strings of
pleasure. BB's clinked against tin objects in the shooting gallery. Hawkers with
greased hands and pudgy fingers tried to lure suckers toward their gaudy booths.
A backboard thudded and a hoop clanked as still another young man tried to win
the enormous purple teddy bear which smiled down mockingly from its perch
above. The sound of sizzling hot dogs, cooking on a grease-spattered grill, gave
way to the whirling buzz of a cotton-candy machine. Fascinated, we watched as
the white cardboard cone was slowly transformed into a pink, fluffy cloud. Despite its Fiberglas appearance, the sticky puffs melted on my tongue into sweet
sugar. Soon our faces and hands were gummed with goo.

We scuffled along with the rhythm of the crowd and before long arrived   6
at those metallic contraptions of nuts and bolts—the rides. The sounds of metal
clanging and banging filled the air. Sparks shot out from where the metal pieces
slapped together. Swirling and whirling, these pieces caught the reflection of the
neon lights, and together with the sparks produced a world of spectrum colors.

This was it. The Ferris wheel stood towering before us. As the seat gently   7
swayed, we waited for the ride to begin. The motor belched and then slowly
started to turn; goose bumps formed on my brother's bare arms, and his eyes
grew larger as the ride picked up speed. The fairground was soon a kaleidoscope
of fantastic images and colors. The wind whipped through my hair and snapped
it back, stinging my face at times. Both of us were screaming uncontrollably. Suddenly, with no apparent slowdown, the ride was over, and we made our way diz-
zily to the car.

My brother talked about the big one for weeks. For me it brought back   8
many fond memories and let me, just for an evening, be a child again.

DISCUSSION QUESTIONS

1. This description features a moving observer. Where are the writer's movements indicated?
2. Point out details that appeal to each of the five senses.
3. Reread paragraph 7. Identify perceptive observations used to describe the Ferris wheel ride.
4. How is the essay organized? For its purpose, is this pattern appropriate?

When the Full Moon Shines Its Magic over Monument Valley
JOHN V. YOUNG

PROFESSIONAL WRITING

We were camped here in early spring, by one of those open-faced shelters   1
that the Navajos have provided for tourists in this part of their vast tribal park on
the Arizona–Utah border, 25 miles north of Kayenta. It was cool but pleasant,
and we were alone, three men in a truck.

We were here for a purpose; to see the full moon rise over this most mys-   2 terious and lonely of scenic wonders, where fantastically eroded red and yellow sandstone shapes soar to the sky like a giant's chess pieces and where people—especially white strangers—come quickly to feel like pretty small change indeed.

3   Because all Navajo dwellings face east, our camp faced east—toward the rising sun and the rising moon and across a limitless expanse of tawny desert, that ancient sea, framed by the towering nearby twin pinnacles called The Mittens. We began to feel the magic even before the sun was fully down. It occurred when a diminutive wraith of a Navajo girl wearing a long, dark, velvet dress gleaming with silver ornaments drifted silently by, herding a flock of ghostly sheep to a waterhole somewhere. A bell on one of the rams tinkled faintly, and then its music was lost in the soft rustle of the night wind, leaving us with an impression that perhaps we had really seen nothing at all.

4   Just then, a large woolly dog appeared out of the gloom, seeming to materialize on the spot. It sat quietly on the edge of the glow from our campfire, its eyes shining like mirrors. It made no sound but when we offered food, it accepted the gift gravely and with much dignity. The dog then vanished again, probably to join the girl and her flock. We were not certain it was not part of the illusion.

5   As the sun disappeared entirely, the evening afterglow brush tipped all the spires and cliffs with magenta, deepening to purple, and the sand ripples stood out like miniature ocean waves in darkening shades of orange. Off to the east on the edge of the desert, a pale saffron glow told us the moon was about to rise behind a thin layer of clouds, slashed by the white contrail of an invisible jet airplane miles away.

6   We had our cameras on tripods and were fussing with light meters, making casual bets as to the exact place where the moon would first appear, when it happened—instant enchantment. Precisely between the twin spires of The Mittens, the enormous globe loomed suddenly, seeming as big as the sun itself, behind a coppery curtain on the rim of creation.

7   We were as totally unprepared for the great size of the moon as we were for its flaming color, nor could we have prepared ourselves for the improbable setting. We felt like the wizards of Stonehenge, commanding the planets to send their light through the magic orifices in line at the equinox. Had the Navajo medicine men contrived this for our benefit?

8   The massive disk of the moon seemed to rise very fast at first, an optical effect magnified by the crystalline air and the flatness of the landscape between us and the distant, ragged skyline. Then it seemed to pause for a moment, as if it were pinioned on one of the pinnacles or impaled on a sharply upthrusting rocky point. Its blazing light made inky shadows all around us, split by the brilliant wedge of the moon's path between the spires. The wind had stopped. There was not a sound anywhere, nor even a whisper. If a drum had sounded just then, it would not have been out of place, I suppose, but it would have frightened us half to death.

9   Before the moon had cleared the tops of The Mittens, the show was over and the magic was gone. A thin veil of clouds spread over the sky, ending the spell as suddenly as it had come upon us. It was as if the gods had decided that

we had seen enough for mere mortals on one spring night, and I must confess it was something of a relief to find ourselves back on mundane earth again, with sand in our shoes and a chill in the air.

1. What dominant impression emerges from this description? Does Young identify the impression for his readers or allow them to determine it from his descriptive language?
2. From what position does Young observe the rising moon? How does he orient the reader to his vantage point?
3. Point out why the language in paragraph 5 is effective.
4. How does the last sentence in paragraph 7 ("Had the Navajo medicine men contrived this for our benefit?") relate to the purpose of the essay?
5. What sense impressions dominate in this essay? What other sensory impressions does Young use? Where are these other impressions found?
6. This description takes the form of a narrative and includes a climax. Where does the climax occur and how does it affect the viewers?

Choose one of the following topics or another that your instructor approves for an essay of description. Create a dominant impression by using carefully chosen, well-organized details observed from an appropriate vantage point. Try to write so that the reader actually experiences your description.

1. Holiday shopping
2. A rock concert
3. An exercise class
4. A graduation audience
5. A shopping center
6. A pet store or zoo
7. A busy city intersection
8. The view from your bedroom window
9. Getting caught in a storm
10. A fast-food restaurant
11. Your house after a party
12. An outdoor place of special importance to you
13. A run-down part of town
14. An automobile
15. An arcade

CHAPTER FOUR

Showing Relationships

CLASSIFICATION
AND
COMPARISON

CLASSIFICATION

Help Wanted, Situations Wanted, Real Estate, Personal. Do these terms look familiar? They do if you've ever scanned the classified ads of the newspaper. Ads are grouped into categories, and each category is then subdivided. The people who assemble this layout are *classifying.* Figure 4.1 shows the main divisions of a typical classified ad section and a further breakdown of one of them.

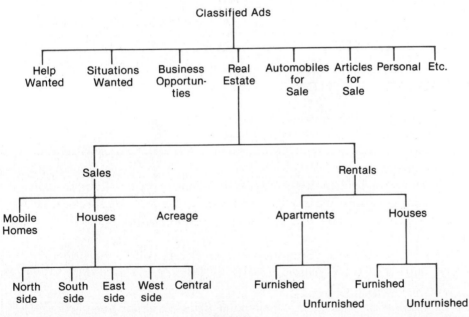

Figure 4.1

As this figure indicates, grouping allows the people who handle ads to divide entries according to a logical scheme and aids readers in finding what they are looking for. Imagine the trouble you would have checking the real estate ads if all the entries were run in the order the ads were placed.

Our minds naturally sort and arrange information into categories. Within a few weeks, newborn infants can tell the faces of family members from those of outsiders. Later, toddlers learn to distinguish between cats, dogs, and rabbits. In both cases the classification rests solely on physical differences. As we mature we start classifying in more abstract ways, and by adulthood we are constantly sorting things into categories: dates or mates, eating places, oddballs, friends, investments, jobs, political views.

Classification also helps writers and readers come to grips with a large or complex topic. A classification paper breaks a broad topic into categories according to some specific principle, presents the distinctive features of each category, and shows how the features vary among categories. Segmenting the topic simplifies the discussion by presenting the information in small, neatly sorted piles, rather than in one jumbled and confusing heap.

Furthermore, classification helps us choose among alternatives. Noting the engine size, maneuverability, seating capacity, and gas mileage of typical subcompact, compact, and intermediate-size cars helps us decide which one to buy. Examining the features of term, whole life, and endowment insurance enables us to select a policy that best fits our needs. As you can see, classification plays an important role in our lives.

WRITING A CLASSIFICATION
CHOOSING A PRINCIPLE
OF CLASSIFICATION

People classify in different ways for different purposes. For instance, a clothing designer might classify women according to their fashion sense; a representative of the National Organization for Women, according to their views on feminism; and the Secretary of Labor, according to their occupations. For your paper, single out and use only one principle of classification for each level of categories, a principle in accord with your purpose. If you break your main categories into subcategories, then it's permissible to shift to another principle (see Fig. 4.2).

Both of these classifications are *proper* because all the groupings at each level share a common ground: country of origin in the first, number of cylinders in the second.

In contrast, applying more than one principle at any one particular level results in overlapping categories. Figure 4.3 shows an *improper* classification. Its scheme is flawed because it groups cars in two ways: by country of origin and by kind. Some small cars, for example, the British Triumph, are both European cars *and* sports cars.

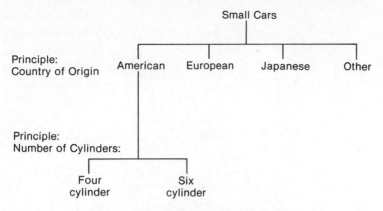

Figure 4.2   Proper Classification of Small Cars

Figure 4.3   Improper Classification of Small Cars

---

1. **How would each of the following people be most likely to classify the families in Anytown, USA?**   **EXERCISE**

   a. The bishop of the Roman Catholic diocese in which the city is located
   b. The state senator who represents the city
   c. A field worker for the NAACP
   d. The director of the local credit bureau

2. **The following lists contain overlapping categories. Identify the inconsistent item in each list and explain why it is faulty.**

Nurses	*Pictures*	*Electorate in Midville*
Surgical nurses	Oil paintings	Republicans
Psychiatric nurses	Magazine illustrations	Democrats
Emergency room nurses	Lithographs	Nonvoters
Terminal care nurses	Watercolors	Independents
Night nurses	Etchings	

"People who wish to register their irritation should go to Room 203. People who want to express their anger should proceed to Room 210. And those who would like to give vent to their frustration must wait here."

Drawing by Koren; ©1982 The New Yorker Magazine, Inc.

DETERMINING THE NUMBER OF CATEGORIES

Once you've targeted a classification principle, turn your attention to how much territory your paper will cover. Sometimes you'll want to discuss every category, at other times only selected ones. Signal your scope in a statement such as this one, taken from a report that identifies and discusses the chief industries in a town: *This study shows that furniture making, food processing, and printing account for 75 percent of the jobs in Lowden.* We can clearly see that the report will not cover all industries.

ORGANIZING THE PAPER

Discuss your categories in whatever order best suits your purpose. Order of climax—least important, more important, and finally most important—frequently works well. Or perhaps your topic will suggest arranging the categories by behavior, income, education, physical characteristics, or the like. In any case, supply the details that treat your reader to a clear picture of each category and the relationships among them.

REVISION CHECKLIST

Ponder these questions as you revise your classification paper.

✔ Why am I classifying? To help the reader understand a complex topic? To choose among alternatives?

✔ Is my principle of classification in line with my purpose?

✔ Do my categories overlap?

✔ Have I developed an appropriate number of categories?

✔ What do my categories have in common? How do they differ?

✔ Have I arranged my categories in an effective order?

✔ Have I developed each one with effective details?

EXAMPLE ESSAYS OF CLASSIFICATION

Undesirable Produce Market Customers
CLARENCE DeLONG

STUDENT WRITING

1   You will find almost as large a variety of customers at a produce market as you will find fruits and vegetables. Undesirable produce market customers fall into three main categories—those who squeeze the fruit, those who complain constantly, and those who try to cheat the market—and when you meet them all in one day, you have one big headache. Perhaps you will recognize these people as I describe them.

2   "Sammy Squeezer" is the least annoying of these undesirables. He wants to make sure that everything he buys is "just right." He pokes his thumbs into the top of a cantaloupe. If they penetrate very deeply, he won't buy this particular specimen, considering it to be overripe. He squeezes the peaches, plums, nectarines, and any other fruit he can get his hands on. After ten of these people squeeze one piece of fruit, it will surely be soft, even if it wasn't originally. Moving on to the corn, Sammy carefully peels back the husk to examine the kernels inside. If they don't suit him, he doesn't bother to fold the husk back to protect the kernels; he simply tosses the ear back into the basket. The problems he creates for the employees are primarily physical—removing the damaged items after he leaves.

3   A more annoying customer is "Betty Bitcher." She is never satisfied with the quality of the produce: the bananas are too green, the lettuce has brown spots, the berries are too ripe, and the potatoes have green spots. Sometimes you wonder if Betty would have been satisfied with the fruit grown in the Garden of Eden.

4   The produce has no monopoly on her complaints, however. Betty also finds fault with the service she receives from the employees. Talking to other customers or directly to the clerks, she can be heard saying such things as "Why is this the only place I ever have to wait in line? They must have trouble getting good help here." Even as she leaves the market, which is none too soon, she must make one last complaint: "You mean I have to carry my own potatoes to the car?" The problems she creates for the employees are primarily mental—she can make your nerves quite active.

5   Perhaps the most annoying customer of all is "Charlie Cheater." You have to keep your eye on him constantly because he knows all the tricks of cheating. He will add berries onto an already full basket. He will take 6/79¢ oranges and tell you they're the 6/59¢ ones. He will put expensive grapes in the bottom of a sack and add cheaper ones on top. Then he'll tell you that they are all the cheaper variety. Likewise, he will put expensive nectarines in a sack, place a few cheaper peaches on top, and try to pass them all off as peaches. If he is caught, he usually says, "I don't know how that happened. My little girl (or boy) must have put them in there." The child usually looks dumbfounded.

6   The problem Charlie creates for the market is twofold: financial and legal. If you don't catch him, your profits suffer. If you do catch him, you almost have to prosecute, usually for amounts of only a dollar or two, or you'll have every Charlie in town at your door.

7   Did you recognize any of these customers? If you didn't and would like to see some of them in action, stop in at Steve's Produce Market. That's where I work, and that's where I meet them.

DISCUSSION QUESTIONS

1. What is the writer's purpose in developing this classification? Where does he state it?
2. In what order has he arranged his categories? Refer to the essay when answering.
3. Demonstrate that the writer has avoided overlapping categories.
4. How do you know he hasn't discussed every category of undesirable customers?

PROFESSIONAL WRITING

Can People Be Judged by Their Appearance?
ERIC BERNE

1   Everyone knows that a human being, like a chicken, comes from an egg. At a very early stage, the human embryo forms a three-layered tube, the inside layer of which grows into the stomach and lungs, the middle layer into bones, muscle, joints, and blood vessels, and the outside layer into the skin and nervous system.

2   Usually these three grow about equally, so that the average human being is a fair mixture of brains, muscles, and inward organs. In some eggs, however, one layer grows more than the others, and when the angels have finished putting

the child together, he may have more gut than brain, or more brain than muscle. When this happens, the individual's activities will often be mostly with the overgrown layer.

We can thus say that while the average human being is a mixture, some   3 people are mainly "digestion-minded," some "muscle-minded," and some "brain-minded," correspondingly digestion-bodied, muscle-bodied, or brain-bodied. The digestion-bodied people look thick; the muscle-bodied people look wide; and the brain-bodied people look long. This does not mean the taller a man is the brainer he will be. It means that if a man, even a short man, looks long rather than wide or thick, he will often be more concerned about what goes on in his mind than about what he does or what he eats; but the key factor is slenderness and not height. On the other hand, a man who gives the impression of being thick rather than long or wide will usually be more interested in a good steak than in a good idea or a good long walk.

Medical men use Greek words to describe these types of body-build. For   4 the man whose body shape mostly depends on the inside layer of the egg, they use the word *endomorph*. If it depends mostly upon the middle layer, they call him a *mesomorph*. If it depends upon the outside layer they call him an *ectomorph*. We can see the same roots in our English words "enter," "medium," and "exit," which might just as easily have been spelled "ender," "mesium," and "ectit."

Since the inside skin of the human egg, or endoderm, forms the inner or-   5 gans of the belly, the viscera, the endomorph is usually belly-minded; since the middle skin forms the body tissues, or soma, the mesomorph is usually muscle-minded; and since the outside skin forms the brain, or cerebrum, the ectomorph is usually brain-minded. Translating this into Greek, we have the viscerotonic endomorph, the somatotonic mesomorph, and the cerebrotonic ectomorph.

Words are beautiful things to a cerebrotonic, but a viscerotonic knows you   6 cannot eat a menu no matter what language it is printed in, and a somatotonic knows you cannot increase your chest expansion by reading a dictionary. So it is advisable to leave these words and see what kinds of people they actually apply to, remembering again that most individuals are fairly equal mixtures and that what we have to say concerns only the extremes. Up to the present, these types have been thoroughly studied only in the male sex.

If a man is definitely a thick type rather than a broad or long type, he is   7 likely to be round and soft, with a big chest but a bigger belly. He would rather eat than breathe comfortably. He is likely to have a wide face, short, thick neck, big thighs and upper arms, and small hands and feet. He has overdeveloped breasts and looks as though he were blown up a little like a balloon. His skin is soft and smooth, and when he gets bald, as he does usually quite early, he loses the hair in the middle of his head first.

The short, jolly, thickset, red-faced politician with a cigar in his mouth, who   8 always looks as though he were about to have a stroke, is the best example of this type. The reason he often makes a good politician is that he likes people, banquets, baths, and sleep; he is easygoing, soothing, and his feelings are easy to understand.

9   His abdomen is big because he has lots of intestines. He likes to take in things. He likes to take in food, and affection and approval as well. Going to a banquet with people who like him is his idea of a fine time. It is important for a psychiatrist to understand the nature of such men when they come to him for advice.

10   If a man is definitely a broad type rather than a thick or long type, he is likely to be rugged and have lots of muscle. He is apt to have big forearms and legs, and his chest and belly are well formed and firm, with the chest bigger than the belly. He would rather breathe than eat. He has a bony head, big shoulders, and a square jaw. His skin is thick, coarse, and elastic, and tans easily. If he gets bald, it usually starts on the front of the head.

11   Dick Tracy, Li'l Abner, and other men of action belong to this type. Such people make good lifeguards and construction workers. They like to put out energy. They have lots of muscles, and they like to use them. They go in for adventure, exercise, fighting, and getting the upper hand. They are bold and unrestrained, and love to master the people and things around them. If the psychiatrist knows the things which give such people satisfaction, he is able to understand why they may be unhappy in certain situations.

12   The man who is definitely a long type is likely to have thin bones and muscles. His shoulders are apt to sag, and he has a flat belly with a dropped stomach, and long, weak legs. His neck and fingers are long, and his face is shaped like a long egg. His skin is thin, dry, and pale, and he rarely gets bald. He looks like an absent-minded professor and often is one.

13   Though such people are jumpy, they like to keep their energy and don't fancy moving around much. They would rather sit quietly by themselves and keep out of difficulties. Trouble upsets them, and they run away from it. Their friends don't understand them very well. They move jerkily and feel jerkily. The psychiatrist who understands how easily they become anxious is often able to help them get along better in the sociable and aggressive world of endomorphs and mesomorphs.

14   In the special cases where people definitely belong to one type or another, then, one can tell a good deal about their personalities from their appearance. When the human mind is engaged in one of its struggles with itself or with the world outside, the individual's way of handling the struggle will be partly determined by his type. If he is a viscerotonic he will often want to go to a party where he can eat and drink and be in good company at a time when he might be better off attending to business; the somatotonic will want to go out and do something about it, master the situation, even if what he does is foolish and not properly figured out, while the cerebrotonic will go off by himself and think it over, when perhaps he would be better off doing something about it or seeking good company to try to forget it.

15   Since these personality characteristics depend on the growth of the layers of the little egg from which the person developed, they are very difficult to change. Nevertheless, it is important for the individual to know about these types,

so that he can have at least an inkling of what to expect from those around him, and can make allowances for the different kinds of human nature, and so that he can become aware of and learn to control his own natural tendencies, which may sometimes guide him into making the same mistakes over and over again in handling his difficulties.

---

1. According to Berne, most individuals do not fit into the categories he discusses. Why then is the information he presents useful to the average person? Where in the essay does Berne address this question?

2. Even though Berne applies scientific labels to the three categories of people he discusses, the essay isn't written for scientists. What audience is Berne trying to reach? How do you know?

3. Point out the significance of the following sentence in paragraph 6: "So it is advisable to leave these words and see what kinds of people they actually apply to, remembering again that most individuals are fairly equal mixtures and that what we have to say concerns only the extremes."

4. In what order does Berne organize his categories? Would another order have worked as well? Why or why not?

5. How does Berne organize the discussion within each of his categories?

Write a classification paper on one of the topics below or one approved by your instructor. Select a principle of classification, choose appropriate categories, arrange them in an effective order, and develop them with specific details.

1. College teachers
2. Pet owners
3. House designs
4. Drivers
5. Churchgoers
6. Pocket calculators
7. Patrons of singles bars
8. Eating places
9. Parents
10. Sports announcers (or fans)
11. Television comedies
12. Attitudes toward death
13. Salesclerks
14. People waiting in line
15. Bores

COMPARISON

Which candidate for senator should get my vote, Ken Conwell or Jerry Mander?

Let me know whether this new shipment of nylon thread meets specs.

Doesn't this tune remind you of a Kenny Rogers song?

How does high school in Australia stack up against high school in this country?

Everyone makes *comparisons*, not just once in a while but day after day. When we compare, we examine two or more items for likenesses, differences, or both.

Frequently, we compare to choose between alternatives. Many issues are trivial: whether to plunk the first quarter in Space Ace or in Star Wars, whether to order pizza or a sub sandwich. But comparison also influences our more important decisions. We choose between majoring in chemistry or chemical engineering, between remaining single or getting married. We weigh buying against renting, working for Slavedriver Industries against working for Scrooge and Marley. In the classroom, instructors may ask us to write a paper that compares the suitability of two pieces of equipment for a particular application. On the job, an employer may have us weigh two proposals for decreasing employee absenteeism and write a report recommending one of them.

Comparison also acquaints us with unfamiliar things. To help an American audience understand the English sport of rugby, a sportswriter might compare its field, team, rules, and scoring system with those for football. To help students learn about West Germany's government, a political science textbook might discuss the features of the German parliament, the way its members are chosen, and the method of picking its chancellor, using our own government as a backdrop.

Comparison, like classification, satisfies our instinctive desire to understand how things relate to one another. But don't confuse the two. Classification shows the relationships among different categories that make up a larger whole. Comparison shows how individual things are similar or different. To illustrate, we would use classification to present the characteristics of bad or good instructors, but we would use comparison to evaluate the classroom performance of two individual instructors. If a good instructor is fired and a bad one becomes a dean, the two classification categories remain intact.

WRITING A COMPARISON

SELECTING ITEMS FOR COMPARISON

Make sure the items you compare share some common ground. For example, you could compare two golfers on driving ability, putting ability, and sand play, or two cars on appearance, gas mileage, and manufacturer's warranty; but you can't meaningfully compare a golfer with a car, any more than you could compare guacamole with Guadalajara or chicken with charcoal. There's simply no basis for comparison.

Any valid comparison, on the other hand, presents many possibilities. Suppose you are the head of the record and tape department of a large store and have two excellent salespeople working for you. The manager of the store asks you to prepare a one- or two-page report that compares their qualifications for managing the record department in a new branch store. On the spot you can rule out items such as eye color, hair style, and religion, which have nothing to do with job performance. Instead, you would decide what managerial traits the job will require and the extent to which each candidate exhibits them. Your thinking might result in a list like this.

Points of Similarity or Difference	Pat	Mike
1. Ability to deal with customers, sales skills	Excellent	Excellent
2. Effort: regular attendance, hard work on the job	Excellent	Excellent
3. Leadership qualities	Excellent	Good
4. Knowledge of ordering and accounting procedures	Good	Fair
5. Musical knowledge	Excellent	Good

This list tells you which points to emphasize and suggests Pat as the candidate to recommend. You might briefly mention similarities (points 1 and 2) in an introductory paragraph, but the report would focus on differences (points 3, 4, and 5), since you're distinguishing between two employees.

Say you want to compare two good restaurants in order to recommend one of them. List the points of similarity and difference that you might discuss. Differences should predominate because you will base your decision on them.

EXERCISE

ORGANIZING THE PAPER

You can use either of two basic patterns to organize a comparison paper: block or alternating.

The Block Pattern.   With the block pattern, the writer first presents all of the information about one item and then all of the information about the other. Here is the comparison of the two salespeople, Pat and Mike, outlined according to the block pattern.

     I. Introduction: mentions similarities in sales skills and effort but recommends Pat for promotion.
    II. Specific points about Mike
        A. Leadership qualities
        B. Knowledge of ordering and accounting procedures
        C. Musical knowledge
    III. Specific points about Pat
        A. Leadership qualities
        B. Knowledge of ordering and accounting procedures
        C. Musical knowledge
    IV. Conclusion: reasserts that Pat should be promoted.

The block pattern works best with short papers or ones that include only a few points of comparison. The reader can easily remember all the points in the first block while reading the second.

The Alternating Pattern.   A writer using the alternating pattern presents a point about one item, then follows immediately with a similar point about the other. Organized in this way, the Pat and Mike paper would look like this:

     I. Introduction: mentions similarities in sales skills and effort but recommends Pat for promotion.
    II. Leadership qualities
        A. Mike's leadership qualities
        B. Pat's leadership qualities
    III. Knowledge of ordering and accounting procedures
        A. Mike's knowledge
        B. Pat's knowledge
    IV. Musical knowledge
        A. Mike's musical knowledge
        B. Pat's musical knowledge
    V. Conclusion: reasserts that Pat should be promoted.

For longer papers that include many points of comparison, use the alternating method. Discussing each point in one place highlights similarities and differences; your reader doesn't have to pause and reread in order to grasp them. The alternating plan also works well for short papers.

Once you select your pattern, arrange your points of comparison in an appropriate order. Take up closely related points one after the other. Depending on your purpose, you might work from similarities to differences or the reverse. Often, a good writing strategy is to move from the least significant to the most significant point so that you conclude with punch.

Using the points of comparison you selected for the exercise on page 75, prepare outlines for a paper organized according to the block and then the alternating pattern.

EXERCISE

Think about these questions as you revise your paper.

REVISION CHECKLIST

- ✔ What is my purpose? To choose between alternatives? Acquaint the reader with something unfamiliar? Does that purpose govern how I've approached my topic?
- ✔ If I'm clarifying the unfamiliar, are my ideas easy for the reader to grasp? Have I compared the unfamiliar with the familiar?
- ✔ Have I considered all points of similarity and difference that bear directly on my purpose?
- ✔ Have I selected appropriate supporting details?
- ✔ Have I chosen an effective arrangement for presenting the likenesses and differences?

ANALOGY

An *analogy,* a special type of comparison, calls attention to one or more similarities underlying different types of items. Most analogies support other kinds of writing. They follow the same organizational patterns as ordinary comparisons.

An analogy often explains something unfamiliar by likening it to something familiar. Here is an example.

The atmosphere of Earth acts like any window in serving two very important functions. It lets light in, and it permits us to look out. It also serves as a shield to keep out dangerous or uncomfortable things. A normal glazed window lets us keep our houses warm by keeping out cold air, and it prevents rain, dirt, and unwelcome insects and animals from coming in. . . . Earth's atmospheric window also helps to keep our planet at a comfortable temperature by holding back radiated heat and protecting us from dangerous levels of ultraviolet light.

Lester del Ray, The Mysterious Sky

Conversely, an analogy sometimes presents information on something unfamiliar in order to help illuminate the familiar. The following paragraph discusses the qualities and obligations of an unfamiliar person, the mountain guide, to shed light on a familiar practice—teaching:

> The mountain guide, like the true teacher, has a quiet authority. He or she engenders trust and confidence so that one is willing to join the endeavor. The guide accepts his leadership role, yet recognizes that success (measured by the heights that are scaled) depends upon the close cooperation and active participation of each member of the group. He has crossed the terrain before and is familiar with the landmarks, but each trip is new and generates its own anxiety and excitement. Essential skills must be mastered; if they are lacking, disaster looms. The situation demands keen focus and rapt attention: slackness, misjudgment, or laziness can abort the venture.

Nancy K. Hill, "Scaling the Heights:
The Teacher as Mountaineer"

Before undertaking an analogy, make sure that the reader will be acquainted with the "familiar" items, that the items are indeed comparable in significant respects, and that the analogy truly illuminates. You could probably develop a meaningful analogy between a heart and a pump or a mob and a storm, but not between a flicker and a flophouse or a laser and limburger cheese.

EXAMPLE ESSAYS OF COMPARISON AND ANALOGY

STUDENT
WRITING

Cultural Gap
STUDENT UNKNOWN

1   On 14th Street N.W. in Washington, D.C., two polarized cultures exist within ten city blocks of each other. They are separated by the river of traffic that flows day and night along P Street, which intersects 14th Street at right angles.

Little or no communication passes between the two cultures to unify their lives, their purposes, or their concerns; and so, in viewing the two cultures, one sees a marked difference between the environments and the peoples of each.

On 14th Street running south from P Street to the Potomac River are op-   2
ulent department stores, such as Woodward and Lothrop and Julius Garfinkle, and small but expensive clothing stores with richly dressed mannequins in the windows. Modern, skyscraping office buildings harbor banks and travel bureaus on the ground floors and insurance companies and corporation headquarters in the upper stories. Dotting the concretescape are high-priced movie theaters, gourmet restaurants, multilevel parking garages, bookstores, candy-novelty-gift shops, and an occasional landmark such as the renovated Ford's Theater—all ca-tering to the prosperous population of the city. This section of 14th Street is rel-atively clean: the city maintenance crews must clean up after only a nine-to-five populace and the Saturday crowds of shoppers. The pervading mood of the area is one of bustling wealth during the day and, in the night, calm.

Crossing P Street toward the north, one notes a gradual but startling   3
change in the scenery of 14th Street. Two architectural features assault the eyes and automatically register as tokens of trouble: the floodlights which leave no alley or doorway in shadows and the riot screens which cage in the store windows. The buildings are old, condemned, decaying monoliths, each occupying an entire city block. Liquor stores, drugstores, dusty television repair shops, seedy por-nographic bookstores that display photographs of naked bodies with the genital areas blacked out by strips of tape, discount stores smelling perpetually of stale chocolate and cold popcorn, and cluttered pawnshops—businesses such as these occupy the street level. Each is separated from the adjoining stores by a littered entranceway which leads up a decaying wooden stairway to the next two floors. All the buildings are three stories tall, all have most of their windows broken and blocked with boards or newspapers, and all reek of liquor, urine, and unidenti-fiable rot. One monolith, representative of the others, is an asymmetrical maze of crooked stairways, winding corridors, and filthy rooms which are carpeted with musty mattresses, strewn with liquor bottles, beer cans, and greasy paper bags, and veiled with layers of settled dust. In the middle of the structure is a rat-infested courtyard piled high with worn tires, rotted-out mattresses, broken glass, and innumerable bags of trash, all thrown where they will never be collected by the city. This section of 14th Street is perpetually dirty; the city makes only a mea-ger attempt to clean up after the populace, perhaps because of their irregular hours. The streets are occupied by roving mobs from ten o'clock at night until dawn the next morning. The prime time for riots coincides with the working hours of the maintenance crews. And so the general atmosphere of this end of 14th Street is one of decadence and poverty.

The daytime inhabitants of the southern end of 14th Street rarely venture   4
into the wasteland to the north. These are government workers, businesspeople, and white-collar workers who can afford to live in the suburbs of nearby Virginia

and Maryland. The great majority are civil-service workers, college-educated, and living in the suburbs; they are able to educate their children in some of the best school systems in the country. Many of these middle- and upper-middle-class citizens have never really seen Washington, D.C.: they brave the rush-hour traffic from six-thirty to nine-thirty in the morning and often take notice only of the particular building in which they work and its surrounding streets. Then they return in the flood of cars on the clogged superhighways to isolated, comfortable homes and the activities of the reasonably well-off.

5   The nocturnal inhabitants of the northern half of 14th Street, however, are blue-collar workers, poorly paid menial laborers, and persons who are unemployed because they lack the necessary education or because deprivation has robbed them of the will to work. These people live in housing that is owned by absentee landlords who charge unjustly high rents and make no effort to maintain the buildings at a level adequate for human occupancy. Nor are their children able to secure an adequate education: the city of Washington operates at the mercy of the Senate, which allocates just enough money to maintain city services at a low and totally inadequate level, but not enough to improve them.

6   And so, trapped by economic and social squalor, the inhabitants of this urban slum congregate along 14th Street at night, looking for entertainment and temporary escape. It is here that one finds the prostitutes, the junkies, the alcoholics, and the numerous street people who frequent burlesque houses, raw bars, and peep shows. The buildings along 14th Street harbor a transient population of junkies, runaways, and drifters. Here, a scuffle between two people or a parking ticket left by a policeman can spark a spontaneous riot. This is the culture of 14th Street, the closely-knit society of people who share the same lives, where everybody knows everybody else.

7   Thus, a stark contrast exists between the two cultures of 14th Street, which appears to be like an earthworm, with half of its body crushed by poverty, but the other half still alive, wriggling in wealth. The two are alike only in that each communicates little with the other, because of the wide disparity between the lives of the people and the conditions of the environments. The devastating irony of the situation on 14th Street lies in the fact that only ten blocks away sit the very governmental institutions that could alleviate the poverty—the Senate, the House of Representatives, and the White House.

DISCUSSION QUESTIONS

1. What point does the writer want to make by contrasting the two parts of 14th Street? Where is it made clear? By what other means is it suggested?
2. What pattern of organization has the writer used?
3. Point out effective supporting details. What can you learn from them?
4. Why does the essay devote more space to discussing the poor end of the street than to discussing the prosperous part?

That Lean and Hungry Look
SUZANNE BRITT JORDAN

Caesar was right. Thin people need watching. I've been watching them for most of my adult life, and I don't like what I see. When these narrow fellows spring at me, I quiver to my toes. Thin people come in all personalities, most of them menacing. You've got your "together" thin person, your mechanical thin person, your condescending thin person, your tsk-tsk thin person, your efficiency-expert thin person. All of them are dangerous. 1

In the first place, thin people aren't fun. They don't know how to goof off, at least in the best, fat sense of the word. They've always got to be adoing. Give them a coffee break, and they'll jog around the block. Supply them with a quiet evening at home, and they'll fix the screen door and lick S&H green stamps. They say things like "there aren't enough hours in the day." Fat people never say that. Fat people think the day is too damn long already. 2

Thin people make me tired. They've got speedy little metabolisms that cause them to bustle briskly. They're forever rubbing their bony hands together and eying new problems to "tackle." I like to surround myself with sluggish, inert, easygoing fat people, the kind who believe that if you clean it up today, it'll just get dirty again tomorrow. 3

Some people say the business about the jolly fat person is a myth, that all of us chubbies are neurotic, sick, sad people. I disagree. Fat people may not be chortling all day long, but they're a hell of a lot *nicer* than the wizened and shriveled. Thin people turn surly, mean and hard at a young age because they never learn the value of a hot-fudge sundae for easing tension. Thin people don't like gooey soft things because they themselves are neither gooey nor soft. They are crunchy and dull, like carrots. They go straight to the heart of the matter while fat people let things stay all blurry and hazy and vague, the way things actually are. Thin people want to face the truth. Fat people know there is no truth. One of my thin friends is always staring at complex, unsolvable problems and saying, "The key thing is . . ." Fat people never say that. They know there isn't any such thing as the key thing about anything. 4

Thin people believe in logic. Fat people see all sides. The sides fat people see are rounded blobs, usually gray, always nebulous and truly not worth worrying about. But the thin person persists. "If you consume more calories than you burn," says one of my thin friends, "you will gain weight. It's that simple." Fat people always grin when they hear statements like that. They know better. 5

Fat people realize that life is illogical and unfair. They know very well that God is not in his heaven and all is not right with the world. If God was up there, fat people could have two doughnuts and a big orange drink anytime they wanted it. 6

Thin people have a long list of logical things they are always spouting off to me. They hold up one finger at a time as they reel off these things, so I won't 7 lose track. They speak slowly as if to a young child. The list is long and full of holes. It contains tidbits like "get a grip on yourself," "cigarettes kill," "cholesterol clogs," "fit as a fiddle," "ducks in a row," "organize" and "sound fiscal management." Phrases like that.

8   They think these 2,000-point plans lead to happiness. Fat people know happiness is elusive at best and even if they could get the kind thin people talk about, they wouldn't want it. Wisely, fat people see that such programs are too dull, too hard, too off the mark. They are never better than a whole cheesecake.

9   Fat people know all about the mystery of life. They are the ones acquainted with the night, with luck, with fate, with playing it by ear. One thin person I know once suggested that we arrange all the parts of a jigsaw puzzle into groups according to size, shape and color. He figured this would cut the time needed to complete the puzzle by at least 50 percent. I said I wouldn't do it. One, I like to muddle through. Two, what good would it do to finish early? Three, the jigsaw puzzle isn't the important thing. The important thing is the fun of four people (one thin person included) sitting around a card table, working a jigsaw puzzle. My thin friend had no use for my list. Instead of joining us, he went outside and mulched the boxwoods. The three remaining fat people finished the puzzle and made chocolate, double-fudged brownies to celebrate.

10   The main problem with thin people is they oppress. Their good intentions, bony torsos, tight ships, neat corners, cerebral machinations and pat solutions loom like dark clouds over the loose, comfortable, spread-out, soft world of the fat. Long after fat people have removed their coats and shoes and put their feet up on the coffee table, thin people are still sitting on the edge of the sofa, looking neat as a pin, discussing rutabagas. Fat people are heavily into fits of laughter, slapping their thighs and whooping it up, while thin people are still politely waiting for the punch line.

11   Thin people are downers. They like math and morality and reasoned evaluation of the limitations of human beings. They have their skinny little acts together. They expound, prognose, probe and prick.

12   Fat people are convivial. They will like you even if you're irregular and have acne. They will come up with a good reason why you never wrote the great American novel. They will cry in your beer with you. They will put your name in the pot. They will let you off the hook. Fat people will gab, giggle, guffaw, gallumph, gyrate and gossip. They are generous, giving and gallant. They are gluttonous and goodly and great. What you want when you're down is soft and jiggly, not muscled and stable. Fat people know this. Fat people have plenty of room. Fat people will take you in.

DISCUSSION QUESTIONS

1. Cite passages from Jordan's essay to show that she is trying to entertain us.
2. Jordan asserts that thin people have four shortcomings. What are they, and where is each discussed? In what order are these shortcomings arranged?

3. Why do you think Jordan uses the alternating pattern rather than the block pattern to organize her essay.
4. In paragraph 11, Jordan charges that thin people like to make "reasoned evaluation of the limitations of human beings". In what way is this statement ironic?

Nations Can Be Schizoid Too*
CHARLES OSGOOD

PROFESSIONAL
WRITING

One mark of schizophrenia or a schizoid personality according to R.D. Laing, one of the world's experts on the subject, is that a person gets to feeling that at least part of his life and experience is somehow unreal. There's a real self and an unreal self. The real self, his actual core personality, is what he calls me. But it's the me nobody knows. The other part, the unreal, accidental, or artificial self, is the one he projects to the world. The sicker he gets the more he thinks it is the unreal self and not the real self that is acting when he acts. The him that is driving a car, listening to the radio, fighting with his wife, or robbing a bank is not the real him. However, if you have to deal with this individual the real him is the one that's doing these things. What he thinks of as the real him is what is unreal to everybody else. The individual they see walking, talking, acting one way or another, is what that individual really is as far as they are concerned. That inner him that nobody knows, nobody knows—so it is unreal to them.   1

Now all of us are a little bit schizoid. We all do this thing of distinguishing between ourselves as we conceive of ourselves and the superficial, at least from our point of view superficial, us that faces the rest of the world. Of course to the rest of the world that superficial face is us.   2

Nations can be schizoid, too. We can, for example, get to feeling that the real America is something quite distinct from the day-to-day way that America is and acts. We can say yes there are awful problems in the cities but the cities are not the real America. We can say yes there are economic and social problems but that unemployed people, black people, or poor people are not the real Americans. We can say yes there is injustice but the real America is just. We can acknowledge the American military is the biggest, strongest, and most expensive in the world . . . yet know on another level that the real America is not militaristic, is peaceloving and would never act the bully. We can say the polluted lakes and streams and rivers are just an accident of progress—they are not the real American waters—any more than the air over New York or LA is the real American air.   3

To the outside world the real America is what they see and hear—what we say and how we act. To them the real America is homes and radio and newspa-   4 pers, highways, our television, our politicians and policemen, our criminals and prisons—it is our businesses, science, schools, hospitals, cities, suburbs, farms—everything visible, audible, and tangible about us. The point is that we are all these things and that to the extent we disassociate from them and feel that they have nothing to do with us to that extent we are schizoid. Finally if we get to the point where we think that there is a real America only we can see, if our inner vision does not correspond to what other people think about us, we shouldn't be too surprised if they think we are crazy.

DISCUSSION QUESTIONS

1. What point does this analogy make? Is the point stated or unstated? If stated, where does it appear?
2. Why does Osgood begin by citing an authority?
3. Does the essay explain the familiar by likening it to the unfamiliar or the unfamiliar by likening it to the familiar?
4. Why does Osgood emphasize national rather than individual schizophrenia?

SUGGESTIONS FOR WRITING

1. **Write a comparison essay on one of the topics below or another that your instructor approves. List the points you will discuss and then arrange them in a suitable pattern. Emphasize similarities, differences, or both.**

    a. A liberal arts versus a technical education
    b. The physical or mental demands of two jobs
    c. Two advertisements
    d. Parents versus teachers as educators
    e. Something natural and something artificial
    f. A novel and a movie that tell the same story
    g. Two instructors
    h. Two sportscasters or news commentators
    i. A television family and your family
    j. The business, residential, or slum districts of two cities or a wealthy and a working-class residential district in the same city
    k. A favorite social spot during the day and during the evening
    l. Suburban home life versus apartment life
    m. The effectiveness of two pieces of writing
    n. The working conditions on two jobs
    o. Two techniques for doing something in your field

2. **Select one of the following topics or another that your instructor approves for an analogy essay. Proceed as you would for any other comparison.**

    a. The offerings in a college catalog and a restaurant
    b. A conquering army and a swarm of locusts

c. An electric current and water flowing through a pipe
d. A heart and a pump
e. The structure of an atom and that of the solar system
f. A teacher and a merchant
g. Cancer and anarchy
h. A parent and a farmer
i. A brain and a telephone switchboard
j. Earth and a spaceship
k. A camera and the human eye
l. A workaholic and an alcoholic
m. A mob and a storm
n. A kidney and a filter
o. A cluttered attic and a disorderly mind

CHAPTER FIVE

Explaining How and Why

PROCESS ANALYSIS AND CAUSE AND EFFECT

PROCESS ANALYSIS

"Hey Bill, I'd like you to take a look at Mr. Gorgerise's car. He's really fuming. Says the engine's burning too much oil, running rough, and getting poor mileage. Check it out and see what you can find."

Bill begins by removing the spark plugs, hooking a remote-control starter to the starter in the car, and grounding the ignition to prevent the car's starting accidentally. Next, he fits a compression pressure gauge into the sparkplug hole by cylinder number one, starts the engine, and reads and records the pressure; then he does the same for each of the other cylinders. Finally, he compares the readings with one another and the auto maker's engine specs. The verdict? An excessively worn engine that needs rebuilding. Bill has carried out a *process,* just one among many that fill his workdays.

As we pursue our affairs, we perform processes almost constantly, ranging from such daily rituals as brewing a pot of coffee and flossing our teeth to taking a picture, taping a record album, preparing for a date, or replacing a light switch. Often we share our special technique for doing something—for example, making chicken cacciatore—by passing it on to a friend.

Some process analyses give step-by-step directions for doing something; others tell how some procedure is, was, or will be carried out. Like narration, process analysis presents a series of actions, but its purpose is different: to explain the "how" rather than the "what" of the events.

Many popular publications feature process analyses, which help readers to sew zippers in garments, build catamarans, live within their means, and improve their wok technique. Process analysis also frequently helps you meet the writing demands of your courses. A political-science instructor may ask you to explain how Reagan won the presidential nomination in 1980, or a biology instructor may want an explanation of how bees find their way back to the hive. Another instructor may call for directions relating to some process in your field—for example, analyzing a chemical compound, programming a computer, taking fingerprints, or obtaining a blood sample. Later, depending on your job, your employer may require directions for assembling a device or developing a new order-handling procedure.

As these examples show, a process can be nontechnical, historical, scientific, natural, or technical.

WRITING A PROCESS ANALYSIS

The first decision about a process analysis is whether you want your reader to perform the process or simply to understand it. Your choice will dictate how you address the reader and present the material.

PERFORMING A PROCESS

A "how-to" explanation presents instruction in the form of commands and often addresses the reader directly as "you." This approach tends to involve the reader in what you are explaining while emphasizing that the directions must be, not merely should be, followed.

The Introduction.   Start your paper by identifying the process, listing the items needed to carry it out, and noting any special conditions necessary to ensure a successful outcome. You might also note the usefulness or importance of the process or encourage the reader by indicating how easy it is to perform. For scientific and technical processes, follow conventional practice by ending the introduction with a list of the major steps in the process.

Here's how the introduction to a paper on grilling hamburgers might look:

> Grilling hamburgers on an outdoor charcoal grill is a simple process that almost anyone can master. Before starting, you will need a clean grill, charcoal briquets, charcoal lighter fluid and matches, hamburger meat, a plate, a spatula, and some water to put out any flames caused by fat drippings. The sizzling, tasty patties you will have when you finish are a treat that almost everyone will enjoy.

DISCUSSION QUESTIONS

1. How does the writer try to induce the reader to perform the process?
2. Why doesn't this introduction include a listing of steps?

The Body.   The body of a process paper discusses each step in detail. Plan this part by jotting down every step you can think of. Be especially careful not to omit a step that is obvious to you but wouldn't be to your reader. This kind of oversight can doom your efforts to failure.

Armed with your list, now arrange the steps in order. The list for the paper on grilling hamburgers might look like this:

1. Remove grill rack
2. Prepare charcoal
3. Light charcoal
4. Make hamburger patties
5. Wait until briquets turn an ash-white color (thirty to forty-five minutes)
6. Replace grill rack
7. Place patties on it
8. Flip them over
9. Remove patties from grill

In some processes, only one order will work; in others, you'll be able to vary the arrangement somewhat. Changing an automobile tire demands a set procedure. The car must be jacked up before the flat is removed, and the flat must be removed before the spare is put on. When you grill hamburgers, however, it matters little whether you light the charcoal before or after you gather the hamburger ingredients and shape the patties. If you have some leeway, choose whatever order has worked effectively for you.

As you develop each step, indicate its purpose, unless it's obvious. The reader will then work more intelligently and efficiently, without skipping necessary tasks. Flag an especially dangerous or difficult step with a cautionary warning. If two or more steps must be carried out simultaneously, say so at the start of the first one.

Let's see how part of the body of the paper on hamburger grilling might unfold:

> The first step is to get the fire going. Remove the grill rack and stack about twenty charcoal briquets in a pyramid shape in the center of the grill. Stacking allows the briquets to burn off one another and thus produces a hotter fire. Next, squirt charcoal lighter fluid over the briquets. Wait about five minutes so that the fluid has time to soak into the charcoal. Then toss in a lighted match. The flame will burn for a few minutes before it goes out. When this happens, allow the briquets to sit for another fifteen minutes so that the charcoal can start to burn. Once the burning starts, do not squirt on any more lighter fluid. A flame could quickly follow the stream back into the can, causing it to explode. As the briquets begin to turn from pitch black to ash white, spread them out with a stick so that they barely touch one another. Air can circulate and produce a hot, even fire, the type that makes grilling a success.

---

1. At what points has the writer provided reasons for doing things?
2. Where has he included a warning?

DISCUSSION QUESTIONS

EXERCISE   1. **Develop a complete list of the steps involved in one of the following processes; then arrange them in an appropriate order.**

    a. Baking bread
    b. Assembling or repairing some common household device
    c. Carrying out a process related to sports
    d. Breaking a bad habit
    e. Building a fire in a fireplace

    2. **Examine your favorite newspaper or magazine for examples of process analysis. Bring them to class for group discussion of how they illustrate step-by-step directions.**

The Conclusion.   Bring your essay to a close with a few brief remarks that help the reader see the total process more clearly. A conclusion can summarize the process, evaluate its results, or discuss its importance. Choose the type you think most appropriate and helpful. The paper on hamburger grilling might end this way:

> Once the patties are cooked the way you like them, remove them from the grill and place them on buns. Now you are ready to enjoy a mouthwatering treat that you will long remember.
>
> E. M. Pryzblyo

UNDERSTANDING A PROCESS

Sometimes a process analysis explains how some procedure is, was, or will be carried out rather than indicating how to perform it. This type of paper follows the same general pattern as a "how-to" process but differs in a few key ways. First, the introduction seldom lists any steps or mentions special conditions required to perform the process. Nor does the body offer any warnings or statements of purpose. Furthermore, information-only processes do not issue polite commands or address the reader directly as "you." Instead, the writer uses the first person (I, we), third person (he, she, it), or the passive voice, which presents the actions without naming their doers ("two samples were chosen for testing"). Customarily, technical process and lab experiments are written in the passive voice.

EXERCISE   **Read the following excerpts and answer the questions at the end.**

    1.   To define a word . . . the dictionary editor places before him the stack of cards illustrating that word; each of the cards represents the use of the word by

a writer of some literary or historical importance. He reads the cards carefully, discards some, re-reads the rest, and divides up the stack according to what he thinks are the several senses of the word. Finally, he writes his definition, following the hard-and-fast rule that each definition must be based on what the quotations in front of him reveal about the meaning of the word.

S. I. Hayakawa, *Language in Thought and Action*

2.   To prepare a bacterial smear for staining, first use an inoculating loop to place a drop of distilled water on a clean glass microscope slide. Next pass the loop and the opening of the tube containing the bacterial culture to be examined through a Bunsen burner flame to sterilize them. From the tube, remove a small bit of culture with the loop, and rub the loop in the drop of water on the slide until the water covers an area one and one-half inches long and approximately the width of the slide. Next reflame the opening of the culture tube to prevent contamination of the culture, and then plug it shut. Allow the smear to air dry, and then pass the slide, smear side up, through the flame of the burner until it is warm to the touch. The dried smear should have a cloudy, milky-white appearance.

Darryl Williams

3.   Thus, when I now approach a stack of three two-inch cinder blocks to attempt a breaking feat, I do not set myself to "try hard," or to summon up all my strength. Instead I relax, sinking my awareness into my belly and legs, feeling my connection with the ground. I breathe deeply, mentally directing the breath through my torso, legs, and arms. I imagine a line of force coming up from the ground through my legs, down one arm, and out through the stone slabs, and down again into the ground, penetrating to the center of the earth. I do not focus any attention on the objects to be broken. Although when I am lifting or holding them in a normal state of consciousness the blocks seem tremendously dense, heavy, and hard, in the course of my one- or two-minute preparation their reality seems to change, as indeed the reality of the whole situation changes. . . . When I make my final approach to the bricks, if I regard them at all they seem light, airy, and friendly; they do not have the insistent inner drive in them that I do.

I do not hit the bricks; I do not break them. Rather, I take a deep breath, hold it for half a second, then *release* suddenly but smoothly, focusing on the energy line and allowing my arm to express it. My palm passes right through the place where the blocks were, but they have apparently parted just before I get there, and there is no sensation of impact, no shock wave, no pain. . . . Hours later, what remains is not the sense of destructive power but the feeling of attunement with universal forces, of identification with the mysterious but very real power of life itself.

Don Ethan Miller, "A State of Grace: Understanding the Martial Arts"

4.   The analyzer was adjusted so the scale read zero and connected to the short sampling tube which had previously been inserted into the smoke stack. The sample was taken by depressing the bulb the requisite number of times, and the re-

sults were then read and recorded The procedure was repeated, this time using the long sampling tube and sampling through the fire door.

Charles Finnie

Answer questions 1 and 2 about each excerpt above.

1. Does the writer expect a reader to perform or merely understand the process? How do you know?
2. Is the excerpt written in the first, second, or third person? The passive voice? Why?

Questions 3 through 5 refer to specified excerpts above.

3. Excerpt 1 does not explain why the dictionary editor discards some word cards. What reason can you give for this omission?
4. Cite two places in excerpt 2 where the writer notes the purpose of an action. Why are these explanations provided?
5. Why doesn't Miller use polite commands in excerpt 3?

REVISION CHECKLIST

Here are some questions to ask yourself as you revise your process analysis.

- ✔ Do I expect my readers to carry out or merely comprehend the process?
- ✔ Is my explanation complete? Have I included all necessary steps? Have I supplied an explanation where the purpose of a step is not clear? Have I mentioned any special conditions the reader needs to know about? Have I supplied warnings for any steps that are dangerous or might be performed improperly?
- ✔ Are my steps presented in the proper order?
- ✔ Have I developed each step in sufficient detail?

EXAMPLE ESSAYS
OF PROCESS ANALYSIS

STUDENT WRITING

The ABC's of CPR
KATHY PETROSKI

1   A heart attack, drowning, choking, or electrocution—any of these can stop an adult's breathing. The victim, however, need not always die. Many a life that would otherwise be lost could be saved simply by applying the ABC's of CPR—Cardiopulmonary Resuscitation. Here's how it is performed. When you are certain that the victim's breathing and pulse have stopped, begin CPR immediately.

If breathing and circulation are not restored within five minutes, irreversible brain damage occurs. CPR requires no special equipment; presence of mind, however, is absolutely essential.

A stands for opening the airway. Lay the victim in a supine (face up) position on a firm surface. Once the victim is correctly positioned, quickly tilt the head as far back as possible by placing one hand beneath the neck and gently lifting upward. In an unconscious person, the tongue falls to the back of the throat and blocks the air passages. Hyperextending the head in this fashion pulls the tongue from that position, thus allowing air to pass. At the same time tilt the forehead back with the other hand until the chin points straight upward. The relaxed jaw muscles will then tighten, opening the air passage to the lungs. Remove your hand from the forehead and, using your first two fingers, check the mouth for food, dentures, vomitus, or a foreign object. Remove any obstruction with a sweeping motion. These measures may cause the patient to start breathing spontaneously. If they do not, mouth-to-mouth resuscitation must be started.   2

B stands for breathing. While maintaining your grasp behind the neck, pinch the victim's nostrils shut with the index finger and thumb of your other hand. Open your mouth, and place it over the victim's mouth so that a tight seal is formed. Such contact allows air to reach and expand the lungs. If the seal is incomplete, you will hear your own breath escaping. Deliver four quick, full breaths without allowing the victim's lungs to deflate completely between breaths; then remove your mouth and allow him to exhale passively. At this point, check the carotid pulse to determine whether the heart is beating. To do so, place the tips of your index and middle fingers laterally into the groove between the trachea (windpipe) and the muscles at the side of the neck. If no pulse is evident, artificial circulation must be started.   3

C means circulation. Locate the lower end of the sternum (breastbone), and move upward approximately the width of two fingers. At this point, firmly apply the heel of one hand, positioning the fingers at right angles to the length of the body and keeping them slanted upward. If the hand is positioned any higher or lower on the sternum, serious internal injuries in the abdomen or chest are possible. Now place the heel of your second hand on top of your first. The fingers may be interlaced or interlocked, but they must not touch the chest, or the force of your compressions may fracture ribs.   4

Keeping your elbows straight and pushing down from the shoulders, apply firm, heavy pressure until the sternum is depressed approximately one and one-half to two inches. Rock forward and backward in a rhythmic fashion, exerting pressure with the weight of your body. This action squeezes the heart against the immobile spine with enough pressure to pump blood from the left ventricle of the heart into general circulation. Compress the chest, and then immediately release the pressure, fifteen times. Do not, at any point in the cycle, remove your hands from the chest wall. Counting the compressions aloud will help develop a systematic cycle, which is essential for success. When the fifteen have been completed, pinch the nose as described above, seal the victim's mouth with your own, and deliver a quick breath of air. As the victim exhales, inhale another breath and   5 deliver it, and then compress the chest an additional fifteen times. Alternate res-piration and compression steps, timing yourself so as to deliver approximately eighty compressions per minute.

6   At various intervals, quickly check the effectiveness of your CPR technique. Lift the eyelids and notice if the pupils are constricted—a key sign that the brain is receiving enough oxygen. In addition, if the bluish color of the victim is de-creasing and spontaneous breathing and movement are increasing, the victim has responded favorably.

7   To maximize the chances for survival, do not interrupt this technique for more than five or ten seconds. Continue the ABC's of CPR until competent med-ical help or life-support equipment arrives.

DISCUSSION QUESTIONS

1. How does the writer use the letters *A, B,* and *C* from the CPR technique in this paper?
2. How does the opening paragraph prepare the reader for what follows?
3. Where does the essay indicate the purposes of actions?
4. What order has the writer used? Explain why this order is a good choice.
5. Is the purpose of this essay to provide a procedure for the reader to follow or to explain how a process is carried out? Give reasons for your answer.

PROFESSIONAL WRITING

From *The Spider and the Wasp**

ALEXANDER PETRUNKEVITCH

1   In the adult stage the [pepsis] wasp lives only a few months. The female produces but a few eggs, one at a time at intervals of two or three days. For each egg the mother must provide one adult tarantula, alive but paralyzed. The mother wasp attaches the egg to the paralyzed spider's abdomen. Upon hatching from the egg, the larva is many hundreds of times smaller than its living but help-less victim. It eats no other food and drinks no water. By the time it has finished its single Gargantuan meal and become ready for wasphood, nothing remains of the tarantula but its indigestible chitinous skeleton.

2   The mother wasp goes tarantula-hunting when the egg in her ovary is al-most ready to be laid. Flying low over the ground late on a sunny afternoon, the wasp looks for its victim or for the mouth of a tarantula burrow, a round hole edged by a bit of silk. The sex of the spider makes no difference, but the mother is highly discriminating as to species. Each species of Pepsis requires a certain species of tarantula, and the wasp will not attack the wrong species. In a cage with a tarantula which is not its normal prey, the wasp avoids the spider and is usually killed by it in the night.

3   Yet when a wasp finds the correct species, it is the other way about. To iden-tify the species the wasp apparently must explore the spider with her antennae. The tarantula shows an amazing tolerance to this exploration. The wasp crawls under it and walks over it without evoking any hostile response. The molestation

is so great and so persistent that the tarantula often rises on all eight legs, as if it were on stilts. It may stand this way for several minutes. Meanwhile the wasp, having satisfied itself that the victim is of the right species, moves off a few inches to dig the spider's grave. Working vigorously with legs and jaws, it excavates—like a machine—a hole 8 to 10 inches deep with a diameter slightly larger than the spider's girth. Now and again the wasp pops out of the hole to make sure that the spider is still there.

When the grave is finished, the wasp returns to the tarantula to complete   4
her ghastly enterprise. First she feels it all over once more with her antennae. Then her behavior becomes more aggressive. She bends her abdomen, protruding her sting, and searches for the soft membrane at the point where the spider's legs join its body—the only spot where she can penetrate the horny skeleton. From time to time, as the exasperated spider slowly shifts ground, the wasp turns on her back and slides along with the aid of her wings, trying to get under the tarantula for a shot at the vital spot. During all this maneuvering, which can last for several minutes, the tarantula makes no move to save itself. Finally the wasp corners it against some obstruction and grasps one of its legs in her powerful jaws. Now at last the harassed spider tries a desperate but vain defense. The two contestants roll over and over on the ground. It is a terrifying sight and the outcome is always the same. The wasp finally manages to thrust her sting into the soft spot and holds it there for a few seconds while she pumps in the poison. Almost immediately the tarantula falls paralyzed on its back. Its legs stop twitching; its heart stops beating. Yet it is not dead, as is shown by the fact that if taken from the wasp it can be restored to some sensitivity by being kept in a moist chamber for several months.

After paralyzing the tarantula, the wasp cleans herself by dragging her   5
body around the ground and rubbing her feet, sucks the drop of blood oozing from the wound in the spider's abdomen, then grabs a leg of the flabby, helpless animal in her jaws and drags it down to the bottom of the grave. She stays there for many minutes, sometimes for several hours, and what she does all that time in the dark we do not know. Eventually she lays her egg and attaches it to the side of the spider's abdomen with a sticky secretion. Then she emerges, fills the grave with soil carried bit by bit in her jaws, and finally tramples the ground all around to hide any trace of the grave from prowlers. Then she flies away, leaving her descendant safely started in life.

In all this the behavior of the wasp evidently is qualitatively different from   6
that of the spider. The wasp acts like an intelligent animal. This is not to say that instinct plays no part or that she reasons as man does. But her actions are to the point; they are not automatic and can be modified to fit the situation. We do not know for certain how she identifies the tarantula—probably it is by some olfactory or chemo-tactile sense—but she does it purposefully and does not blindly tackle a wrong species.

On the other hand, the tarantula's behavior shows only confusion. Evi-   7
dently the wasp's pawing gives it no pleasure, for it tries to move away. That the wasp is not simulating sexual stimulation is certain because male and female tarantulas react in the same way to its advances. That the spider is not anesthetized by some odorless secretion is easily shown by blowing lightly at the tarantula and

making it jump suddenly. What, then, makes the tarantula behave as stupidly as it does?

8   No clear, simple answer is available. Possibly the stimulation by the wasp's antennae is masked by a heavier pressure on the spider's body, so that it reacts as when prodded by a pencil. But the explanation may be much more complex. Initiative in attack is not in the nature of tarantulas; most species fight only when cornered so that escape is impossible. Their inherited patterns of behavior apparently prompt them to avoid problems rather than attack them. For example, spiders always weave their webs in three dimensions, and when a spider finds that there is insufficient space to attach certain threads in the third dimension, it leaves the place and seeks another, instead of finishing the web in a single plane. This urge to escape seems to arise under all circumstances, in all phases of life, and to take the place of reasoning. For a spider to change the pattern of its web is as impossible as for an inexperienced man to build a bridge across a chasm obstructing his way.

9   In a way the instinctive urge to escape is not only easier but often more efficient than reasoning. The tarantula does exactly what is most efficient in all cases except in an encounter with a ruthless and determined attacker dependent for the existence of her own species on killing as many tarantulas as she can lay eggs. Perhaps in this case the spider follows its usual pattern of trying to escape, instead of seizing and killing the wasp, because it is not aware of its danger. In any case, the survival of the tarantula species as a whole is protected by the fact that the spider is much more fertile than the wasp.

DISCUSSION QUESTIONS

1. Into how many steps is this natural process divided? In which paragraph or paragraphs is each discussed?
2. Characterize Petrunkevitch's attitude toward his topic. Is it completely objective, or does Petrunkevitch sometimes reveal his personal feelings? If he does, indicate where.
3. Petrunkevitch uses a number of transitional words and phrases to ensure a smooth flow of ideas. Indicate those transitional devices and the paragraphs in which they are found.
4. Where does the conclusion begin and what is its purpose?

SUGGESTIONS FOR WRITING

Write a process analysis on one of the topics below or one approved by your instructor. The paper may provide instructions for the reader to follow or tell how a process is performed. Prepare a complete list of steps, arrange them in an appropriate order, and follow them as you write the body of your essay.

1. Succeeding at pinball or your favorite video game
2. Programming a computer
3. Making a good impression on a first date
4. Breaking a bad habit

5. Dealing with a bite of a poisonous snake
6. Training a dog or another pet
7. Preparing for a two-week vacation
8. Growing a particular type of fruit or vegetable in a home garden
9. Carrying out a process related to your hobby
10. Preparing your favorite meal
11. Studying for an examination
12. Performing a process required by your job
13. Achieving some important goal
14. Building the body beautiful
15. Being the life of a party

CAUSE AND EFFECT

"Dad, why do Mexican jumping beans jump?"
"I don't know, Lee."
"Well, then, why do zebras have stripes?"
"You've got me there, too."
"I wonder what happens inside the TV when I turn it on."
"Couldn't tell you. Lots of things, probably."
"Say, Dad, do you mind all these questions?"
"Of course not. If you don't ask questions, how'll you ever learn anything?"

People, of course, do learn lots of things without asking questions. This brief dialogue, for example, shows that *causation,* like a coin or record, has two sides. The first side, cause, probes the reasons why actions, events, attitudes, and conditions occur. Effect, the second side, examines their consequences. Causal analysis explains the operation of devices, the attitudes and actions of individuals and groups, as well as historical events and natural happenings.

All of us ask and answer questions of causation. Scott wonders why Susie *really* broke off their relationship, and fraternity members speculate on the ultimate results of a serious hazing injury. Your instructors ask you to write on topics such as the causes of the American Revolution, the consequences of the 1929 crash, the reasons why so many couples are divorcing, or the effects of different fertilizers on plant growth. An employer may want a report on why a certain product malfunctions, what might happen if a community redesigns its traffic pattern, or how a school closing might affect business. Newspaper headlines proclaim "Oil Glut Drops Gas Prices" or "President Blames Fed for High Interest Rates," both echoing causal relationships. While watching a cable movie you wonder what the reason is behind the wavering picture. Thinking in terms of cause and effect goes on all the time.

Matters of causation almost always feature more than one cause and more than one effect. Sometimes a set of events forms a sequence called a causal chain, with each event the effect of the preceding one and the cause of the next one. Interrupting the chain at any point halts the sequence. Think of this chain as a long row of upright dominoes: push one over, and the rest topple one after the other. One political theory proposed that notion regarding the nations of Southeast Asia, holding that if one fell to the communists, others would follow until all did. Belief in this domino theory helped bring about the United States's entry into the Vietnam war. Causal chains can also help explain how devices function and some social changes proceed.

Often the sequence of causes and effects is too complex to fit the image of a chain. Suppose you are driving to a movie on a rainy night. You approach an intersection screened by bushes and, because you have the right-of-way, start across. Suddenly a car with unlit headlights looms directly in your path. You hit the brakes but skid on the slippery pavement and crash into the other car, crumpling its left fender and damaging your own bumper. Later, as you mull the episode over in your mind, you begin to sense its complexities.

Obviously, the *immediate cause* of the accident was the failure of the other driver to heed the stop sign. But other causes also played a part: the bushes and the unlit headlights that prevented you from seeing the other car sooner, the wet pavement that caused you to skid, and the movie that brought you out in the first place.

Further thinking leads you to recognize still other factors. During your drive, you changed speed many times, slowing down when you encountered a rough stretch of road, speeding up when the rain temporarily slackened. You also halted several times for traffic lights and stop signs. Any significant alteration of this sequence would have brought you to the intersection before or after the other car and thus prevented the accident, as would any similar variations in the other person's driving.

You also realize that the effects of the accident go beyond the fender and bumper damage. After the accident, a policeman arrived and ticketed the other driver. As a result of the delay, you missed the movie. Further, the accident unnerved you so badly that you couldn't attend classes the next day and therefore missed an important writing assignment. Because of a bad driving record, the other driver lost his license for sixty days and had to cancel a long-planned vacation to Colorado. Clearly the effects of this accident rival the causes in complexity.

People who view the same thing from different vantage points often see it differently, sometimes with tunnel vision. For example, a prison guard may believe a man is in the penitentiary because he committed armed robbery and deserves to be there. The prisoner's mother may believe she failed as a parent and blame herself for the imprisonment. The son may feel his partner's confession put him behind bars. And a sociologist may think that a bad early environment sowed the seeds of criminal action.

Such differing slants call to mind the fable of the blind men who touched different parts of an elephant and then tried to describe it. One, after feeling a side, thought that the elephant resembled a wall. Another, who had grasped the tail, called the animal ropelike. A third, taking his cue from a leg, likened the animal to a tree. Understanding a causal relationship calls for "feeling the whole beast," not seizing on one part. Even then, people frequently disagree on the importance of the parts.

---

1. **Read the following selection and then arrange the events in a causal chain.**   EXERCISE

> Although some folk societies still exist today, similar human groups began the slow process of evolving into more complex societies many millennia ago, through settlement in villages and through advances in technology and organizational structure. This gave rise to the second level of organization: civilized preindustrial, or "feudal," society. Here there is a surplus of food because of the selective cultivation of grains—and also because of the practice of animal husbandry. The food surplus permits both the specialization of labor and the kind of class structure that can, for instance, provide the leadership and command the manpower to develop and maintain extensive irrigation systems (which in turn makes possible further increases in the food supply). . . .
>
> Gideon Sjöberg, "The Origin and
> Development of Cities"

2. **Trace the possible effects of the following occurrences:**

   a. You pick out a salad at the cafeteria and sit down to eat. Suddenly you notice a large green worm on one of the lettuce leaves.
   b. As you leave your composition classroom, you trip and break your arm.
   c. Your boss has warned you not to be late to work again. You are driving to work with ten minutes to spare when you get a flat tire.

WRITING A CAUSAL ANALYSIS

Before you start to write, decide whether you want to center on causes, effects, or both. You can signal your intention in a number of ways. To prepare for a focus on causes, you might use the words *cause, reason,* or *stems from,* or you might ask why something has occurred. To signal a paper on effects, you might use *effect, fallout,* or *impact,* or you might ask what has happened since something took place. Read these two examples:

*Signals
causes*   Midville's recent increase in street crime stems primarily from its curtailed educational program, lack of job opportunities for young people, and high rate of drug addition.

Signals
effects   Since my marriage to Rita, how has my social life changed?

Whatever your decision, don't attempt a comprehensive accounting that traces a cause to a more remote cause, then to a still more remote cause. That way madness lies. Determine some cutoff point that accords with your purpose. As you plan your presentation, be alert for three common errors in reasoning.

Ignoring Multiple Causes.   An effect rarely stems from a simple cause. The person who believes that permissive parents have caused the present upsurge of venereal disease or the one who blames television violence for the climbing numbers of emotionally disturbed children oversimplifies the situation. Permissiveness and violence perhaps did contribute to these conditions. Without much doubt, however, numerous other factors played important parts.

Mistaking Chronology for Causation.   Don't assume that just because one event followed another, the first necessarily caused the second. This kind of faulty thinking feeds many popular superstitions. Horace walks under a ladder, subsequently stubs his toe, and thinks that his path caused his pain. Sue breaks a mirror just before Al breaks their engagement; then she blames the cracked mirror. Many people once believed that the election of Herbert Hoover as President in 1928 triggered the Great Depression in 1929. Today some people believe that the testing of atomic weapons has altered our weather patterns. Don't misunderstand: one event *may* cause the next; but before you go on record with your conclusion, make sure that you're not dealing with mere chronology.

Confusing Causes and Effects.   Young children declare that the moving trees make the wind blow. Similarly, some adults may think that Pam and Paul married because they fell in love, when in reality economic necessity mandated the vows that later led to deep feelings for each other. Scan your evidence carefully in order to avoid such faulty assertions.

Close scrutiny may reveal that one cause was indispensable; the rest merely played supporting roles. If so, discuss the main cause first. In analyzing your automobile mishap, which fits this situation, start with the failure of the other driver to yield the right-of-way, then fan out to any other causes that merit mentioning. Sometimes you'll find that no single cause was essential but that all of them helped matters along. Combinations of this kind lie at the heart of many social and economic concerns: inflation, depression, and urban crime rates, to name just a few. Weigh each cause carefully and rank them in importance. If your topic and purpose will profit from building suspense, work from the least important cause to the most important. Otherwise, reverse the order. For analyzing causal chains, chronological order works effectively.

Treat effects as carefully as you do causes. Keeping in mind that effects also generally travel in packs, try to hunt down every significant one and to arrange them in some logical order. If they occur together, consider order of climax. If one follows the other, present them in that sequence.

EXERCISE

1. **Which of the following statements point toward papers that will focus on causes? Which point toward papers focusing on effects? Explain your answers.**

   a. Most of the problems that plague newly married couples are the direct outgrowth of timidity and pride.
   b. The Marshall Plan was designed to aid the economic recovery of Europe after World War II.
   c. The smoke from burning poison ivy can bring on a skin rash and a lung irritation.
   d. Popularity in high school stems largely from good looks, a pleasing personality, participation in school activities, the right friends, and frequent dates.

2. **Identify which of the following paragraphs deals with causes, which with effects. List the causes and effects.**

   a.   Color filters offer three advantages in black-and-white photography. First, a particular color will be lightened by a filter of the same color. For example, in a photograph of a red rose in a dark blue vase, both will appear almost the same shade of gray if no filter is used. However, when photographed through a red filter, the rose will appear much lighter than the vase; and through a blue filter the vase will appear much lighter than the rose. This effect can be useful in emphasizing or muting certain objects in a photograph. Second, a particular color filter will darken its complementary color in the scene. Consequently, any orange object will appear darker than normal if a blue filter is used. Finally, color filters can reduce or increase atmospheric haze. For example, in a distant aerial shot there will often be so much haze that distant detail is obscured. To eliminate haze almost entirely, the photographer can use a deep red filter. On the other hand, if more haze is desired in order to achieve an artistic effect, varying shades of blue filters can be used.

   Timothy Kelly

   b.   Overeating, which has become a national pastime for millions of Americans, has several roots. For example, parents who are concerned that their children get enough to eat during the growing years overfeed them and thereby establish a lifetime overeating habit. The child who is constantly praised for cleaning up his plate experiences a sort of gratification later on as he cleans up all too many plates. The easy availability of so much food is a constant temptation for many people, especially the types of food served at fast food restaurants and merchandised in the frozen food departments of supermarkets. Equally tempting are all the snack foods constantly advertised on TV. But many people don't need temptation from the outside; their overeating arises from such psychological factors as nervousness, boredom, loneliness, insecurity, an overall discontent with life, or an aversion to exercise. Thus, overeating can actually be a symptom of psychological surrender to, or withdrawal from, the complexities and competition of modern life.

Kenneth Reichow

REVISION CHECKLIST

Answer these questions as you revise your causal analysis.

- ✔ Have I made the right decision in electing to focus on causes, effects, or both?
- ✔ Have I ferreted out all important causes and effects? Mistakenly labeled something as an effect merely because it follows something else? Confused causes and effects?
- ✔ Am I dealing with a causal chain? An essential cause and several supporting causes? A group of causes that contribute to the effect without being essential to it?
- ✔ Have I presented my causes and effects in an appropriate order?
- ✔ Have I supported my discussion with sufficient details?

EXAMPLE ESSAYS OF CAUSE AND EFFECT

STUDENT WRITING

Backpacking
STUDENT UNKNOWN

1   For decades, Americans have been accepting John Muir's invitation to "climb the Mountains, get their glad tidings." Until fairly recently, the mountains attracted only rugged individuals who were prepared to face considerable hardship in order to hike and climb. Since the early 1970s, however, the mountains have changed from the sanctuary of the dedicated few to the playground of the multitudes, as shown by the booming backpacking-equipment industry and the crowded trails. Why this sudden increase in the number of mountain-climbing enthusiasts? I believe there are three reasons—backpacking is inexpensive, provides exercise, and involves little physical discomfort.

2   In a decade that has seen the price of entertainment rise to outrageous levels, the mountains are a very economical place to vacation. A backpacker need spend only about two hundred and fifty dollars to obtain an outfit suitable for all seasons but winter. After that, the only expenses are for food and transportation. A reasonably economical shopper can buy a week's worth of high-nutrition, low-weight food from the local supermarket for about thirty to forty dollars, much

less than the cost of eating in restaurants. Because backpackers travel under their own power, the only transportation expenses are those of driving to and from a trailhead. And because backpackers carry their own shelter, there are no motel bills—only the occasional camping permit or park entry fee. Overall, backpacking costs much less per day than most conventional forms of entertainment. Consequently, as compared to his tourist counterpart, the backpacker can "get away from it all" for more days, without spending any more money.

Growing numbers of people are also coming to realize that backpacking   3 provides very good exercise. Since mountain terrain varies from level meadows to sheer rock faces, the physical challenges in backpacking are boundless. Virtually anyone wanting exercise can participate—from those content with the mild exertion involved in exploring the meadows to those who crave the arduous task of scaling a high-altitude peak or pass.

But probably the major lure of the mountains for today's backpackers is   4 that conquering them involves much less physical discomfort than it once did. Technology has made it possible to be reasonably comfortable in harsh weather if the proper gear is used. A nylon tent or a tarpaulin will keep the rain from dampening one's spirits or gear, a good frame pack will comfortably carry everything needed for a few days, a small gasoline stove will allow hot meals to be cooked under almost any circumstances, and a well-fitting pair of boots will keep the feet comfortable and protect them too. All the items mentioned are so light that one can be fully protected from the elements without having to carry more than twenty pounds of equipment.

When I first started backpacking about six years ago, I encountered few   5 people. Those who did backpack made every effort to leave no trace of their presence and treated the mountains with deference and respect. But as more people have taken to the mountains, trash, defoliation, and erosion have increased. Let's hope that as time passes, the new backpackers will also come to respect the mountains.

DISCUSSION QUESTIONS

1. Does this paper focus on causes, effects, or both? Show how the opening paragraph signals the writer's intention.
2. Discuss the organization of the essay.
3. Explain how the conclusion supports the point made in the introduction to the paper.

From *The Politics of Energy*
BARRY COMMONER

PROFESSIONAL WRITING

The high and growing cost of nuclear power plants is due not so much to   1 the difficulties associated with the technology that it has in common with non-nuclear plants—that is, the conversion of energy of steam into electricity—but rather to its unique feature, the use of fission to supply the heat needed to produce steam. The accident at Harrisburg showed that a failure in the steam-to-electricity section of the plant that would have caused very little trouble in a conventional power plant came close to producing a catastrophic disaster in the nuclear one and has shut down the plant for a long time, and possibly permanently.

2   The Three Mile Island Power Plant produced the steam needed to drive its electric turbines in a pressurized-water reactor. In such a reactor, water is circulated through the reactor's fuel core, where—because it is under pressure—it is heated far above its normal boiling point by the heat generated by the fission reaction. The superheated water flows through the reactor's "primary loop" into a heat exchanger where it brings water, which circulates in a "secondary loop," to the boiling point, and the resulting steam flows into the turbine to generate electricity. The spent steam is recondensed and pumped back to the heat exchanger, where it is again coverted to steam, and so on. A third loop of cooling water is used to condense the steam, carrying off the excess heat to a cooling tower where it is finally released into the air. This arrangement is much more complex than the design of a conventional power system, where the steam generated in the boiler passes directly into the turbine. In this type of nuclear plant the water that circulates through the reactor (which is equivalent to the boiler in a conventional plant) becomes intensely radioactive, and the complex successive circulation loops are essential to keep that radioactivity from leaving the reactor.

3   On March 28, 1979, at 3:53 A.M., a pump at the Harrisburg plant failed. Because the pump failed, the reactor's heat was not drawn off in the heat exchanger and the very hot water in the primary loop overheated. The pressure in the loop increased, opening a release valve that was supposed to counteract such an event. But the valve stuck open and the primary loop system lost so much water (which ended up as a highly radioactive pool, six feet deep, on the floor of the reactor building) that it was unable to carry off all the heat generated within the reactor core. Under these circumstances, the intense heat held within the reactor could, in theory, melt its fuel rods, and the resulting "meltdown" could then carry a hugely radioactive mass through the floor of the reactor. The reactor's emergency cooling system, which is designed to prevent this disaster, was then automatically activated; but when it was, apparently, turned off too soon, some of the fuel rods overheated. This produced a bubble of hydrogen gas at the top of the reactor. (The hydrogen is dissolved in the water in order to react with oxygen that is produced when the intense reactor radiation splits water molecules into their atomic constituents. When heated, the dissolved hydrogen bubbles out of the solution.) This bubble blocked the flow of cooling water so that despite the action of the emergency cooling system the reactor core was again in danger of melting down. Another danger was that the gas might contain enough oxygen to cause an explosion that could rupture the huge containers that surround the reactor and release a deadly cloud of radioactive material into the surrounding countryside. Working desperately, technicians were able to gradually reduce the size of the gas bubble, using a special apparatus brought in from the atomic laboratory at Oak Ridge, Tennessee, and the danger of a catastrophic release of radioactive materials subsided. But the sealed-off plant was now so radioactive that no one could enter it for many months—or, according to some observers, for years—without being exposed to a lethal dose of radiation.

Some radioactive gases did escape from the plant, prompting the governor   4
of Pennsylvania, Richard Thornburgh, to ask that pregnant women and children
leave the area five miles around the plant. Many other people decided to leave as
well, and within a week 60,000 or more residents had left the area, drawing
money from their banks and leaving state offices and a local hospital short-
handed.

Like the horseshoe nail that lost a kingdom, the failure of a pump at the   5
Three Mile Island Nuclear Power Plant may have lost the entire industry. It dra-
matized the vulnerability of the complex system that is embodied in the elaborate
technology of nuclear power. In that design, the normally benign and easily controlled process of producing steam to drive an electric generator turned into a
trigger for a radioactive catastrophe. . . .

DISCUSSION QUESTIONS

1. What purpose does the information in paragraph 1 serve? Paragraph 2?
2. Which paragraph focuses on the causes and effects involved in the accident? Did the accident stem from one initial cause or several?
3. List the items that would be included in a causal chain depicting this accident.
4. This selection traces two other causal chains besides the one involved in the accident. What are they and where are they discussed?

SUGGESTIONS FOR WRITING

Use one of the topics below, or another that your instructor approves, to develop a causal analysis. Think carefully about your topic. Determine which causes or effects, or both, are important. Set a limit on how far you will trace your reasons and results. Scrutinize your analysis for errors in reasoning, settle on an organization, and write the essay.

1. Reasons why students fail college
2. The effect of some friend, acquaintance, or public figure on your life
3. Causes behind some disciplinary action
4. Effects of some choice you made
5. Why are you a _____ major
6. Effects of living in a dormitory, in your own apartment, or at home
7. Reasons why you are a Democrat, a Republican, or an Independent
8. Effects of pollution in your hometown or some other familiar place
9. Effects of your choice of college or of your decision to go to college
10. Reasons why you have a particular habit or participate in a particular sport
11. Effects on your life of winning the grand prize in a state lottery
12. Reasons why _____ is a popular public figure
13. Effects of some family crisis on your life
14. Causes or effects or both of some disease
15. Causes or consequences or both of some decision made by you or your family

CHAPTER SIX

Making Yourself Clear

ILLUSTRATION
AND
DEFINITION

ILLUSTRATION

"It doesn't pay to fight City Hall. For example, my friend Josie. . . ."

"Many intelligent people lack common sense. Take Dr. Brandon. . . ."

"Topnotch women tennis players are among the biggest moneymakers in sports. Last year, for instance, Chris Evert Lloyd. . . ."

"Predicting the weather is far from an exact science. Two winters ago, a surprise snowstorm. . . ."

Have you ever noticed how often people use *illustrations* (examples) to clarify a general statement?

Everyday conversations teem with "for example" or "for instance," often in response to a furrowed brow or puzzled look. Hank Cassidy serves as the perfect example of a good ole boy, or Millionaires' Meadows illustrates how the wealthy live. Teachers frequently lead with an abstract principle or general law followed by examples that bring it down to earth. Advertisers trot out typical satisfied users of their product as inducements for us to buy.

The old saw that a picture is worth a thousand words best explains the popularity of illustration. The concrete is always easier to grasp than the abstract, and illustrations help us communicate our ideas more effectively.

WRITING AN ILLUSTRATION

The following guidelines will help you write effective illustrations.

SELECTING APPROPRIATE EXAMPLES

The first guideline for effective illustration is to select examples that stay on target and do not veer off into an intriguing side issue. For instance, when

"Teacher burnout."

Drawing by Booth. © 1982 The New Yorker Magazine, Inc.

illustrating that the lyrics in a rock group's latest album are not in good taste, resist the temptation to inject comments on the widely publicized night life of one of its members. Furthermore, see that your examples display the features associated with whatever you are illustrating. Don't offer Hank Cassidy as an example of a typical good ole boy unless he fits the general mold by being a fun-loving, easy-going beer guzzler who likes to hang out with other men. Finally, spark your reader's interest by adding details that enliven your examples and bring them into sharper focus.

In the essay "Computer Addicts," Dina Ingber offers several illustrations of "hackers"—compulsive computer programmers with "a drive so consuming it overshadows nearly every other part of their lives and forms the focal point of their existence." Here is one such illustration:

Bob Shaw, a 15-year-old high-school student, is a case in point. Bob was temporarily pulled off the computers at school when he began failing his other

ILLUSTRATION   109

courses. But instead of hitting the books, he continues to sulk outside the computer center, peering longingly through the glass door at the consoles within.

Pale and drawn, his brown hair unkempt, Bob speaks only in monosyllables, avoiding eye contact. In answer to questions about friends, hobbies, school, he merely shrugs or mumbles a few words aimed at his sneakered feet. But when the conversation turns to the subject of computers, he brightens—and blurts out a few full sentences about the computer he's building and the projects he plans.

Dina Ingber, "Computer Addicts"

DETERMINING THE NUMBER OF EXAMPLES

How many examples should you include? One long one or several briefer backups? Look to your thesis for the answer. To make the point that a good nurse must be compassionate, conscientious, and competent, your best bet would probably be one example, since one person must display all these traits. But if you're showing the different ways that Hemingway handled the initiation theme in his fiction, you'll need several examples.

EXERCISE

1. **Choose one of the following topic sentences. Select an appropriate example and write the rest of the paragraph.**

   a. Sometimes a minor incident drastically changes a person's life.
   b. _____'s name exactly suits (her/his) personality.
   c. I still get embarrassed when I remember _____.
   d. Not all education goes on in the classroom.
   e. I learned the value of _____ the hard way.

2. **Explain why you would use one extended illustration or several shorter ones to develop each of the following statements. Suggest appropriate illustrations.**

   a. Many parents I know think for their children.
   b. The hamburger isn't what it used to be.
   c. The ideal pet is small, quiet, and affectionate.
   d. College students view their responsibilities differently.
   e. The hotels in Gotham City run the gamut from sumptuous to seedy.

ORGANIZING THE EXAMPLES

A simple extended illustration often assumes narrative form, presenting a series of events in time sequence. Sets of illustrations that trace trends also rely on time sequence, moving either forward or backward. This arrangement would work nicely if you wanted to show that over the last forty years parents have become more permissive in raising their children. On the other hand, showing that people in an occupational group exhibit some particular characteristic in varying degrees would logically be done in order of climax (from least to greatest or vice versa). To demonstrate how salesclerks differ in their attitude toward customers, you might describe first a hostile clerk, then a pleasant one, and finally an outstandingly courteous and helpful one. Sometimes any arrangement will work equally well. Suppose you're showing that Americans are taking various precautions to ward off heart attacks. Although you might move from a person who exercises to one who diets and finally to one who practices relaxation techniques, no special order is inherently preferable.

REVISION CHECKLIST

Think about these questions as you revise your illustration paper.

- ✔ Exactly what idea am I trying to put across? Have I used the examples that best typify it?
- ✔ Do my examples illustrate my idea without introducing irrelevant material?
- ✔ Are my examples interesting?
- ✔ Have I used an appropriate number of illustrations?
- ✔ Have I organized my paper effectively?

EXAMPLE ESSAYS
OF ILLUSTRATION

STUDENT
WRITING

A Lesson from Nature
MIKE BRAENDLE

1   As I was growing up, my parents often passed along little maximlike sayings to me. Most of these have since slipped my mind, but I still remember the exact words of my father's favorite: "The door to success is labeled Push." Although for a while these were just words to me, I came to understand their true meaning as I observed the struggles of a crayfish while I was fishing one day.

2   There it lay, trapped in the small plastic compartment of my steel tackle box, which was sitting on the bank of the river. The sun had been shining for some time, and the plastic of the compartment surrounding the crayfish intensified the heat. In fact, the heat had become so great that the skin covering the small hard-shelled body was beginning to wrinkle. Nevertheless, the pinching claws continually groped about, trying to find something to grasp, some means

ILLUSTRATION   111

of escape. The hard and heavy shell, acting like an anchor, burdened the crayfish greatly. The two small eyes, always moving, searched wildly for some way out, but found none. The segmented tail, as large as the rest of the body, was constantly pushing, trying to hoist the heavy body over the edge of the compartment.

The eyes at last fell upon a possibility for escape: the back wall of the compartment was slightly lower than the other three walls. Sensing an advantage, the crayfish seemed to labor more deliberately. The tail, pushing vigorously, tried to lift the heavy shell out of the plastic compartment. As the tail struggled, the claws slashed savagely back and forth, searching for something to grab. 3

Finally, after some time and struggle, the crayfish grasped the back wall. As it pulled, with every muscle straining, the hard shell edged up and over the wall of the compartment. Stopping abruptly and gazing at its surroundings, the crayfish tried to orient itself. Off to one side in another compartment lay a strange-looking creature, unmoving. The crayfish did not recognize this odd-shaped thing as a fishing lure, but it did sense that the creature, with its bright metallic tint and protruding hooks, was not alive. 4

It took only a moment for the determined crustacean to figure out which way to go. It moved, as if driven by instinct, across this compartment and then others, occasionally getting caught on a protruding hook. These hooks slowed its progress, scratching grooves and gouges in the hard shell. 5

As the crayfish moved steadily toward the edge of the box, the thought of cold water seemed to excite it. It moved faster, more deliberately now. When reaching the edge of the box, it stopped for a moment, as if pondering what to do next. Then, defiantly, it flopped over the edge, landing on its hard shell. It stayed on its back for some time, but then turned over and dragged itself to the water. 6

The crayfish lay there for a long time, soaking in the cool and refreshing river. Then with a powerful flap of its tail, it disappeared into the depths. Here, where there was no threat of drying out, it could and probably would recuperate from this tiring experience. 7

---

1. What general statement does this essay illustrate?
2. Why is one extended illustration effective here?
3. Explain the organization of the essay and why it is appropriate.
4. In paragraph 2, the writer says the crayfish "continually groped" and "searched wildly" with its tail "contantly pushing." How do these descriptions relate to the writer's purpose?
5. Point out specific sentences in paragraphs 3 and 4 that seem particularly effective in engaging the reader's interest.
6. Would a concluding paragraph which restated the main idea make this essay more effective? Why or why not?

DISCUSSION QUESTIONS

Old Folks at Home
BERNARD SLOAN

1   I once felt sorry for people in old-age homes. I accepted their portrayal on television specials as helpless innocents cast aside by their young, paying the price of growing old in America. I thought all these lonely old men and women were victims of the indifference and selfishness of the younger generation.

2   No more.

3   I have learned through personal experience why so many grandmothers and grandfathers end up in institutions for the aged, unwanted and unvisited. It isn't always their children who put them there. Sometimes they put themselves there.

4   These are the selfish, demanding elderly who are impossible to live with. Often they are people who were difficult to live with when they were younger, but now they have age on their side. Their families, torn with pain and guilt, spend months or years struggling to do "the right thing." Finally, they give up.

5   I have been through it. I have friends who are going through it. Caring, concerned sons and daughters who try, God knows they try, but the harder they try the harder it gets. Their elderly parents who should know better carp and criticize and complain. Instead of compromising, they constantly test their children, forever setting up new challenges for them to meet, assuming the one-sided game can go on forever.

6   It comes as a shock to them when the special privileges conferred by their age and relationship run out, and their son or daughter tolerates their tyranny no longer. "How can you do this to me?" the parent cries, bags packed.

7   It is not easy.

8   We have friends who spent a fortune remodeling their home to provide an apartment for the wife's aging mother. The daughter was determined to overcome their differences for the chance to be close to her mother, to give her mother the love of a family rather than the services of a mercenary. Instead, she provided herself and her family with a three-year nightmare, the old woman seizing every opportunity to demean her daughter's husband, criticize the children, and turn every family argument into a screaming fight.

9   "She's tearing our family apart," the daughter cries. "I'm going to be the villain by casting her out, but she has to go, or it's the end of my marriage."

10   Our friend is now searching for a suitable home. In her desperation she will settle for the best home available, which will not necessarily be the best home.

11   Another friend not only brings her father-in-law cooked meals, she cleans his apartment every week. Not once has he thanked her. But he has managed to find fault with everything she does. How long will he be able to live by himself? Another year, perhaps. And then what? Who will he blame when he winds up in an institution? Not himself.

12   A business acquaintance makes solitary visits to his angry mother in her lonely apartment. His wife will no longer submit to the old woman's hostility. The old woman, an Italian Catholic, cannot forgive her son for marrying a French

ILLUSTRATION 113

Catholic. Mixed marriages, she still proclaims regularly, don't work. Twenty-five years and three delightful children don't count.

Can't she read the handwriting on the wall? She is busy writing her own future. 13

When my mother became ill, I moved her from her Sun Belt apartment to our home so that she could spend her remaining time with her only family, her only grandchildren. Although she never approved of my wife (the wrong religion again), we were positive she would relinquish her prejudices in exchange for love and care. No such luck. Instead of making an attempt to adjust to our household, my mother tried to manipulate the four of us to center our lives around her. 14

My wife took her to the doctor regularly, supervised her medication, bought and prepared special foods for her—all while working full time—yet my mother found nothing right about anything she did. Our refrigerator could be bulging, but my mother managed to crave the one thing missing. We were made to feel guilty if we left her alone for an evening, and were maneuvered into quarrels if we stayed. After five months of this, we began to investigate "homes." 15

Even the most relentlessly cheerful were depressing. Amidst flowered walls and piped-in music ("Heaven, I'm in Heaven") old people stared at television or gathered in activity rooms where they were kept busy with the arts and crafts taught in the third grade. They were not bedridden, these people; they required no nursing, no special care. Although unable to shop, cook and take care of a home of their own, they were quite capable of participating in the life of a family. Yet they were separated from their families. 16

How many of these people had driven their families to drive them out? How many felt that reaching 60 or 70 or 80 entitled them to behave in a manner that would never be tolerated in the young? As if the very fact of being old excused them from the rules of common decency. As if the right to be demanding and complaining was conferred upon them along with half fares on buses and discount days at the market. 17

That cantankerous old man may be a laugh riot on the stage as he sends comic characters scurrying at his every command, but he is hell to live with. That feisty old lady may be hilarious when company comes, but she can drive a family crazy. They are candidates for being "put away" as soon as the family being destroyed gets up the courage. 18

I don't mean to suggest that there are not great numbers of old people who must live in institutions because they are victims—victims of infirmity and, yes, victims of callous, selfish children. But for our own sakes, and for our children, it is pointless to ignore the fact that many of the elderly bear some responsibility for their fate. After all, warm, loving, sharing people are a joy to live with whatever their age. 19

---

1. What general idea does this essay illustrate? State it as a thesis sentence.
2. Why are several illustrations a good choice here?
3. Discuss the arrangement of these illustrations. Would it be more logical to re-

DISCUSSION QUESTIONS

position the final illustration earlier in the essay? Why or why not? How can you account for the greater length of the final illustration?

4. Point out the significance of the following statements, found at the start of paragraph 5: "I have been through it. I have friends who are going through it."

5. Write a sentence or two explaining why the title of this essay is effective.

SUGGESTIONS FOR WRITING   **Use one of the ideas below or another that your instructor approves for your illustration essay. Select appropriate examples, determine how many you will use, and decide how you will organize them.**

1. Americans are a wasteful people.
2. If you want something done, ask the busiest person around.
3. People often choose strange places to vacation.
4. Women are becoming increasingly prominent (in politics, business, sports, or some other field).
5. Dedication is the secret of success for many athletes (or use any other field or occupation).
6. People have many strange remedies for hangovers.
7. An adult never stands so tall as when stooping to help a child.
8. A good nurse must be compassionate, conscientious, and competent (or use another occupation with appropriate characteristics).
9. _____ is a demanding profession.
10. Many intelligent people lack common sense.
11. It does not (or does) pay to fight City Hall.
12. Successful people are often self-made.
13. "Doing your thing" does not always work out for the best.
14. _____ is the most (or least) effective teacher I have ever had.
15. Not to decide is to decide.

DEFINITION

Eschew obfuscation sedulously.

Once the bandage is off the wound, swab the proud flesh with the disinfectant.

Speaking on national television, anti-drug crusader Mary Jane Potter recommended that convicted drug pushers serve at least twenty years in prison.

Got questions? You're not alone. Almost anyone would question the sentences above: "What in the world does 'Eschew blah blah' mean?" "How can flesh be *proud?*" "What does Potter mean by *drug pusher*? Would she send some kid up for twenty years just because he sold a friend one marijuana cigarette?" To avoid puzzling and provoking your own readers, you'll often need to explain the meaning of some term. The term may be unfamiliar to your audience (eschew blah blah), used in an uncommon sense (proud), or mean different things to different people (drug pusher). Whenever you clarify the meaning of some term, you are *defining*.

We humans are instinctively curious; we start asking about meanings as soon as we start talking. Told that a parent works in a factory, a child inquires, "What's a factory?" Upon hearing the story of Hansel and Gretel, children want to know about woodcutters and witches. As we grow past the moppet stage and head toward maturity, we continue to seek, as well as supply, definitions. Instructors expect us to learn and explain all sorts of literary, historical, social, scientific, and technical terms. An employer asks us to define terms like *corporate responsibility, product stewardship*, or *cost-benefit analysis* for new employees. A newspaper story about a new earth-orbiting astronomical observatory sends us to a neighborhood astronomy buff for an explanation of *supernova, quasar*, or *black hole*. In our reflective moments we ponder ultimate questions: What do we mean by good and evil? What is the nature of God?

Sometimes a word or phrase will nicely settle a definition question. To clear up the mystery of "proud flesh," all you'd need to do is insert the parenthetical phrase (excessively swollen and grainy) after the word *proud*. But often, especially when you're dealing with new terms, brief definitions just leave the reader confused. Recent social, political, and technological developments have spawned throngs of new expressions: *punk rock, gentrification, supply side economics, new federalism, neoliberal, breeder reactor, clone,* and *macroengineering* are a few. When you use a new and unfamiliar term in a piece of writing, you'll probably need more than a single sentence to explain it. Your readers may know nothing about the term, and dismissing it in a single sentence would leave them stranded.

Abstract terms—those standing for things we can't see, feel, or otherwise experience with our five senses—often require special attention, too. It's impossible to capture the essence of *democracy* or *hatred* or *freedom* in a single sentence. These concepts are so complex and people have such differing notions about what they mean that they simply can't be crowded into such cramped quarters. Some concrete terms—those standing for actions and things we can perceive with our five senses—also have multiple meanings and require more than passing treatment. *Drug pusher* provides an example. Some people limit the term to full-time sellers of hard drugs like cocaine and heroin. Others, at the opposite extreme, extend it to everyone who sells any drug in any quantity, whether full or part-time. Without knowing just what Mary Jane Potter means by *drug pusher*, you have no real grounds for judging her recommendations. The many dimensions of the epithet *nurd*, captured in the following poster from *The National Lampoon*, suggest just how difficult defining can be.

nurd also **nerd** / nerd:/ n [ME, fr. OE *neord*, perforated earthen jar or gourd] : an adolescent male possessing any of a number of socially objectionable characteristics, including passivity, disregard for personal appearance, obsessive neatness, introversion, undue respect for authority, sexual ignorance, disinterest in athletics, fidgeting, kooties, anality, infantilism, orality, pusillanimity, obsequiousness, and using big words; *see:* TWINK, WONK, FINK, TWIT, [*greasy*], GRIND, FLAMER, WIMP, WEENIE, DINK, CREEP, FLYER, GEEK, DIP, LEMUR, Q-BALL, SIMP, TWIRP, DRIP, WOMBAT, ZOOMER, SCREAMER.

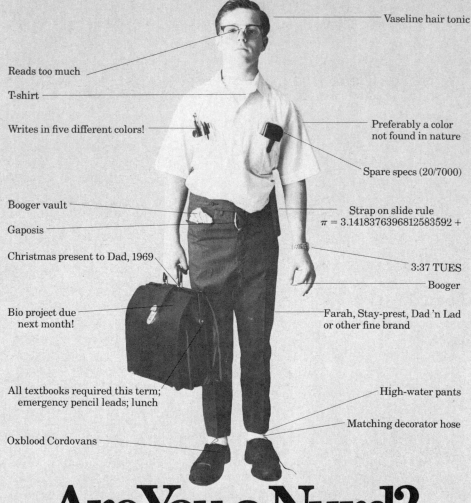

Vaseline hair tonic

Reads too much

T-shirt

Writes in five different colors!

Preferably a color not found in nature

Spare specs (20/7000)

Booger vault

Gaposis

Strap on slide rule
$\pi = 3.1418376396812583592 +$

Christmas present to Dad, 1969

3:37 TUES

Booger

Bio project due next month!

Farah, Stay-prest, Dad 'n Lad or other fine brand

All textbooks required this term; emergency pencil leads; lunch

High-water pants

Matching decorator hose

Oxblood Cordovans

Are You a Nurd?

...Let's hope not. But just in case you've begun to notice telltale signs, such as a reawakened fascination with word problems or scratching mosquito bites until they bleed, take this simple test. If you have less than five (5) of these dead giveaways, you're probably a cool guy. If you have eight (8) or more, you're just kind of flakey. Ten (10) or more? Check for a leper colony near you.

NATIONAL LAMPOON

TYPES OF DEFINITIONS

Three types of definitions—synonyms, essential definitions, and extended definitions—serve writers' needs. Although the first two seldom require more than a word or a sentence, an extended definition can run to several pages. The three types, however, are related. Synonyms and essential definitions share quarters between the covers of dictionaries, and both furnish starting points for extended definitions.

SYNONYMS

Synonyms are words with very nearly the same meanings. *Lissome* is synonymous with *lithe* or *nimble,* and *condign* is a synonym of *worthy* and *suitable.* Synonyms allow writers to clarify the meanings of unfamiliar words without cumbersome explanations. To clarify the term *expostulation* in a quoted passage, all you'd have to do is add the word *objection,* in brackets, after it. Because synonyms are not identical twins, using them puts a slightly different shade of meaning on a message: *objection* means "strong disapproval," whereas *expostulation* also implies a desire to change another's thinking. Nonetheless, synonyms provide an easy, convenient means of breaking communications logjams.

ESSENTIAL DEFINITION

An essential, or formal, definition places the item being defined in a broad category, then shows how it differs from other items in that category. Here are three examples.

A howdah is a covered seat for riding on the back of an elephant or camel.

A voiceprint is a graphical record of a person's voice characteristics.

To parboil is to boil meat, vegetables, or fruits until they are partially cooked.

Writing a good essential definition demands keen attention to details. It's not enough to define a vacuum cleaner as "an appliance that cleans floors, furniture, and upholstery." Brooms and carpet sweepers also clean floors, and whisk brooms clean upholstery. To establish the proper boundaries, you'd need to note that a vacuum cleaner runs on electricity and cleans with suction. Here's how the amended definition might then look.

A vacuum cleaner is an electrical appliance that uses suction to clean floors, carpets, and upholstery.

Limitations of Essential Definitions.   Essential definitions have certain built-in limitations. Because of their brevity, they often can't do full justice to abstract terms such as *cowardice, love, jealousy, power.* Problems also arise with terms that have several settled meanings. To explain *jam* adequately, you'd need at least three essential definitions: (1) a closely packed crowd, (2) preserves, and (3) a difficult situation. But despite these limitations, an essential definition can be useful by itself or as part of a longer definition. Writers often build an extended definition around an essential definition.

Pitfalls in Preparing Essential Definitions.   When you prepare an essential definition, guard against these flaws:

Circular definition. Don't define a term by repeating it or changing its form slightly. Saying that a psychiatrist is "a physician who practices psychiatry" will only frustrate someone who's never heard of psychiatry. Repress circularity and provide the proper insight by choosing terms the reader can relate to; for example, "A psychiatrist is a physician who diagnoses and treats mental disorders."

Overly broad definition. Shy away from definitions that embrace too much territory. If you define a skunk as "an animal that has a bushy tail and black fur with white markings," your definition is not precise. Many cats and dogs also fit this description. But if you add "and that ejects a foul-smelling secretion when threatened," you will clear the air, of any misconceptions at least.

Overly narrow definition. Don't hem in your definition too closely, either. "A kitchen blender is a bladed electrical appliance used to chop foods" illustrates this error. Blenders perform other operations, too. To correct the error, add the missing information. "A kitchen blender is a bladed electrical appliance used to chop, mix, whip, liquefy, or otherwise process foods."

Omission of main category. Avoid using "is where" or "is when" instead of naming the main category. Here are examples of this error. "A bistro is where food and wine are served" and "An ordination is when a person is formally recognized as a minister, priest, or rabbi." The reader will not know exactly what sort of thing (a bar? a party?) a bistro is and may think that *ordination* means a time. Note the improvement when the broad categories are named: "A bistro is a small restaurant where both food and wine are served" and "An ordination is a ceremony at which a person is formally recognized as a minister, priest, or rabbi."

EXERCISE   1. **Identify the broad category and the distinguishing traits in each of these essential definitions.**

a. Gangue is useless rock accompanying valuable minerals in a deposit.
b. A catbird is a small American songbird with a slate-colored body, a black cap, and a catlike cry.

c. A soldier is a man or woman serving in an army.

d. Myelin is a white fatty substance that forms a sheath around some nerve fibers.

e. A gargoyle is a waterspout carved in the likeness of a grotesque animal or imaginary creature and projecting from the gutter of a building.

f. A magnum is a wine bottle that holds about two-fifths of a gallon.

2. **Indicate which of the following statements are acceptable essential definitions. Explain what is wrong with those that are not. Correct them.**

a. A scalpel is a small knife that has a sharp blade used for surgery and anatomical dissections.

b. A puritan is a person with puritanical beliefs.

c. A kraal is where South African tribespeople keep large domestic animals.

d. A rifle is a firearm that has a grooved barrel and is used for hunting large game.

e. A motorcycle is a two-wheeled vehicle used mainly for human transportation.

f. Fainting is when a person loses consciousness owing to inadequate flow of blood to the brain.

3. **Write an essential definition for each of the following terms.**

a. groupie   d. jock
b. happy hour   e. pushover
c. hit man   f. hard grader

EXTENDED DEFINITION

Extended definitions allow you to deal adequately with new terms as well as terms that have multiple meanings. Other situations that require their use include explaining how a term has been misused, contrasting its ideal and common meanings, and emphasizing some neglected aspect of a meaning.

Extended definitions are montages of other methods of development. Often they also define negatively by fencing out rather than fencing in. The following paragraphs show how one writer handled an extended definition of "sudden infant death syndrome." The student began by presenting a specific illustration, which also incorporated an essential definition and two synonyms.

Jane and Dick Smith were proud, new parents of an eight-pound, ten-ounce baby girl named Jenny. One summer night, Jane put Jenny to bed at 8:00. When she went to check on her at 3:00 A.M., Jane found Jenny dead. The baby had given no cry of pain, shown no sign of trouble. Even the doctor did not know why she had died, for she was healthy and strong. The autopsy report confirmed the doctor's suspicion—the infant was a victim of the "sudden infant death syndrome," also known as SIDS or crib death. SIDS is the sudden and unexplainable death of an apparently healthy, sleeping infant. It is the number-one cause of death in infants after the first week of life and as a result has been the subject of numerous research studies.

DISCUSSION QUESTIONS

1. What synonyms does the writer use?
2. Which sentence presents an essential definition?

In the next paragraph, the writer turned to negation, pointing out some of the things that researchers have ruled out about SIDS.

Although researchers do not know what SIDS is, they do know what it is *not.* They know it cannot be predicted; it strikes like a thief in the night. Crib deaths occur in seconds, with no sound of pain, and they always happen when the child is sleeping. Suffocation is *not* the cause, nor is aspiration or regurgitation. Researchers have found no correlation between the incidence of SIDS and the mother's use of birth control pills or tobacco or the presence of fluoride in water. Since it is not hereditary or contagious, only a slim chance exists that SIDS will strike twice in the same family.

Finally, the student explored several proposed causes of SIDS as well as how parents may react to the loss of their child.

As might be expected, researchers have offered many theories concerning the cause of crib death. Dr. R. C. Reisinger, a National Cancer Institute scientist, has linked crib deaths to the growth of a common bacterium, *E. coli,* in the intestines of newborn babies. The organisms multiply in the intestines, manufacturing a toxin that is absorbed by the intestinal wall and passes into the bloodstream. Breast milk stops the growth of the organism, whereas cow's milk permits it. Therefore, Dr. Reisinger believes, bottle-fed babies run a higher risk of crib death than other babies. . . .

The loss of a child through crib death is an especially traumatic experience. Parents often develop feelings of guilt and depression, thinking they somehow caused the child's death. To alleviate such feelings, organizations have been established to help parents accept the fact that they did not cause the death.

Trudy Stelter

Different topics demand different combinations of methods. A paper on drag racing might describe the hectic scene as the cars line up for a race, then classify the different categories of vehicles, and finally explain the steps in a race.

WRITING A DEFINITION PAPER

If you choose your own topic, pick an abstract term or one about which your reader can learn something. Defining the word *table*, for instance, is not a promising idea. If the topic and reader are total strangers, a short definition often provides a convenient introduction. If you do lead off with a short definition taken from the dictionary, don't introduce it with an expression like "*Webster* says . . ." or "Webster's dictionary says . . ." Several dictionaries have the name *Webster* in their titles, and your reader won't know which one you mean. Use the dictionary's full name: *"Webster's New World Dictionary* says. . . ."

Think hard about what methods of development to use. Each method has its own set of special strengths, as the following list shows.

> *Narration.* Tracing the history of a new development or the changing meaning of a term
>
> *Description.* Pointing out interesting or important features of a device, event, or occurrence
>
> *Illustration.* Tracing changes in meaning and defining abstract terms
>
> *Comparison.* Distinguishing between an unfamiliar and a familiar item
>
> *Classification.* Pointing out the different categories into which an item or an event can be grouped
>
> *Process.* Explaining what a device does or how it is used, how a procedure is carried out, or how a natural event takes place
>
> *Cause and effect.* Explaining the origins and consequences of events, conditions, problems, and attitudes
>
> *Negation.* Placing limitations on conditions and events and correcting popular misconceptions

Examine your topic in light of this listing and select the methods of development that seem most promising. Don't hesitate to use a method of development for some purpose not mentioned here. If you decide a comparison will help your reader understand some abstract term, use it.

Definition papers can end in a number of ways. If you're defining some undesirable condition or event (such as the sudden infant death syndrome), you might express hope for some speedy solution. If you're reporting on some new development (like macroengineering), you might predict its economic and social impact. Often, a summary of your main points is effective. Choose whichever type of ending best supports your main idea.

REVISION
CHECKLIST

Consider each of these questions as you revise your extended definition.

- ✔ Am I satisfied with the type of term I've chosen to define?
- ✔ If I've started with an essential definition, have I made certain that it's not overly broad, overly narrow, or circular? That it names a broad category? If I've started with a dictionary definition, have I supplied the full name of the dictionary?
- ✔ Have I used appropriate methods of development? Are there additional methods I might consider?
- ✔ Is my paper organized effectively?

EXAMPLE ESSAYS OF DEFINITION

STUDENT
WRITING

A Word to the Wise
STUDENT UNKNOWN

1   Believe it or not, the Now Generation is head over heels in love with a whole flock of expressions that are old as the hills. These expressions, none the worse for wear, continue to rear their ugly heads day in and day out. But let's quit beating around the bush and call a spade a spade. Or rather, let's call these golden oldies by their true name—clichés. According to *Webster's New World Dictionary*, a cliché is "an expression or idea that has become trite"—you might say it's become a household word. The English professor who comes face to face with these expressions whenever he turns around is likely to regard clichés as pure poison, something he wouldn't touch with a ten-foot pole even if his life depended on it. But let's give the devil his due and look at the other side of the coin. To the student who would otherwise have to burn the midnight oil—the supreme sacrifice—the cliché is indeed a true-blue friend.

2   Beauty is in the eye of the beholder, and a cliché is a thing of beauty to nine students out of ten. It is just what the doctor ordered for those students who, not knowing beans about using fresh, colorful expressions, would otherwise find themselves completely over their heads in their composition classes. A friend in need is a friend indeed. If the professor is asleep at the switch, these students can pass their writing assignments with flying colors—without working like a beaver or even breathing hard.

3   The cliché is not merely a fair-weather friend. From morning till night, through thick and thin, it stands ready to lend a helping hand to each and every student in our institutions of higher learning. Once in a blue moon, a student who doesn't know which side his bread is buttered on will turn in a paper in which clichés are conspicuous by their absence. But such students are as scarce as hen's teeth, and professors don't hold their breath waiting for them; the professors know beyond a shadow of a doubt that that would be the height of foolishness.

4   Because using clichés is as easy as falling off a log, it goes without saying

that it would be duck soup to continue in this vein till hell freezes over. However, since that would be carrying coals to Newcastle, let's ring down the curtain and bid adieu to the fair topic of the cliché. (No use beating a dead horse.)

1. Identify the essential definition in this essay.
2. Point out the methods that the writer uses to develop the definition.
3. Explain how the writer has achieved unity; that is, has welded the clichés together to produce a unified paper.
4. Underline all the clichés. Does the paper effectively define its topic? Why or why not?

The Bureaucrat
CITICORP N.A.

1   Bureaucracy is a state of mind. True, every bureaucrat needs an organization, a milieu—to choose another useful word from the French—but it is the bureaucrat who makes the milieu, not the other way around.

2   Most of us associate bureaucracy and all its attendant evils with large organizations, especially governments, and we are not surprised to see it getting worse. As the earth's population grows and computers multiply along with the people, burgeoning bureaucracy appears a natural consequence. What Thomas Carlyle, a hundred years ago, could dismiss contemptuously as "the Continental nuisance called 'Bureaucracy' is now to become the fate of all humanity because there are so many of us.

3   Before resigning ourselves to the inevitable, however, we might pause to consider that one of the most pervasive bureaucracies the world has ever known was oppressing the population of the Nile Valley 5,000 years ago, when there were fewer people in the entire world than now live in North America. Add to this the thought that the same number of people can be organized into (*a*) an army, (*b*) a crowd or (*c*) a mob, and it is clear that something more must be involved than time and numbers.

4   What distinguishes each of the aforementioned groups is not how many people it contains, nor where they happen to congregate, but their purpose for being there. And so it is with the bureaucrat.

5   The true bureaucrat is any individual who has lost sight of the underlying purpose of the job at hand, whether in government, industry—or a bank. The purpose of a library, for example, is to facilitate the reading of books. Yet to a certain type of librarian, perfection consists of a well-stocked library with a place for every book—and every book in its place. The reader who insists on taking books home, leaving empty spaces on shelves, is this librarian's natural enemy.

6   It is a cast of mind invulnerable even to the vicissitudes of war. We see it in James Jones's novel *From Here to Eternity* where American soldiers under surprise

attack by Japanese planes at the outbreak of World War II rush to the arsenal for weapons, only to find the door barred by a comrade-in-arms loudly proclaiming that he cannot pass out live ammunition without a written request signed by a commissioned officer.

7   One of these custodians forgot the purpose of a library, the other, the purpose of an army. Both illustrate how, in institutionalized endeavors, means have a way of displacing the ends they are originally designed to serve. In fact, it is one of the bureaucrat's distinguishing features that, for him or for her, the means *become* the ends.

8   The struggle to prevent this subtle subversion is—or should be—a continual challenge to every policy maker in any organization, public or private. Bureaucrats love any policy and can be counted on to enforce it faithfully, as in, "I'm sorry, but that's the policy here." Unfortunately, they don't understand what a policy is.

9   A policy is a standard solution to a constantly recurring problem, not an inviolable law. As a weapon in the hands of literal-minded people, however, a "firm policy" can be as deadly as a repeating rifle. When matters finally become intolerable, the harassed administrator will usually "change the policy." Of course, this never helps because the problem was not the policy in the first place, but the manner of its application.

10   Every college student seeking entry into a course for which he lacks the exact prerequisite, every shopper trying to return a gift without receipt of purchase, every bank customer seeking to correct an error in an account is in danger of discovering that the rules imagined by Joseph Heller are in service wherever rote is more revered than reason.

11   The application of binary logic to human affairs through electronic computers has done nothing to retard the spread of *Catch 22* into the wider world. And thus the thought occurs that modern bureaucracy does, after all, present some problems new to history. Nothing lends itself so readily to "a standard solution to a constantly recurring problem" as a computer.

12   In the best of all possible worlds we might look forward to the day when computers handle all standard solutions, freeing human brains to concentrate on the singular and the exceptional. In the real world, it does not always work out that way—as anyone knows who has ever become trapped in a two-way correspondence with a computer and appealed in vain for human intervention.

13   A favorite student protest sign of the sixties read, "I am a Human Being. Do not fold, spindle or mutilate." What they objected to is real, only the fault is not in our computers, but in ourselves. It lies in our human propensity to let means become ends, and all too often to resemble Santayana's description of a fanatic: one who, having forgotten his purpose, redoubles his efforts.

14   We can denounce the bureaucrats and condemn their works, but they will not go away. They have been with us since the dawn of history, and if they seem to be getting worse, it is because *we* are getting worse. For, in the words of the comic strip *Pogo:* "We has met the enemy, and they is us."

15   Bureaucracy is a state of mind, and the best way to fight it—whether you work for government, industry, a private foundation or a bank—is not to be a bureaucrat. Or at least try not to.

1. Where does the essential definition of *bureaucrat* appear? The essential definition of *policy*?
2. What methods of writing are used to develop paragraphs 3, 5, and 6?
3. What seems to be the purpose of this essay? Refer to the text to explain your answer.
4. To what audience is it addressed? Again, when answering cite appropriate examples.

Write a definition essay using one of the following suggestions or one approved by your instructor. Develop your extended definition by any combination of the methods discussed in this chapter. You might define a word that is new, that has been misused or misunderstood, or that has a disputed meaning. If you pick a word with a disputed meaning, use your definition to support your position.

1. Liberal arts education
2. Vocational education
3. Routine
4. Culture
5. Stress
6. Charisma
7. Marriage
8. A boss
9. A client or customer
10. Freshman
11. Male chauvinist
12. Feminist
13. Police officer
14. The macho man
15. The "together" lady

CHAPTER SEVEN

Convincing Others

ARGUMENT

"What did you think of that movie?"

"Great!"

"What do you mean, *great*? I thought the acting was wooden and the story completely unbelievable."

"That's about what I'd expect from you. You wouldn't know a good movie if it walked up and bit you."

"Oh yeah? What makes you think you're such a great. . . ."

Argument or quarrel? Many people would ask, "What's the difference?" To them, the two terms convey the same meaning, both calling to mind two angry, red-faced people, shouting, trading insults, and sometimes slugging it out. In writing, however, *argument* stands for something quite different: a paper, grounded on logical, structured evidence, that attempts to convince the reader to accept an opinion, take some action, or do both.

We constantly attempt to win others over to our way of thinking. Children try to talk their parents into doing all sorts of things: taking them to the movies, buying them balloons or bicycles, letting them stay up beyond their usual bedtimes. Adults urge city councils to control mosquitoes by spraying, exhort their friends to change positions on nuclear disarmament or capital punishment, or propose that a company change its billing system or buy some new piece of equipment.

As we press our own arguments, we are bombarded with those of others. Advertisers flood us with pitches for jeans and jackets, autos and albums, all the presumed necessities of a healthy, fulfilled life. Spouses press claims for lakeside vacations. Politicians vie for our votes. Rectors and rabbis try to enlist us on the side of righteousness. Mastering the skills of argument can help you gain your own ends and avoid the snares of unscrupulous persuaders.

Certain kinds of topics just aren't arguable. There's no point, for instance, in trying to tackle questions of personal preference or taste (is red prettier than blue?) Such contests quickly turn into "it is," "it isn't" exchanges that establish nothing except the silliness of the contenders. Questions of simple fact (Was Eisenhower first elected President in 1952?) don't qualify either; one side has all the ammunition. Bickering will never settle these issues; reference books quickly will.

Because argument involves conflict, there's always a chance we'll lose some contests. Our parents might turn thumbs down on the bike because they can't afford it. The city might claim that spraying will kill certain desirable insects. Our friends hear what we have to say but hold stubbornly to their original views. The boss refuses to buy the equipment, citing poor company profits. To score a win, we need to present a case more compelling than that of our opposition.

Most successful arguments rest on a firm, logical foundation. To supplement this rational base, writers often enlist emotion to arouse their readers' passions and sympathies. Furthermore, writers make ethical appeals by projecting favorable images of themselves.

THE RATIONAL APPEAL

When you appeal to reason, you appeal to the reader's ability to think logically. You say, in effect, "If you examine my thinking on this issue, you will agree with me." Logical thinking proceeds by leading the reader from some point that both reader and writer accept as true to other points that follow from it. Without such a starting point, the process can't get under way. Rational appeals include three reasoning strategies: induction, deduction, and analogy.

INDUCTION

Induction moves from separate bits of evidence to a general observation. Suppose that on a hot, humid summer day you go to the kitchen to eat some potato chips from a bag opened the day before. As you start to munch, you make these observations:

Chip #1: limp and stale
Chip #2: limp and stale
Chip #3: limp and stale
Chip #4: limp and stale
Chip #5: limp and stale

At this point, you decide that the rest of the chips are probably stale too, and you stop eating. Inductive reasoning has led you, stale chip by stale chip, to a conclusion about the whole bag.

But probability is not proof. To prove something by induction, we must check every bit of evidence, and often that's just not practical or possible. Nonetheless, induction has great value for the conduct of human affairs. Say a food company has test marketed a new spaghetti sauce and now wants to decide whether it should start selling the product nationwide. A poll of 1200 users, representing a cross section of the market, indicates that 78 percent rate the sauce "excellent." As a result, the company decides to go ahead. Induction has led them to conclude that future customers will savor the sauce as much as past customers did. Polls that sample political preferences and other public attitudes also operate inductively.

DEDUCTION

Deduction reverses the pattern of induction by moving from a general observation to a more specific observation. Often it takes the form of a categorical syllogism, a set of three statements that follow a set pattern to ensure sound reasoning. The general observation, or *major premise,* names a category of things and says that all or none of them share a certain characteristic. The *minor premise* notes that a thing or group of things belongs to that category. The *conclusion* states that the thing or group shares the characteristics of the category. Here are two examples:

Major premise: All persons are mortal.

Minor premise: Sue Davis is a person.

Conclusion: Therefore, Sue Davis is mortal.

Major premise: No dogs have feathers.

Minor premise: Spot is a dog.

Conclusion: Therefore, Spot does not have feathers.

Syllogisms frequently appear in stripped-down form, with one of the premises or the conclusion omitted. The following example omits the major premise: "Because Wilma is a civil engineer, she has a strong background in mathematics." Here is the entire syllogism.

All civil engineers have strong backgrounds in mathematics.

Wilma is a civil engineer.

Therefore, Wilma has a strong background in mathematics.

Syllogistic Argument at Work.   To see how the syllogism works in an actual argument essay, read the following excerpt from Martin Luther King, Jr.'s "Letter from Birmingham Jail." King wrote the letter after his arrest during a civil-rights demonstration in Birmingham, Alabama. He addressed it to eight Birmingham clergymen who had published a letter that defended his war on racial discrimination but deplored his "nonviolent direct action" which included sit-ins and protest marches. In answering the clergymen, King draws a difference between just and unjust laws, then uses it to justify his willingness to defy segregation laws but not others.

> . . . How does one determine whether a law is just or unjust? A just law is a man-made code that squares with the moral law or the law of God. An unjust law is a code that is out of harmony with the moral law. To put it in the terms of St. Thomas Aquinas: An unjust law is a human law that is not rooted in eternal law and natural law. Any law that degrades human personality is unjust. All segregation statutes are unjust because segregation distorts the soul and damages the personality. It gives the segregator a false sense of superiority and the segregated a false sense of inferiority. . . . Thus it is that I can urge men to obey the 1954 decision of the Supreme Court, for it is morally right; and I can urge them to disobey segregation ordinances, for they are morally wrong.

Stated in syllogistic form, King's reasoning goes as follows:

> All laws that degrade human personality are unjust.
>
> All segregation laws are laws that degrade human personality.
>
> Therefore, all segregation laws are unjust.

This syllogism is readily apparent and likely to win acceptance from the Birmingham clergymen because King enlists a religious authority to support his definitions of just and unjust laws. Indeed, most readers, not just these clergymen, would probably accept the syllogism.

Avoiding Misuse of Syllogisms.   When using syllogisms in an argument, make sure they follow the proper order. The writer of the following passage ignores this caution.

> And that's not all. Newton has stated openly that he favors federally funded abortions for the poor. Just the other day, the American Socialist party took this same stand. In my book, Newton's position puts him squarely in the Socialist camp. I strongly urge anyone supporting this man's candidacy to reconsider. . . .

Restated in syllogistic form, the writer's argument goes like this:

> Socialists favor federally funded abortions for the poor.
>
> Newton favors federally funded abortions for the poor.
>
> Therefore, Newton is a Socialist.

The last two statements reverse the proper order, and as a result the syllogism proves nothing about Newton's politics: he may or may not be "in the Socialist camp."

Launching an argument with a false but widely believed major premise is another error to avoid. Note this example:

> All conservatives are opposed to environmental protection.
>
> Mary is a conservative.
>
> Therefore, Mary is opposed to environmental protection.

But is every conservative an environmental Jack the Ripper? In some communities, political conservatives have led fights against air and water pollution, and most conservatives agree that at least some controls are worthwhile. Mary's sympathies, then, may well lie with those who want to heal, rather than hack, the environment.

This type of flaw becomes much harder to detect when the syllogism omits the major premise:

> Professor Snarf is a poor instructor; she grades her students so hard.

Expanding the statement into a full-blown syllogism exposes the shaky underpinnings on which the original rests.

> All instructors who grade hard are poor instructors.
>
> Professor Snarf grades her students hard.
>
> Therefore, Professor Snarf is a poor instructor.

Following this procedure with any stripped-down syllogism will quickly show whether it is trying to sneak across a faulty idea.

EXERCISE   **Which of these syllogisms is satisfactory, which have false major premises, and which is faulty because the last two statements reverse the proper order?**

1. All singers are happy people.
   Mary Harper is a singer.
   Therefore, Mary Harper is a happy person.

2. All cowards fear danger.
   "Chicken" Cacciatore is a coward.
   Therefore, "Chicken" Cacciatore fears danger.

3. All cats like meat.
   Towser likes meat.
   Therefore, Towser is a cat.

4. No salesperson would ever misrepresent a product to a customer.
   Sabrina is a salesperson.
   Therefore, Sabrina would never misrepresent a product to a customer.

ANALOGY

An analogy compares two unlike situations or things. Arguers often use analogies to contend that because two items share one or more likenesses, the items resemble each other in additional ways. Familiar analogies assume that humans respond to chemicals as rats do and that success in school predicts success on the job.

With analogy, the conclusion about one thing rests upon observations of some different thing; therefore, this method of reasoning is the weakest kind of rational appeal. Analogies never conclusively prove anything. But they often help explain and show probability and therefore are quite persuasive.

Judge the value of any analogy by two touchstones. First, its points of similarity must bear directly upon the issue. Second, it must account for any significant differences between the two things. Here's an effective analogy, used to back an argument that a liberal education is the best kind to help us cope successfully with life.

Suppose it were perfectly certain that the life and fortune of everyone of us would, one day or other, depend upon his winning or losing a game of chess. Don't you think that we should all consider it to be a primary duty to learn at least the names and the moves of the pieces; to have a notion of a gambit, and a keen eye for all the means of giving and getting out of check? Do you not think that we should look with a disapprobation amounting to scorn, upon the father who allowed his son, or the state which allowed its members, to grow up without knowing a pawn from a knight?

Yet it is a very plain and elementary truth, that the life, the fortune, and the happiness of every one of us, and, more or less, of those who are connected with us, do depend upon our knowing something of the rules of a game infinitely more difficult and complicated than chess. It is a game which has been played for untold ages, every man and woman of us being one of the two players in a game of his or her own. The chessboard is the world, the pieces are the phenomena of the universe, the rules of the game are what we call the laws of Nature. The player on the other side is hidden from us. We know that his play is always fair, just, and patient. But also we know, to our cost, that he never overlooks a mistake, or makes the smallest allowance for ignorance. To the man who plays well, the highest stakes are paid, with that sort of overflowing generosity with which the strong shows delight in strength. And one who plays ill is checkmated—without haste, but without remorse. . . .

Well, what I mean by Education is learning the rules of this mighty game. In other words, education is the instruction of the intellect in the law of Nature, under which name I include not merely things and their forces, but men and their ways; and the fashioning of the affections and of the will into an earnest and loving desire to move in harmony with those laws. For me, education means neither more nor less than this. Anything which professes to call itself education must be tried by this standard, and if it fails to stand the test, I will not call it education, whatever may be the force of authority, or of numbers, upon the other side.

Thomas Henry Huxley, "A Liberal
Education and Where to Find it"

THE EMOTIONAL APPEAL

Although effective argument relies mainly on reason, an emotional appeal can lend powerful reinforcement. Indeed, emotion can win the heart and the help of people who would otherwise passively accept a logical argument but take no action. Each Christmas, newspapers raise large sums for local charity by running stark case histories of destitute families. Organizations raise funds to fight famine by displaying brochures that feature skeletal, swollenbellied children. Still other groups use emotion-charged stories and pictures to solicit support for environmental protection, to combat various diseases, and so on. Less benignly, advertisers use emotion to play upon our hopes, fears, and vanities in order to sell mouthwash, cars, clothes, and other products. Politicians paint themselves as God-fearing, honest toilers for the public good while lambasting their opponents as the uncaring tools of special interests. In evaluating or writing an argument, ask yourself whether the facts warrant the emotion. Is the condition of the destitute family truly cause for pity? Is any politician unwaveringly good, any other irredeemably bad?

The following paragraph from "Letter from Birmingham Jail" illustrates an appropriate use of emotion:

> We have waited for more than 340 years for our constitutional and God-given rights. The nations of Asia and Africa are moving with jetlike speed toward gaining political independence, but we still creep at horse-and-buggy pace toward gaining a cup of coffee at a lunch counter. Perhaps it is easy for those who have never felt the stinging darts of segregation to say, "Wait." But when you have seen vicious mobs lynch your mothers and fathers at will and drown your sisters and brothers at whim; when you have seen hate-filled policemen curse, kick, and even kill your black brothers and sisters; when you see the vast majority of your twenty million Negro brothers smothering in an airtight cage of poverty in the midst of an affluent society; when you suddenly find your tongue twisted and your speech stammering as you seek to explain to your six-year-old daughter why she can't go to the public amusement park that has just been advertised on television, and see tears welling up in her eyes when she is told that Funtown is closed to colored children, and see ominous clouds of inferiority beginning to form in her little mental sky, and see her beginning to distort her personality by developing an unconscious bitterness toward white people; when you have to concoct an answer for a five-year-old son who is asking, "Daddy, why do white people treat colored people so mean?"; when you take a cross-country drive and find it necessary to sleep night after night in the uncomfortable corners of your automobile because no motel will accept you; when you are humiliated day in and day out by nagging signs reading "white" and "colored"; when your first name becomes "nigger," your middle name becomes "boy" (however old you are) and your last name becomes "John," and your wife and mother are never given the respected title "Mrs."; when you are harried by day and haunted by night by the fact that you are a Negro, living constantly at tiptoe stance, never quite knowing what to expect next, and are plagued with inner fears and outer resentments, when you are forever fighting a degenerating sense of "nobodiness"—then you will understand why we find it difficult to wait. There comes a time when the cup of endurance runs over, and men are no longer willing to be plunged into the abyss of despair. I hope, sirs, you can understand our legitimate and unavoidable impatience.
>
> Martin Luther King, Jr., "Letter from Birmingham Jail"

THE ETHICAL APPEAL

Ethical appeals derive from the image a writer projects. Before logic can do its work, the audience must be willing to consider the argument. If a writer's tone offends the audience, the reasoning, however brilliant, will fail to penetrate. But if the writer comes across as pleasant, moral, fair-minded, decent, worthwhile—any of a number of positive characteristics appropriate to the seriousness of the argument—gaining reader support is much easier.

In "Letter from Birmingham Jail," King wisely enlists the force of ethical appeal, starting in the opening paragraph. King knows that his clergymen audience opposes his actions, if not his ends; that his wider audience includes many people who violently oppose the civil rights movement; and that he must therefore build a respectable character from the disadvantageous position of an inmate in a jail.

King first notes that his journey to Birmingham and his activities there grew out of his desire for justice. In making this point, he draws a parallel between himself and biblical bearers of the Gospel.

> . . . I am in Birmingham because injustice is here. Just as the prophets of the eighth century B.C. left their villages and carried their "thus saith the Lord" far beyond the boundaries of their home towns, and just as the Apostle Paul left his village of Tarsus and carried the gospel of Jesus Christ to the far corners of the Greco–Roman world, so am I compelled to carry the gospel of freedom beyond my own home town. Like Paul, I must constantly respond to the Macedonian call for aid.

King points out that he and his followers turned to direct action only after it had become clear that the city fathers would not negotiate in good faith. He further declares that he postponed his direct action program several times before finally putting it into effect. Then he defends his action as a necessary prelude to moral growth.

> . . . I have earnestly opposed violent tension, but there is a type of constructive, nonviolent tension which is necessary for growth. Just as Socrates felt that it was necessary to create a tension in the mind so that individuals could rise from the bondage of myths and half-truths to the unfettered realm of creative analysis and objective appraisal, so must we see the need for nonviolent gadflies to create the kind of tension in society that will help men rise from the dark depths of prejudice and racism to the majestic heights of understanding and brotherhood.

Here King offers a needed explanation without sacrificing his dignity. He comes across as rational, religious, and peace-loving, a person who mirrors the qualities his audience would be most likely to accept.

WRITING AN ARGUMENT
SIZING UP YOUR OPPOSITION AND AUDIENCE

Like most people, you'll probably have strong feelings about your position. But don't for that reason ignore the other side. Before starting to write, draw up a list of pros and cons and inspect them carefully. You may decide to switch your position. Even if you don't, knowing the opposition's strengths allows you to counter or neutralize them. Suppose you favor a nationwide ban on the sale of handguns. You need to know that half of our state constitutions grant citizens the right to own guns. Unless you acknowledge and somehow counter this fact, your case will suffer and perhaps even founder.

As with other essays, aim your argument at a specific audience. Select a group of readers who are either neutral or who oppose your position; there's no point in preaching to the converted. Take a little time to weigh the attitudes, needs, and expectations of your readers so that you can tailor your arguments accordingly. Exchange places with them and view the issue through their eyes. Ask yourself: How are they likely to respond to what I say? What types of evidence would bring them around to my way of thinking? To convince an audience of farmers that the federal school lunch program needs expanding, you might stress the added income they would gain. Speak to nutritionists about health benefits; tell school officials that the program could improve class performance.

DEVELOPING AND SUPPORTING AN ARGUMENT

The heart of your argument is the evidence supporting your position. Evidence falls into several categories: established truths, opinions of authorities, statistical findings, and personal experience. The strongest arguments usually combine several types of evidence.

Established Truths.   These are facts that no one can seriously dispute. Here are some examples.

Historical fact	The first amendment of the United States Constitution prohibits Congress from abridging freedom of the press.
Scientific fact	The layer of ozone in the earth's upper atmosphere protects us against the sun's harmful ultraviolet radiation.
Geographical fact	The western part of the United States has tremendous reserves of coal.

Established truths aren't arguable themselves but do provide strong backup for argumentative propositions. For example, citing the abundant coal supply in the western regions could support an argument that the United States should return to coal to supply our energy needs.

Some established truths, having grown out of careful observations and thinking over a period of years, amount basically to enlightened common sense. The notion that everyone possesses a unique combination of interests, abilities, and personality characteristics illustrates this kind of established truth. Few people would seriously question it.

Opinions of Authorities.   An authority is a recognized expert in some field. Authoritative opinions—the only kind to use—play a powerful role in winning readers over to your side. The views of metropolitan police chiefs and experienced criminologists could support your position on ways to control urban crime. Researchers who have investigated the effects of air pollution could help you argue for stricter smog control laws. Whatever your argument, don't settle for less than a heavyweight authority. And show your reader just why those you cite are authorities.

The following paragraph, from an article arguing that extra-high-voltage electric transmission lines pose a health hazard, illustrates the use of authority.

> Robert Becker, a physician and director of the Orthopedic–Biophysics Laboratory at the Syracuse, New York, Veterans Administration Hospital—Upstate Medical Center, has been researching the effects of low-frequency electric fields (60 Hz) for fifteen years. Testifying at health and safety hearings for proposed lines in New York, he said that exposure to the fields can produce physiological and functional changes in humans—anything from increased irritability and fatigue to raised cholesterol levels, hypertension and ulcers. Studies of rats exposed to low-level electric fields showed tumor growths and abnormalities in development. Dr. Becker believes we are performing unauthorized medical experiments by exposing people to the electromagnetic fields surrounding the transmission lines.
>
> Kelly Davis, "Health and High Voltage: 765 KV Lines"

Beware of opinions from those who stand to profit if their views prevail. The agribusiness executive who favors farm price supports or the labor leader who opposes any restrictions on picketing may be writing merely to guard old privileges or garner new ones. Unless the opinion can stand especially close scrutiny, don't put it in your paper; it will just weaken your case with perceptive readers.

Because authorities don't always see eye to eye, their views lack the finality of established truths. Furthermore, their opinions will convince only if the audience accepts the authority *as* authoritative. Although advertisers succeed in presenting football stars as authorities on shaving cream and credit cards, most people would not accept their views on the safety of nuclear energy.

Statistical Findings. Statistics—data showing how much, how many, or how often—can also buttress your argument. Most statistics come from books, magazines, newspapers, handbooks, encyclopedias, and reports, but you can use data from your own investigations as well.

Because statistics are so often misused, many people distrust them. Therefore, any statistics you offer must be reliable. First, make sure your sample isn't too small. Don't use the results of a one-day traffic count to argue for a traffic light at a certain intersection. City Hall might counter by contending that the results were atypical. To make your case, you'd need to count traffic for perhaps two or three weeks. Take care not to push statistical claims too far. You may know that two-thirds of Tarrytown's factories pollute the air excessively, but don't argue that the same figures probably apply to your town. There's simply no carryover. Keep alert for biased statistics; they can cause as serious a credibility gap as biased opinions. As a general rule, recent data are better than old data, but either must come from a reliable source. Older information from *The New York Times* would probably be more accurate than current data from some publication that trades on sensationalism. Here's how one student used statistics:

> Otto Friedrich, writing in *Time* magazine, underscores the magnitude of the tax-cheating problem. According to the IRS, he says, Americans will deliberately underpay their 1982 federal taxes by $100 billion, up from $29 billion just ten years ago. To make matters worse, only 1.55 percent of all taxpayers will receive an audit, as compared to 2.55 percent in 1976. Thus, the odds for successful tax evasion keep getting better.
>
> Dana Mandolari

Personal Experience. Sometimes personal experience can deliver an argumentative message more forcefully than any other kind of evidence. Suppose that two years ago a speeder ran into your car and almost killed you. Today you're arguing for stiffer laws against speeding. Chances are you'll rely mainly on expert opinions and on statistics showing the number of people killed and injured each year in speeding accidents. Describing the crash, however, the slow, pain-filled weeks in the hospital, and the months spent hobbling around on crutches may well provide the persuasive nudge that's needed to win over your reader. Personal experience generally reinforces but does not replace other kinds of evidence. Unless it has other backup, readers may reject the evidence of personal experience as atypical or trivial.

ORGANIZING YOUR ARGUMENT

A typical introduction arouses the reader's interest, makes an ethical appeal, and states the proposition. A *proposition* is a special thesis statement that names the issue and indicates which side the writer will take. It can declare that something is a fact, call for certain action, or assert that something has greater value than something else. Here are examples.

1. Carron College does not provide adequate recreational facilities for its students. *(declares something is fact)*
2. Because the present building is overcrowded and unsafe, the people of Midville should vote funds for a new junior high school. *(calls for action)*
3. The new photocopier provides sharper, cheaper photocopies than those from the machine we now have. *(notes value)*

Depending on the argument, you may want to trace briefly the background or look at the consequences of the issue. If your essay will be long, you could preview the points you'll present.

After the introduction comes the evidence, arranged in whatever order you think will work best. If one of your points is likely to trigger resistance, hold it back until you've first presented points that are easier to accept. If not, you could begin or end with your most compelling argument.

Also use this part of your paper to refute; that is, to point out weaknesses or errors in the opposing position. You can sprinkle refutations throughout the body of the paper or group them together just ahead of the conclusion. Whatever you decide, don't adopt a gloating or sarcastic tone that will alienate a fair-minded reader. Resist the urge to engage in straw man tactics—calling attention to imaginary or trivial weaknesses of the opposing side so that you can demolish them. Shrewd readers easily spot such ploys. Finally, don't be afraid to concede secondary or insignificant points to the opposition. Arguments have two or more sides; you can't have all the ammunition on your side. (If you discover you must concede major points, however, consider switching sides.) Here is a sample refutation from a student paper.

Despite its good features, no-fault divorce has not lacked critics, who most commonly charge that it increases divorce, thereby cheapening marriage. Although the divorce rate has risen each time a state has liberalized its divorce law, it does not necessarily follow that the number of broken marriages has increased. When New Jersey liberalized its divorce laws in 1971, as Rose DeWolf reports in *Nation* magazine, twice as many people divorced as in the previous year. Most of the couples, however, had been separated over ten years and could not divorce under the old law.

Dominic DeLuca

Conclude in a manner that will sway the reader to your side. In addition to restating your position, you could summarize your main points, predict consequences if your position does (or does not) prevail, or make an emotional appeal for support or action. If your proposition is sure to generate a strong emotional response, you might defer it until the end, until you've softened your audience with the evidence.

FERRETING OUT FALLACIES

After you've written the first draft of your paper, scan it for fallacies—lapses in logic that reflect on your ability to think clearly. They weaken your argument. The fallacies described below are among the most common. Correct any you find in your own arguments, and call attention to those you turn up on the other side.

Hasty Generalization.   Hasty generalization results when someone draws a conclusion after considering too little evidence. For example, a student tries to see an instructor during one of her office hours, but the instructor is not in. The student goes away muttering, "She's never there when she should be." That is hasty generalization. Perhaps the instructor was delayed by another student, attended a special department meeting, or went home ill. Even if she merely went shopping, that's not a good reason for saying she always shirks her responsibility. Half a dozen or more unsuccessful office visits would be needed to make such a charge stick.

Non Sequitur.   From the Latin "It does not follow," this fallacy draws unwarranted conclusions from seemingly ample evidence. Consider this example: "Bill's been out almost every night for the last two weeks. Who is she?" These evening excursions, numerous though they may be, point to no particular conclusion. Bill may be studying in the library, participating in campus organizations, taking night classes, or walking. Of course, he *could* be charmed by a new date, but that conclusion requires other evidence.

Stereotyping.   A person who commits this fallacy attaches one or more supposed characteristics to a group or one of its members. Typical stereotypes include "Latins make better lovers," "blondes have more fun," and "women are lousy drivers." Stereotyping racial, religious, ethnic, or nationality groups can destroy an argument. The images are often malicious and always offensive to fair-minded readers.

Either/or Fallacy.   The either/or fallacy asserts that only two choices exist when, in fact, several options are possible. A salesperson who wants you to buy snow tires may claim, "Either buy these tires or plan on getting stuck a lot this winter." But are you really that boxed in? You might drive only on main roads that are plowed immediately after every snowstorm. You could use public transportation when it snows. You could buy radial tires for year-round use. If very little snow falls, you might not need special tires at all.

     Not all either/or statements are fallacies. The instructor who checks a student's record and then issues a warning, "Make at least a *C* on your final or you'll fail the course," is not guilty of a reasoning error. No other alternatives exist. Most situations, however, offer more than two choices.

Begging the Question.   A person who begs the question asserts the truth of some unproven statement. Here is an example: "Vitamin A is harmful to your health, and all bottles should carry a warning label. If enough of us write the Food and Drug Administration, we can get the labeling we need." But how do we know Vitamin A does harm users? No evidence is offered. People lacking principles often use this fallacy to hit opponents below the belt: "We shouldn't allow a right-wing sympathizer like Mary Dailey to represent us in Congress." Despite a lack of suitable evidence, voters often accept such faulty logic and vote for the other candidate.

Circular Argument.   Circular argument, a first cousin to begging the question, supports a position merely by restating it. "Pauline is a good manager because she runs the company effectively" says, in effect, that "something is because something is." Repetition replaces evidence.

The Argument Ad Hominem.   The Latin term "to the man" designates an argument that attacks an individual rather than that individual's opinions or qualifications. Note this example: "Sam Bernhart doesn't deserve promotion to Personnel Manager. His divorce was a disgrace, and he's always writing letters to the editor. The company should find someone more suitable." This attack completely skirts the real issue—whether Sam's job performance entitles him to the promotion. Unless his personal conduct has caused his work to suffer, it should not enter into the decision.

Appeal to the Crowd.   An appeal of this sort arouses an emotional response by playing on the irrational fears and prejudices of the audience. Terms like *communists, fascists, bleeding hearts, right-winger, welfare chiselers*, and *law and order* are tossed about freely to sway the audience for or against something. Consider:

> The streets of our country are in turmoil. The universities are filled with students rebelling and rioting. Communists are seeking to destroy our country. Russia is threatening us with her might, and the public is in danger. Yes, danger from within and without. We need law and order. Yes, without law and order our nation cannot survive. Elect us, and we shall by law and order be respected among the nations of the world. Without law and order our republic shall fall.

Tapping the emotions of the crowd can succeed in swaying large groups and in winning acceptance for positions that rational thinking would reject. Think what Adolf Hitler, the author of the foregoing excerpt, brought about in Germany.

Guilt by Association.   This fallacy points out some similarity or connection between one person or group and another. It tags the first with the sins, real or imagined, of the second. The following excerpt from a letter protesting a speaker at a lecture series illustrates this technique:

> The next slated speaker, Dr. Sylvester Crampton, was for years a member of the Economic Information Committee. This foundation has very strong ties with other ultraright-wing groups, some of which have been labeled fascistic. When he speaks next Thursday, whose brand of Americanism will he be selling?

Post Hoc, ergo Propter Hoc.   The Latin meaning, "after this, therefore because of this," refers to the fallacy of assuming that because one event follows another, the first caused the second. Such shoddy thinking underlies many popular superstitions ("If a black cat crosses your path, you'll have bad luck") and many connections that cannot be substantiated ("I always catch cold on Easter"). Sometimes one event does cause another: a sudden thunderclap might startle a person into dropping a dish. At other times, coincidence is the only connection. Careful thinking will usually lay farfetched causal notions to rest.

Faulty Analogy.   This is the error of assuming that two circumstances or things are similar in all important respects, when in fact they are not. Here's an example. Harvey Thompson, high school football coach, tells his players, "Vince Lombardi won two Super Bowls by insisting on perfect execution of plays and enforcing strict disciplinary measures. We're going to win the conference championship by following the same methods." Thompson assumes that because he and Lombardi are coaches, he can duplicate Lombardi's achievements by using Lombardi's methods. Several important differences, however, mark the two situations:

1. Lombardi had very talented players, obtained through the player draft or trades; Thompson can choose only from the students in high school.
2. Lombardi's players were paid professionals who very likely were motivated at least in part by the financial rewards that came from winning the Super Bowl; Thompson's players are amateurs.
3. "Perfect execution of plays" is probably easier to attain on the professional level than in high school because of the players' experience.
4. Despite Lombardi's rigid disciplinary measures, very few of his players quit, perhaps because they were under contract. Could Thompson expect his players, essentially volunteers, to accept the kind of verbal and physical rigors Lombardi was famous for?

Identify and explain the fallacies in the following examples. Remember that understanding the faulty reasoning is more important than merely naming the fallacy.   **EXERCISE**

1. While eating a Golden Glow orange, Nancy discovers that it is rotten. "I'll never buy another Golden Glow product," she declares emphatically.
2. A campaigning politician states that unless the federal government appropriates funds to help people living in poverty, they will all starve.
3. A husband and wife see an X-rated movie called *Swinging Wives*. A week later the husband discovers that his wife, while supposedly attending an evening class, has been unfaithful to him. He blames the movie for her infidelity.
4. Look at those two motorcycle riders trying to pick a fight. All those cycle bums are troublemakers.
5. Bill really loves to eat. Some day he'll have a serious weight problem.
6. Because no-fault divorce is responsible for today's skyrocketing divorce rate, it should be abolished.
7. This is the best-looking picture in the exhibit; it's so much more attractive than the others.
8. I do not support this school millage proposal. It's sponsored by James McAndrews, who's about the most ill-tempered, quarrelsome person I've ever met. I'd never favor anything he supports.

9. My position on social and economic issues is easy to state. I am against wooly-brained do-gooders and big-spending, pie-in-the-sky welfare programs that have brought us to the brink of social disaster. I stand foursquare behind our free enterprise system, which has given us a standard of living the whole world envies, and if elected, I will defend it with everything at my command.

REVISION CHECKLIST

Ponder these questions as you revise your argument paper.

✔ Is my topic controversial? Have I examined both sides of the issue? Assessed and countered the opposition's special strengths?

✔ Is the paper aimed at the audience I want to reach? Have I tailored my argument to appeal to that audience?

✔ If I've reasoned inductively, have I observed enough examples to justify my conclusion? If I've reasoned deductively, are my deductions sound? If they are faulty, have I started with a faulty premise or reversed the last two statements of the syllogism? If I've used analogy, are my points of comparison pertinent to the issue? Have I noted any significant differences between the items being compared?

✔ If I've included an emotional appeal, does it center on those emotions most likely to sway the reader?

✔ Have I made a conscious effort to present myself in a favorable light?

✔ Is my evidence sound, adequate, and appropriate to the argument? Are my authorities qualified? Have I established their expertise? Are they biased? Will my audience accept them as authorities? Do my statistics adequately support my position? Have I pushed my statistical claims too far?

✔ Is my proposition clearly evident and the appropriate type; i.e., one of fact, action, or value?

✔ Is my evidence effectively structured? Have I adequately refuted opposing arguments?

✔ Is my argument free of fallacies?

EXAMPLE ESSAYS OF ARGUMENT

STUDENT WRITING

The Right to Bear Arms
BRENDA BUEHRLE

1   The right of citizens to bear arms is often discussed in heated tones and emotional language. Political assassinations, for example, inevitably spark an outcry for control of firearms, as do soaring crime statistics. These appeals are fre-

quently countered by jingles such as "When guns are outlawed, only outlaws will have guns." If we bypass such purely emotional pleas and examine the issue objectively, we find that there is ample legal justification for the right to bear arms.

The first thing we should consider is the original intent of the Second Amendment to the United States Constitution, which states: "A well-regulated militia being necessary to the security of a free State, the right of the people to keep and bear arms shall not be infringed." When the purpose of any constitutional provision or law is in question, a good procedure is to return to the thoughts and words of those who originally framed it. For the Second Amendment, it is necessary to examine the ideas of George Mason, the Virginia constitutionalist. Mason wrote several specific safeguards of individual rights into the Virginia constitution of 1776. The Bill of Rights—that is, the first ten amendments added to the United States Constitution in 1791—incorporates many of Mason's safeguards. R.A. Rutland's edition of Mason's papers reveals clearly that his conception of the militia—that group empowered by law to bear arms—went far beyond an organized group of men in uniform. During a debate in Richmond on June 16, 1788, Mason rhetorically said: "I ask who are the militia?" and then answered his own question with these words: "They consist now of the whole people, except a few public officials." There can be little doubt that George Mason, "Father of the Bill of Rights," never intended to restrict the right to bear arms to a relatively few men in uniform. Therefore, the original concept of the Second Amendment was that the militia consisted of all people; and to ensure security of a free country, the people had the right to keep and bear arms.

2

Early in this century Congress interpreted the militia more narrowly than Mason did. On January 23, 1903, Congress defined the militia as all able-bodied male citizens more than eighteen and less than forty-five years of age. These men were divided into two classes: the organized militia, to be known as the National Guard of the State, Territory, or District of Columbia, and the remainder, to be known as the Reserve Militia. Thus, the Congress classified all males within certain age limits, and not in the National Guard, as members of the militia. These men would now seem to be the "people to keep and bear arms" whose right to firearms "shall not be infringed" under the Second Amendment. Furthermore, under the broad doctrine of equal rights, it would appear that women should also be included, if they fall into the proper age groups eligible for military service.

3

Since no definite laws in the United States Constitution define the rights of gun owners throughout the fifty states, the state constitutions certainly would seem to be the highest law in such cases, as provided in the Ninth and Tenth Amendments. These reserve, to the states and the people, all rights and powers not spelled out in the United States Constitution. Because the Second Amendment does not definitely state the rights of gun owners, the federal government cannot alter the rights that are defined in individual state constitutions. At least half of these state constitutions go beyond the Second Amendment by spelling out that the right to bear arms is an individual right for personal protection or defense of home and property and has nothing to do with a "well-regulated mi-

4

litia." Among these states are Arizona, Michigan, and Pennsylvania. For example, Arizona's constitution states, "The right of the individual citizen to bear arms in defense of himself or the State shall not be impaired. . . ." Michigan's says, "Every person has a right to keep and bear arms for the defense of himself and the State." Pennsylvania's constitution is emphatic: "The right of the citizens to bear arms in defense of themselves and the State shall not be questioned." Given such declarations, the states with these and similar provisions could not possibly prohibit ownership of hand guns or any other arms.

5   It should be clear that the Second Amendment was not originally intended to apply only to militia, but to the "whole people." In addition, Congress has indicated that the militia consists of all able-bodied young and middle-aged males (and now perhaps females also). Furthermore, 50 percent of the state constitutions define and protect the rights of individual gun owners. Is it not evident that the right to bear arms is rooted in solid legal precedent?

DISCUSSION QUESTIONS

1. Identify the writer's proposition. Is it one of fact, action, or value?
2. In paragraph 1, the writer cites two approaches to the issue. What are they? Could they have been presented in reverse order? Why or why not?
3. What type of evidence does the writer use in her argument?
4. Reread the last two sentences in paragraph 3. Indicate why the phrasing "would now seem" and "it would appear" is appropriate here.
5. What type of conclusion does the writer use? Why is the question that ends it effective?

PROFESSIONAL WRITING

What Running Can't Do For You
JAMES FIXX

1   Not long ago, with a perfectly straight face, the author of a book on running wondered aloud whether the sport might not now qualify as a bona fide religion, right up there, one gathered, with Christianity, Judaism, and the planet's other major faiths.

2   This is only one instance of a rapidly developing theme in the current running literature. In fact, some of the most articulate and respected figures in running have spoken out in support of it. In "The Joy of Running," for example, the psychiatrist Thaddeus Kostrubala identifies running with the search for the Holy Grail ("If we find the Grail, the wasteland is redeemed"). In "Running & Being," Dr. George Sheehan writes, "My danger is that I will fail to reach my limits and find God. But here my body helps." And in "Beyond Jogging," Esalen's Mike Spino is similarly sanguine about the transcendental benefits derivable from putting one foot in front of the other. "The quest of spirit through the body," he insists, "has just begun."

This spiritual strain in runners isn't, of course, a new development. Its be- 3
ginnings were apparent several years ago, long before the sport acquired the
trendy ubiquity it has today. I first noticed it while conducting interviews for "The
Complete Book of Running." One woman spoke solemnly of having become a
"convert" to running. Then, lest I mistake her meaning, she added, "I don't think
I'm far off in equating my experience with a conversion." And the wife of a middle-aged runner, shaking her head in wry puzzlement, said, "Tom used to be a
Methodist. Now he's a runner."

No, what is new today isn't that an occasional runner is claiming spiritual 4
benefits from the sport. It is that almost all runners are, and that mystical visions
have become as common as blisters. By the thousands, the faithful listen to lectures on shinsplints, and do so with a bright-eyed intensity once witnessed mostly
at revival meetings. Books about running are declared to be "bibles." Authorities
on the sport are introduced to audiences as "gurus." In at least one case I know
of, the author of a book on running—all right, I'll confess it: it was me—was described as "the high priest."

I'd like to argue, as a member in more or less good standing of the vast 5
congregation of runners, that this sort of windy hyperbole is just plain silly. And
maybe slightly dangerous, too. Even, if we realize what we're up to, downright
wicked.

It's easy enough to see how running got confused with religion. Running 6
can, it's true, make you imagine yourself a better person than you are. Yesterday,
I ran for an hour through a seaside park near my home in Connecticut. The last
of the leaves were tumbling in the wind. I ran past three imperturbable skunks,
a raccoon, a family of squirrels busily laying in a winter's supplies. A pheasant
noisily took to the air at the sound of running shoes on gravel. By the time I got
home, I felt refreshed and beatified. I know of no human activity, except perhaps
sex, that can do so much in so brief a time, and do it so wonderfully.

Think, on the other hand, of what running can't do. Running has nothing, 7
absolutely nothing, to do with caring about other people, or with compassion or
with self-sacrifice. On the contrary, devotees of the sport are likely to be incor-
rigible loners, sufficient unto themselves in their sweaty enjoyments. To the extent, therefore, that we let ourselves equate those enjoyments with the traditional
pursuits and hard-won satisfactions of religion, we deflect our attention from
concerns that are far more important than getting into a pair of Adidases and
breathing hard before breakfast.

Don't imagine, incidentally, that the loneliness of the long-distance runner 8
is nothing but a literary fancy. It's true; runners do tend to be solitary souls. Furthermore, far from being troubled by their solitude, they revel in it.

A few years ago, researchers at Purdue University recruited 60 sedentary 9
staff members for an experiment to explore the psychological effects of regular
exercise. The scientists first evaluated their subjects' personalities, then put them
on an exercise program consisting mainly of running. At the end of four months,
they conducted a second evaluation—and found striking changes. Along with the

inevitable physical improvement, the runners had become more stable emotionally, more confident and, perhaps most significantly, more self-sufficient.

10   Fine. It need hardly be pointed out, however, that self-sufficiency is the opposite of commitment to the human community that is at the heart of the religious impulse. It is a mistake to confuse cardiovascular fitness with *caritas*.

11   Fellow marathon-runner Colman McCarthy put the matter deftly when he wrote, "Running . . . is really little more than another of man's hobbies that help distract him from the toil of earning a living, pondering life's mysteries, and living in a world where three-fourths of the people are chronically ill and will die that way." Amen. A sweat suit is not a surplice. Gatorade is not Communion wine. The Verrazano Bridge is not a cathedral.

12   I think I know why so many people are running today. It's not just that running is good for you, or even that it's fun. For the very best of reasons our generation has lost faith in many of society's pivotal institutions—government, the law, marriage and religion among them. It's only natural, therefore, that we should find ourselves wistfully searching for substitutes. The potential substitute closest at hand is ourselves. If we can't expect perfection in our institutions, why not try to create it in ourselves? It's no accident that one longtime runner has written, "I have found my hero and he is me."

13   Serving as your own hero has its risks. It may make perfectly good sense if you're a Jesus, a Moses or a Muhammad. But most of us are likely to wind up with a somewhat flimsy example of heroism. Far more promising, it seems to me, to look for heroes somewhere else than in our own steamy warm-up suits.

14   When we run, some remarkable things happen. We feel better, look better, have more energy, and think more clearly. We lose weight, increase our resistance to heart attack and alter our blood chemistry for the better. We even delay certain of the body's aging processes and, some researchers say, probably live longer than we would if we didn't run.

15   Aren't those gifts enough? Why ask running for benefits that are plainly beyond its capacity to bestow?

DISCUSSION QUESTIONS

1. Fixx does not state his proposition at the start of the argument. What is it, and where is it stated? Is it a proposition of fact, action, or value? Why did he delay stating it?
2. Which paragraphs refute opposing arguments?
3. What type of evidence does Fixx use in paragraph 9?
4. Does Fixx address a general or specialized audience? How do you know?
5. Discuss the ethical appeal of the author. What image of him emerges? Cite specific parts of the essay to explain your answer.

Write an argument on some topic you feel strongly about. Study all sides of the issue so you can argue effectively and appeal to a particular audience. Support your proposition with logical evidence. Begin with one of the following subjects or another your instructor approves. **SUGGESTIONS FOR WRITING**

1. Compulsory composition courses in college
2. Living together unmarried
3. Banning whale hunting
4. Requiring students to pass a general competency test to graduate from high school
5. Some aspect of native American affairs
6. Capital punishment
7. Government funding of noncommercial television
8. Gay rights
9. Legislation banning throwaway bottles
10. Bilingual instruction in schools
11. Legalizing prostitution (or gambling)
12. Mandatory airbags in cars
13. Guardian Angels patrolling city streets
14. Sobriety checklanes for nabbing drunk drivers
15. A local or campus issue

CHAPTER EIGHT

Paragraphs

Some paragraphs launch, others wrap up pieces of writing; still others establish links between parts. Paragraphs can break long discussions of one idea into segments that provide rest stops for readers. Paragraphs can also consolidate several briefly developed ideas into a single reading unit. Occasionally a paragraph stands by itself as an essay in miniature. Most paragraphs, though, are blocks of sentences that develop and clarify one idea. As the major units in an essay, paragraphs relate to one another and reflect the controlling purpose of the whole piece.

THE TOPIC SENTENCE

The topic sentence states the main idea of the paragraph. Think of the topic sentence as a rallying point, with all supporting sentences developing the idea it expresses. A good topic sentence helps you, the writer, gauge what information belongs in a paragraph; at the same time, it informs your reader about the point you're making.

Placement varies from paragraph to paragraph, as the following examples show. As you read each, note how supporting information develops the topic sentence, which is italicized.

TOPIC SENTENCE STATED FIRST

Many paragraphs open with the topic sentence. The writer reveals the central idea immediately and then builds from a solid base.

Starting about one million years ago, the fossil record shows an accelerating growth of the human brain. It expanded at first at the rate of one cubic inch of additional gray matter every hundred thousand years; then the growth rate doubled; it doubled again; and finally it doubled once more. Five hundred thousand years ago

the rate of growth hit its peak. At that time, the brain was expanding at the phe-
nomenal rate of ten cubic inches every hundred thousand years. No other organ
in the history of life is known to have grown as fast as this.

Robert Jastrow, Until the Sun Dies

TOPIC SENTENCE STATED LAST

In order to emphasize the support and build gradually to a conclusion,
a topic sentence can end the paragraph. This position creates suspense as the
reader anticipates the summarizing remark.

An experience of my own comes handily to mind. Some years ago, when
the Restaurant de la Pyramide in Vienne was without question one of the best
half-dozen restaurants in the world, I visited it for the first time. After I had ordered my meal, the sommelier [wine steward] appeared to set before me a wine
list of surpassing amplitude and excellence. But as I cast my eyes down this unbelievable offering of the world's most tantalizing wines, the sommelier bent over
me and pointed out a wine of which I had never heard, ticketed at a price one-
fifth that of its illustrious neighbors. "Monsieur," said the sommelier, "I would
suggest this one. It is a local wine, a very good wine. It is not a great wine, but
after all, monsieur, you are likely to pass this way only once. The great wines you
will find everywhere; this wine you will find only in Vienne. I would like you to
try it, while you have the opportunity." *This, to my mind, was true sophistication—on
the part of M. Point for having the wine and on the part of the waiter for offering it.*

Stephen White, "The New Sophistication:
Defining the Terms"

TOPIC SENTENCE STATED
FIRST AND LAST

Some paragraphs lead with the main idea and then restate it, usually in
different words, at the end. This technique allows the writer to repeat an especially important idea.

*Federal control over the need-based [student aid] grant system seems likely to expand,
throwing into doubt the continued existence of the private needs-analysis services.* Pressures
of accountability and the need to rationalize procedures governing this multi-bil-
lion-dollar operation will increase the tensions of maintaining separate private
and public services, and a single system for determining financial need is inevitable. *Control over the policies governing the distribution of grant aid will shift decisively
from private to public hands.*

David W. Breneman, "The Outlook for
Student Finance"

TOPIC SENTENCE STATED
IN THE MIDDLE

On occasion, the topic sentence falls between one clump of sentences that provides background information and a followup clump that develops the central idea. This arrangement allows the writer to shift the emphasis and at the same time preserve close ties between what precedes and follows the topic sentence.

Over the centuries, China has often been the subject of Western fantasy. In their own way, a number of scholars, journalists, and other travelers have perpetuated this tradition in recent years, rushing to rediscover the country after its long period of isolation. Some of these visitors, justifiably impressed by the Communists' achievements in eliminating the exploitative aspects of pre-1949 mandarin society, propagated the view that the revolution, after its initial successes, had continued to "serve the people," and that China was "the wave of the future"—a compelling alternative to the disorder and materialism of contemporary Western society. Human rights were not at issue, they argued, because such Western concepts were inapplicable to China. *In the past year, however, the Chinese have begun to speak for themselves, and they are conveying quite a different picture.* In the view of many of its own people, China is a backward and repressive nation. "China is Asia's Gulag Archipelago," an elderly Chinese scholar said to me shortly after I had arrived in China last spring. "I was in Germany right after the Second World War, and I saw the horrors of Buchenwald and other concentration camps. In a way—in its destruction of the human spirit these past two decades—China has been even worse."

David Finkelstein, "When the Snow Thaws"

TOPIC SENTENCE IMPLIED

Some paragraphs, particularly in narrative and descriptive writing, have no topic sentence. Rather, all sentences point toward a main idea that readers must grasp for themselves.

[Captain Robert Barclay] once went out at 5 in the morning to do a little grouse shooting. He walked at least 30 miles while he potted away, and then after dinner set out on a walk of 60 miles that he accomplished in 11 hours without a halt. Barclay did not sleep after this but went through the following day as if nothing had happened until the afternoon, when he walked 16 miles to a ball. He danced all night, and then in early morning walked home and spent a day partridge shooting. Finally he did get to bed—but only after a period of two nights and nearly three days had elapsed and he had walked 130 miles.

John Lovesey, "A Myth Is as Good as a Mile"

The details in this paragraph collectively suggest a clear central idea: that Barclay had incredible physical endurance. But writing effective paragraphs without topic sentences challenges even the best writers. Therefore, control most of your paragraphs with clearly expressed topic sentences.

EXERCISE   Identify the topic sentences in each of the following paragraphs and explain how you arrived at your decision. If the topic sentence is implied, state the central idea in your own words.

1.   Last winter, while leafing through the *Guinness Book of World Records*, I came across an item stating that the tallest sunflower ever had been grown by G. E. Hocking, an Englishman. Fired by a competitive urge, I planted a half acre of sunflower seeds. That half acre is now a magnificent 22,000 square feet of green and gold flora. From the elevated rear deck of my apartment, I can look out over the swaying mass of thick, hairy green stalks and see each stalk thrusting up through the darker heart-shaped leaves below and supporting an ever-bobbing imitation of the sun. In this dwarf forest, some of the flower heads measure almost a foot in diameter. Though almost all my plants are now blooming, none will top the sixteen feet, two inches reached by Hocking's plant. My tallest is just thirteen feet even, but I don't think that's too bad for the first time out. Next year, however, will be another matter. I plan to have an automatic watering system to feed my babies.

Joseph Wheeler

2.   What my mother never told me was how fast time passes in adult life. I remember, when I was little, thinking I would live to be at least as old as my grandmother, who was dynamic even at ninety-two, the age at which she died. Now I see those ninety-two years hurtling by me. And my mother never told me how much fun sex could be, or what a discovery it is. Of course, I'm of an age when mothers really didn't tell you much about anything. My mother never told me the facts of life.

Joyce Susskind, "Surprises in a Woman's Life"

3.   In fact, the separation between the scientists and non-scientists is much less bridgeable among the young than it was even thirty years ago. Thirty years ago the cultures had long ceased to speak to each other: but at least they managed a kind of frozen smile across the gulf. Now the politeness has gone, and they just make faces. It is not only that the young scientists now feel that they are part of a culture on the rise while the other is in retreat. It is also, to be brutal, that the young scientists know that with an indifferent degree they'll get a comfortable job, while their contemporaries and counterparts in English or History will be lucky to earn 60 percent as much. No young scientist of any talent would feel that he isn't wanted or that his work is ridiculous, as did the hero of *Lucky Jim;* and in

After reading the next two paragraphs, answer the questions that follow.

1.   The legend—in Africa—that all elephants over a large geographical area go to a common "graveyard" when they sense death is approaching led many hunters to treat them with special cruelty. Ivory hunters, believing the myth and trying to locate such graveyards, often intentionally wounded an elephant in the hopes of following the suffering beast as it made its way to the place where it wanted to die. The idea was to wound the elephant seriously enough so that it thought it was going to die but not so seriously that it died in a very short time. All too often, the process resulted in a single elephant being shot or speared many times and relentlessly pursued until it either fell dead or was killed when it finally turned and charged its attackers. In any case, no wounded elephant ever led its pursuers to the mythical graveyard with its hoped-for booty of ivory tusks.

                                                                      Kris Hurrell

2.   When I was growing up, I spent many happy hours with my brothers and sisters playing jungle games in the woodlot behind our farm home. This lot, ten acres of dense-set poplars and birches standing amidst the blackened stumps of an old pine forest, provided a perfect setting for our jungle adventures. At times we acted out African versions of cowboys and Indians; at others we sought the long lost riches of lost gold and diamond mines. Often our adventures pitted Tarzan against tomb robbers and poachers. Besides serving as a playground, our woodlot furnished most of the fuel for the iron stoves in our kitchen and living room. I can still remember the back-breaking work of chopping up stumps and fallen trees and hauling them to the house. In the winter, the woodlot offered fine small-game hunting. In the summer, it provided a cool refuge from the heat that blistered the fields and farmhouse. Today, farm and woodlot are gone, swallowed up by a sprawling suburb. I wonder whether the children who live there ever want to play jungle games or regret that there's no place for them.

                                                                  Beverly Timmons

1. By referring specifically to the paragraphs, show that one is unified and one is not.
2. How would you improve the paragraph that lacks unity?
3. Identify the topic sentence of each paragraph.

ORGANIZATION

        Besides displaying unity, effective paragraphs follow some clear pattern of organization. The options for organizing paragraphs span a wide range:

1. The strategies discussed in Part II (chapters 3 through 7)
2. Coordination, subordination, or a combination of the two
3. Order of climax

The choice you make depends upon your material and your purpose in writing.

Earlier Strategies.   These include all of the following patterns:

Time sequence (narration)	Cause and effect
Space sequence (description)	Illustration
Comparison	Definition
Classification	Argument
Process analysis	

Four example paragraphs follow. The first, organized by *time sequence*, traces the final years of the Model T Ford, concluding with a topic sentence that sums up its impact.

> In 1917 the Model T lost much of its attraction when its exterior appearance was drastically altered. The famous flat-sided brass radiator disappeared and the new style featured (in the words of the catalogue) "The stream-line hood, large radiator and enclosed fan, crown fenders, black finish and nickel trimmings" ("crown fenders" would be described in England as domed mudguards). Electric lighting and starting followed in 1919, and the model then continued with little alteration until 1927, when it was finally withdrawn. After a considerable pause it was replaced by the Model A, a very conventional machine with wire wheels, three-speed gearbox and four-wheel brakes (the "T" had never made this concession to progress and continued to the last with two minute brake drums on the back wheels only). While it was in preparation, others had taken the lead and the "A" never replaced the immortal "T" in the public fancy. Indeed, the "Tin Lizzy" or "Flivver" had become almost a national characteristic, and at the end of its eighteen years in production the total number sold was fifteen million.
>
> Cecil Clutton and John Stanford,
> *The Vintage Motor-Car*

The next paragraph, oganized by *space sequence*, describes a ceramic elf, starting from the bottom and working up to the top. Other common spatial arrangements include top to bottom, left to right, right to left, nearby to far away, far away to nearby, clockwise, and counterclockwise.

> The ceramic elf in our family room is quite a character. His reddish-brown slippers, which hang over the mantel shelf, taper to a slender point. Pudgy, yellow-stockinged legs disappear into a wrinkled tunic-style, olive-green jacket, gathered at the waist with a thick brown belt that fits snugly around his roly-poly belly. His short, meaty arms hang comfortably, one hand resting on the knapsack at his side and the other clutching the bowl of an old black pipe. An unkempt, snow-white beard, dotted by occasional snarls, trails patriarch-fashion from his lower lip to his belt line. A button nose capped with a smudge of gold dust, mis-

chievous black eyes, and an unruly snatch of hair peeking out from under his burnt-orange stocking cap complete Bartholomew's appearance.

Maria Sanchez

Although descriptive paragraphs, like those developed by narration, often lack topic sentences, our example leads off with the central idea.

The next example illustrates development by *comparison*. Like the preceding one, it proceeds from an opening topic sentence.

There is an essential difference between a news story, as understood by a newspaperman or a wire-service writer, and the newsmagazine story. The chief purpose of the conventional news story is to tell what happened. It starts with the most important information and continues into increasingly inconsequential details, not only because the reader may not read beyond the first paragraph but because an editor working on galley proofs a few minutes before press time likes to be able to cut freely from the end of the story. A newsmagazine is very different. It is written to be read consecutively from beginning to end, and each of its stories is designed, following the critical theories of Edgar Allan Poe, to create one emotional effect. The news, what happened that week, may be told in the beginning, the middle, or the end; for the purpose is not to throw information at the reader but to seduce him into reading the whole story, and into accepting the dramatic (and often political) point being made.

Otto Friedrich, "There are 00 Trees in Russia"

And here is a paragraph smoothly organized by steps in a *process:*

Making beer nuts is a quick, simple procedure that provides a delicious evening snack. You'll need six cups of raw peanuts, three cups of sugar, and one-and-one-half cups of water. To begin, combine the sugar and water in a two-quart saucepan and stir to dissolve the sugar. Next, add the peanuts and stir again until all of the peanuts are covered by the sugar-water solution. Place the pan, uncovered, on a burner set at medium-high heat for ten to twelve minutes, until the sugar crystallizes and coats the peanuts thoroughly. Stay at the stove during the heating process and stir the mixture every two or three minutes to ensure even coating of the nuts. When the peanuts are thoroughly coated, pour them onto an ungreased cookie sheet and bake at 350 degrees for about thirty minutes, stirring and lightly salting at ten-minute intervals. Serve your beer nuts fresh out of the oven or eat them at room temperature after allowing them to cool.

Kimberlee Walters

Again, the topic sentence comes first.

Coordination and Subordination.   Another good way of looking at a paragraph is to see its sentences as coordinate or subordinate. In a coordinate paragraph, all the supporting sentences carry the same weight. Together, they form a sort of list, with each developing a different facet of the main idea. Often, though not always, all follow the same grammatical form. Here's an example of a coordinate paragraph. To help you see the structure, we've indented, numbered, and stacked the supporting sentences.

1. As he opens the door to the crowded gymnasium, Dave is blasted by the familiar noises of the junior varsity basketball game.

    2. Hundreds of voices blend together to form one huge roar, which reaches a peak whenever the home team makes a basket.

    2. Suddenly, a shrill whistle silences the crowd, and then a stabbing buzzer signals a time out.

    2. With a break in the action, the pep band strikes up the school fight song.

                                                                    Mike Hogan

This paragraph opens with a topic sentence that focuses on the noises of the basketball game. Each of the supporting sentences then describes a different noise.

In a paragraph developed by subordination, each of the supporting sentences throws light on something in the sentence just ahead of it. Of all the supporting sentences, only the first one has a direct connection to the topic sentence. Here's an example:

1. The microorganisms that seem to have it in for us in the worst way—the ones that really appear to wish us ill—turn out on close examination to be rather more like bystanders, strays, strangers in from the cold.

    2. They will invade and replicate if given the choice, and some of them will get into our deepest tissues and set forth in our blood, but it is our response to their presence that makes the disease.

        3. Our arsenals for fighting off bacteria are so powerful, and involve so many different defense mechanisms, that we are in more danger from them than from the invaders.

            4. We live in the midst of explosive devices; we are mined.

                                              Lewis Thomas, *Lives of a Cell: Notes of a Biology-Watcher*

They, them, and *their* in the second sentence refer to *microorganisms* in the topic sentence. The phrases *arsenals for fighting off bacteria* and *defense mechanisms* in the third sentence are linked to *response to their presence* in the second. *Explosive devices* and *mined* in the final sentence tie in with *danger* in the next to last sentence. As we move from one supporting sentence to the next, the link with the topic sentence becomes more and more indirect.

Many paragraphs mix coordinate and subordinate sentences, the subordinate sentences adding depth to the coordinate.

1. My roommate Leonard is the most high-strung person I've ever met.

  2. Spending one evening with him is about all that most people can take.

    3. At the supper table, Leonard constantly drums his fingers on the table in a staccato beat, pausing only occasionally to gulp down some hunks of food.

      4. Those hunks are no doubt well churned in the most active stomach west of Walla Walla.

    3. Later, when it's time for a few hands of cards before cracking the books, you'd swear Leonard is shuffling the spots right off the cards.

      4. Nobody ever asks to cut the deck when he deals.

    3. These nervous mannerisms carry over into his studying.

      4. It's a unique experience to watch Leonard pace the floor, turn abruptly, and mutter something like "suburb located right outside city limits, exurb located farther out."

    3. Only when this bundle of nerves winds down and goes to bed does peace come to our room.

                                                           Steve Lintemuth

Here each of the four coordinate sentences, identified by the number 3, ties back to the second sentence of the paragraph, and each deals with a separate evening activity. Each of the fourth-level sentences supplements the point made in the sentence immediately preceding.

When you suspect that one of your paragraphs lacks unity, check its structure by trying to rewrite it in indented form. Unless each of its sentences is linked clearly to the topic sentence or develops an aspect of the preceding sentence, the paragraph is not unified and needs revision.

Order of Climax.   Climactic order creates a crescendo pattern, starting with the least emphatic detail and progressing to the most emphatic. The topic sentence can begin or end the paragraph, or it can remain implied. This pattern holds the reader's interest by building suspense. On occasion, writers reverse the order, landing the heaviest punch first; but such paragraphs can trail off, leaving the reader dissatisfied.

Here is a paragraph illustrating climactic order:

The speaking errors I hear affect me to different degrees. I'm so conditioned to hearing "It don't make any difference" and "There's three ways to solve the problem" that I've almost accepted such usage. However, errors such as "Just between you and I, Arnold loves Edna" and "I'm going back to my room to lay down" still offend my sensibility. When hearing them, I usually just chuckle to myself and walk away. The "Twin I's"—*irrevelant* and *irregardless* are another matter. More than any other errors, they really grate on my ear. Whenever I hear "that may be true, but it's irrevelant" or "Irregardless of how much I study, I still get *C*'s," I have the urge to correct the speaker. It's really surprising that more people don't clean up their language act.

Valerie Sonntag

EXERCISE   From a magazine or newspaper article, select four paragraphs that illustrate different patterns of organization. Identify the topic sentence in each case; or if it is implied, state it in your own words. Point out the organization of each paragraph.

COHERENCE

Coherent writing flows smoothly and easily from sentence to sentence and paragraph to paragraph, making clear the relationships among ideas and thus allowing the reader to grasp connections. Because incoherent writing fails to supply those needed connections, it jerks forward by fits and starts, confusing and ultimately irritating the reader.

Here is a paragraph that lacks coherence:

> I woke up late. I had been so tired the night before that I had forgotten to set the alarm. All I could think of was the report I had stayed up until 3 A.M. typing, and how I could possibly get twenty copies ready for next morning's 9 o'clock sales meeting. I panicked and ran out the door. My bus was so crowded I had to stand. Jumping off the bus, I raced back up the street. The meeting was already underway. Mr. Jackson gestured for me to come into the conference room. Inserting the first page of the report into the copier, I set the dial for twenty copies and pressed the print button. The sign started flashing CALL KEY OPERATOR. The machine was out of order. Mr. Jackson asked whether the report was ready. I pointed to the flashing red words. Mr. Jackson nodded grimly without saying anything. He left me alone with the broken machine.

This paragraph has some degree of unity: most of its sentences relate to the writer's disastrous experience with the sales report. Unfortunately, though, its many gaps in logic create rather than answer questions, and in very bumpy prose, at that. Note, for instance, the gap between the third and fourth sentences. Did the writer jump out of bed and rush right out the door? Of course not, but the reader has no real clue to what the sequence of events really was. Another gap occurs between the next two sentences, leaving the reader to puzzle over the connection between having to stand while on the bus and having to race up the street when he got off. And who is Mr. Jackson? The paragraph never tells, but the reader will want to know.

Now read this rewritten version, additions italicized:

> I woke up late *because* I had been so tired the night before that I had forgotten to set the alarm. All I could think of was the report I had stayed up until 3 A.M. typing, and how I could possibly get twenty copies ready for next morning's 9 o'clock sales meeting. *When I realized it was 8:30,* I panicked. *Jumping out of bed, I threw on some clothes, grabbed the report,* and ran out the door. My bus was so crowded I had to stand *and could not see out the window. Two blocks beyond my stop, I realized I should have gotten off.* "Stop!" *I cried and,* jumping off the bus, raced back up the street. *When I reached the office, it was 9:15, and* the meeting was already underway. Mr. Jackson, *the sales manager, saw me and* gestured for me to come into the conference room. *"One moment," I said as calmly as I could and hurried to the copier.* Inserting the first page of the report into it, I set the dial for twenty copies and pressed the print button. *Immediately,* the sign started flashing CALL KEY OPERATOR. The machine was out of order. *The next thing I knew,* Mr. Jackson *was at my side* asking whether the report was ready. I pointed to the flashing red words, *and* Mr. Jackson nodded grimly without saying anything. *Turning on his heel,* he *walked away and* left me alone with the broken machine.

As this example shows, correcting an incoherent paragraph may call for anything from a single word to a whole sentence or more.

Coherence derives from a sufficient supply of supporting details and your firm sense of the way your ideas go together. If you brainstorm your topic thoroughly and think carefully about the relationships between sentences, incoherence isn't likely to haunt your paragraphs. As you write and revise, signal connections to the reader by using *transitions*—devices that link sentences to one another. These are the most common transitional devices:

1. Connecting words and phrases
2. Repeated key words
3. Pronouns and demonstrative adjectives
4. Parallelism

You can use them to furnish links both within and between paragraphs.

Connecting Words and Phrases. These connectors clarify relationships between sentences. The following list groups them according to function:

> *Showing similarity:* in like manner, likewise, moreover, similarly
> *Showing contrast:* at the same time, but, even so, however, in contrast, instead, nevertheless, still, on the contrary, on the other hand, otherwise, yet

Showing results or effects: accordingly, as a result, because, consequently, hence, since, therefore, thus

Adding ideas together: also, besides, first (second, third . . .), furthermore, in addition, in the first place, likewise, moreover, similarly, too

Drawing conclusions: as a result, finally, in brief, in conclusion, in short, to summarize

Pointing out examples: for example, for instance, to illustrate

Showing emphasis and clarity: above all, after all, again, as a matter of fact, besides, in fact, in other words, indeed, nonetheless, that is

Indicating time: at times, after, afterward, from then on, immediately, later, meanwhile, next, now, once, previously, subsequently, then, until, while

Conceding a point: granted that, of course, to be sure, admittedly

Use these connectors to fill gaps when necessary, but don't overload your writing with them. In well-planned prose, the message flows clearly with only an occasional assist from connectors.

In the following example, the connecting words and phrases are italicized. Earlier in the article, the writer defends the idea of being a "woman workaholic." In this excerpt, she clarifies the difference between hard workers and workaholics.

> My efforts to define workaholism and to distinguish workaholics from other hard workers proved difficult. *While* workaholics do work hard, not all hard workers are workaholics. Moonlighters, *for example,* may work 16 hours a day to make ends meet, but most of them will stop working when their financial circumstances permit. Accountants, *too,* seem to work non-stop, but many slow down after the April 15 tax deadline. Workaholics, *on the other hand,* always devote more time and thought to their work than their situation demands. Even in the absence of deadlines to meet, mortgages to pay, promotions to earn, or bosses to please, workaholics still work hard. What sets them apart is their attitude toward work, not the number of hours they work.
>
> Marilyn Machlowitz, "Workaholism: What's Wrong with Being Married to Your Work?"

DISCUSSION QUESTIONS

1. What ideas does each of the italicized words and phrases connect?
2. What relationship does each show?

Repeated Key Words.   Repeating key words, especially those that convey a paragraph's central idea, can help smooth the reader's path through a piece of writing. The words may appear in differing form and with differing intentions, but their presence keeps the main issues before the reader. In the following paragraph, the repetition of *majority, minority,* and *will* enhances coherence, as does the more limited repetition of *government* and *interests.*

> Whatever fine-spun theories we may devise to resolve or obscure the difficulty, there is no use blinking the fact that the *will* of the *majority* is not the same thing as the *will* of all. *Majority* rule works well only so long as the *minority* is *willing* to accept the *will* of the *majority* as the *will* of the *nation* and let it go at that. Generally speaking, the *minority* will be *willing* to let it go at that so long as it feels that its essential *interests* and rights are not fundamentally different from those of the current *majority,* and so long as it can, in any case, look forward with confidence to mustering enough votes within four or six years to become itself the *majority* and so redress the balance. But if it comes to pass that a large *minority* feels that it has no such chance, that it is a fixed and permanent *minority* and that another group or class with rights and *interests* fundamentally hostile to its own is in permanent control, then *government* by *majority* vote ceases in any sense to be *government* by the *will* of the people for the good of all, and becomes *government* by the *will* of some of the people for their own *interests* at the expense of the others.
>
> Carl Becker, *Freedom and Responsibility in the American Way of Life*

EXERCISE

Write a paragraph using one of the following sentences as your topic sentence. Having inserted the missing key word, repeat it in your paragraph to help link your sentences together.

1. _____ is my favorite relative.
2. I wish I had (a, an, some, more) _____.
3. _____ changed my life.
4. _____ is more trouble that it's worth.
5. A visit to _____ always depresses me.
6. Eating _____ is a challenge.
7. I admire _____.

Pronouns and Demonstrative Adjectives.   Pronouns stand in for nouns that appear earlier in the sentence or in previous sentences. Alternating pronouns and their nouns throughout the paragraph prevents monotony and promotes clarity. We have italicized the pronouns in the following excerpt, taken from an article about the efforts of Dolores Huerta and Cesar Chavez to organize the United Farm Workers into a strong union.

> A book could be written on *their* [Huerta's and Chavez's] complex relationship. *Both* are stubborn and opinionated. *She* is notorious in the union for com-

bativeness. (Stories are told of growers begging to face anyone at the negotiating table except Huerta.) Chavez jokes of "unleashing Dolores"; but *he* respects *her* opinons and *they* generally agree on larger issues. Dolores says *they* fight a lot because *"he* knows *I*'ll never quit, so *he* uses *me* to let off steam; *he* knows *I*'ll fight back anyway." Chavez, a traditionalist in *his* own home life, is said to privately disapprove of Dolores's divorces, *her* living now with *his* brother Richard, and *her* chaotic way of raising *her* kids. But *he* knows that the union is the center of *her* life, just as *it* is with *his*. "Dolores is absolutely fearless, physically and emotionally," *he* says.

> Judith Coburn, "Dolores Huerta: La
> Pasionaria of the Farm Workers"

Except for *it* in the second sentence from the end, all the pronouns refer to Huerta, Chavez, or both.

Four demonstrative adjectives—*this, that, these,* and *those*—also help hook ideas together. Demonstratives are special adjectives that identify or point out nouns rather than describe them. Here is an example from the Declaration of Independence:

> We hold *these* truths to be self-evident, that all men are created equal, that they are endowed by their Creator with certain unalienable Rights, that among *these* are Life, Liberty, and the pursuit of Happiness. That to secure *these* rights, Governments are instituted among Men, deriving their just powers from the consent of the governed. That whenever any Form of Government becomes destructive of *these* ends, it is the Right of the People to alter or to abolish it, and to institute new Government, laying its foundation on such principles and organizing its power in such form, as to them shall seem most likely to effect their Safety and Happiness.

EXERCISE   **In a magazine, newspaper, textbook, or some other written source, find two paragraphs that use pronouns and demonstrative adjectives to increase coherence. Copy the paragraphs, underline the pronouns and demonstrative adjectives, and explain what each refers to.**

Parallelism.   Parallelism uses repetition of grammatical form to express a series of equivalent ideas. Besides giving continuity, the repetition adds rhythm and balance to the writing. Note how the italicized constructions in the following paragraph tie together the unfolding definition of poverty.

> *Poverty is staying* up all night on cold nights to watch the fire, knowing one spark on the newspaper covering the walls means your sleeping children die in flames. In summer *poverty is watching* gnats and flies devour your baby's tears

when he cries. The screens are torn and you pay so little rent you know they will never be fixed. *Poverty means* insects in your food, in your nose, in your eyes, and crawling over you when you sleep. *Poverty is hoping* it never rains because diapers won't dry when it rains and soon you are using newspapers. *Poverty is seeing* your children forever with runny noses. Paper handkerchiefs cost money and all your rags you need for other things. Even more costly are antihistamines. *Poverty is cooking* without food and cleaning without soap.

Jo Goodwin Parker, "What Is Poverty?"

ADEQUATE DEVELOPMENT

Students often ask for guidelines on paragraph length: "Should I aim for fifty to sixty words? Seven to ten sentences? About one-fourth of a page?" The questions are natural, but the approach is wrong. Instead of targeting a particular length, ask yourself what the reader needs to know. Then supply just enough information to make your point clearly. Inadequate development results in fuzziness, forcing the reader to grope for understanding. A swollen paragraph, on the other hand, dilutes emphasis. Why load up with four or five examples when two or three will do?

Here are two versions of a paragraph, the first inadequately developed.

Underdeveloped Paragraph

Most of the delegates to the Constitutional Convention of 1787 feared too much democracy. As a result, they drafted the Constitution as a document outlining a limited democracy. Indeed, some of the provisions were simply undemocratic. But despite reflecting the delegates' distrust of popular rule, the Constitution did provide a framework in which democracy could evolve.

Adequately Developed Paragraph

Most of the delegates to the Constitutional Convention of 1787 feared too much democracy. As a result, they drafted the Constitution as a document outlining a limited democracy. Indeed, some of the provisions were simply undemocratic: *universal suffrage was denied; voting qualifications were left to the states; and women, blacks, and persons without property were denied the federal franchise. Until the passage of the Seventeenth Amendment in 1913, senators were not popularly elected but were chosen by state legislators.* But despite reflecting the delegates' distrust of popular rule, the Constitution did provide a framework in which democracy could evolve.

The writer of the first paragraph fails to provide examples of undemocratic provisions, whereas the writer of the second paragraph, anticipating the reader's needs, adds the necessary information.

Readability also plays a role in setting paragraph length. Within a paper, paragraphs signal natural dividing places, allowing the reader to pause and absorb the material presented up to that point. Too little paragraphing overwhelms the reader with long blocks of material. Too much creates a choppy Dick-and-Jane effect that may seem simplistic, even irritating. To counter these problems, writers sometimes use several paragraphs for an idea that needs extended development, or they combine several short paragraphs into one.

EXERCISE

1. **Indicate where the ideas in this long block of material divide logically; explain your choices.**

During the summer following graduation from high school, I could hardly wait to get to college and "be on my own." In the first weeks of my freshman year at State University, however, I found that independence can be tough and painful. I had expected raucous good times and a carefree collegiate life, the sort depicted in old beach movies and suggested by the selective memories of sentimental alumni. Instead, all I felt at first was the burden of increasing responsibilities and the loneliness of "a man without a country." I discovered that being independent of parents who kept at me to do my homework and expected me to accomplish certain household chores did not mean I was free to do as I pleased. On the contrary, living on my own meant that I had to perform for myself all the tasks that the family used to share. Studying became a full-time occupation rather than a nightly duty to be accomplished in an hour or two, and my college instructors made it clear that they would have little sympathy for negligence or even for my inability to do an assignment. But what was more troubling about my early college life than having to do laundry, prepare meals, and complete stacks of homework, though, was the terrifying sense of being all alone. I was independent, no longer a part of the world that had seemed to confine me, but I soon realized that confinement had also meant security. I never liked the feeling that people were watching over me, but I knew that my family and friends were also watching out for me—and that's a good feeling to have. At the university no one seemed particularly to be watching, though professors constantly evaluated the quality of my work. I felt estranged from people in those first weeks of college life, desperately needing a confidant but fearful that the new and tenuous friendships I had made would be damaged if I were to confess my fears and problems. It was simply too early for me to feel a part of the university. So there I was, independent in the fullest sense, and thus "a man without a country."

2. **The following short, choppy units are inadequately developed. List some details you could use to expand one of them into a good paragraph.**

I like living in a small town because the people are so friendly. I can always get the latest gossip from the local busybody. In addition, there's always the telephone party line.

In a big city, people are afraid to get too friendly. Everything is very private, and nobody knows anything about anybody else.

3. Scan the compositions you have written for other classes for paragraphs that are over- or underdeveloped. Revise any you find.

PARAGRAPHS WITH SPECIAL FUNCTIONS

Special-function paragraphs include introductions, transitional paragraphs, and conclusions. One-paragraph introductions and conclusions appear in short, multiparagraph essays. Transitional paragraphs occur primarily in long compositions.

INTRODUCTIONS

A good introduction acquaints and coaxes. It announces the essay's topic, and it may directly state the thesis. In addition, the introduction sets the tone—somber, lighthearted, angry—of what will follow. An amusing anecdote would not be an appropriate opening for a paper about political torture.

With essays, as with people, first impressions are important. If your opening rouses interest, it will draw the reader into the essay and pave the way for your ideas. If, instead, you'd like to try your hand at turning the reader away, search for a beginning that is mechanical, plodding, and dull. Your success will astonish you. Here are some bad openings.

In this paper I intend to . . .

Wars have always afflicted mankind.

As you may know, inflation is a problem for many of us.

In the modern world of today . . .

How would you respond to these openings? Ask yourself that same question about every opening you write.

Gear the length of the introduction to the length of the essay. Although longer papers sometimes begin with two or more introductory paragraphs, generally the lead-in for a short essay is a single paragraph. Here are some possibilities for launching an essay. The type you select depends on your purpose, subject, audience, and personality.

A Directly Stated Thesis. This is common type of opening, orienting the reader to what will follow. After providing some general background, the writer of our example narrows her scope to a thesis that previews the upcoming sections of her essay.

> An increasing number of mid-life women are reentering the workforce, pursuing college degrees, and getting more involved in the public arena. Several labels besides "mid-life" have been attached to this type of person: the mature woman, the older woman, and, more recently, the reentry woman. By definition, she is between thirty-five and fifty-five years old and has been away from the business or academic scene for anywhere from fifteen to thirty years. The academic community, the media, marketing people, and employers are giving her close scrutiny, and it is apparent that she is having a greater impact on our society than she realizes.
>
> Jo Ann Harris

A Definition.   This kind of introduction works particularly well in a paper that acquaints the reader with an unfamiliar topic.

> You are completely alone in a large open space and are struck by a terrifying, unreasoning fear. You sweat, your heart beats, you cannot breathe. You fear you may die of a heart attack, although you do not have heart disease. Suppose you decide you will never get yourself in this helpless situation again. You go home and refuse to leave its secure confines. Your family has to support you. You have agoraphobia—a disabling terror of open spaces.
>
> "Controlling Phobias Through
> Behavior Modification"

A Quotation.   A beginning quotation, particularly from an authority in the field, can be an effective springboard to the ideas that follow. Make sure any quote you use relates clearly to your topic.

> The director of the census made a dramatic announcement in 1890. The Nation's unsettled area, he revealed, "has been so broken into by isolated bodies of settlement that there can hardly be said to be a frontier line." These words sounded the close of one period of America's history. For three centuries before, men had marched westward, seeking in the forests and plains that lay beyond the settled areas a chance to begin anew. For three centuries they had driven back the wilderness as their conquest of the continent went on. Now, in 1890, they were told that a frontier line separating the settled and unsettled portions of the United States no longer existed. The west was won, and the expansion that had been the most distinctive feature of the country's past was at an end.
>
> Ray Allen Billington, "The Frontier
> Disappears"

An Anecdote or Personal Experience.   A well-told personal incident or experience serves as a sort of Pied Piper of Hamelin, luring readers into the rest of the paper. Like other introductions, an anecdote should bear on what comes afterward. Engle's anecdote, like the stories she reviews, demonstrates that "women also have dark hearts."

> My mother used to have a little china cream and sugar set that was given to her by a woman who later killed her children with an axe. It sat cheerfully in the china cabinet, as inadequate a symbol as I have ever seen of the dark mysteries within us. Yet at least it was there to remind us that no matter how much Jesus wanted us for a sunbeam, we would still have some day to cope with a deeper reality than common sense could explain. It stood for strange cars not to get into, running shoes to wear when you were out alone at night and the backs of Chinese restaurants you were not supposed to go into.
>
> Marian Engle, review of *The Goddess and Other Women* by Joyce Carol Oates

An Arresting Statement.   Sometimes you can jolt the reader into attention, using content, language, or both, particularly if your essay develops an unusual or extreme position.

> Students are niggers. When you get that straight, our schools begin to make sense. It's important, though, to understand why they're niggers. If we follow that question seriously enough, it will lead us past the zone of academic bullshit, where dedicated teachers pass their knowledge on to a new generation, and into the nitty-gritty of human needs and hang-ups. And from there we can go on to consider whether it might ever be possible for students to come up from slavery.
>
> Jerry Farber, "The Student as Nigger"

Interesting Details.   These details pique curiosity and draw the reader into the paper.

> It is Friday night at any of the ten thousand watering holes of the small towns and crossroads hamlets of the South. The room is a cacophony of the ping-pong-ding-dingding of the pinball machine, the pop-fizz of another round of Pabst, the refrain of "Red Necks, White Socks and Blue Ribbon Beer" on the juke box, the insolent roar of a souped-up engine outside and, above it all, the sound of easy laughter. The good ole boys have gathered for their fraternal ritual—the aimless diversion that they have elevated into a life-style.
>
> Bonnie Angelo, "Those Good Ole Boys"

A Question.   A provocative question can entice the reader into the essay to find the answer.

> When you leave your apartment or house, do you begin to feel better? If you leave for a week-long trip, do you find your head clears, your migraine disappears, dizziness stops, your aches and pains subside, depression fades away,

and your entire attitude is better? If so, chemical pollution of the atmosphere in your home may be making you ill.

> Marshall Mandell, "Are You Allergic to Your House?"

---

1. **Explain why each of the preceding introductions interests or does not interest you. Does your response stem from the topic or the way the author introduces it?**

2. **Find magazine articles with effective introductory paragraphs illustrating at least three different techniques. Write a paragraph explaining why each impresses you.**

TRANSITIONAL PARAGRAPHS

In the midst of a lengthy essay, you may need a short paragraph that announces a shift from one group of ideas to another. Transitional paragraphs summarize previously explained ideas, repeat the thesis, or point to ideas that follow. In our example, Bruno Bettelheim has been discussing a young boy named Joey who has turned into a kind of human machine. After describing Joey's assorted delusions, Bettelheim signals his switch from the delusions to the fears that caused them.

> What deep-seated fears and needs underlay Joey's delusional system? We were long in finding out, for Joey's preventions effectively concealed the secret of his autistic behavior. In the meantime we dealt with his peripheral problems one by one.

> Bruno Bettelheim, "Joey: 'A Mechanical Boy' "

The following transitional paragraph looks back as well as ahead.

> Certainly these three factors—exercise, economy, convenience of short-cuts—help explain the popularity of bicycling today. But a fourth attraction sometimes overrides the others: the lure of the open road.

> Mike Bernstein

CONCLUSIONS

A conclusion rounds out a paper and signals that the discussion has been completed. Not all papers require a separate concluding paragraph; narratives and descriptions, for example, generally end when the writer finishes the story or concludes the impression. But many essays benefit from a conclusion that drives the point home a final time. To be effective, a conclusion must mesh logically and stylistically with what comes earlier. A long, complex paper often ends with a summary of the main points, but any of several other options may be appropriate for shorter papers with easy-to-grasp ideas. Most short essays have single-paragraph conclusions; longer papers may require a two- or three-paragraph wrap-up.

Here are some cautions about writing your conclusion:

1. Don't introduce new material. Draw together, round out, but don't take off in a new direction.
2. Don't tack on an ending in desperation when the hour is late and the paper is due tomorrow—the so-called midnight special. Your reader deserves better than "All in all, skiing is a great sport" or "Thus we can see that motorcycle racing isn't for everyone."
3. Don't apologize. Saying that you could have done a better job makes a reader wonder why you didn't.
4. Don't moralize. A preachy conclusion can undermine the position you have established in the rest of your composition.

The following examples illustrate several common types of conclusions.

Restatement of the Thesis.   The following conclusion reasserts Jordan's thesis that "a mood of antisocial negativism is creeping through the structure of American life, corroding our ideals, and suffocating the hopes of poor people and minorities."

> There is room for honest differences about each of these key issues, but the new negativism's overt greed and the implicit racism of its loud "No" to minority aspirations indicate that this is a poisonous movement that denies the moral ideals and humane values that characterize the best in America's heritage.
>
> Vernon E. Jordan, Jr., "The New Negativism"

A Summary.   A summary draws together and reinforces the main points of a paper.

> There are, of course, many other arguments against capital punishment, including its high cost and its failure to deter crime. But I believe the most important points against the death penalty are the possibility of executing an innocent man, the discriminatory manner in which it is applied, and the barbaric methods of carrying it out. In my opinion, capital punishment is, in effect, premeditated murder by society as a whole. As the old saying goes, two wrongs don't make a right.
>
> Diane Trathen

A Question.   The paragraph below concludes an argument that running should not be elevated to a religion, that its other benefits are sufficient. A final question often prompts the reader to think further on the topic. If your essay is meant to be persuasive, be sure to phrase a concluding question so that the way a reasonable person would answer emphasizes your point of view.

> Aren't those gifts enough? Why ask running for benefits that are plainly beyond its capacity to bestow?
>
> James Fixx, "What Running Can't Do For You"

A Quotation.   A quotation can capture the essence of your thought and end the essay with authority.

> "We had no idea of the emotional involvement and the commitment of these women," Richard says. "Suddenly a constituency arose. Suddenly there are thousands and thousands of women who don't care about your moral position or mine—they want a baby."
>
> David Zimmerman, "Are Test-Tube Babies the Answer for the Childless?"

Ironic Twist or Surprising Observation.   These approaches prompt the reader to think further about a paper's topic. The following paragraph points out the ironic refusal of the government to confront poverty that exists a mere ten blocks away from its offices.

> Thus, a stark contrast exists between the two cultures of 14th Street, which appears to be like an earthworm, with half of its body crushed by poverty, but the other half still alive, wriggling in wealth. The two are alike only in that each communicates little with the other, because of the wide disparity between the lives of the people and the conditions of the environments. The devastating irony of the situation on 14th Street lies in the fact that only ten blocks away sit the very governmental institutions that could alleviate the poverty—the Senate, the House of Representatives, and the White House.
>
> Student unknown

Clever or Lighthearted Ending.   The writer, capitalizing on the essay's topic, ends by exaggerating the fault being criticized.

> Because using clichés is as easy as falling off a log, it goes without saying that it would be duck soup to continue in this vein till hell freezes over. However, since that would be carrying coals to Newcastle, let's ring down the curtain and bid adieu to the fair topic of the cliché. (No use beating a dead horse.)
>
> Student unknown

Personal Challenge.   A challenge often prompts the reader to take some action.

> And therein lies the challenge. You can't merely puff hard for a few days and then revert to the Lazy Boy recliner, smugly thinking that you're "in shape." You must sweat and strain and puff regularly, week in and week out. They're your muscles, your lungs, your heart. The only caretaker they have is you.
>
> Monica Duvall

Hope or Recommendation.   Both a hope and a recommendation may restate points already made in the essay or suggest actions to take in order to arrive at a solution.

> Periodically my pilot and I climb into our aircraft and head out over the Minnesota wilderness, following a succession of electronic beeps that lead to some of the last remaining wolves in the lower 48 states. We hope that the data we collect will provide a better understanding of the wolf. We especially hope that our work will help guide authorities into a management program that will insure the perpetuation of the species in the last vestiges of its former range.
>
> L. David Mech, "Where Can the
Wolves Survive?"

> I who am blind can give one hint to those who can see—one admonition to those who would make full use of the gift of sight: Use your eyes as if tomorrow you would be stricken blind. And the same method can be applied to the other senses. Hear the music of voices, the song of the bird, the mighty strains of an orchestra, as if you would be stricken deaf tomorrow. Touch each object you want to touch as if tomorrow your tactile sense would fail. Smell the perfume of flowers, taste with relish each morsel, as if tomorrow you could never smell and taste again. Make the most of every sense; glory in all the facets of pleasure and beauty which the world reveals to you through the several means of contact which Nature provides. But of all the senses, I am sure that sight must be the most delightful.
>
> Helen Keller, "Three Days to See"

---

1. **Explain why each of the foregoing introductions does or does not interest you. Does your response stem from the topic or from the author's handling of it?**   **EXERCISE**

2. **Copy effective concluding paragraphs, illustrating at least three different techniques, from magazine articles. Then write a paragraph explaining why each impresses you.**

CHAPTER NINE

Effective Sentences

A sentence is a group of words that begins with a capital letter, ends with a period, question mark, or exclamation point, and makes sense by itself. Sentences take many forms, some straightforward and unadorned, others intricate and ornate, each with its own stylistic strengths. Becoming familiar with these forms and their uses gives you the option to

- emphasize or deemphasize an idea
- combine ideas into one sentence or keep them separate in more than one sentence
- make sentences sound formal or informal
- emphasize the actor or the action
- achieve rhythm, variety, and contrast

Effective sentences bring both exactness and flair to your writing.

SENTENCE PARTS

Before moving to sentences and style, let's briefly brush up on sentence elements. These elements include subjects, predicates, direct objects, indirect objects, subject complements, phrases, and clauses.

SUBJECT AND PREDICATE

A simple sentence has two main parts, a subject and a predicate. The *subject*, which names something, can carry out an action, receive action, or just exist. It consists of one or more naming words and often one or more other words that describe it. The *predicate* tells something about the subject and completes the thought expressed by the sentence. It includes one or more verbs, often accompanied by one or more words that expand or modify its meaning. In the following examples, the naming words are underlined once, and the verbs are underlined twice.

Subjects	Predicates
Barney	blushed.
The king	is in the counting house.
Politics	makes strange bedfellows.
The tall, slender spires	were glittering in the sun.
Operating the jackhammer	left me exhausted.

A simple sentence can have a compound subject (two or more separate naming words), a compound predicate (two or more separate predicates), or both:

John and Mary ate lunch and washed the dishes.

DIRECT OBJECT

A direct object names whatever receives, or results from, the action of a verb.

Freddy bought a car.

Lou made punch for the party.

INDIRECT OBJECT

An indirect object identifies someone or something that receives whatever is named by the direct object.

They built the dog a kennel.

The interviewer offered Anita the job.

SUBJECT COMPLEMENT

Subject complements follow verbs that show existence: *is, are, was, were,* and all other forms of *be,* as well as *seem, appear,* and a few others. Subject complements rename or describe the subject.

Samantha is an architect.

Samantha is efficient.

PHRASE

In a phrase, words are grouped to work together, but the group has no subject or predicate. Some phrases serve as adjectives, others as adverbs or nouns.

The girl <u>at the microscope</u> is my sister. *(phrase as adjective)*

<u>Being a selfish child</u>, young Francis Macomber ate the lion's share of the dessert. *(phrase as adverb)*

<u>Running this store</u> takes all my time. *(phrase as noun)*

CLAUSE

A clause is a group of words that includes a subject and a predicate. An independent (or main) clause expresses a complete thought and can stand alone as a simple sentence. A dependent (or subordinate) clause functions as an adjective, adverb, or noun and accompanies or forms part of an independent clause.

<u>The cat chased a mouse</u>. *(independent clause)*

I'm switching to Dr. Jekyll <u>because I don't like Dr. Fell</u>. *(dependent clause as adverb)*

The hand <u>that rocked the cradle</u> has just kicked the bucket. *(dependent clause as adjective)*

<u>Whoever wins the lottery</u> will receive one million dollars. *(dependent clause as noun)*

MODIFIER

A modifier is a word, phrase, or clause that adds information about the element it goes with.

The clerk <u>handling the reservations</u> is our newest employee.

<u>After graduating</u> from college, Ivan worked in a bakery <u>because he couldn't find an engineering job</u>.

The first sentence contains a phrase that modifies *clerk* by identifying which one. The second starts with a phrase that tells when Ivan worked and ends with a subordinate clause that shows why he took the position.

Some modifiers can be moved about in the sentence; others can't. The phrase *handling the reservations* in the first sentence cannot be moved. The positions of the phrase and clause in the second sentence, however, can be switched.

SENTENCE STRATEGIES

Effective sentences stem, at least in part, from selecting the right word order for independent clauses, using subordination and coordination of ideas, correctly positioning movable modifiers, using parallel structures, choosing the right verb voice, and using fragments only intentionally for particular effects. Usually it's best to work on these different strategies as you revise. Don't pause to refine each sentence after you write it.

WORD ORDER IN INDEPENDENT CLAUSES

Look back at the independent clauses in the preceding section, and you'll see that the basic parts follow a similar arrangement. First comes the subject, then the verb, and finally any other element needed to convey the main message.

> Barney blushed. *(subject, verb)*
>
> They built the dog a kennel. *(subject, verb, indirect object, direct object)*
>
> Samantha is an architect. *(subject, verb, subject complement)*

This arrangement puts the emphasis on the subject, right where it's usually wanted.

But the pattern doesn't work in every situation. Occasionally a writer wants to emphasize some element that follows the verb, create an artistic effect, or give the subject unusual emphasis. Enter inverted order and the expletive construction.

Inverted order.   To invert a sentence, move to the front the element you want to emphasize. Sometimes the rest of the sentence follows in regular subject-then-verb order; sometimes the verb precedes the subject.

> Lovable he isn't. *(subject complement, subject, verb)*
>
> This I just don't understand. *(direct object, subject, verb)*
>
> Tall grow the pines in the mountains. *(subject complement, verb, subject)*

Sentences that ask questions typically follow an inverted pattern.

> Is this your coat? *(verb, subject, subject complement)*
>
> Will you let the cat out? *(verb, subject, verb, direct object)*

Expletives.   An expletive fills a vacancy in a sentence without contributing to the meaning. English has two common expletives, *there* and *it*. Ordinarily, *there* functions as an adverb, *it* as a pronoun, and either can appear anywhere in a sentence. As expletives, however, they alter normal sentence order by beginning sentences and anticipating the real subjects or objects.

Expletives are often used unnecessarily, as in the following example:

There were twenty persons attending the sales meeting.

This sentence errs on two counts: its subject needs no extra emphasis, and it is very clumsy. Notice the improvement without the expletive and the un-needed words:

Twenty persons attended the sales meeting.

When the subject or object needs highlighting, leading off with an expletive will, by altering normal order, call it more forcefully to the reader's attention.

Normal order	A fly is in my soup.
	He seeks her happiness.
Expletive construction	There is a fly in my soup. *(expletive anticipating subject)*
	It is her happiness he seeks. *(expletive anticipating object)*

Once in a while you'll find that something just can't be said unless you use an expletive.

There is no reason for such foolishness.

No other construction can express exactly the same thought.

Indicate which of these sentences follow normal order, which are inverted, and which have expletive constructions. Rewrite so that all will be in normal order.   **EXERCISE**

1. Dick Lewis is a true friend. *N*
2. It was her Mustang he stole.
3. An intelligent person is she. *inv* She is an intelligent person
4. May I go to the movie with you? *N*
5. A sadder but wiser man he became. *inv* He became a sadder but wiser man
6. There are many dead fish on the beach. *ex* many dead fishes are on the beach
7. The instructor gave the class a long reading assignment.
8. The Willetts have bought a new house. *N*
9. It is Marianne's aim to become a lawyer. Marianne wants to be a lawyer
10. Harry works at a supermarket. *N*

COORDINATION AND SUBORDINATION

Coordination and subordination are ways to rank ideas in sentences. When we coordinate, we make ideas equal; when we subordinate, we make them unequal. These techniques come into play with four kinds of sentences: simple, compound, complex, and compound-complex.

Simple Sentences.   A simple sentence has one subject and one predicate. Some simple sentences consist merely of a single noun and a single verb.

> Millicent shouted.

Others can include elements such as compound subjects, compound verbs, direct objects, indirect objects, and subject complements.

> Jim and Sue have bought a car. *(compound subject, direct object)*
>
> Lucretia Borgia smiled and mixed her guests a cocktail. *(compound verb, indirect object, direct object)*
>
> Autumn is a sad season. *(subject complement)*

Most simple sentences are rather short and easy to understand. This trimness can add punch to your writing, but it can also make your writing sound childish and waste words.

> The audience was young and friendly. It was responsive. It cheered for each speaker.

Combined into a single simple sentence, the information is easier to follow and more interesting to read:

> The young, friendly, responsive audience cheered for each speaker.

Compound Sentences.   A compound sentence contains two or more independent clauses, each holding the same (coordinate) rank. In other words, the writer regards the ideas in the clauses as equally important.

In some cases, a comma and a coordinating conjunction *(and, but, or, nor, for, yet, so)* link successive clauses.

> Name the baby Huey, *or* I'll cut you out of my will.
>
> Lee wanted an *A* in Algebra, *so* she studied eight hours for the final test.

In others, a semicolon and a conjunctive adverb *(for example, however, in fact, likewise, meanwhile, instead,* and the like) furnish the connection.

> Tod wants to see the play; *in fact,* he's talked about it for weeks.
>
> Today, many young women do not rush into marriage and motherhood; *instead,* they spend several years establishing careers.

Finally, a writer may omit any connecting word and separate the clauses with a semicolon.

> The sky grew pitch black; the wind died; an ominous quiet hung over the whole city.

> Be sure to read this Hemingway novel; it suggests how to cope gracefully with pressure.

Compound sentences allow writers to express simple relationships among simple ideas.

> The young, friendly audience was responsive, so it cheered for each speaker.

This sentence gives a single, simple reason for a single action.

Compound sentences have one important limitation: they prevent the highlighting of particular ideas. In conversation, people often talk in compound sentences.

> The grass was dry, so I started to water it. Liz came along, and we discussed stock options.

Was the discussion about stock options more important than watering the lawn? Less important? Equally important? We simply can't tell. To clear the matter up, we need to use a complex sentence.

Complex Sentences. A complex sentence has one independent clause and one or more dependent clauses. Relegating an idea to a dependent clause shows that the writer considers it less important than the idea in the main clause.

> *Because the young, friendly audience was responsive,* it cheered for each speaker.

> *After the ball was over,* Arthur collapsed on the sofa.

> *Once they had reached the lakeshore,* the campers found a level spot *where they could pitch their tent.*

Unlike compound sentences, complex ones allow writers to vary the emphasis of ideas.

> While I watered the grass, I discussed stock options with Liz.

> I watered the grass while I discussed stock options with Liz.

The first sentence emphasizes the talk with Liz, the second watering the lawn.

Often, shifting sights allows a writer to make changes in meaning as well as in emphasis.

While his bicycle was damaged, Pat walked to work.

While Pat walked to work, his bicycle was damaged.

Furthermore, complex sentences signal *how* ideas relate. Note the various relationships in the following sentences:

Because she was swimming well, Millicent did 200 laps today. *(reason)*

The Sears Tower is taller *than the Empire State Building. (extent).*

Ms. Yoshira is the executive *for whom I am working. (relationship between persons)*

Compound-Complex Sentences.   This type of sentence features two or more independent clauses and one or more dependent clauses. Here are two examples with the dependent clauses underlined.

Ms. Harris works as an investment manager, and Mr. Williams, who lives next door to her, owns a jewelry store.

Because his mother said so, Melvin believes nice young men don't buy lingerie for the women they date; instead, they give presents like flowers and candy.

Compound-complex sentences allow writers to present more intricate relationships than complex sentences do. Read the following sentences and then their rewording into a compound-complex sentence. Note how subordination contributes to the compactness and greater smoothness of the single-sentence version.

Mary hated to be seen in ugly clothing. Nevertheless, she wore an ugly dress with red polka dots. She had received the dress as a Christmas present. Her Aunt Ida had given it to her.

Although Mary hated to be seen in ugly clothing, she nevertheless wore an ugly red-polka-dot dress that her Aunt Ida had given her for Christmas.

The second version condenses thirty-five words to twenty-seven.

EXERCISE   **A. Label the independent and dependent clauses in the sentences below. Then identify each sentence as simple, compound, complex, or compound–complex.**

1. A career in broadcasting requires good verbal skills, an extensive wardrobe, and a pleasant smile.
2. Because its bag was too full, the vacuum cleaner backfired, leaving the room dirtier than it had been before.

3. Leave your boots in the back hall, please. *Please leave your boots in the back hall*

4. When Tom arrived home, his roommate asked him where he had really gone; six hours seemed too long a time to spend in the library.

5. My orange tree blossomed last week; however, the grapefruit trees have withered, probably because of the freeze last month.

6. Kites make good gifts for children; even if a child already has a kite, a second one will come in handy if the first one becomes tangled in a tree.

7. It's risky to confide in a co-worker because you never can be sure that the confidence will be kept.

8. I think I know why he moved here: he likes having the only dental practice in this part of the state.

9. The pencil and the stapler are on the table next to the window in Mr. Brigg's office.

10. Don't add bleach to your load of colored shirts; the colors will fade and the fibers will weaken.

B. Using coordination and subordination, rewrite the following passages to reduce words and improve smoothness.

1. He played the piano. He played the organ. He played the French horn. He did not play the viola.

2. The weather was icy cold and windy. Lee was wearing only a T-shirt and athletic shorts.

3. Life on Venus may be possible. It will not be the kind of life we know on Earth. Life on Mars may be possible. It will not be the kind of life we know on Earth. *but not like that of Earth*

4. He felt his classmates were laughing at his error. He ran out of the room. He vowed never to return to that class.

5. Albert lay in bed. He stared at the ceiling. Albert thought about the previous afternoon. He had asked Kathy to go to dinner with him. She is a pretty, blonde-haired woman. She sits at the desk next to his. They work at Hemphill's. She had refused.

6. I went to the store to buy a box of detergent. I saw Bill there, and we talked about last night's game.

7. Tim went to the newsstand. He bought a magazine there. While he was on the way home, he lost it. He had nothing to read. *Tim bought a magazine at t*

POSITIONING OF MOVABLE MODIFIERS

Movable modifiers can appear on either side of the main statement or within it.

Modifiers After Main Statement.   Sentences that follow this arrangement, frequently called *loose sentences*, occur more commonly than either of the others. They mirror conversation, in which a speaker first makes a statement and then adds on further thoughts. Often, the main statement has just one modifier.

Our company will have to file for bankruptcy *because of this year's huge losses. (phrase as modifier)*

Or it can head up a whole train of them.

He burst suddenly into the party, *loud, angry, obscene. (words as modifiers)*

The family used to gather around the hearth, *doing such chores as polishing shoes, mending ripped clothing, reading, chatting, always warmed by one another's presence as much as by the flames. (words and phrases as modifiers)*

Sally stared in disbelief, and then she smiled, *slowly, tremulously, as if she couldn't believe her good fortune. (words and clause as modifiers)*

There are three essential qualities for buzzard country: *a rich supply of unburied corpses, high mountains, a strong sun. (noun-base groups as modifiers)*

John D. Stewart, "Vulture Country"

A sentence may contain several layers of modifiers. In the following example, we've indented and numbered to show the different layers.

1. The men struggled to the top of the hill,
2. thirsty,
2. drenched in sweat,
2. and cursing in pain
   3. as their knapsack straps cut into their raw, chafed shoulders
      4. with every step.

In this sentence, the terms numbered 2 refer back to *men* in the item numbered 1. Item 3 is linked to *cursing* in the preceding item 2, and item 4 is linked to *cut* in item 3.

The modifiers-last arrangement works well for injecting descriptive details into narratives and also for qualifying, explaining, and presenting lists in other kinds of writing.

Modifiers Before Main Statement.   Sentences that delay the main point until the end are called *periodic*. In contrast to loose sentences, periodic sentences lend a formal note to what is said, slowing its pace, adding cadence, and making it more serious.

If you can keep your head when everyone around you is panicking, you probably don't understand the situation. *(clauses as modifiers)*

From the onset of his journey to the heart of darkness, Marlow witnesses many incidents that reveal the human capacity for evil. *(phrases as modifiers)*

The danger of sideswiping another vehicle, the knowledge that a hidden bump or hole could throw me from the dune buggy, both of these things added to the thrill of the race. *(noun plus phrase and noun plus clause as modifiers)*

When so large a percentage of our college students admits to cheating, when so many professors practice grade inflation, when administrators fail to face up to these problems, our colleges are in serious trouble. (*clauses as modifiers*)

1.   *When the public protests,*
  2.   *confronted with some obvious evidence of the damaging results of pesticide applications,*
  it is fed little tranquilizing pills of half truth. (*clause and phrase as modifiers*)

Rachel Carson, *Silent Spring*

As shown in the Carson example, periodic sentences can also have layers of modifiers.

Positioning the modifiers before the main point throws the emphasis upon the end of the sentence, helping to make the main point with greater force. The delay also lets a writer create sentences that, like the first example, carry stings, ironic or humorous, in their tails.

Modifiers within Main Statement.   Inserting one or more modifiers into a main statement creates a sentence with *interrupted order*. The material may come between the subject and the verb or between the verb and the rest of the predicate.

The young girl, *wearing a tattered dress and looking anything but well-off herself,* gave the beggar a ten-dollar bill. (*phrases between subject and verb*)

Dewey declared, *in a loud, happy voice,* that the concert was the best he'd ever heard. (*phrase between verb and rest of predicate*)

The bedsprings, *bent and rusted, festooned with spider webs,* lay on top of the heap. (*words and phrase between subject and verb*)

The evolutionists, *piercing beneath the show of momentary stability,* discovered, *hidden in rudimentary organs,* the discarded rubbish of the past. (*one phrase between subject and verb, another between verb and rest of predicate*)

By stretching out the main idea, inserted modifiers slow the forward pace of the sentence, giving it some of the formality and force of a periodic sentence.

Identify each sentence as loose, periodic, or interrupted. Rewrite each as one of the other kinds.   **EXERCISE**

interrupted order

1.   Victoria, cast out by family and friends, without the strength to make a new life in a new place, calmly and carefully injected the lethal drug into her thigh.
2.   When told that she had to have her spleen removed, the woman gasped.
3.   Tom missed the bus because his wife had forgotten to reset the alarm after she got up and he had cut himself several times shaving. *periodic*

4. Good health, warm friends, a beautiful summer evening—the best things cannot be purchased.
5. A customer, red-faced and perspiring, stormed up to the claims desk.
6. Stopping just short of the tunnel entrance, the freight train avoided a collision with the crowded commuter train stalled inside.
7. The new kid hammered away at the fading champ, determination in his eyes and glory in his fists.
8. The new tract house sparkled in the sunlight, pink and trim, its lawn immaculate, its two bushes and newly planted crab apple tree, by their very tininess, making the yard look vaster than its actual size.
9. Bright red and skin stinging after a day at the beach, Steve will remember the tanning oil next time.
10. Saloons, gaudily painted and beckoning with promises of extraordinary pleasures, lined the town's main street.
11. In being whisked from Lyons, France, to Tel Aviv to Sri Lanka for location shots, the Hollywood star gave new force to the phrase "international celebrity."
12. The first graders stood in line, talking and giggling, pushing at one another's caps and pencil boxes and kicking one another's shins, unmindful of the drudgery that awaited them within the old schoolhouse.

USING PARALLELISM

Parallelism presents equivalent ideas in grammatically equivalent form. Dressing them in the same grammatical garb calls attention to their kinship and adds smoothness and polish. The following sentence pairs demonstrate the improvement that parallelism brings:

Nonparallel   James's outfit was *wrinkled, mismatched,* and *he needed to wash it. (words and independent clause)*

Parallel   James's outfit was *wrinkled, mismatched,* and *dirty. (words)*

Nonparallel   Oscar likes *reading books, attending plays,* and *to search for antiques. (different kinds of phrases)*

Parallel   Oscar likes *reading books, attending plays,* and *searching for antiques. (same kind of phrases)*

Nonparallel   Beth performs her tasks *quickly, willingly,* and *with accuracy. (words and phrase)*

Parallel   Beth performs her tasks *quickly, willingly,* and *accurately. (words)*

Nonparallel   The instructor complimented me *for taking part in class discussions and because I had written a superb theme. (phrase and clause)*

Parallel   The instructor complimented me *for taking part in class discussions and for writing a superb theme. (phrases)*

As the examples show, revising nonparallel sentences smooths out bumpiness while binding the ideas together more closely and lending them a more finished look.

Parallelism doesn't always stop with a single sentence. Writers sometimes extend it to a series of sentences or even an entire paragraph.

> He had never lost his childlike innocence. He had never lost his sense of wonder. He had never lost his sense of joy in nature's simplest gifts.

> . . . Brownsville [a part of Brooklyn, New York] in that model quarter looks like an old crone who has had a plastic operation, and to my amazement I miss her old, sly, and withered face. I miss all those ratty little wooden tenements, born with the smell of damp in them, in which there grew up how many schoolteachers, city accountants, rabbis, cancer specialists, functionaries of the revolution, and strong-arm men for Murder, Inc.; I miss that affected squirt who always wore a paste diamond on his left pinky and one unforgotten day, taught me to say *children* for *kids*; I miss the sinister "Coney Island" dives where before, during, and after the school day we all anxiously gobbled down hot dogs soggy in sauerkraut and mustard, and I slid along the sawdust floor fighting to get back the violin the tough guys always stole from my locker for a joke; I miss the poisonous sweetness I used to breathe in from the caramels inside the paper cartons every time I passed the candy wholesaler's on my way back from school; I miss the liturgical refrain *Kosher-Bosher* lettered on the windows of the butcher shop; the ducks at Thanksgiving hanging down the doorways of the chicken store; the clouds of white dust that rose up behind the windows of the mattress factory. Above all I miss the fence to the junk yard where I would wait with my store of little red volumes, *THE WORLD'S GREATEST SELECTED SHORT STORIES*, given us gratis by the *Literary Digest,* hoping for a glimpse of a girl named Deborah. . . .
>
> Alfred Kazin, *A Walker in the City*

Repeating a structure through several sentences of a paragraph beats a tattoo that drums the points home more forcefully and adds rhythm to the prose. But don't overuse the technique, or it will lose its impact and seem irritating and artificial.

Balance, a special form of parallelism, positions two grammatically equivalent ideas on opposite sides of some pivot point, such as a word or punctuation mark.

> Hope for the best, and prepare for the worst.
>
> Many are called, but few are chosen.
>
> When I'm right, nobody ever notices; when I'm wrong, nobody ever forgets.
>
> The sheep are in the meadow, and the cows are in the corn.

Like regular parallel sentences, balanced sentences sometimes come in series:

> The tension in this city is not between white people and Negro people. The tension is, at bottom, between justice and injustice, between the forces of light and the forces of darkness. And if there is a victory, it will be a victory not merely for fifty thousand Negroes, but a victory for justice and the forces of light.
>
> Martin Luther King, Jr., "Pilgrimage to Nonviolence"

Balance works especially well for pitting contrasting or clashing ideas against each other. It sharpens the difference between them while achieving compactness and lending an air of insight to what is said.

EXERCISE   **Identify each sentence as nonparallel, parallel, or balanced; then rewrite each nonparallel sentence to make it parallel.**

1. Professor Bartlett enjoys helping students, counseling advisees, and participation in faculty meetings.
2. I can still see Aunt Alva striding into the corral, cornering a cow against a fencepost, try to balance herself on a one-legged milking stool, and butt her head into the cow's belly.
3. The city plans on building a new fishing pier and on dredging the channel of the river.
4. Elton plans on vacationing in New York, but Noreen wants to raft down the Colorado River.
5. Being half drunk and because he was already late for work, Tom called his boss and said he was too ill to come in that day.
6. The novel's chief character peers through a tangle of long hair, slouches along in a shambling gait, and gets into trouble constantly.
7. You can take the boy out of the country, but you can't take the country out of the boy.
8. Joe's problem is not that he earns too little money but spending it foolishly.
9. The room was dark, gloomy, and everything was dusty.
10. The apparition glided through the wall, across the room, and up the fireplace chimney.

CHOOSING THE RIGHT VERB VOICE

A sentence's verb voice derives from the relationship between the subject and the action. A sentence in the *active voice* has a subject that does something plus a verb that shows action.

The boy hit the target.

The girl painted the garage.

This pattern keeps the key information in the key part of the sentence, making it strong and vigorous and giving the reader a close-up look at the action.

The *passive voice* reverses the subject–action relationship by having the subject receive, rather than perform, the action. Instead of an action verb, it uses a form of the verb *to be*; for example, *is, are, was, were*. Some sentences identify the actor in a prepositional phrase; others don't mention the actor at all.

The target was hit by the boy.

The federal debt is to be increased.

Demoting or banishing the actor dilutes the force of the sentence, puts greater distance between the action and the reader, and almost always adds extra words to the message.

Most writers who overuse the passive voice simply don't realize its effects on their writing. Read the following paragraph, written mainly in the passive voice.

> Graft becomes possible when gifts are given to police officers or favors are done for them by persons who expect preferential treatment in return. Gifts of many kinds may be received by officers. Often free meals are given to them by the owners of restaurants on their beats. During the Christmas season, they may be given liquor, food, or theater tickets by merchants. If favored treatment is not received by the donors, no great harm is done. But if traffic offenses, safety code violations, and other infractions are overlooked by the officers, corruption results. When such corruption is exposed by the newspapers, faith is lost in law enforcement agencies.

This impersonal, very wordy passage plods across the page and therefore lacks any real, persuasive impact. Now note the livelier, more forceful tone of this rewritten version.

> Graft becomes possible when police officers accept gifts or favors from persons who expect preferential treatment in return. Officers may receive gifts of many kinds. Restaurant owners often provide free meals for officers on the beat. During the Christmas season, merchants may give them liquor, food, or theater tickets. If donors do not receive favored treatment, no great harm is done. But if officers overlook traffic offenses, safety code violations, and other infractions, corruption results. When the newspapers expose such corruption, citizens lose faith in law enforcement agencies.

Don't misunderstand: the passive voice does have its uses. It can mask identities—or at least try to. A child may try to dodge responsibility by saying "Mother, while you were out, the living room lamp got broken." Less manipulatively, reporters may use it to conceal the identity of a source.

Technical and scientific writing customarily uses the passive voice to explain processes.

> In the production of steel, iron ore is first converted into pig iron by combining it with limestone and coke and then heating the mixture in a blast furnace. Pig iron, however, contains too many impurities to be useful to industry, and as a result must be refined and converted to steel. In the refining process, manganese, silicon, and aluminum are heated with the pig iron in order to degas it; that is, to remove excess oxygen and impurities from it. The manganese, silicon, and aluminum are vaporized while the iron remains in the liquid state, and the impurities are carried away by the vapors. Once this step has been completed, the molten steel is poured into ingots and allowed to cool. The steel is now ready for further processing.
>
> Greg Langford

Putting such writing in the passive voice provides a desirable objective tone and puts the emphasis where it's most important: on the action, not the actor.

On occasion, everyday writing also uses the passive voice. To illustrate:

The garbage is collected once a week, on Monday.

These caves were formed about 10 million years ago.

In the first case, there's no need to tell who collects the garbage; obviously, garbage collectors do. In the second, the writer may not know what caused the formation, and saying "Something formed these caves about 10 million years ago" would sound ridiculous. In both situations, the action, not the actor, is paramount.

Unless special circumstances call for the passive voice, however, use the active voice.

EXERCISE **After determining whether each sentence below is in active or passive voice, rewrite the passive sentences as active ones.**

1. Mary's parents gave her a sports car for her sixteenth birthday.
2. Fires were left burning by negligent campers.
3. The new ice arena will be opened by the city in about two weeks.
4. Harry left the open toolbox out in the rain.
5. Corn was introduced to the Pilgrims by friendly American Indians.

6. Maude took a trip to Sante Fe, New Mexico.
7. We have just installed a new computer in our main office.
8. The club president awarded Tompkins the Order of the Golden Mace.
9. The sound of war drums was heard by the missionaries as they floated down the river.
10. Objections were raised by some members of the legislature to the ratification of the proposed amendment.

USING FRAGMENTS

A fragment is only a part of a sentence, but it is capitalized and punctuated as if it were a complete sentence.

Although fragments are seldom used in formal prose, they form the backbone of most conversations. Here's how a typical bit of dialogue might go:

"Where are you going tonight?" *(sentence)*
"To Woodland Mall." *(fragment)*
"What for?" *(fragment)*
"To buy some shoes." *(fragment)*
"Alone?" *(fragment)*
"No, with Maisie Perkins." *(fragment)*
"Can I come too?" *(sentence)*
"Sure." *(fragment)*

As with most conversations, the sprinkling of complete sentences makes the fragments clear.

Writers of nonfiction use fragments to create special effects. In the following passage, the fragment emphasizes the importance of the question it asks and varies the pace of the writing:

> Before kidney transplants, people had an ethical unease about renal dialysis—the artificial kidney machine. Unquestionably it was a great technical advance making it possible to treat kidney dysfunctions from which thousands die. But the machine was, and is, expensive and involves intensive care of the patient by doctors and nurses. For whom the machine? In the United States the dilemma was evaded but not solved by having lay panels, like juries, making life-or-death choices. In Britain, where the National Health Service entitles everyone, rich or poor, to have access to any necessary treatment, the responsibility rests on the medical staff. It was (and still is) a difficult decision.
>
> Lord Ritchie-Calder, "The Doctor's Dilemma"

Once in a while, as in the following examples, a writer will use not one fragment but a whole series. In the Ciardi selection, the fragments heighten the ironic effect that the author intends. In the other one, they create a kaleidoscopic effect that mirrors the kaleidoscopic impressions offered by the Jazz Age itself.

> Or look at any of the women's magazines. There, as Bernard DeVoto once pointed out, advertising begins as poetry in the front pages and ends as pharmacopoeia and therapy in the back pages. The poetry of the front matter is the dream of perfect beauty that must be hers. These, the flawless teeth. This, the baby skin that must be hers. This, the perfumed breath she must exhale. This, the sixteen-year-old figure she must display at forty, at fifty, at sixty, and forever.
>
> John Ciardi, "What Is Happiness?"

> The Jazz Age offers a kaleidoscope of shifting impressions. Of novelties quickly embraced and quickly discarded. Of flappers flaunting bobbed hair and short skirts. Of hip flasks and bootleg whisky, fast cars and coonskin coats, jazz and dancing till dawn. And overall a sense of futility, an uneasy conviction that all the gods were dead.
>
> Elliott L. Smith and Andrew W. Hart,
> *The Short Story: A Contemporary Looking Glass*

Before using any fragment in your own writing, think carefully about your intended effect and explore other ways of achieving it. Unless only a fragment will serve your needs, don't use one; fragments are likely to be viewed as unintentional—and thus errors—in the work of inexperienced writers.

EXERCISE   **Each of the following passages includes one or more fragments. Identify each and explain its function.**

1.   Anthropologists came to Indian country only after the tribes had agreed to live on reservations and had given up their warlike ways. Had the tribes been given a choice of fighting the cavalry or the anthropologists, there is little doubt as to whom they would have chosen. In a crisis situation, men always attack the biggest threat to their existence. A warrior killed in battle could always go to the happy hunting grounds. But where does an Indian laid low by an anthro go? To the library?

> Vine Deloria, Jr., "Custer Died for Your Sins"

2.   He [Richard Wagner] wrote operas; and no sooner did he have the synopsis of a story, but he would invite—or rather summon—a crowd of his friends to his house and read it aloud to them. Not for criticism. For applause. When the complete poem was written, the friends had to come again, and hear *that* read aloud. Then he would publish the poem, sometimes years before the music that went with it was written. He played the piano like a composer, in the worst sense of

what that implies, and he would sit down at the piano before parties that included some of the finest pianists of his time, and play for them, by the hour, his own music, needless to say. He had a composer's voice. And he would invite eminent vocalists to his house, and sing them his operas, taking all the parts.

Deems Taylor, "The Monster"

BEYOND THE SINGLE SENTENCE

What makes a team successful? Skilled players, to be sure, but teamwork as well. Most sentences are part of a team; and unless they work in harmony, the composition will suffer, however good each of them may be.

Harmony—the rhythmic interplay of sentences—demands, first of all, sentences of different lengths. If all your sentences drag on and on, your reader may bog down and lose the train of thought. If all are clipped, the ideas may seem simplistic, and the sentences will jerk along like a standard transmission car under the foot of an automatic transmission driver. And if all of them are middling long, their plodding, monotonous pace may bring boredom and inattention.

Content sets the pattern of sentence lengths, and often your ideas will lead naturally to the proper mix of long and short sentences. But don't count on it. Chances are, you will need to assert your skills. Once you have finished a draft of your paper, read it over, see how its rhythms strike your inner ear, and put check marks by stretches that "sound" wrong. For instance, you might need to condense a set of jolting primer-book sentences into a single sentence that presents their ideas in a series:

Original Version

> Members of the Unification Church actively recruit converts. They do it in shopping malls. College campuses are also recruiting sites. They talk about the benefits of world unity and sell books as well as records. Donations are also solicited. Listeners receive invitations to a dinner. There the guests learn more about the sect.

Revised Version

> Members of the Unification Church recruit converts in such places as shopping malls and college campuses. They talk about the benefits of world unity, sell books and records, ask for donations, and invite listeners to a dinner to learn more about the sect.

If a key point is submerged in a long sentence, lift it out and set it up as a separate thought, thereby giving it the recognition it deserves. For example:

Original Version

Employers find mature women to be valuable members of their organizations. They are conscientious, have excellent attendance records, and stay calm when things go awry, <u>but unfortunately many employers exploit them</u>. Despite their desirable qualities, most remain mired in clerical, sales, and elementary teaching positions. On the average they earn two-thirds as much as men.

Revised Version

Employers find mature women to be valuable members of their organizations. They are conscientious, have excellent attendance records, and stay calm when things go awry. <u>Unfortunately, though, many employers exploit them</u>. Despite their desirable qualities, most remain mired in clerical, sales, and elementary teaching positions. On the average they earn two-thirds as much as men.

In the following paragraph, the sentences differ considerably in length.

To protest that some fairly improbable people, some people who could not possibly respect themselves, seem to sleep easily enough is to miss the point entirely, as surely as those people miss it who think that self-respect has necessarily to do with not having safety pins in one's underwear. There is a common superstition that "self-respect" is a kind of charm against snakes, something that keeps those who have it locked in some unblighted Eden, out of strange beds, ambivalent conversations, and trouble in general. It does not at all. It has nothing to do with the face of things, but concerns instead a separate peace, a private reconciliation.

Joan Didion, "On Self-Respect"

Much of the appealing rhythm of this passage stems from varied sentence length. The first two rather long sentences (49 and 36 words) are followed by the very brief "It does not at all," which gains emphasis by its position. The last sentence adds variety by means of its moderate length (19 words), quite apart from its interesting observation on the real nature of self-respect.

Look to the structures of your sentences as well as their length. Do they resemble a streetful of row houses built from the same blueprint? If they are all simple, with few modifiers, your readers may underrate the importance of your message. To correct row-house sentences, draw upon the patterns you learned about earlier in this chapter. Try inverting sentence order or positioning modifiers at different points. Combine sentences. Turn a statement into a question. Build from several blueprints. Try anything as long as the structures go together and you don't warp meanings.

The following example illustrates how sentence combining adds smoothness and interest to a piece of writing.

Original Version

Before deaf children can speak, they must learn the speech sounds of the English language. This is a process that requires them to practice breath control, to mouth vowels, and to study the speech positions of the mouth and tongue for many hours. A speech specialist helped my brother do these things. The specialist started with him before he was two years old. She built up his vocabulary by teaching him a series of related words. Each of these words identified something in his environment. My brother proved to be an apt student. He soon learned to talk.

Revised Version

Before deaf children can speak, they must learn the speech sounds of the English language, a process that requires them to practice breath control, mouth vowels, and study the speech positions of the mouth and tongue for many hours. A speech specialist helped my brother do these things. Starting before he was two years old, she built up his vocabulary by teaching him a series of related words, each identified with something in his environment. My brother proved to be an apt student and soon learned to talk.

Revise the following passages to improve their style.   **EXERCISE**

1. Andrew Carnegie came to America from Scotland. He worked as a factory hand, a telegrapher, and a railway clerk to support himself. His savings from these jobs were invested in oil and later in the largest steel works in the country. Historians do not agree in their assessments of Carnegie. Some have considered him as a cruel taskmaster and others as a benevolent benefactor. His contributions to American society, however, cannot be denied. He established public libraries all across the country and spent much time in promoting peace. Good or bad, he ranks as one of our most noteworthy nineteenth-century immigrants.

2. She went to the seashore. She found some seashells. She picked up the seashells. She put the seashells into a basket. She had a whole basketful of seashells. She went home with the basket. She took the shells out of the basket. She put the shells on a dinette table. She brought jeweler's tools to the table. She pierced holes in the shells. She strung the shells on small chains. The chains were gold and silver. She made twenty necklaces. The selling price of the necklaces was $10 apiece. She earned $175 profit. She used her profits to go to the shore again. She could afford to stay for a week this time.

CHAPTER TEN

Diction, Tone, Style

The decisions you make about words and sentences set the tone and style of your writing. Not only do you choose sentence strategies for correctness and effectiveness, but you also choose words for accuracy and effect. Sentences must be clear and effective; so must words. The choices parallel each other. Diction deals broadly with words, not in isolation but as parts of sentences, paragraphs, and essays. Every time you write and revise, diction comes into play.

TOWARD CLEAR DICTION

Clear diction stems from selecting words with the right meanings, using abstract and concrete words appropriately, and picking terms that are neither too specific nor too general. Dictionaries and thesauruses can help guide your choices.

WORD MEANINGS

Make sure the words you use mean what you think they do, so that inaccurate words will not distort your message. If you use *in tandem,* meaning "in single file," to describe a pair of horses hitched together in the usual fashion, you'll confuse the reader. The same holds true if you use *willy-nilly* (willingly or unwillingly) to mean "haphazard" (unplanned, by chance) or *livid* (lead-colored, bluish gray) to mean "flushed" (red-faced, blushing). Sound-alike word pairs often trip up unwary writers. Take *continually* and *continuously,* for example. *Continually* means "again and again"; *continuously,* "without letup or a break." If we want to say that Dr. Mitty received one phone call after another, but we write "The phone rang continuously," we're really saying that the phone kept ringing even though no one answered it. Pages 435–438 present a list of commonly confused words. Study this list, refer to it as you revise your writing, and use a dictionary if you have the slightest doubt about meaning.

CONCRETE AND ABSTRACT WORDS

A concrete word names or describes something that we can perceive with one or more of our five senses. A thing is concrete if we can weigh it, measure it, hold it in our hands, photograph it, taste it, sniff it, add salt to it, drop it, smash into it, or borrow it from a neighbor. If it's abstract, we can't do any of these things. *Bob Seger* is a concrete term, as are *Swiss cheese, petroleum, maple syrup,* and *Dallas.* On the other hand, *jealousy, power, conservatism, size,* and *sadness* are abstract terms.

Concrete words evoke precise, vivid, mental images and as a result help convey a message. The images that abstract terms create differ from person to person. Try this test: ask several of your friends to describe what comes to mind when they think of *joy, dignity, hatred,* or some other abstract term.

In the following passage, the concrete diction is italicized:

> To do without self-respect . . . is to be an unwilling *audience of one* to an interminable *documentary* that details one's failings, both real and imagined, with *fresh footage spliced* in for every *screening.* There's *the glass you broke* in anger, there's *the hurt on X's face; watch now, this next scene, the night Y came back from Houston,* see how you muff this one. To live without self-respect is to *lie awake* some *night,* beyond the reach of *warm milk, phenobarbital,* and *the sleeping hand on the coverlet,* counting up the sins of commission and omission, the trusts betrayed, the promises subtly broken, the gifts irrevocably wasted through sloth or cowardice or carelessness. However long we postpone it, we eventually lie down alone in that notoriously *uncomfortable bed,* the one we make ourselves. Whether or not we sleep in it depends, of course, on whether or not we respect ourselves.
>
> Joan Didion, "On Self-Respect"

Now read a version of this passage that omits the concrete diction and note how vague and colorless it seems.

> To do without self-respect is to be continuously aware of your failings, both real and imagined. Incidents stay in your mind long after they are over. To live without self-respect means being bothered by intentional or unintentional failings, trusts betrayed, promises subtly broken, and gifts irrevocably wasted through sloth or cowardice or carelessness. However long we postpone it, we eventually must come to terms with who we are. How we respond to this situation depends, of course, on whether or not we respect ourselves.

EXERCISE   **Underline the concrete terms in the following passage.**

> The fog which rises from the river has no color, no texture, no taste, smell, or sound. It is sheer vision, a vision of purity, a slow, mesmeric, inexorable erasure of the slate. You see fog mushrooming along the river's course. Gently, it

obliterates the alders tangled on the banks, wipes out the road. Buildings without foundations, trees without trunks, hang in the air like mirages. Sun may be shining brightly on them, or rain drenching them, or stars twinkling above or among them. Slowly the fog reaches higher and spreads. Ridgepoles, small topmost branches, and your own dooryard vanish. There is nothing left now but shining mist. It is all, and you float on it, utterly alone, as one imagines he might in empty space if flung off by earth; as the mind does, drifting into sleep; as the spirit does, having escaped its mortal frame.

Gladys Hasty Carroll, *Sing Out the Glory*

SPECIFIC AND GENERAL TERMS

One concrete term can be more specific or more general than some other concrete term. As we move from *Lassie* to *collie* to *dog* to *mammal* and finally to *animal,* we become less and less specific, ending with a term that specifies not one particular animal but rather encompasses every animal on earth. With each step we retain only those features that fit the more general term. Thus, when we move from *collie* to *dog,* we leave out everything that makes collies different from terriers, greyhounds, and other breeds.

The more specific the term, the less difference among the images it calls to mind. If you say *animal* to a group of friends, one may think of a dog, another of a horse, and a third of a gorilla. *Collie,* on the other hand, triggers images of a large, long-haired, brown and white dog with a pointed muzzle. When you have a choice, always pick the more specific term. You'll connect better with your reader if you do.

EXERCISE

1. **Arrange each set of words from less specific to more specific.**

   a. man, ex-President, human being, Jimmy Carter, American
   b. Forest Hills Apartments, building, structure, condominium, dwelling

2. **Expand each of the following words into a series of four or more that become progressively more specific. Use 1*a* or 1*b* as a pattern.**

   a. activity   d. institution
   b. event   e. device
   c. political party f. reading matter

DICTIONARIES AND THESAURUSES

Get the dictionary habit and learn to use a thesaurus. They'll increase your vocabulary as well as your skill at using words you already know.

Dictionaries.   Dictionaries are storehouses of word meanings. In general, dictionary makers do not try to dictate how words should be used. Instead, they note current and past meanings. When a word gains or loses a meaning, or a newly minted word enjoys wide circulation, dictionary makers observe and record. Most users, however, regard dictionaries as authorities on correctness.

But dictionaries supply much more than word meanings. Figure 10.1 on page 203, an annotated entry from a college-level dictionary, shows what they provide.

Some dictionary entries include information beyond that in the figure.

Idioms. Expressing meanings that differ from those of the words that make them up, idioms are used in the following sentences:

I won't *put up with* any foolishness.

The dowager *gave me the cold shoulder*.

In the first example, *put up with* means "tolerate"; in the second, *gave me the cold shoulder* means "snubbed me." Looking up the most prominent word of an unfamiliar idiom may lead you to a listing and a definition.

Irregular forms. Any irregular forms are indicated. In *Webster's New World Dictionary,* the entry for the verb *spring* notes that the other forms are *sprang, sprung,* and *springing.* This information helps you use correct forms in your writing.

Usage labels. Usage labels help you determine whether a word suits the circumstances of your writing. Here are the most common labels:

Label	*Meaning*
Colloquial	Characteristic of informal writing and speaking; should not be considered nonstandard.
Slang	Informal, newly coined words and expressions, or old expressions with new meanings.
Obsolete	No longer in use but found in past writing.
Archaic	Still finds restricted use; for example, in legal documents; otherwise not appropriate.
Poetic	Used only in poetry and in prose with a poetic tone.
Dialect	Used regularly only in a particular geographical location such as the southeastern United States or the Scottish Lowlands.

Pronunciation. Dictionaries indicate preferred as well as secondary pronunciations. Accent marks (ˈ) show which syllable gets the primary stress and which the secondary stress, if any. To determine the pronunciation, follow the key at the bottom of the page.

Parts of Speech. Each word is classified by grammatical function. Usually, abbreviations such as *n* (noun), *adj.* (adjective), and *vt.* (transitive verb) identify the part of speech.

Spelling, Syllabication. When a word has variant spellings, some dictionaries indicate a preferred version. Alphabetically close variants appear in the same entry. Dots or hyphens separate syllables and tell where to divide a word written on two lines.

Etymology. This term means the origin and development of words. Most college dictionaries limit the entry to the root (original) word and an abbreviation for the original language. The abbreviation key near the front of the dictionary identifies the language.

man·i·fold (manʹə fōldʹ) *adj.* [ME. < OE. *manigfeald:* see MANY & -FOLD] **1.** having many and various forms, features, parts, etc. [*manifold* wisdom] **2.** of many sorts; many and varied; multifarious: used with a plural noun [*manifold* duties] **3.** being such in many and various ways or for many reasons [a *manifold* villain] **4.** comprising, consisting of, or operating several units or parts of one kind: said of certain devices —*n.* **1.** something that is manifold **2.** a pipe with one inlet and several outlets or with one outlet and several inlets, for connecting with other pipes, as, in an automobile, for conducting exhausts from each cylinder into a single exhaust pipe —*vt.* **1.** to make manifold; multiply **2.** to make more than one copy of [to *manifold* a letter with carbon paper] —*SYN.* see MANY. —**manʹi·foldʹer** *n.* —**manʹi·foldʹly** *adv.* —**manʹi·foldʹness** *n.*

MANIFOLD
(A. manifold; B. cylinders)

Meanings. Meanings are grouped by parts of speech. Sometimes usage is briefly illustrated (*manifold* duties). Some dictionaries list meanings in historical order, others according to frequency of use. The front part of the dictionary specifies the arrangement.

Synonyms. These are words close in meaning to the one being defined. Although no synonym carries exactly the same meaning as the original, the two may be interchangeable in some situations.

Additional Word Formations. These are words derived from the one being defined. Their parts of speech are also indicated. Because they have the same basic meaning as the parent word, definitions are omitted.

Figure 10.1

From *Webster's New World Dictionary of the American Language*, Second College Edition.

While any dictionary is better than none, some clearly outrank others in usefulness. A pocket dictionary is handy but not as comprehensive as a desk dictionary. Excellent desk-sized dictionaries include:

The American Heritage Dictionary
Funk and Wagnall's Standard College Dictionary
The Random House Dictionary of the English Language
Webster's Ninth New Collegiate Dictionary
Webster's New World Dictionary of the American Language

Unabridged (complete) dictionaries, such as *Webster's Third New International Dictionary,* can be found in college and public libraries. There you'll also find a variety of specialized dictionaries, including the following:

Comprehensive Etymological Dictionary of the English Language, Ernest Klein
Dictionary of American Slang, ed. Harold Wentworth and Stuart B. Flexner
Dictionary of Clichés, Eric Partridge
A Dictionary of Contemporary American Usage, Bergen and Cornelia Evans
A Dictionary of Foreign Words and Phrases, A. J. Bliss
A Dictionary of Slang and Unconventional English, Eric Partridge
Handbook of American Idioms and Idiomatic Usage, Harold C. Whitford and Robert J. Dixson
Modern American Usage: A Guide, Jacques Barzun et al.
The Oxford Dictionary of English Etymology, C. T. Onions et al.

Your librarian can direct you to dictionaries that list terms in particular fields.

EXERCISE   **Use a good desk dictionary to look up the specified information for each of the following lists of words.**

1. Variant spellings:

airplane	gray
color	theater
aesthete	tornadoes
gaily	usable

2. Syllabication and the syllable that receives the main stress:

anacrusis	harbinger
baccalaureate	ionize
cadenza	misanthrope
exclamation	sequester

3. Parts of speech:

before	separate
deep	then
fair	to
here	where

4. Etymology:

carnival	phenomenon
fiduciary	sabotage
Icarian	supercilious
lethargy	tawdry

5. Idiomatic phrases:

beat	jump
ear	make
get	put
high	set

6. Synonyms:

attack	mercy
distress	object
ghastly	plot
keep	range

Thesauruses.   Thesauruses list synonyms for words but omit definitions and the other elements in dictionary entries. Figure 10.2 on page 206 shows a typical entry. Note that the items are grouped according to parts of speech, and some are cross-indexed.

A thesaurus is valuable for finding a word to convey an exact shade of meaning or for finding a synonym when you want to avoid repetition. But synonyms are never exactly equal, nor are they always interchangeable. To illustrate: *offend* means "to cause displeasure or resentment either intentionally or unintentionally"; *outrage* means "to commit a deliberate and extreme offense against someone else's sense of justice or propriety." Therefore, a word of caution: use the thesaurus with the dictionary. Only in that way can you distinguish which synonym fits a specific sentence.

Excellent guides to synonyms include the following:

Roget's Thesaurus
Webster's New Dictionary of Synonyms
Modern Guide to Synonyms and Related Words, S. I. Hayakawa

247. FORMLESSNESS

.1 NOUNS **formlessness, shapelessness;** amorphousness, amorphism, amorphia; **chaos,** confusion, messiness, orderlessness; **disorder** 62; entropy; anarchy 740.2; **indeterminateness, indefiniteness,** indecisiveness, vagueness, mistiness, haziness, fuzziness, blurriness, unclearness, obscurity.

.2 unlicked cub, diamond in the rough.

.3 VERBS **deform, distort** 249.5; unform, unshape; disorder, jumble, mess up, muddle, confuse; obfuscate, obscure, fog up, blur.

.4 ADJS **formless, shapeless,** featureless, characterless, nondescript, inchoate, lumpen, blobby or baggy [both informal], inform; amorphous, amorphic, amorph(o)–; **chaotic, orderless,** disorderly 62.13, unordered, unorganized, confused, anarchic 740.6; kaleidoscopic; **indeterminate, indefinite,** undefined, indecisive, vague, misty, hazy, fuzzy, blurred or blurry, unclear, obscure.

.5 **unformed, unshaped,** unshapen, unfashioned, unlicked; uncut, unhewn.

Figure 10.2

From *Roget's International Thesaurus,* 4th edition, revised by Robert L. Chapman (Thomas Y. Crowell). Copyright © 1977 by Harper & Row, Publishers, Inc. Reprinted by permission of Harper & Row, Publishers, Inc.

TOWARD RHETORICAL EFFECT

"Rhetorical effect" refers to the response that the manner of writing, not the message, generates in the reader. Successful writers trigger a desired response through the level of their diction and the tone of their writing.

LEVEL OF DICTION

What level of diction is best? The answer depends upon the writer's audience and the writing situation. Think for a minute about a safety engineer who investigates a serious industrial accident on which he must write two reports: one for the safety director of the company, who represents a technical audience, and another for the local newspaper, read by a general audience. Although the two accounts would cover nearly identical ground, clearly they'd use very different language, specialized and formal in the first case, everyday and more relaxed in the second. In each case, the language would reflect the background of the audience. As you write, always tailor your language to audience and purpose.

Standard English, the language that educated people use in both formal and informal settings, follows the familiar grammatical rules. Generally speaking, everything you write should be in Standard English. *Nonstandard English* refers to any version of the language that deviates from these rules. Here is an example from Twain's *Huckleberry Finn.*

> You don't know about me without you have read a book by the name of *The Adventures of Tom Sawyer;* but that ain't no matter. That book was made by Mr. Mark Twain, and he told the truth, mainly. There was things which he stretched, but mainly he told the truth. That is nothing. I never seen anybody but lied one time or another, without it was Aunt Polly, or the widow, or maybe Mary. Aunt Polly—Tom's Aunt Polly, she is—and Mary, and the Widow Douglas is all told about in that book, which is mostly a true book, with some stretchers, as I said before.

Nonstandard English does have a place in writing. Fiction writers use it to narrate the talk of characters who, if real, would speak that way. Journalists use it to report eyewitness reactions to accidents and crimes, and people who compile oral histories use it to record the recollections of people they interview. But avoid it in other writing.

Standard English includes three levels of usage: formal, informal, and technical.

Formal Level.   The formal level, dignified and serious, is suitable for important political, business, and academic occasions. Its vocabulary is marked by many abstract and multisyllabic words, but no slang or contractions. Long sentences and deliberately varied sentence patterns help give it a strong, rhythmic flow. Sentences are often periodic, and many have parallel or balanced structures. (See pages 186–190.) Overall, formal prose impresses the reader as authoritative, stately, and graceful.

The Declaration of Independence, as well as the following excerpt from John F. Kennedy's inaugural address, illustrates the formal level.

> Now the trumpet summons us again—not as a call to bear arms, though arms we need; not as a call to battle, though embattled we are; but a call to bear the burden of a long twilight struggle, year in and year out, "rejoicing in hope, patient in tribulation," a struggle against the common enemies of man: tyranny, poverty, disease, and war itself. . . .
>
> In the long history of the world, only a few generations have been granted the role of defending freedom in its hour of maximum danger. I do not shrink from this responsibility; I welcome it. I do not believe that any of us would exchange places with any other people or any other generation. The energy, the

faith, the devotion which we bring to this endeavor will light our country and all who serve it, and the glow from that fire can truly light the world.

And so, my fellow Americans, ask not what your country can do for you; ask what you can do for your country.

John F. Kennedy, "Inaugural Address"

The first sentence opens with parallelism to show contrast: "not as a call to bear arms, though arms we need" and "not as a call to battle, though embattled we are." In the second paragraph, parallelism in the second sentence shows contrast; in the last sentence it does not. Except for the second sentence in paragraph two, all of the sentences are periodic rather than loose. Thus, not until the end of the opening sentence do we learn the nature of the "long twilight struggle" to which the "trumpet summons us." Time and again Kennedy uses elevated diction—polysyllabic words like *embattled, rejoicing, tribulation, tyranny, poverty, generations, devotion,* and *endeavor,* along with shorter abstract words like *hope, freedom,* and *faith.* These carefully controlled sentence patterns, along with this wording, lend rhythmical dignity to the whole passage.

Informal Level.   Informal writing resembles orderly, intelligent conversation. Earmarked by relatively ordinary words, frequent use of loose sentences, and shorter, less varied sentence structures than formal prose, informal writing may include contractions or even slang, and it is more likely than formal writing to use the pronouns *I, me, my, you,* and *yours.* Casual and familiar rather than dignified and rhythmic, informal writing does not usually call attention to itself. Nevertheless, the language is precise and effective. Here is an example:

There was a distressing story in the paper a few months ago. I wish I'd clipped it out and saved it. As it is, I can only hope I remember it fairly accurately. There was a group of people who wanted a particular dictionary removed from the shelves of the local library because it contained a lot of obscenity. I think they said there were sixty-five or so dirty words in it. Some poor woman who was acting as a spokesman for the group had a list of offending words, which she started to read aloud at a hearing. She managed to read about twenty of them before she started sobbing uncontrollably and couldn't continue.

Thomas H. Middleton, "The Magic Power of Words"

Unlike the Kennedy excerpt, this one has relatively uncomplicated sentences. Three of them—the fourth, sixth, and seventh—are loose rather than periodic. The passage includes two contractions, *I'd* and *couldn't,* one casual expression, *a lot of,* and the pronoun *I.* Most of the words are very short, and none would be out of place in an ordinary conversation.

Formal–Informal Level.   As life has become less formal, informal diction has become increasingly widespread. Today many articles and books, even ones on relatively serious topics, mix informal and formal elements. To illustrate:

> . . . faith in sports has been vigorously promoted by industry, the military, government, the media. The value of the arena and the locker room has been imposed on our national life. Coaches and sportswriters are speaking for generals and businessmen, too, when they tell us that a man must be physically and psychologically "tough" to succeed, that he must be clean and punctual and honest, that he must bear pain, bad luck, and defeat without whimpering or making excuses. A man must prove his faith in sports and the American Way by whipping himself into shape, playing by the rules, being part of the team, and putting out all the way. If his faith is strong, he will triumph. It's his own fault if he loses, fails, remains poor.
>
> Robert Lipsyte, *Sports World*

All these sentences except the next to last are loose. Two are quite long, four quite short, and only two have parallel phrases or clauses. Although a few expressions—"bear," "the American Way," "triumph"—echo formal diction, most of the words have an informal ring, and two expressions, "whipping himself into shape" and "putting out all the way," skirt the edges of slang.

Technical Level.   A specialist writing for others in the same field or for sophisticated nonspecialists writes on the technical level, a cousin to the formal level. Technical language uses specialized words that may be esoteric and difficult for a general audience. Its sentences tend to be long and complex, but unlike formal diction it doesn't lean toward periodic sentences, parallelism, and balance. Read this example from the field of entomology, the study of insects:

> The light organs of fireflies are complex structures, and recent studies using the electron microscope show them to be even more complex than once supposed. Each is composed of three layers: an outer "window," simply a transparent portion of the body wall; the light organ proper; and an inner layer of opaque, whitish cells filled with granules of uric acid, the so-called "reflector." The light organ proper contains large, slablike light cells, each of them filled with large granules and much smaller, dark granules, the latter tending to be concentrated around the numerous air tubes and nerves penetrating the light organ. These smaller granules were once assumed by some persons to be luminous bacteria, but we now know that they are mitochondria, the source of ATP [adenosine triphosphate] and therefore of the energy of light production. The much larger granules that fill most of the light cells are still of unknown function; perhaps they serve as the source of luciferin.
>
> Howard Ensign Evans, *Life on a Little-Known Planet*

Note the specialized vocabulary—*granules, uric acid, mitochondria,* and *luciferin*—as well as the length and complexity of the sentences. Five sentences make up the passage, the shortest having twenty-four words. None is periodic, and none has a parallel or balanced structure.

Every field has *jargon,* specialized terms or inside talk that provides a convenient shorthand for communication among its members. For an audience of biologists, you may write that two organisms have a *symbiotic relationship,* meaning "mutually beneficial"; for psychology majors, you might use *catalepsy* instead of "a temporary loss of consciousness and feeling, often accompanied by muscular rigidity." As a general rule, use technical terms only when you're writing for an audience that knows their meanings. If unfamiliar words are necessary in a paper aimed at a general audience, define them the first time they appear.

Colloquial Language and Slang.   *Colloquial* originally meant "the language of ordinary conversation between people of a particular region." *Slang,* according to *Webster's Eighth New Collegiate Dictionary,* is "an informal nonstandard vocabulary composed typically of coinages, changed words, and extravagant, forced, or facetious figures of speech." These two categories shade into each other, and even authorities sometimes disagree on whether to label a term *colloquial* or *slang.* The word *bender,* meaning "a drinking spree," seems firmly in the colloquial camp, and *bummer,* a term recently used by young people to mean "a bad time," is just as clearly slang. *Break a leg* is theater slang used to wish a performer success. But what about *guy* and *kid*? Once they were slang, but so many people have used them for so long that they have now become colloquial.

Regardless of their labels, colloquial and slang terms are almost never appropriate in formal writing. They sometimes serve a useful purpose in informal writing by creating a special effect or increasing audience appeal. Even so, careful writers use them sparingly. Some readers may not understand some colloquial language, and slang usually becomes dated quickly. The following paragraph uses colloquial and slang expressions successfully:

> . . . When I was just a kid on Eighth Avenue in knee pants . . . [Big Bill] was trying to get himself killed. He was always in some fight with a knife. He was always cutting or trying to cut sombody's throat. He was always getting cut or getting shot. Every Saturday night that he was out there, something happened. If you heard on Sunday morning that somebody had gotten shot or stabbed, you didn't usually ask who did it. You'd ask if Big Bill did it. If he did it, no one paid much attention to it, because he was always doing something like that. They'd say, "Yeah, man. That cat is crazy."
>
> Claude Brown, *Manchild in the Promised Land*

Kid, yeah, and *cat* reflect the speech of Brown's characters and thus add authenticity to his account. Despite the informal diction, Brown uses parallelism in the second, third, and fourth sentences; repetition of "he was always" emphasizes the single-minded self-destructiveness of Big Bill's behavior.

Indicate whether each of the following passages is an example of formal, informal, or technical diction. Support your answers with examples from the passages. Point out slang or colloquial expressions.   **EXERCISE**

1.   We may now recapitulate the reasons which have made it necessary to substitute "space-time" for space and time. The old separation of space and time rested upon the belief that there was no ambiguity in saying that two events in distant places happened at the same time; consequently it was thought that we could describe the topography of the universe at a given instant in purely spatial terms. But now that simultaneity has become relative to a particular observer, this is no longer possible. What is, for one observer, a description of the state of the world at a given instant, is, for another observer, a series of events at various different times, whose relations are not merely spatial but also temporal.

Bertrand Russell, *The ABC of Relativity*

2.   In some ways I am an exceptionally privileged woman of thirty-seven. I am in the room of a private, legal abortion hospital, where a surgeon, a friend of many years, is waiting for me in the operating room. I am only five weeks pregnant. Last week I walked out of another hospital, unaborted, because I had suddenly changed my mind. I have a husband who cares for me. He yells because my indecisiveness makes him anxious, but basically he has permitted the final choice to rest in my hands: "It would be very tough, especially for you, and it is absolutely insane, but yes, we could have another baby." I have a mother who cares. I have two young sons, whose small faces are the most moving arguments I have against going through with this abortion. I have a doctorate in psychology, which among other advantages, assures me of the professional courtesy of special passes in hospitals, passes that at this moment enable my husband and my mother to stand in my room at a nonvisiting hour and yell at each other over my head while I sob.

Magda Denes, *In Necessity and Sorrow:*
Life and Death in an Abortion Hospital

3.   A quibble [pun] is to Shakespeare what luminous vapours are to the traveller; he follows it at all adventures, it is sure to lead him out of his way, and sure to engulf him in the mire. It has some malignant power over his mind, and its fascinations are irresistible. Whatever be the dignity or profundity of his disquisition, whether he be enlarging knowledge or exalting affection, whether he

be amusing attention with incidents, or enchaining it in suspense, let but a quibble spring up before him, and he leaves his work unfinished. A quibble is the golden apple for which he will always turn aside from his career, or stoop from his elevation. A quibble, poor and barren as it is, gave him such delight, that he was content to purchase it, by the sacrifice of reason, propriety, and truth. A quibble was to him the fatal Cleopatra for which he lost the world, and was content to lose it.

Samuel Johnson, *Preface to*
The Plays of William Shakespeare

4.   I have just spent two days with Edward T. Hall, an anthropologist, watching thousands of my fellow New Yorkers short-circuiting themselves into hot little twitching death balls with jolts of their own adrenalin. Dr. Hall says it is overcrowding that does it. Overcrowding gets the adrenalin going, and the adrenalin gets them queer, autistic, sadistic, barren, batty, sloppy, hot-in-the-pants, charred-in-the-flankers, leering, puling, numb—the usual in New York, in other words, and God knows where else. Dr. Hall has the theory that overcrowding has already thrown New York into a state of behavioral sink. Behavioral sink is a term from ethology, which is the study of how animals relate to their environment. Among animals, the sink winds up with a "population collapse" or "massive die-off." O rotten Gotham.

Tom Wolfe, *The Pump House Gang*

TONE

Tone reveals the author's attitude toward the topic and the reader. Every piece of writing has a tone, intended or otherwise, which stems from the meanings and connotations of words, the sentence patterns, and the rhythm of the prose.

Denotation and Connotation.   The denotation of a word is its direct, essential meaning: what the word always stands for. The word *book,* for example, denotes "a set of printed or blank sheets bound together along one edge to form a volume." This definition is objective and neutral: it does not assign any special value or convey any particular attitude toward either the word or what the word stands for. But when the self-made man snorts "book-learnin' " at his better-educated junior partner, he does assign a value and an attitude—that he ranks experience higher than education.

Some words almost always carry strong connotations or emotional associations. *Death,* for instance, is rich in associations. *Webster's Eighth New Collegiate Dictionary* defines it as "a permanent cessation of all vital functions" or "the end of life," but it means much more. All of us have hopes, fears, and memories about death, feelings that color our responses whenever we hear or read the word. Likewise, we have personal responses to words like *sexy, cheap, radical, politician,* and *mother.* Such connotations develop by association: our experiences determine, to a considerable extent, how we feel and think about something. To an Olympic swimmer who has won a gold medal, *swimming* may stir pleasant memories of the victory and the plaudits that went with it. The victim of a near-drowning, however, might react to the same word with something approaching horror.

Nonetheless, cultural connotations are more important than personal ones. Cultural connotations develop the way individual ones do, but on a much larger scale, growing out of the common experiences of many speakers and writers, and changing with usage and circumstances.

Context, the parts of a passage that precede and follow a word, also affects connotation. Note, for instance, the different associations of *dog* in the following sentences.

That movie is a real dog.

I sure am putting on the dog!

It's a dog-eat-dog world.

Your dog-in-the-manger attitude makes you very unpopular.

Denotation is sometimes called the language of science and technology; connotation, the language of art. But we need both to communicate effectively. Denotation allows us to convey precise, essential meanings. Connotation adds richness, warmth, and bite. Without them our language would be bland and sterile, our lives bleak and mechanical.

Objective Tone. An objective tone keeps the writer's personality and opinions out of the message. Here is an example.

> Myopia is a condition of the eye which makes distant vision blurry. In brief, the myopic individual is nearsighted. When the eye is normal, rays of light pass through it and come to focus on the retina, located at the back of the eye. With the myopic eye, however, the rays of light come together a little in front of the retina. As a result, the distant image is not seen clearly. Myopia may result from the eye itself being too long or the lens of the eye being too flat. In either case, the rays converge in front of the retina, and the nearsighted individual is likely to have difficulty making out distant objects.
>
> Janine Neumann

This tone suits a popular explanation of a medical condition. The prose is businesslike and authoritative, the sentence patterns uncomplicated, and nothing reveals the person behind the words.

Other Attitudes.   Sometimes you write merely to inform, sometimes to persuade. In persuasive writing, let your attitude toward your topic set the tone. Decide how subtle, flamboyant, or formal your writing should be and what special tone—satiric, cynical, serious, mock pompous, bawdy, playful—will win your reader over.

Ultimately, every essay has combined characteristics that give it a special tone. The following excerpts illustrate some of tone's many dimensions:

> Unless you have led an abnormally isolated adulthood, the chances are excellent that you know many people who have at one time or another committed an act, or consorted with someone who was committing an act, for which they might have been sent to prison. We do not consider most of these people, or ourselves, criminals; the act is one thing, the criminality of it quite something else. Homicide, for example, is in our law not a crime; murder only is proscribed. The difference between the two is the intention, or to be more accurate, society's decision about the nature of that intention.
>
> Bruce Jackson, "Who Goes to Prison: Caste
and Careerism in Crime"

Here we have a sophisticated and rather formal tone. Terms like *consorted* and *proscribed,* while exactly suited to Jackson's meaning, do not form part of most people's word kits. The complexity of the first sentence and the varied patterns of those that follow contribute to the air of sophistication. The emphatic *quite,* meaning "entirely," is cultivated usage; and along with *society's decision,* it lends the tone a wry touch.

> Cans. Beer cans. Glinting on the verges of a million miles of roadways, lying in scrub, grass, dirt, leaves, sand, mud, but never hidden. Piels, Rheingold, Ballantine, Schaeffer, Schlitz, shining in the sun or picked by moon or the beams of headlights at night; washed by rain or flattened by wheels, but never dulled, never buried, never destroyed. Here is the mark of savages, the testament of wasters, the stain of prosperity.
>
> Who are these men who defile the grassy borders of our roads and lanes, who pollute our ponds, who spoil the purity of our ocean beaches with the empty vessels of their thirst? Who are the men who make these vessels in millions and then say, "Drink and discard"? What society is this that can afford to cast away a million tons of metal and to make a wild and fruitful land a garbage heap?
>
> Marya Mannes, "Wasteland"

Rhythm and word choice contribute equally to the tone of this passage. The excerpt opens with imagistic sentence fragments that create a panoramic word picture of our littered roadways. Then complete sentences and somber commentary follow. Words and patterns are repeated, mixing the dignified language of epic and religion with common derogatory terms—*testament, pu-*

rity, vessels, and *fruitful* set against *savages, wasters, defile,* and *garbage heap*—to convey the contradictions Mannes deplores. The rhetorical questions, used instead of accusations, further distance the author, making her outrage seem lofty. Mannes's tone is at once majestic and disdainful.

> *Erethizon dorsatus,* an antisocial character of the Northern U.S. and Canadian forest, commonly called a porcupine, looks like an uncombed head, has a grumpy personality, fights with his tail, hides his head when he's in trouble, attacks backing up, retreats going ahead, and eats toilet seats as if they were Post Toasties. It's a sad commentary on his personality that people are always trying to do him in.
>
> R. T. Allen, "The Porcupine"

The tone of this passage is affectionately humorous. Allen sets this tone by taking note of the porcupine's tousled appearance, testy personality, and peculiar habits, such as eating outdoor toilet seats (for their salt content, as Allen later explains). The net effect is to personify porcupines, making them seem like the eccentric reprobate human that others regard with amused toleration.

The final passage begins by referring to a "promissory note": the Constitution and the promise of life, liberty, and the pursuit of happiness spelled out in the Declaration of Independence:

> It is obvious today that America has defaulted on this promissory note insofar as her citizens of color are concerned. Instead of honoring this sacred obligation, America has given the Negro people a bad check; a check which has come back marked "insufficient funds." But we refuse to believe that the bank of justice is bankrupt. We refuse to believe that there are insufficient funds in the great vaults of opportunity in this nation. So we have come to cash this check—a check that will give us upon demand the riches of freedom and the security of justice. We have also come to this hallowed spot to remind America of the fierce urgency of *now.* This is no time to engage in the luxury of cooling off or to take the tranquilizing drug of gradualism. *Now* is the time to make real the promises of Democracy. *Now* is the time to rise from the dark and desolate valley of segregation to the sunlit path of racial justice. *Now* is the time to open the doors of opportunity to all of God's children. *Now* is the time to lift our nation from the quicksands of racial injustice to the solid rock of brotherhood.
>
> Martin Luther King, Jr., "I Have a Dream"

This writing speaks passionately for freedom and justice. Its most obvious rhetorical strategy is metaphor, first the extended one of the promissory note, then brief separate metaphors that make the same point. The repetition of *now* sharpens the insistent tone. Eloquence comes through parallelism, repetition, and words like *sacred* and *hallowed;* vividness through figures of speech like "vaults of opportunity" and "sunlit path of racial justice." Like George Orwell,

Mark Twain, Joseph Conrad, and other masters of tonal effects whose work appears in this book, King uses both rhythm and diction to create a tone that infuses and invigorates his message.

EXERCISE   **Characterize the tone of each of the following paragraphs. Point out how word choice, sentence structure, rhythm, and other elements contribute to it.**

1.   When I awoke, dimly aware of some commotion and outcry in the clearing, the light was slanting down through the pines in such a way that the glade was lit like some vast cathedral. I could see the dust motes of wood pollen in the long shaft of light, and there on the extended branch sat an enormous raven with a red and squirming nestling in its beak.

    The sound that awoke me was the outraged cries of the nestling's parents, who flew helplessly in circles around the clearing. . . . And he, the murderer, the black bird at the heart of life, sat there, glistening in the common light, formidable, unperturbed, untouchable. The sighing died. It was then I saw the judgment. It was the judgment of life against death. I will never see it again so forcefully presented. I will never hear it again in notes so tragically prolonged. For in the midst of protest, they forgot the violence. There, in that clearing, the crystal note of a song sparrow lifted hesitantly in the hush. And, finally, after painful fluttering, another took the song, and then another, the song passing from one bird to another, doubtfully at first, as though some evil thing was being slowly forgotten. Till suddenly they took heart and sang from many throats joyously together as birds are known to sing. They sang under the brooding shadow of the raven. In simple truth they had forgotten the raven, for they were the singers of life, and not of death.

    Loren Eiseley, "The Judgment of the Birds"

2.   America, which leads the world in almost every economic category, leads it above all in the production of schlock. Christmas toys broken before New Year's, wash-n-wear suits that neither wash well nor wear well, appliances that expire a month after the guarantee, Barbie dolls, frozen pizza—these are but a few of the shoddy goods whose main contribution to our civilization, apart from a momentary satisfaction to the purchaser, is to swell the sanitary-fill schlock heaps that are the feces of our Gross (and how!) National Product.

    Robert Claiborne, "Future Schlock"

3.   Babe Ruth was ***The Sultan of Swat***
    Babe Ruth was ***THE BAMBINO***
    Babe Ruth was what you came to see!!!!

    It was like going to a carnival, with Babe as both the star performer and the side-show attraction. Hell, that's what we called him: "You big ape." He was what a home-run hitter was supposed to look like. Wide, flat nose. Big feet. Little ankles. Belly hanging over his belt. All he had to do was walk on to the field and everybody would applaud. The air became charged with electricity. You just felt that something great was going to happen.

He'd twirl that big 48-ounce bat around in little circles up at the plate as if he were cranking it up for the Biggest Home Run Ever Hit—*you felt that*—and when he'd hit one he would hit it like nobody has hit it before or since. A mile high and a mile out. I can see him now, as I did so many times, just look up, drop the bat and start to trot, the little pitter-patter pigeon-toed, high-bellied trot that seemed to say, I've done it before and I'll do it again, but this one was for you.

Leo Durocher, Nice Guys Finish Last

SPECIAL STYLISTIC TECHNIQUES

The style of a piece of writing is its character or personality. Like people, writing can be many things: dull, stuffy, discordant, sedate, lively, flamboyant, eccentric, and so on. Figurative language, puns, and irony can contribute to your own distinctive writing style.

FIGURATIVE LANGUAGE

Figurative language, a special category of concrete diction, uses words in a nonliteral way to create sharply etched sensory images that catch and hold the reader's attention. Besides energizing the writing, figurative language helps to strengthen the reader's grip on its ideas. Five figurative devices are especially important: simile, metaphor, personification, overstatement, and understatement.

Simile and Metaphor.   A *simile* directly compares two unlike things by the use of *like* or *as*. "Todd is as restless as an aspen leaf in a breeze" and "Her smile flicked on and off like a sunbeam flashing momentarily through a cloudbank" are similes. A *metaphor* also compares unlike things, but indirectly rather than directly. Some metaphors include a linking verb (*is, are, were,* and so on); others do not. "The moon was a wind-tossed bark" and "The curtain of darkness fell over the land" are both metaphors. Here is an excerpt that contains similes and metaphors.

The field is a sea of deep, dark green, a sea made up of millions of small blades of grass blended together as one. Each blade is a dark green spear, broad at the bottom and narrowing to a needle point at the tip. Its full length is arched so that, viewed from one end, it looks like a shallow trough with paper-thin sides. On the inner side of this trough, small ridges and shallow valleys run from base to tip. To a finger rubbed across them, they feel like short bristly hairs.

Daniel Kinney

**DISCUSSION
QUESTIONS**

1. Locate the similes in this passage and explain how they help the reader.
2. Locate the metaphors and point out how each heightens the sensory impact of the writing.

Writers too often snatch hastily at the first similes and metaphors that come to mind and end up strewing their pages with overused and enfeebled specimens. Johnny is "as blind as a bat," Mary runs around "like a chicken with its head cut off"—and the writing slips into trite gear. Other ineffective comparisons link items that are too dissimilar. For example, "The wind whistled through the trees like a herd of galloping horses" would only puzzle a reader.

Personification.   This is a special sort of metaphor that assigns human qualities or traits to something nonhuman: a plant, an abstraction, a nonliving thing. Here are some examples.

> The vine clung stubbornly to the trunk of the tree.

> May fortune smile upon you.

> The waves lapped sullenly against the base of the cliff.

Each of these sentences assigns its subject a different emotional quality—stubbornness, friendliness, gloom—each figurative rather than literal: vines aren't stubborn, fortune doesn't smile, and waves aren't sullen.

Personification sometimes extends beyond a single sentence. To illustrate, the following passage carries a single image through two paragraphs:

> "I figured when my legislative program passed the Congress," [Lyndon] Johnson said in 1971, "that the Great Society had a real chance to grow into a beautiful woman. And I figured her growth and development would be as natural and inevitable as any small child's. In the first year, as we got the laws on the books, she'd begin to crawl. Then in the second year, as we got more laws on the books, she'd begin to walk, and the year after that, she'd be off and running, all the time growing bigger and healthier and fatter. And when she grew up, I figured she'd be so big and beautiful that the American people couldn't help but fall in love with her, and once they did, they'd want to keep her around forever, making her a permanent part of American life, more permanent than the New Deal.

> "But now Nixon has come along and everything I've worked for is ruined. There's a story in the paper every day about him slashing another one of my Great Society programs. I can just see him waking up in the morning, making that victory sign of his and deciding which program to kill. It's a terrible thing for me to sit by and watch someone else starve my Great Society to death. She's getting thinner and thinner and uglier and uglier all the time; now her bones are beginning to stick out and her wrinkles are beginning to show. Soon she'll be so

ugly that the American people will refuse to look at her; they'll stick her in a closet to hide her away and there she'll die. And when she dies, I too will die."

Doris Kearns, "Who *Was* Lyndon Baines Johnson?"

Through personification, Johnson expresses affection for his social program, disapproval of Nixon's policies, and sorrow over the coming demise of the "child" he has so carefully nurtured.

Personification works best when it is used in moderation and doesn't make outrageous comparisons. Dishes don't run away with spoons except in nursery rhymes.

Overstatement.   Overstatement, sometimes called hyperbole, deliberately and drastically exaggerates in order to make a point. An example is "Wilfred is the world's biggest fool."

One of the best examples of sustained overstatement is Mark Twain's essay "Fenimore Cooper's Literary Offences." In it, Twain claims, "In one place in *Deerslayer,* and in the restricted space of two-thirds of a page, Cooper has scored 114 offences against literary art out of a possible 115." Twain also asserts, "There have been daring people in the world who claimed that Cooper could write English, but they are all dead now. . . ." Through such exaggerations, Twain mocks the shortcomings of Cooper's novels.

Used sparingly, overstatement is emphatic, adding real force to an event or situation. Writers who consistently exaggerate, however, risk losing their credibility.

Understatement.   Understatement makes an assertion in a humble manner without giving something its due, as when a sportscaster calls a team's 23–2 record "pretty fair." By drawing attention to the thing it appears to slight, this soft-spoken approach offers writers a shrewd rhetorical strategy. To illustrate:

> To assume that Heidi Mansfield lacks the qualifications for this position is not unwarranted.

Without ever actually calling Mansfield unqualified, the statement suggests that she is. Similarly, when a meat company executive says, "It is not unlikely that beef prices will jump ten cents a pound in the next two months," we might as well count on spending another dime. As these statements show, understatement not infrequently has an ulterior motive.

Identify the similes, metaphors, personifications, overstatements, or understatements in these sentences.   **EXERCISE**

1. The old table greedily sucked up the linseed oil.
2. Russia's social and economic system is a giant staircase that leads nowhere.

3. Stanley has the bile of human meanness by the quart in every vein.
4. Their music sounds like the drumming of an infant's fists against the sides of a crib.
5. The foundations of our divorce are as strong as ever.
6. It is not unlike Muriel to be late.
7. You're the world's biggest liar!
8. "Fashion, though folly's child, and guide of fools, Rules e'en the wisest, and in learning rules."
9. Einstein's theories have had some impact on modern science.
10. I'm as tired as a horse at sunset.

Puns.   A pun is a play on words. Generally, the same word has a double-barreled meaning, as in "The president of the Rockville Gun Club has blasted the state's plans to shorten the deer-hunting season." But on occasion, a pun juggles two words having the same, or nearly the same, sound but different meanings. The title "The Mourning After" for a paper on hangover remedies suggests that time when the effects of overdrinking come to a head. Don't use a pun that seems forced or is in bad taste. Few readers would probably object to "One current problem for Americans is the rising cost of electrical energy." But many would groan at "The professional tennis racket is one that people should avoid." And nearly all would rightly feel distaste if a paper about capital punishment talked about condemned prisoners "dying for news that the governor had commuted their sentences."

Irony.   Irony occurs when a writer intentionally states one thing but actually means something different or even opposite. A certain point is thus highlighted. The sportswriter who refers to the "ideal conditions" for a tennis tournament when rain has drenched the courts and forced cancellation of matches speaks ironically. Washington Irving illustrates a longer example of the same sort of irony:

> The baron, though a small man, had a large soul, and it swelled with satisfaction at the consciousness of being the greatest man in the little world about him. He loved to tell long stories about the dark old warriors whose portraits looked grimly down from the walls around, and he found no listeners equal to those that fed at his expense. He was much given to the marvellous, and a firm believer in all those supernatural tales with which every mountain and valley in Germany abounds. The faith of his guests exceeded even his own; they listened to every tale of wonder with open eyes and mouths, and never failed to be astonished, even though repeated for the hundredth time. Thus lived the Baron Von Landshort, the oracle of his table, the absolute monarch of his little territory, and happy, above all things, in the persuasion that he was the wisest man of the age.
>
> Washington Irving, "The Spectre Bridegroom"

Irving never directly states the baron's shortcomings. Rather, suggestive details such as the swelling of the baron's soul, his belief in the supernatural, and his deception by the sponging guests portray one who, far from being "the wisest man of the age," is pompous, superstitious, and gullible.

ELIMINATING INEFFECTIVE DICTION

Wordiness, euphemisms, clichés, and mixed metaphors are flaws that can rob your writing of crispness and clarity. As you revise, stay alert for these culprits and eliminate any that you find.

WORDINESS

Wordiness is verbal obesity, and like physical obesity it has more than one cause. Some writers overnourish their prose to make it sound more impressive, some to pad an assignment, and some simply because they don't realize they're doing it. Whatever the reason, the results are the same: ponderous, slow-moving papers that lack punch. To inject vigor, strip your prose down to fighting weight by cutting out every word that doesn't serve a purpose. If five words are doing the work of one, drop four.

The two major forms of wordiness, deadwood and gobbledygook, often occur together. *Deadwood,* which does nothing but take up space and clutter the writing, is bracketed in the following sentence:

Responsible parents [of today] neither allow their children [to have] absolute freedom [to do as they please] nor severely restrict their children's activities.

Now read the sentence without the deadwood.

Responsible parents neither allow their children absolute freedom nor severely restrict their children's activities.

Careful revision has increased the clarity and reduced the words from twenty-three to fourteen.

Gobbledygook consists of long, abstract, or technical words that help create unnecessarily long and complex sentences. Some people who write it mistakenly believe it "dignifies" their thoughts. Others want to conceal their meanings by clouding their statements. And some naively think that long words are better than short ones. All of these writers use gobbledygook, but none of their readers appreciate it. Here are some samples of gobbledygook followed by revised versions in plain English:

Original Version
The fish exhibited a 100 percent mortality response.

Revised Version
All of the fish died.

Original Version
We have been made cognizant of the fact that the experiment will be terminated in the near future.

Revised Version
We have learned that the experiment will end soon.

EUPHEMISMS

Euphemisms take the sting out of something unpleasant or add stature to something humble. Familiar expressions include *pass away* for *die, preowned* for *used, sanitation engineer* for *garbage collector,* and *exceptional* for *retarded* or *physically handicapped.*

In most cases, the writer simply intends to cushion reality. But euphemisms also have grisly uses. Mobsters don't *beat up* merchants who refuse *protection* (itself a euphemism); they *lean on* them. Hitler didn't talk about *exterminating the Jews* but about *the final solution to the Jewish problem.* These euphemisms don't just blur reality; they blot out images of horror. Of merchants with broken limbs and bloodied faces. Of cattle cars crammed with men, women, and children enroute to death camps. Of barbed wire and gas ovens and starved corpses in the millions.

Any euphemism, however well-intentioned, probably obscures an issue. On occasion you may need one in order to protect the sensitive reader, but usually you will serve readers best by using direct expressions that present reality, not a tidied-up version.

CLICHÉS AND MIXED METAPHORS

Clichés.   Rather than responding to experience with their own perceptions, writers often fall back on stock, well-worn observations. They use clichés, the verbal knee-jerk responses triggered by patterned thinking. Dullness follows. Daily conversation teems with stale, trite expressions, because talk is unplanned; but writing allows you time to find fresh, effective language. Your individual response is what commands the reader's attention, and only thinking will generate that response. The following list of clichés barely "scratches the surface."

acid test
almighty dollar
apple of his eye
beat a hasty retreat
beating around the bush

better late than never
black sheep
blind as a bat
budding genius
burn the midnight oil

chip off the old block

clear as a bell

conspicuous by its absence

cool as a cucumber

each and every

easier said than done

exception proves the rule

fast and furious

goes without saying

green with envy

hit the nail on the head

honesty is the best policy

innocent as a lamb

in the last analysis

last but not least

make hay while the sun shines

nipped in the bud

no sooner said than done

perfect specimen

picture of health

put in an appearance

rears its ugly head

scrape the bottom of the barrel

set the world on fire

sick as a dog

slowly but surely

strike while the iron is hot

when my ship comes in

wine, women, and song

worse for the wear

Mixed Metaphors.   Clichéd writing often suffers as well from mixed metaphors—inappropriate combinations that startle or amuse the reader. How would you respond if you came across these?

> When he opened that can of worms, he bit off more than he could chew.

> Female chauvinist sows, acting like chickens with their heads cut off, are jumping the gun in the battle of the sexes.

Can you visualize pigs flopping like headless chickens and prematurely starting a race that turns into a battle? The point is obvious.

The following sentences are flawed by wordiness, euphemisms, clichés, and mixed metaphors. When you have identified the faults, revise the sentences.   **EXERCISE**

1. The American eagle will never, in the face of foreign threats, pull in its horns or draw back into its shell.
2. Last summer, I was engaged in the repair of automobiles.
3. You're looking as bright as a button this morning.
4. My mother was called to her heavenly reward last winter.
5. My brother is in the process of pursuing a curriculum of industrial chemistry.
6. The ball's in your court, and if you strike out, don't expect me to pick up the pieces.
7. Winning first prize for her essay was a real feather in Peggy's cap.
8. Our company plans to confer retirement on 200 employees by year's end.

CHAPTER ELEVEN

The Essay Examination

Instructors use essay examinations to gauge your grasp of ideas, noting how well you apply, analyze, challenge, compare, or otherwise handle them. Facts and figures, on the other hand, are more often tested by objective examinations. Writing essay answers under pressure and with minimal time to rethink and revise differs from writing at home. Instructors expect reasonably complete and coherent answers but not models of style or neatness. They do expect legibility. An effective presentation greatly increases your chances for success; and, provided you know the material, the skills learned in composition class can help you present your answers effectively. A plan, a thesis, specific support, staying on track, and the pointers presented in this chapter—all are grade boosters.

STUDYING FOR THE EXAMINATION

Some pointers for studying:

1. Allow adequate preparation time. For a comprehensive test, start reviewing several days in advance. For one that covers a small segment of the course, a day or two should be enough.
2. Reread the key points you've marked in your class notes and textbook. Use them to develop a set of basic concepts.
3. Make up a set of sample questions related to these concepts and do some free writing to answer them. Even if none of the questions appears on the test, your efforts will ease pretest jitters and supply insights that apply to other questions.
4. Answer your questions by drawing upon your concepts and supplying details from your notes and textbook.

TYPES OF TEST QUESTIONS

Test questions differ greatly. Some instructors favor narrow, highly focused items with detailed answering instructions. Others like broad items, perhaps with simple directions such as "write for twenty minutes." The sample questions below range from very broad to very narrow.

1. Analyze the influences of the industrial revolution on European society.
2. Discuss the most important causes of the Spanish–American War.
3. Compare and contrast the David statues of Michelangelo and Bernini.
4. Select three different camera shots used in the movie *All That Jazz.* Identify at least one scene that illustrates each shot; then explain how each shot functions by describing the relationship between the shot and the action or dialogue.
5. Define the relationship between setting and meaning in Joyce's "Araby." Discuss three different settings in the story, such as North Richmond Street, the front parlor or back drawing room of the boy's house, the train, Araby as the boy imagines it, and Araby as it is. Show how each setting relates to the events and theme of the story. Unify your essay by connecting each of your points to your thesis statement.

A highly focused question such as item 5 suggests how to organize and develop the essay. If you know the answer, you can begin writing quickly. In contrast, item 1 forces you to focus and narrow the subject before you respond. A response to this type of item requires careful planning.

PREPARING TO WRITE

You can't get from Pocatello to Poughkeepsie without first consulting a map and then following the appropriate route. The same principle applies to writing an exam. Often students fail to read general directions or to answer what is asked. Low grades follow. To avoid penalizing yourself, scan the test items, noting how many must be answered in each part and which ones are optional. When you have a choice, select the questions you can answer most thoroughly. Pay attention to any suggestions or requirements concerning length (one paragraph, two pages) or relative weight (25 points, 30 minutes, 40 percent), and budget your time accordingly.

The first requirement for most essay tests is to read the question for *key words.* Does the instructor want you to analyze, compare, criticize, defend, describe, discuss, evaluate, illustrate, explain, justify, trace, or summarize? If you are asked to explain how Darwin's theory of evolution affected nineteenth-century thinking, do just that; you won't be happy with your grade if, instead, you summarize the theory. Merely putting ideas on paper, even if they are perceptive, does not substitute for addressing the question.

Indicate what each of the following questions calls for. What is required? By what methods—arguing, describing, or the like—would you develop the answer?   **EXERCISE**

1. Distinguish between mild depression and severe depression. You might focus on the nature, the symptoms, or the potential treatments of each condition.
2. Trace Owen Warland's search for values and a sense of self-worth in "The Artist of the Beautiful." Consider Owen's motivation, the methods he uses, the difficulties he confronts, and his ultimate achievement. You might also refer to characters in other stories you have read for this class in order to clarify Owen's situation.
3. Explain how to clean an automobile carburetor.
4. Briefly relate the events in the Book of Job and then explain the significance of the tale. Could the tale be called symbolic? Why or why not?

When you have the essay question clearly in mind, don't immediately start writing. A jack-rabbit start spells trouble. Instead, take a few moments to plan your answer. If you don't know your route and destination before you start writing, you jeopardize your chances for arriving at a correct response.

Follow these steps in planning your answer:

1. Prepare a thesis statement that responds to the question and will control your answer.
2. Make a rough outline that sketches the main points you'll cover and an effective order for presenting them.
3. Make a mental or written list of specific supporting details, based on required reading and lecture notes, that you can use to develop these points.

Writing an essay exam, like writing an essay, is a front-end-loaded process. Much of the brain work occurs before you put your answer on paper. You won't get to Poughkeepsie just by starting to drive.

WRITING THE EXAMINATION

If you follow the foregoing plan, you'll be able to write quickly and coherently. Position your thesis statement at the start of your answer. Make sure each paragraph is controlled by a topic sentence tied to the thesis statement, and stick to your topic as you write. Fight the impulse to jot down everything you know about the general subject. The grader doesn't want to plow through verbiage to arrive at your answer.

The following essay illustrates these guidelines.

Question:	Discuss the various appeals described by classical rhetoric that an orator can use. Give a brief example of each kind of appeal.
Answer: *Thesis statement previews focus and order of answer*	Classical rhetoric defines three major appeals—logical, emotional, and ethical—that an orator may use to win support from his audience.
Topic sentence *Example 1* *Example 2*	Most rhetoricians agree that any argument must be based on logic; that is, it must appeal to the intellect of the listeners. Unless it does, the orator will fail to convince them. For example, if a speaker who is urging the election of a candidate presents the candidate's voting record, he is appealing to logic. He asks the audience to understand that the voting record predicts how the candidate will continue to vote if elected. Likewise, if a candidate for public office describes how a tax cut will stimulate the economy and create new jobs, he is using a logical appeal.
Topic sentence *Example 1* *Example 2*	In addition to logic, emotional appeals are a powerful means of swaying people, especially groups. Though emotional appeals work along with logical appeals, they are quite different, because they are directed at the listener's hopes, fears, and sympathies. When a presidential candidate indicates that a vote for his opponent is a vote to escalate the arms race and risk nuclear holocaust, he is making an emotional appeal. So, too, is the candidate who asserts that inflation can be whipped and American industry revitalized and that our country can assume its rightful place as economic leader of the free world.
Topic sentence *Example 1* *Example 2*	The ethical appeal is more subtle than either of the other two, but probably just as important. The orator must strike the audience as a sensible, good person if they are to believe the message. Sometimes the speaker's logic and also the tone—moderate, sensible, or wise—will convey sufficient ethical appeal. At other times, a speaker will use statements that are deliberately intended to create ethical appeal. "In developing this program, I will work closely with both houses of the legislature, including the members of both political parties" and "Despite our differences, I believe my opponent to be a decent, honest person" are examples of such statements.

Restatement   In any speech, all these appeals—logical, emotional, and
of thesis   ethical—work together to convince an audience.

Student unknown

In contrast, the next two responses to the same question illustrate common faults of examination essays.

Answer A

There are three basic appeals that a speaker can make to captivate his audience. These are the ethical appeal, the logical appeal, and the emotional appeal. 1

The first of these—the ethical appeal—includes all the speaker's efforts to have his audience regard him as rational, wise, good, and generous. Needless to say, the ethical appeal is very important. Without it, no one would pay attention to the speaker's argument. 2

The second appeal—logical—is also extremely important. It carries the burden of the argument from speaker to listener and appeals to the intellect of the audience. 3

Emotional appeal—the third and final one—is made to the passions and feelings of the listeners. The significance of such an appeal is obvious. 4

A speaker often uses all three appeals to win an audience over. 5

Answer *A* starts with a thesis statement and includes brief definitions of the three appeals; however, it omits any concrete examples and includes no specific details. As a result, the significance of the emotional appeal is not "obvious," as paragraph 4 claims, nor does the answer offer any hints as to why the other appeals are important. This response resembles an outline more than an answer and suggests the student lacked the knowledge to do a good job.

Answer B

Orators may make three different kinds of appeals to win favor from an audience: emotional appeal, logical appeal, and ethical appeal. 1

Let's start with emotional appeal because this is the one that is not essential to a speech. Logical and ethical appeals are always included; emotional appeal may be used to help sway an audience, but without logical and ethical appeals no argument is accepted. This simply makes sense: if there is no logic, there is no argument; and if the speaker doesn't come across as an ethical person—someone to be relied upon—then no one will accept what he or she says. But emotional appeal is different. Unemotional arguments may be accepted. 2

Nevertheless, emotional appeal is important. It includes whatever a speaker does to move the feelings of the audience. The speaker asks, "Don't you want to protect your families?" In doing so, he or she appeals emotionally. A speaker may 3 appeal to the prejudices or biases of listeners. Someone at a Ku Klux Klan rally does that. So does a minister who exhorts people to be "saved." Both speakers address the emotions of the groups they talk to.

4   There is a very fine use of emotional appeal in the "Letter from Birmingham Jail" by Martin Luther King, Jr. At one point King asks his audience of white clergy how they would feel if, like blacks, they had to deny their children treats such as amusement parks and had to fear for the lives of their families, and so on. He also describes the bombings and burnings that blacks are subjected to. All the details move readers emotionally, so that they come to sympathize with blacks who live in fear.

5   Logical appeal, as noted earlier, is crucial. The speaker must seem to have an intelligent plan. The listeners want the plan to meet their needs.

6   The other appeal is the ethical one. It is made when a speaker makes him- or herself seem generous, good and wise.

7   All three appeals can be used in one speech, although the logical and ethical appeals are essential to it.

Although this answer opens with an acceptable thesis statement, the writer has skipped the planning stage and leaped directly into writing. Does it make sense to lead off in paragraph 2 with an appeal tagged "not essential"? And note how paragraph 2 also drifts from the emotional appeal to the other two types, despite its topic sentence. Paragraphs 3 and 4 again focus on the emotional appeal, and ironically, through specific examples, make a good case for its importance. Paragraphs 5 and 6 shortchange logical and ethical appeals, offering discussions that are too thin to convince the grader that the student understands these concepts. The essay contradicts itself: if logical and ethical appeals are the essential ones and emotional appeals "not essential," why is more than half the essay about emotional appeals?

EXERCISE   1. **Read the examination question and answer below, then answer the questions that follow the essay.**

Question

Analyze the significant relationships between imagination and reality in Coleridge's "This Lime-Tree Bower My Prison." In your answer, you might consider some of the following questions. What is the importance of setting in the poem? Is the speaker's mind a form of setting? How is reality implicitly defined in the poem? How, and through what agencies, can reality be transmitted? What relationship is finally perceived between the spiritual and the concrete? How does friendship or fellow-feeling trigger the essential insights revealed in the poem?

Answer

Coleridge's "This Lime-Tree Bower My Prison" shows imagination to be a powerful force that can control one's perception of reality and that is, in itself, a kind of reality—perhaps the most important reality. Thus, imagination and reality are more intimately linked and more similar in Coleridge's poem than they are ordinarily thought to be.

The relationship between imagination and reality is revealed by the speaker of "Lime-Tree Bower," although he doesn't openly state it. The technique for revelation is dramatic monologue, with the speaker seemingly talking spontaneously as his situation gives rise to a series of thoughts.

As the poem begins, the speaker finds himself "trapped" at home in his lime-tree bower, while his friends go on a walk he had hoped to take with them. This situation at first bothers the speaker, causing him to feel imprisoned. As the poem progresses, however, the speaker begins to imagine all the places his friends are visiting on their walk. Though he laments not being with them, he shows excitement as he describes the scenes his friends are viewing: the "roaring dell," the sea, and so on. Thus the speaker recognizes that he is able to participate imaginatively in the walk and, in doing so, to escape his "prison" reality and enter the reality of his friends.

The moment of recognition occurs at the beginning of stanza three: "A delight / Comes sudden on my heart, and I am glad / As I myself was there!" Interestingly, however, this point marks a turn in the speaker's thoughts. Once again he realizes where he actually is—the lime-tree bower. But now he appreciates its beauties. The natural beauties he imagined have taught him to appreciate the beauties of nature right before him. He has learned that there is "No plot so narrow, be but Nature there." The lime-tree bower is no longer a prison, but a rich and beautiful, if somewhat small, world.

Imagination has again shaped the speaker's perceptions of reality. It controls the perception of circumstances—whether one views a place as a prison or a microcosm of a larger world, with beauties and possibilities in its own right. The use of imagination can teach one about reality, as it has Coleridge's speaker. And, if one surrenders to it completely—as the speaker does when he envisons the world of the walkers—imagination is a delightful reality, as valid as the reality of the place in which one sits.

Imagination and reality are merged in "This Lime-Tree Bower My Prison," and though this identification is apparently temporary, one may learn through imagination how to cope with and enjoy reality. Thus, imagination is intimately involved in shaping the perception of reality.

Lori McCue

a. Which of the possible approaches suggested in the question does the student select?

b. Which of the other questions does she indirectly answer? Which ones are not addressed?

c. Identify the thesis statement and explain how it controls the answer.

d. Show how the answer demonstrates careful planning.

e. Point out some effective supporting details.

2. **Read the following answers to the examination question "What factors account for the rise of Methodism in eighteenth-century England?" Explain specifically why each answer is good or poor.**

Answer A

1   Methodism, a cult that became a religion, was founded in eighteenth-century England by John Wesley, with the aid of his brother Charles and of George Whitefield. The features of Methodism that accounted for its great success can best be understood by contrasting them with the features of Anglicanism, the state religion of England.

2   The eighteenth-century Anglican church was characterized by extreme complacency. Perhaps the religious traumas during the previous century encouraged the de-emphasizing of religious fervor that might stir up new trouble. Perhaps philosophical and scientific developments led to a decline of active interest in the church. And perhaps, finally, the new wealth and worldliness of the period worked against religious development within the state church. Whatever the reason or reasons might have been, most intellectuals and authorities were content to let the church be a quiet, social institution. Granted, the Anglican church was no place for the sort of religious enthusiasm that John Wesley tried to bring to it. But for a long time he did try to work within the church, turning his cult into a new religion only after years of effort to revitalize the Anglican church.

3   Wesley's attitudes seem somewhat contradictory; he believed in personal and immediate salvation through Christ, the sort of conversion that brought weeping, wailing, gnashing of teeth, and hysterical joy; at the same time, Wesley was a stern, ascetic individual, who did not even believe in play for children. Yet these seemingly contradictory attitudes indicate a depth of religious emotion that was out of place in the comfortable, even-keeled, socially oriented Anglican church and that was regarded with distaste by party-line clergymen.

4   Typically, Anglican clergymen were very different from Wesley and his colleagues. They were gentlemanly and, on the whole, they adopted a subdued approach in the pulpit. The Wesleys and Whitefield, on the other hand, preached provocatively, stirring the emotions more than the intellects of their audiences.

5   The typical Anglican church and churchmen appealed to educated upper- and middle-class people. And they continued to hold the allegiance of rural people, whose need for community was satisfied by their extended families, their friends, and their lifelong ties to their birthplace. But the rise of industrialism during the eighteenth century produced a large group of people to whom the spiritual and emotional community of Methodism appealed. These were the poor, uprooted individuals and nuclear families who had been forced to leave

their birthplace, migrate to crowded, unsanitary cities, and labor long hours under sweatshop conditions. They needed something to hold on to and to inspire them, but the state church spoke dispassionately and over their heads. Wesley spoke to their hearts and won them over, usually with just one sermon.

Thus, traditional needs of people, combined with new social, political, philosophical, and religious situations, encouraged the development of Methodism. For certain people in eighteenth-century England (especially poor city workers), John Wesley's religion met the needs that the dominant religion no longer satisfied.   6

Answer B

Methodism began and grew with amazing rapidity during the eighteenth century in England. It was founded by John Wesley, with the help of Charles Wesley and George Whitefield.   1

One of the factors in the rise of Methodism was the movement of many people to cities to take jobs in industry. These people were no longer secure in their surroundings and could not rely on parish priests for help. Thus, they were ripe for conversion to Methodism.   2

John Wesley was a stern man who loved organization and who could develop a strong church. He might seem grim to us because he opposed games and treats, even coming out against play for children. He believed equally strongly in salvation. He could get people to see sin and salvation as he did and thus get them to convert to his faith.   3

The Anglican church during this period was not active. People went to church, but only out of duty. Ministers were more interested in scholarship or socializing or hunting than in their jobs. Thus, the church declined.   4

Imagine hearing a moving sermon on the horrible qualities of sin or one on the joys of going to heaven. Thinking such thoughts, you can easily imagine how John Wesley's and George Whitefield's hearers felt.   5

The Age of Reason caused Methodism to rise, too. The state church was a victim in the philosophical and scientific drive toward reason. The church became reasonable. But churches are supposed to be emotional supports, and reason and faith are different ways of knowing. Methodism appealed to faith. Thus, it rose.   6

For all the reasons given above, Methodism prospered in eighteenth-century England.   7

CHAPTER TWELVE

Writing About Literature

Teachers of literature generally expect you to write about what you've read. Typically, they might ask you to

- show how an author handled one of the elements in a short story, play, or poem
- weigh several of the elements and tell what the work means
- compare the handling of a particular element in two different works
- air your reactions to some work

Writing about literary topics is rewarding in several ways. Weighing and recording your thoughts on the different elements sharpen your critical thinking ability. Literary papers pay artistic dividends, also, as careful reading and subsequent writing deepen your appreciation of the craftsmanship that permeates a short story, poem, play, essay, or novel. And a literature paper offers you yet another opportunity to apply the writing guidelines discussed in Part One. Focusing, organizing, developing—the old familiar trail leads to success here, too.

THE ELEMENTS OF LITERATURE

Most writing assignments on literature will probably feature one or more of the following elements:

Plot
Narrator and point of view
Character
Setting
Symbols
Irony
Language
Theme

Depending on the work, some of these will be more important than others. Read the following story by Stephen Crane, "The Bride Comes to Yellow Sky." The discussions that follow it point out the basic features of each element and offer useful writing suggestions.

The Bride Comes to Yellow Sky
STEPHEN CRANE

I

The great Pullman was whirling onward with such dignity of motion that a glance from the window seemed simply to prove that the plains of Texas were pouring eastward. Vast flats of green grass, dull-hued spaces of mesquit and cactus, little groups of frame houses, woods of light and tender trees, all were sweeping into the east, sweeping over the horizon, a precipice.

A newly married pair had boarded this coach at San Antonio. The man's face was reddened from many days in the wind and sun, and a direct result of his new black clothes was that his brick-colored hands were constantly performing in a most conscious fashion. From time to time he looked down respectfully at his attire. He sat with a hand on each knee, like a man waiting in a barber's shop. The glances he devoted to other passengers were furtive and shy.

The bride was not pretty, nor was she very young. She wore a dress of blue cashmere, with small reservations of velvet here and there, and with steel buttons abounding. She continually twisted her head to regard her puff sleeves, very stiff, straight, and high. They embarrassed her. It was quite apparent that she had cooked, and that she expected to cook, dutifully. The blushes caused by the careless scrutiny of some passengers as she had entered the car were strange to see upon this plain, under-class countenance, which was drawn in placid, almost emotionless lines.

They were evidently very happy. "Ever been in a parlor-car before?" he asked, smiling with delight.

"No," she answered; "I never was. It's fine, ain't it?"

"Great! And then after a while we'll go forward to the diner, and get a big lay-out. Finest meal in the world. Charge a dollar."

"Oh, do they?" cried the bride. "Charge a dollar? Why, that's too much—for us—ain't it, Jack?"

"Not this trip, anyhow," he answered bravely. "We're going to go the whole thing."

Later he explained to her about the trains. "You see, it's a thousand miles from one end of Texas to the other; and this train runs right across it and never stops but four times." He had the pride of an owner. He pointed out to her the dazzling fittings of the coach; and in truth her eyes opened wider as she contemplated the sea-green figured velvet, the shining brass, silver, and glass, the wood that gleamed as darkly brilliant as the surface of a pool of oil. At one end a bronze figure sturdily held a support for a separated chamber, and at convenient places on the ceiling were frescos in olive and silver.

To the minds of the pair, their surroundings reflected the glory of their marriage that morning in San Antonio; this was the environment of their new estate; and the man's face in particular beamed with an elation that made him appear ridiculous to the negro porter. This individual at times surveyed them from afar with an amused and superior grin. On other occasions he bullied them with skill in ways that did not make it exactly plain to them that they were being bullied. He subtly used all the manners of the most unconquerable kind of snobbery. He oppressed them; but of this oppression they had small knowledge, and they speedily forgot that infrequently a number of travellers covered them with stares of derisive enjoyment. Historically there was supposed to be something infinitely humorous in their situation.

"We are due in Yellow Sky at 3:42," he said, looking tenderly into her eyes.

"Oh, are we?" she said, as if she had not been aware of it. To evince surprise at her husband's statement was part of her wifely amiability. She took from a pocket a little silver watch; and as she held it before her, and stared at it with a frown of attention, the new husband's face shone.

"I bought it in San Anton' from a friend of mine," he told her gleefully.

"It's seventeen minutes past twelve," she said, looking up at him with a kind of shy and clumsy coquetry. A passenger, noting this play, grew excessively sardonic, and winked at himself in one of the numerous mirrors.

At last they went to the dining car. Two rows of negro waiters, in glowing white suits, surveyed their entrance with the interest, and also the equanimity, of men who had been forewarned. The pair fell to the lot of a waiter who happened to feel pleasure in steering them through their meal. He viewed them with the manner of a fatherly pilot, his countenance radiant with benevolence. The patronage, entwined with the ordinary deference, was not plain to them. And yet, as they returned to their coach, they showed in their faces a sense of escape.

To the left, miles down a long purple slope, was a little ribbon of mist where moved the keening Rio Grande. The train was approaching it at an angle, and the apex was Yellow Sky. Presently it was apparent that, as the distance from Yellow Sky grew shorter, the husband became commensurately restless. His brick-red hands were more insistent in their prominence. Occasionally he was even rather absent-minded and far-away when the bride leaned forward and addressed him.

As a matter of truth, Jack Potter was beginning to find the shadow of a deed weigh upon him like a leaden slab. He, the town marshal of Yellow Sky, a man known, liked, and feared in his corner, a prominent person, had gone to San Antonio to meet a girl he believed he loved, and there, after the usual prayers, had actually induced her to marry him, without consulting Yellow Sky for any part of the transaction. He was now bringing his bride before an innocent and unsuspecting community.

Of course people in Yellow Sky married as it pleased them, in accordance with a general custom; but such was Potter's thought of his duty to his friends, or of their idea of his duty, or of an unspoken form which does not control men in these matters, that he felt he was heinous. He had committed an extraordinary crime. Face to face with this girl in San Antonio, and spurred by his sharp impulse, he had gone headlong over all the social hedges. At San Antonio he was like a man hidden in the dark. A knife to sever any friendly duty, any form, was easy to his hand in that remote city. But the hour of Yellow Sky—the hour of daylight—was approaching.

He knew full well that his marriage was an important thing to his town. It could only be exceeded by the burning of the new hotel. His friends could not forgive him. Frequently he had reflected on the advisability of telling them by telegraph, but a new cowardice had been upon him. He feared to do it. And now the train was hurrying him toward a scene of amazement, glee, and reproach. He glanced out of the window at the line of haze swinging slowly in toward the train.

Yellow Sky had a kind of brass band, which played painfully, to the delight of the populace. He laughed without heart as he thought of it. If the citizens could dream of his prospective arrival with his bride, they would parade the band at the station and escort them, amid cheers and laughing congratulations, to his adobe home.

He resolved that he would use all the devices of speed and plainscraft in making the journey from the station to his house. Once within that safe citadel, he could issue some sort of vocal bulletin, and then not go among the citizens until they had time to wear off a little of their enthusiasm.

The bride looked anxiously at him. "What's worrying you, Jack?"

He laughed again. "I'm not worrying, girl; I'm only thinking of Yellow Sky."

She flushed in comprehension.

A sense of mutual guilt invaded their minds and developed a finer tenderness. They looked at each other, with eyes softly aglow. But Potter often laughed the same nervous laugh; the flush upon the bride's face seemed quite permanent.

The traitor to the feelings of Yellow Sky narrowly watched the speeding landscape. "We're nearly there," he said.

Presently the porter came and announced the proximity of Potter's home. He held a brush in his hand, and, with all his airy superiority gone, he brushed Potter's new clothes as the latter slowly turned this way and that way. Potter tumbled out a coin and gave it to the porter, as he had seen others do. It was a heavy and muscle-bound business, as that of a man shoeing his first horse.

The porter took their bag, and as the train began to slow they moved forward to the hooded platform of the car. Presently the two engines and their long string of coaches rushed into the station of Yellow Sky.

"They have to take water here," said Potter, from a constricted throat and in mournful cadence, as one announcing death. Before the train stopped his eye had swept the length of the platform, and he was glad and astonished to see there was none upon it but the station-agent, who, with a slightly hurried and anxious air, was walking toward the water-tanks. When the train had halted, the porter alighted first, and placed in position a little temporary step.

"Come on, girl," said Potter, hoarsely. As he helped her down they each laughed on a false note. He took the bag from the negro, and bade his wife cling to his arm. As they slunk rapidly away, his hang-dog glance perceived that they were unloading the two trunks, and also that the station-agent, far ahead near the baggage-car, had turned and was running toward him, making gestures. He laughed, and groaned as he laughed, when he noted the first effect of his marital bliss upon Yellow Sky. He gripped his wife's arm firmly to his side, and they fled. Behind them the porter stood, chuckling fatuously.

II

The California express on the Southern Railway was due at Yellow Sky in twenty-one minutes. There were six men at the bar of the Weary Gentleman saloon. One was a drummer* who talked a great deal and rapidly; three were Texans who did not care to talk at that time; and two were Mexican sheep-herders, who did not talk as a general practice in the Weary Gentleman saloon. The barkeeper's dog lay on the boardwalk that crossed in front of the door. His head was on his paws, and he glanced drowsily here and there with the constant vigilance of a dog that is kicked on occasion. Across the sandy street were some vivid green grass-plots, so wonderful in appearance, amid the sands that burned near them in a blazing sun, that they caused a doubt in the mind. They exactly resembled the grass mats used to represent lawns on the stage. At the cooler end of the railway station, a man without a coat sat in a tilted chair and smoked his pipe. The fresh-cut bank of the Rio Grande circled near the town, and there could be seen beyond it a great plum-colored plain of mesquit.

Save for the busy drummer and his companions in the saloon, Yellow Sky was dozing. The new-comer leaned gracefully upon the bar, and recited many tales with the confidence of a bard who has come upon a new field.

"—and at the moment that the old man fell downstairs with the bureau in his arms, the old woman was coming up with two scuttles of coal, and of course— "

The drummer's tale was interrupted by a young man who suddenly appeared in the open door. He cried: "Scratchy Wilson's drunk, and has turned loose with both hands." The two Mexicans at once set down their glasses and faded out of the rear entrance of the saloon.

The drummer, innocent and jocular, answered: "All right, old man. S'pose he has? Come in and have a drink, anyhow."

But the information had made such an obvious cleft in every skull in the room that the drummer was obliged to see its importance. All had become instantly solemn. "Say," said he, mystified, "what is this?" His three companions

*Traveling salesman.

made the introductory gesture of eloquent speech; but the young man at the door forestalled them.

"It means, my friend," he answered, as he came into the saloon, "that for the next two hours this town won't be a health resort."

The barkeeper went to the door, and locked and barred it; reaching out of the window, he pulled in heavy wooden shutters, and barred them. Immediately a solemn, chapel-like gloom was upon the place. The drummer was looking from one to another.

"But say," he cried, "what is this, anyhow? You don't mean there is going to be a gun-fight?"

"Don't know whether there'll be a fight or not," answered one man, grimly; "but there'll be some shootin'—some good shootin'."

The young man who had warned them waved his hand. "Oh, there'll be a fight fast enough, if any one wants it. Anybody can get a fight out there in the street. There's a fight just waiting."

The drummer seemed to be swayed between the interest of a foreigner and a perception of personal danger.

"What did you say his name was?" he asked.

"Scratchy Wilson," they answered in chorus.

"And will he kill anybody? What are you going to do? Does this happen often? Does he rampage around like this once a week or so? Can he break in that door?"

"No; he can't break down that door," replied the barkeeper. "He's tried it three times. But when he comes you'd better lay down on the floor, stranger. He's dead sure to shoot at it, and a bullet may come through."

Thereafter the drummer kept a strict eye upon the door. The time had not yet been called for him to hug the floor, but, as a minor precaution, he sidled near to the wall. "Will he kill anybody?" he said again.

The men laughed low and scornfully at the question.

"He's out to shoot, and he's out for trouble. Don't see any good in experimentin' with him."

"But what do you do in a case like this? What do you do?"

A man responded: "Why, he and Jack Potter—"

"But," in chorus the other men interrupted, "Jack Potter's in San Anton'."

"Well, who is he? What's he got to do with it?"

"Oh, he's the town marshal. He goes out and fights Scratchy when he gets on one of these tears."

"Wow!" said the drummer, mopping his brow. "Nice job he's got."

The voices had toned away to mere whisperings. The drummer wished to ask further questions, which were born of an increasing anxiety and bewilderment; but when he attempted them, the men merely looked at him in irritation and motioned him to remain silent. A tense waiting hush was upon them. In the deep shadows of the room their eyes shone as they listened for sounds from the street. One man made three gestures at the barkeeper; and the latter, moving like a ghost, handed him a glass and a bottle. The man poured a full glass of whisky, and set down the bottle noiselessly. He gulped the whisky in a swallow, and turned again toward the door in immovable silence. The drummer saw that the barkeeper, without a sound, had taken a Winchester from beneath the bar. Later he saw this individual beckoning to him, so he tiptoed across the room.

"You better come with me back of the bar."

"No, thanks," said the drummer, perspiring; "I'd rather be where I can made a break for the back door."

Whereupon the man of bottles made a kindly but peremptory gesture. The drummer obeyed it, and, finding himself seated on a box with his head below the level of the bar, balm was laid upon his soul at sight of various zinc and copper fittings that bore a resemblance to armorplate. The barkeeper took a seat comfortably upon an adjacent box.

"You see," he whispered, "this here Scratchy Wilson is a wonder with a gun—a perfect wonder; and when he goes on the wartrail, we hunt our holes—naturally. He's about the last one of the old gang that used to hang out along the river here. He's a terror when he's drunk. When he's sober he's all right—kind of simple—wouldn't hurt a fly—nicest fellow in town. But when he's drunk—whoo!"

There were periods of stillness. "I wish Jack Potter was back from San Anton'," said the barkeeper. "He shot Wilson up once—in the leg—and he would sail in and pull out the kinks in this thing."

Presently they heard from a distance the sound of a shot, followed by three wild yowls. It instantly removed a bond from the men in the darkened saloon. There was a shuffling of feet. They looked at each other. "Here he comes," they said.

III

A man in a maroon-colored flannel shirt, which had been purchased for purposes of decoration, and made principally by some Jewish women on the East Side of New York, rounded a corner and walked into the middle of the main street of Yellow Sky. In either hand the man held a long, heavy, blue-black revolver. Often he yelled, and these cries rang through a semblance of a deserted village, shrilly flying over the roofs in a volume that seemed to have no relation to the ordinary vocal strength of a man. It was as if the surrounding stillness formed the arch of a tomb over him. These cries of ferocious challenge rang against walls of silence. And his boots had red tops with gilded imprints, of the kind beloved in winter by little sledding boys on the hillsides of New England.

The man's face flamed in a rage begot of whisky. His eyes, rolling, and yet keen for ambush, hunted the still doorways and windows. He walked with the creeping movement of the midnight cat. As it occurred to him, he roared menacing information. The long revolvers in his hands were as easy as straws; they were moved with an electric swiftness. The little fingers of each hand played sometimes in a musician's way. Plain from the low collar of the shirt, the cords of his neck straightened and sank, straightened and sank, as passion moved him. They only sounds were his terrible invitations. The calm adobes preserved their demeanor at the passing of this small thing in the middle of the street.

There was no offer of fight—no offer of fight. The man called to the sky. There were no attractions. He bellowed and fumed and swayed his revolvers here and everywhere.

The dog of the barkeeper of the Weary Gentleman saloon had not appreciated the advance of events. He yet lay dozing in front of his master's door. At sight of the dog, the man paused and raised his revolver humorously. At sight of the man, the dog sprang up and walked diagonally away, with a sullen head, and growling. The man yelled, and the dog broke into a gallop. As it was about to enter an alley, there was a loud noise, a whistling, and something spat the ground directly before it. The dog screamed, and, wheeling in terror, galloped headlong in a new direction. Again there was a noise, a whistling, and sand was kicked viciously before it. Fear-stricken, the dog turned and flurried like an animal in a pen. The man stood laughing, his weapons at his hips.

Ultimately the man was attracted by the closed door of the Weary Gentleman saloon. He went to it and, hammering with a revolver, demanded drink.

The door remaining imperturbable, he picked a bit of paper from the walk, and nailed it to the framework with a knife. He then turned his back contemptuously upon this popular resort and, walking to the opposite side of the street and spinning there on his heel quickly and lithely, fired at the bit of paper. He missed it by a half-inch. He swore at himself, and went away. Later he comfortably fusilladed the windows of his most intimate friend. The man was playing with this town; it was a toy for him.

But still there was no offer of fight. The name of Jack Potter, his ancient antagonist, entered his mind, and he concluded that it would be a glad thing if he should go to Potter's house, and by bombardment induce him to come out and fight. He moved in the direction of his desire, chanting Apache scalp-music.

When he arrived at it, Potter's house presented the same still front as had the other adobes. Taking up a strategic position, the man howled a challenge. But this house regarded him as might a great stone god. It gave no sign. After a decent wait, the man howled further challenges, mingling with them wonderful epithets.

Presently there came the spectacle of a man churning himself into deepest rage over the immobility of a house. He fumed at it as the winter wind attacks a prairie cabin in the North. To the distance there should have gone the sound of a tumult like the fighting of two hundred Mexicans. As necessity bade him, he paused for breath or to reload his revolvers.

IV

Potter and his bride walked sheepishly and with speed. Sometimes they laughed together shamefacedly and low.

"Next corner, dear," he said finally.

They put forth the efforts of a pair walking bowed against a strong wind. Potter was about to raise a finger to point the first appearance of the new home when, as they circled the corner, they came face to face with a man in a maroon-colored shirt, who was feverishly pushing cartridges into a large revolver. Upon the instant the man dropped his revolver to the ground and, like lightning, whipped another from its holster. The second weapon was aimed at the bridegroom's chest.

There was a silence. Potter's mouth seemed to be merely a grave for his tongue. He exhibited an instinct to at once loosen his arm from the woman's grip, and he dropped the bag to the sand. As for the bride, her face had gone as yellow as old cloth. She was a slave to hideous rites, gazing at the apparitional snake.

The two men faced each other at a distance of three paces. He of the revolver smiled with a new and quiet ferocity.

"Tried to sneak up on me," he said. "Tried to sneak up on me!" His eyes grew more baleful. As Potter made a slight movement, the man thrust his revolver venomously forward. "No; don't you do it, Jack Potter. Don't you move a finger toward a gun just yet. Don't you move an eyelash. The time has come for me to settle with you, and I'm goin' to do it my own way, and loaf along with no interferin'. So if you don't want a gun bent on you, just mind what I tell you."

Potter looked at his enemy. "I ain't got a gun on me, Scratchy," he said. "Honest, I ain't." He was stiffening and steadying, but yet somewhere at the back of his mind a vision of the Pullman floated: the seagreen figured velvet, the shining brass, silver, and glass, the wood that gleamed as darkly brilliant as the surface of a pool of oil—all the glory of the marriage, the environment of the new estate. "You know I fight when it comes to fighting, Scratchy Wilson; but I ain't got a gun on me. You'll have to do all the shootin' yourself."

His enemy's face went livid. He stepped forward, and lashed his weapon to and fro before Potter's chest. "Don't tell me you ain't got no gun on you, you whelp. Don't tell me no lie like that. There ain't a man in Texas ever seen you without no gun. Don't take me for no kid." His eyes blazed with light, and his throat worked like a pump.

"I ain't takin' you for no kid," answered Potter. His heels had not moved an inch backward. "I'm takin' you for a damn fool. I tell you I ain't got a gun, and I ain't. If you're goin' to shoot me up, you better begin now, you'll never get a chance like this again."

So much enforced reasoning had told on Wilson's rage; he was calmer. "If you ain't got a gun, why ain't you got a gun?" he sneered. "Been to Sunday-school?"

"I ain't got a gun because I've just come from San Anton' with my wife. I'm married," said Potter. "And if I'd thought there was going to be any galoots like you prowling around when I brought my wife home, I'd had a gun, and don't you forget it."

"Married!" said Scratchy, not at all comprehending.

"Yes, married. I'm married," said Potter, distinctly.

"Married?" said Scratchy. Seemingly for the first time, he saw the drooping, drowning woman at the other man's side. "No!" he said. He was like a creature allowed a glimpse of another world. He moved a pace backward, and his arm, with the revolver, dropped to his side. "Is this the lady?" he asked.

"Yes; this is the lady," answered Potter.

There was another period of silence.

"Well," said Wilson at last, slowly, "I s'pose it's all off now."

"It's all off if you say so, Scratchy. You know I didn't make the trouble." Potter lifted his valise.

"Well, I 'low it's off, Jack," said Wilson. He was looking at the ground. "Married!" He was not a student of chivalry; it was merely that in the presence of this foreign condition he was a simple child of the earlier plains. He picked up his starboard revolver, and, placing both weapons in their holsters, he went away. His feet made funnel-shaped tracks in the heavy sand.

PLOT

Plot is the series of events that moves a narrative along. The opening of a story with a conventional plot introduces important characters and sets the stage for what happens. Then one or more conflicts develop, some pitting person against person, others setting characters against society, nature, fate or themselves. Action gradually builds to a climax, where events take a decisive turn. The ending can do a number of things—clear up unanswered questions, hint at the future, state a theme, or reestablish some sort of relationship between two foes. In "The Bride," Potter experiences two conflicts: one with Scratchy Wilson and the other within himself over his marriage. The climax comes when Potter and Scratchy meet face to face, and Scratchy learns about his old adversary's marriage. As Scratchy walks away, we sense that the two old foes have had their last confrontation, that Potter's marriage has altered forever the relationship between them.

Not every plot follows such a clear line. Many modern works lack distinct plot divisions and focus on psychological rather than physical conflicts. In extreme cases, writers may abandon the traditional plot structure entirely and present events in a disorganized sequence that helps accomplish some literary purpose, such as reflecting a character's disturbed state of mind. As you might expect, these works are much harder to read and interpret than those with strong, conventional plots.

A poem sometimes includes a series of actions and events, as Edgar Allan Poe's "Annabel Lee" illustrates.

Annabel Lee

It was many and many a year ago,
  In a kingdom by the sea,
That a maiden there lived whom you may know
  By the name of Annabel Lee;—
And this maiden she lived with no other thought
  Than to love and be loved by me.

I was a child and she was a child,
　　In this kingdom by the sea,
But we loved with a love that was more than love—
　　I and my Annabel Lee—
With a love that the wingèd seraphs of Heaven
　　Coveted her and me.

And this was the reason that, long ago,
　　In this kingdom by the sea,
A wind blew out of a cloud by night
　　Chilling my Annabel Lee;
So that her highborn kinsman came
　　And bore her away from me
To shut her up in a sepulcher
　　In this kingdom by the sea.

The angels, not half so happy in heaven,
　　Went envying her and me:—
Yes! that was the reason (as all men know,
　　In this kingdom by the sea)
That the wind came out of the clouds, chilling
　　And killing my Annabel Lee.

But our love it was stronger by far than the love
　　Of those who were older than we—
　　Of many far wiser than we—
And neither the angels in heaven above
　　Nor the demons down under the sea
Can ever dissever my soul from the soul
　　Of the beautiful Annabel Lee:—

For the moon never beams without bringing me dreams
　　Of the beautiful Annabel Lee;
And the stars never rise but I feel the bright eyes
　　Of the beautiful Annabel Lee;
And so, all the night-tide, I lie down by the side
Of my darling, my darling, my life and my bride,
　　In her sepulcher there by the sea,
　　In her tomb by the side of the sea.

Most poems, however, move from image to image, building statements that constitute their meaning, rather than tell a classically plotted story.

When writing about plot, don't merely repeat what happens. Instead, you might show how the action affects a character, shapes a conflict, or helps the writer reveal a theme.

As you read, note any incidents that seem important and how they relate to your topic. If the story seems disjointed and incoherent, rearrange the events so that they make sense and ask yourself why the writer chose that sequence. To mirror the main character's disordered state of mind? To show that life is chaotic and almost impossible to understand?

Don't overlook any instances of foreshadowing, a technique by which the writer hints at later developments, thus creating interest and building suspense. In H. H. Munro's short story "The Open Window," a visitor to a country house observes that "An undefinable something about the room seemed to suggest masculine habitation." Yet he accepts the story of a young girl that her uncle, the man of the house, had lost his life in a bog three years before. Because he ignores his observation and accepts the girl's story at face value, the visitor is terrified by the sudden appearance of the uncle, who seems to be a ghost. The careful reader, however, senses what's coming and enjoys the trick more for having been in on it.

Note any plot weakness. A character's actions might run counter to his or her personality, or they might not fit the situation. Or a writer might rely excessively on chance or coincidence to resolve a conflict or problem. O. Henry's "The Gift of the Magi" illustrates improbable coincidence. A young wife and husband each have a prized possession: she, her beautiful hair; he, a gold watch. To buy a chain and fob for her husband's watch, the wife sells her hair. At the same time, the husband sells his watch and uses the money to buy a set of fancy combs for his wife's hair. This double coincidence weakens the plot and damages the story's credibility with perceptive readers. Coincidence can help a writer make a point, however, as it does when it's used to show that chance rules human affairs.

EXERCISE   **In a short story with a strong plot line, identify conflicts and climax and tell what the ending does.**

NARRATOR AND POINT OF VIEW

The point of view of a literary work is the vantage point from which the writer views the events. A writer may adopt either a first-person or a third-person point of view. In *first-person* narration, someone in the work tells what happens and is identified by words like *I, me, mine,* and *my.* A *third-person* narrator stays completely out of the story and is never mentioned in any way. "The Bride Comes to Yellow Sky" illustrates third-person narration.

Both first-person and third-person narration have several variants, each with its own special purpose. Of these variants, five are particularly important for fiction.

The most common form of first-person narration features a narrator who takes part in the action. This technique puts the readers directly on the scene and is excellent for tracing the growth or deterioration of a character. Instead of participating in the action, the narrator may view it from the sideline, an approach that preserves on-the-scene directness and allows the narrator to comment on the characters and issues in conflict.

Most third-person narratives reveal the thoughts of just one character, usually the main one. Like the first-person-as-participant, this type of narrative can be used to trace changes in character. Third-person narration, however, can rove freely over the whole literary landscape and report directly upon events that a first-person narrator would know only by hearsay. Instead of presenting just one character's thoughts, a third-person narrator can enter the minds of two, several, or all of the characters. This technique allows the writer to contrast two or more sets of thoughts and feelings and draw some general conclusions from them. Finally, the narrator may, like a motion picture camera, move about and record only what happens and what the characters say, not entering anyone's head. Stories with surprise endings often use this technique.

Begin any discussion of point of view by establishing which one the writer has used and, if it's third-person, how many minds the narrator enters. Then think about possible reasons for the writer's choice. For example, an author might use the first person to show a character's mental deterioration. A third-person narrator might enter two minds to contrast opposing attitudes toward some incident or enter no minds at all, in order to heighten the emotional impact of a story's climax.

First-person narrators are sometimes unreliable; that is, they offer the reader a warped view of things. To gauge reliability, compare the narrator's version of the facts with what the work otherwise reveals. The narrator may come off as stupid, psychologically warped, or too biased to view events fairly. If so, speculate on the reasons. A mentally unreliable narrator may be meant to heighten the horror of events, a highly biased one to point up the folly of prejudice.

As you proceed, try to pinpoint a character who seems to reflect the writer's outlook—someone probably sympathetic, thoughtful, and mature. In third-person narratives, typically this will be someone whose thoughts are presented in detail. In first-person narratives, it's usually the "I" who relates the events, unless that person is unreliable. When no one's thoughts are given, determine the writer's outlook from the other elements of the work.

If a point of view seems unsuitable, say so and suggest why. Suppose a man is planning an elopement that will create a surprise ending. A point of view that revealed the man's thoughts would give away that ending.

Read the following two excerpts and answer the questions that follow them.

He had burned several times to enlist. Tales of great movements shook the land. . . . He had read of marches, sieges, conflicts, and he had longed to see it all. His busy mind had drawn for him large pictures, extravagant with color, lurid with breathless deeds.

But his mother had discouraged him. She had affected to look with some contempt on the quality of his war ardor and patriotism. She would calmly seat herself, and with no apparent difficulty give him many hundreds of reasons why he was of vastly more importance on the farm than he was on the field of battle. She had had certain ways of expression that told him that her statements on the subject came from a deep conviction. Moreover, on her side, was his belief that her ethical motive in the argument was impregnable.

Stephen Crane, *The Red Badge of Courage*

Daddy helped me up onto the line and we hurried home. He said, "That was strange. What train was that, I wonder? And I didn't know the driver either." Then he didn't say any more.

I was shaking all over. That had been for me—for my sake. I guessed what it meant. It was all the fear which would come to me, all the unknowns; all that Daddy didn't know about and couldn't save me from. That was how the world would be for me. . . .

Pär Lagerkvist, "Father and I"

1. In Crane's third-person stance, the narrator enters the son's mind but not the mother's. How does he convey the mother's attitude toward her son's desire to enlist?
2. What does Lagerkvist accomplish by using the first-person point of view?

CHARACTER

Characters are the people in a literary work. Some characters play leading roles, while others back them by doing such things as furnishing humor, acting as narrators, presenting needed information, highlighting main characters by contrast, or simply peopling the landscape. In "The Bride," the drummer helps Crane funnel information to the reader. He asks questions, the bartender answers them, and the reader learns all about Scratchy.

Writers present character in several ways. Some tell the reader point-blank that a person is brave, stupid, self-serving, or the like. But most authors take an indirect approach by indicating how their characters look and act, what they think and say, how they live, and how other characters regard them. Sometimes, of course, one character may misjudge another.

In picturing Potter, Crane first notes his appearance and self-conscious behavior, then delves into his mind to show the turmoil his marriage has stirred. Somewhat later, the bartender adds his brushstrokes to Potter's portrait. At the confrontation, we again observe Potter's thoughts and behavior, as well as what he says to Scratchy. From all this, Potter emerges not as a mere stick figure lawman but as someone with a recognizably lifelike personality.

Some characters remain static; others mature, gain insight, or deteriorate in some telling way. Potter changes. As the story unfolds he abandons his doubts about the course he's charted and ends up fully committed to "the environment of the new estate." Scratchy, on the other hand, ends just as he started, "a simple child of the earlier plains."

A good character analysis identifies the character's role and explains how the author reveals personality. Usually you'll write about the main character, but on occasion you might choose the chief antagonist or some minor character. For a lesser character, point out how that individual interacts with the main character.

Note whether the character changes or remains static. Most main characters change; most lesser ones do not. But sometimes a main character remains frozen, allowing the writer to make an important point. To show that a certain social group suffers from paralysis of the will, an author might create a main character who begins and ends weak and ineffectual. Whatever the situation, when you determine what purpose your character serves, tell the reader.

Think hard about your character's credibility. Ask yourself if he or she is true to life. Cruel stepmothers, brilliant but eccentric detectives, mad scientists, masked seekers after justice—these and other stereotyped figures don't square with real-life people, who are complex mixtures of many traits. Inconsistent acts or unexplained and unmotivated personality changes don't ring true: most people behave the same in similar situations and change only when properly motivated. Not every character needs to be a full-dress creation, but all require enough development to justify their roles.

Write a paragraph describing the personality of the character in the following passage.   **EXERCISE**

The thousand injuries of Fortunato I had borne as I best could, but when he ventured upon insult, I vowed revenge. You, who so well know the nature of my soul, will not suppose, however, that I gave utterance to a threat. *At length* I would be avenged; this was a point definitely settled—but the very definiteness with which it was resolved precluded the idea of risk. I must not only punish, but punish with impunity. A wrong is unredressed when retribution overtakes its redresser. It is equally unredressed when the avenger fails to make himself felt as such to the one who has done the wrong.

Edgar Allan Poe, "The Cask of Amontillado"

SETTING

Setting locates characters in a time, place, and culture so they can think, feel, and act against this background. Writers can generate feelings and moods by describing settings. Sunny spring landscapes signal hope or happiness, dark alleys are foreboding, and thunderstorms suggest violent possibilities. Poetry, especially, uses setting to create mood. In the sonnet "Composed upon Westminster Bridge," William Wordsworth evokes the serenity and grandeur of London as the sun breaks over the sleeping city:

Earth has not anything to show more fair:
Dull would he be of soul who could pass by
A sight so touching in its majesty:
This city now doth, like a garment, wear
The beauty of the morning: silent, bare,
Ships, towers, domes, theaters, and temples lie
Open unto the fields, and to the sky;
All bright and glittering in the smokeless air.
Never did sun more beautifully steep
In his first splendor, valley, rock, or hill;
Ne'er saw I, never felt, a calm so deep!
The river glideth at his own sweet will:
Dear God! the very houses seem asleep;
And all that mighty heart is lying still!

Setting can also help reveal character. In this excerpt from Sinclair Lewis's novel *Babbitt,* the contents and atmosphere of the library mirror the stiff, self-satisfied formality of its banker-owner:

. . . The books were most of them standard sets, with the correct and traditional touch of dim blue, dim gold, and glossy calf-skin. The fire was exactly correct and traditional; a small, quiet, steady fire, reflected by polished fire-irons. The oak desk was dark and altogether perfect; the chairs were gently supercilious.

Shifts in setting often trigger shifts in a character's emotional or psychological state. Jack Potter, typically calm and assured in Yellow Sky, displays great awkwardness and embarrassment in the unfamiliar environment of the Pullman car.

Settings sometimes function as symbols, reinforcing the workings of the other elements. A broad, slowly flowing river may stand for time or fate, a craggy cliff for strength of character, a blizzard-swept plain for the overwhelming power of nature. The following section, a discussion of symbols, points out some symbolic settings in "The Bride."

When you analyze setting, note the geographical region and particular spots where the events unfold, as well as the occupations, life-styles, and social positions of the characters. Then try to establish connections between settings and characters. If an emotionally barren individual always appears against backdrops of gloomy furnished rooms, cheerless restaurants, and decaying slums, you can assume that the writer is using setting to convey character. Look for links between changes in characters and changes in settings. If the setting remains the same, point out any shifts in the way the character views it.

Check the impact of setting on mood by seeing how well the two match up for each setting. Sometimes, as in "The Bride," the two bear little or no relationship to each other. In other cases, the two intertwine throughout the work.

Occasionally, a writer drums home settings so insistently that they overpower the characters and story line. A novel about the super rich may linger so lovingly over their extravagant surroundings that the plot lacks force and the characters seem mere puppets. If the setting hobbles the other elements, identify this flaw in your analysis.

EXERCISE

What mood does the following description of a room generate? What does it suggest about the situation of the room's inhabitants, two women in an Old Ladies' Home?

Marian stood enclosed by a bed, a washstand, and a chair; the tiny room had altogether too much furniture. Everything smelled wet—even the bare floor. She held onto the back of the chair, which was wicker and felt soft and damp. . . . How dark it was! The window shade was down, and the only door was shut. Marian looked at the ceiling. . . . It was like being caught in a robbers' cave. . . .

Eudora Welty, "A Visit of Charity"

SYMBOLS

To strengthen and deepen their messages, writers use symbols: names, persons, objects, places, colors, or actions that have a significance beyond their surface meaning. A symbol may be very obvious—as a name like Mr. Grimm, suggesting the person's character—or quite subtle, as an object representing a universal human emotion.

Some symbols are private and others conventional. A private symbol has special significance within a literary work but not outside it. Conventional symbols are deeply rooted in our culture, and almost everyone knows what they represent. We associate crosses with Christianity and limousines with wealth and power. In "The Bride," the plains pouring eastward past the Pullman windows, Scratchy's eastern clothing, and the mirage-like grass plots in front of the saloon are all private symbols that stand for the passing of the Old West. Because people of Crane's time associated Pullman cars with an urbane, eastern life-style, the Pullman is a conventional symbol that represents the new order of things. Like the Pullman, a symbol may appear more than once in a literary work.

Whether or not a recurring item is a symbol depends upon its associations. In Ernest Hemingway's novel *A Farewell to Arms,* rain may fairly be said to symbolize doom because it consistently accompanies disasters, and one of the main characters says that she has visions of herself lying dead in the rain. But if rain is randomly associated with a rundown lakeside resort, a spirited business meeting, a cozy weekend, and the twentieth-anniversary celebration of a happy marriage, the writer probably intends no symbolism.

Because symbols wear so many guises and mean so many things, don't start to write without first reviewing the literary work thoroughly. Look for anything that seems to have a subterranean meaning. You might, for example, discover that the cracked walls of a crumbling mansion symbolize some character's disordered mental state or that a voyage symbolizes the human journey from birth to death. Several symbols often mean the same thing; writers frequently use them in sets. In "Bartleby the Scrivener," for instance, Herman Melville uses windows that look upon walls, a folding screen, and a prison to symbolize Bartleby's alienated condition; that is, his mental separation from those around him.

Sometimes a symbol changes meaning during the course of a work. A woman who regards her lover's large, strong hands as symbols of passion may, following an illness that leaves him a dangerous madman, view them as symbols of danger and brute strength. Note any changes you discover, and suggest what they signify.

A word of caution: don't go on a witch hunt for symbols. Before you assert that something has a different and deeper meaning than its surface application, make sure evidence in the work backs your claim.

EXERCISE   **Read the following excerpts from Edward Fitzgerald's *The Rubáiyát of Omar Khayyám* and answer the questions that follow.**

> Strange, is it not? that of the myriads who
> Before us passed the door of Darkness through,
> Not one returns to tell us of the Road,
> Which to discover we must travel too.

The Moving Finger writes; and, having writ,
Moves on: nor all your Piety nor Wit
Shall lure it back to cancel half a line,
Nor all your Tears wash out a Word of it.

1. What does the door of Darkness symbolize? The Road? The Moving Finger?
2. What messages are these symbols meant to convey?

IRONY

Irony features some discrepancy, some difference between appearance and reality, expectation and outcome. Sometimes a character says one thing but means something else. The critic who, tongue in cheek, says that a clumsy dancer is "poetry in motion" speaks ironically.

Irony also results when the reader or a character recognizes something as important, but another character does not. In "The Bride" this situation occurs when Potter, not knowing that Scratchy is on a rampage, flees the station agent who tries to let him know. A character's behavior sometimes offers ironic contrasts, too. There's high irony in the contrast between Potter's unflinching face-off with Scratchy and his fear of telling the townsfolk about his marriage.

At times the ending of a work doesn't square with what the reader expects: the confrontation between Potter and Scratchy ends not in a fusillade of bullets but a flurry of words. To add to the irony, Potter wins because he is armed with a new and unfamiliar weapon—his wife. The emotional impact of an ironic ending depends upon the circumstances of plot and character. As Scratchy walks off, we're likely to view matters with amusement. In other cases, we might register joy, horror, gloom, or almost anything else.

In probing for irony, check for statements that say one thing and mean something else, situations in which one character knows something that another doesn't, and contrasts between the ways characters should and do behave. Review the plot to see whether the outcome matches the expectations. For each example you find, tell the reader what the irony accomplishes.

Discuss the irony in this poem. What emotion is the writer trying to evoke?   **EXERCISE**

Do Not Weep, Maiden, For War Is Kind
STEPHEN CRANE

Do not weep, maiden, for war is kind.
Because your lover threw wild hands toward the sky
And the affrighted steed ran on alone,

Do not weep.
War is kind.

Hoarse, booming drums of the regiment,
Little souls who thirst for fight,
These men were born to drill and die.
The unexplained glory flies above them,

Great is the battle-god, great, and his kingdom—
A field where a thousand corpses lie.

Do not weep, babe, for war is kind.
Because your father tumbled in the yellow trenches,
Raged at his breast, gulped and died,
Do not weep.
War is kind.

Swift blazing flag of the regiment,
Eagle with crest of red and gold,
These men were born to drill and die.
Point for them the virtue of slaughter,
Make plain to them the excellence of killing
And a field where a thousand corpses lie.

Mother whose heart hung humble as a button
On the bright splendid shroud of your son,
Do not weep.
War is kind.

LANGUAGE

Imaginative literature relies heavily on images, figures of speech, and tone to add vividness to the writing and convey the author's attitudes.

Images. An image is a vivid representation of a person, object, scene, or action. Unlike a symbol, an image has no meaning beyond itself. In this excerpt from "When Lilacs Last in the Dooryard Bloomed," Walt Whitman summons up an unforgettable series of images as he describes the journey of Abraham Lincoln's body to its final resting place.

Coffin that passes through lanes and streets,
Through day and night with the great cloud darkening the land,
With the pomp of the inlooped flags with the cities draped in black,
With the show of the States themselves as of crepe-veiled women standing,
With processions long and winding and the flambeaus of the night,
With the countless torches lit, with the silent sea of faces and the unbared heads,

With the waiting depot, the arriving coffin, and the somber faces,
With dirges through the night, with the thousand voices rising strong and solemn,
With all the mournful voices of the dirges poured around the coffin,
The dim-lit churches and the shuddering organs—where amid these you jour-
    ney,
With the tolling tolling bells' perpetual clang,
Here, coffin that slowly passes,
I give you my sprig of lilac.

Fiction writers also draw heavily upon images. Crane, a master of im-
agery, sprinkles them through "The Bride." Noteworthy examples occur when
he describes the Pullman car, the view from the saloon, and the rampaging
Scratchy. Images add sharpness and force to descriptions of characters and
settings.

Figures of Speech.   As Chapter Ten notes, these expressions use language in
a nonliteral sense to create special images. Writers rely particularly on three
figures: similes, metaphors, and personification. Similes and metaphors compare unlike things, the first by using *like* or *as*, the second by indicating, directly
or indirectly, that one thing *is* another. Personification assigns human qualities
to something nonhuman.

Figures of speech crowd the stanzas of poetry. Here are two similes from
Robert Burns's "A Red, Red Rose."

O my Luve's like a red, red rose,
    That's newly sprung in June:
O my Luve's like the melodie
    That's sweetly play'd in tune.

And John Crowe Ransom uses these metaphors to describe a dead boy in his
poem of the same title.

A black cloud full of storms too hot for keeping,
A sword beneath his mother's heart . . .

Figurative language looms large in prose as well as in poetry. Crane took
the same delight in figurative language that he did in ordinary images, and he
used it brilliantly in "The Bride." Potter's marriage weighs upon him "like a
leaden slab." When he tips the porter, the transaction is "a heavy and muscle-
bound business, as that of a man shoeing his first horse." During Scratchy's
passage through town, the "calm adobes" maintain their usual demeanor. The
first two examples are similes; the last is a personification. Like images, they
add strength and sparkle to Crane's prose.

Tone.   The tone of a work reflects the writer's attitude toward characters, setting, events, and theme. Grim, angry, cheerful, sarcastic, playful, haughty—these are but some of the tones a writer may adopt. Algernon Swinburne's attitude is one of weariness verging on despair in this excerpt from "The Garden of Proserpine":

> I am tired of tears and laughter,
>   And men that laugh and weep;
> Of what may come hereafter
>   For men that sow to reap:
> I am weary of days and hours,
> Blown buds of barren flowers,
> Desires and dreams and powers
>   And everything but sleep.

In "The Bride," Crane adopts a lighthearted tone by poking fun at his characters and by exaggerating. All of them, major and minor, cut ludicrous figures at one point or another: the nervous newlyweds on the train, the men huddling in the Weary Gentleman saloon, the raging, drunken Scratchy. Potter exaggerates when he regards his marriage as "heinous . . an extraordinary crime." The tumult Scratchy creates in front of Potter's door resembles "the fighting of two hundred Mexicans." This tone anticipates and supports the burlesque confrontation, which mocks the shootouts that ended so many western tales of Crane's time.

Begin a language analysis by examining the writer's use of sensory impressions. Look for passages that arouse sensations of sight, smell, hearing, taste, and touch. Note whether the author gains these effects through images, similes, metaphors, or personifications and why he or she wanted a strong sensory impact. Try to identify the tone and the reason the writer used it. For example, an author may give an unsympathetic first-person narrator a sarcastic tone to generate sympathy for a "good" character. Note any shift in tone and ask yourself why. Has the author shifted from one character to another? Has the character grown and matured?

EXERCISE   **Characterize the tone of the following passage and supply reasons for your answer.**

He closed the trap door shut. The flashlight, snapped on, was company enough. Yes, here was all of Time compressed in a Japanese paper flower. At the touch of memory, everything would unfold into the clear water of the mind, in beautiful blooms, in spring breezes, larger than life. Each of the bureau drawers slid forth, might contain aunts and cousins and grandmamas, ermined in dust. Yes, Time was here. You could feel it breathing, an atmospheric instead of a mechanical clock. . . . It was indeed a great machine of Time, this attic, he knew, he felt, he was sure, and if you touched prisms here, doorknobs there, plucked tassels, chimed crystals, swirled dust, punched trunk hasps and gusted the vox humana of the old hearth bellows until it puffed the soot of a thousand ancient fires into your eyes, if, indeed, you played this instrument, this warm machine of parts, if you fondled all of its bits and pieces, its levers and changers and movers, then, then, *then!*

Ray Bradbury, "A Scent of Sarsaparilla"

THEME

The theme of a literary work is its controlling idea—some point it makes. On occasion, the writer or a character states the theme directly. Mrs. Alving, the main character in Henrik Ibsen's play *Ghosts,* notes that the dead past plays a powerful and evil role in shaping human lives.

> . . . I am half inclined to think that we are all ghosts, Mr. Manders. It is not only what we have inherited from our fathers and mothers that exists again in us, but all sorts of old dead ideas and all kinds of old dead beliefs and things of that kind. They are not actually alive in us; but there they are dormant, all the same, and we can never be rid of them. Whenever I pick up a newspaper and read it, I fancy I see ghosts creeping between the lines. . . . They must be as countless as the grains of sand, it seems to me. And we are so miserably afraid of the light, all of us.

But direct statements are the exception, not the rule. To determine the writer's point, play detective and examine the other elements for clues. Crane never tells us that the theme of "The Bride" is the passing of the Old West, the replacement of anarchy with civilization, and the impact of the change on those who experience it. We can, however, deduce it by analyzing such things as the story's settings and symbols and the behavior of its characters—of Potter, who adapts to the new order, and Scratchy Wilson, who doesn't.

Begin any discussion of theme by determining whether the narrator or a character states the theme directly. If not, examine the characters, events, setting, symbols, and other elements and then explain how they create the theme. If there is a statement, show how the other elements support it.

Let's see how the elements of Nathaniel Hawthorne's short story "Young Goodman Brown" work together to yield the theme. The story has four characters—Goodman Brown; his wife, Faith; Deacon Gookin; and Goody

Cloyse—whose names symbolically suggest that they are completely good. Another symbol, Faith's pink hair ribbon, at first suggests innocence and later its loss. The story relates Brown's nighttime journey into a forest at the edge of a Puritan village and subsequent attendance at a baptismal ceremony for new converts to the Devil. He proceeds into the forest, suggestive of mystery and lawlessness, during a dark night, suggestive of evil, where he meets his guide, the Devil in the guise of his grandfather. As he proceeds, Goodman vacillates between reluctance to join the Devil's party and fascination with it. Innocent and ignorant, he is horrified when he finds that the deacon and Goody seem to be in league with the Devil. Goodman tries to preserve his pure image of his wife, Faith, but her pink ribbon falls out of a tumultuous sky seemingly filled with demons, and Goodman sees her at the baptismal ceremony. He shrieks out to her to "resist the wicked one" and is suddenly alone in the woods, not knowing whether she obeyed. The end of the story finds Brown back in his village, unable to view his wife and neighbors as anything but totally evil.

In light of these happenings, it's probably safe to say that the theme of the story is somewhat as follows:

> Human beings are a mixture of good and evil, but some individuals can't accept this fact. Once they realize that "good" people are susceptible to sin, they decide that everyone is evil, and they become embittered for life.

Point out any thematic weakness that you find. Including a completely innocent major character in a story written to show that people are mixtures of good and evil would contradict the writer's intention.

EXERCISE   **Ralph Waldo Emerson's "Days" offers an observation on how people should occupy their time. Read the poem carefully, checking any unfamiliar words in your dictionary. Then state Emerson's observation in your own words.**

Daughters of Time, the hypocritic Days,
Muffled and dumb like barefoot dervishes,
And marching single in an endless file,
Bring diadems and fagots in their hands.
To each they offer gifts after his will,
Bread, kingdom, stars, and sky that holds them all.

I, in my pleached garden, watched the pomp,
Forgot my morning wishes, hastily
Took a few herbs and apples, and the Day
Turned and departed silent. I, too late,
Under her solemn fillet saw the scorn.

WRITING A PAPER
ON LITERATURE

Here are some tips for planning and writing your paper.

Audience.   Direct your paper at your classmates or instructors, not at some outside expert on the author you're dealing with. Use moderately formal language and a tone that is impersonal but not aloof or pompous. The sample paper on pages 260–262 provides an example.

Focus and Evidence.   Focus on a limited aspect of the work and signal your intention in a clear thesis statement. Then back your position and any general statements about the work with evidence drawn from the work itself. If necessary, search out critical articles or books in your library. Usually, though, you won't need outside sources.

Handling Quotations.   Like aspirin, quotations should be used when necessary, but not to excess. Cite brief, relevant passages to support key ideas, but fight the urge to quote huge blocks of material. Sandwich short quotations, less than five lines long, within quotation marks and run them into the text. For longer quotes, omit the quotation marks and indent the material ten spaces from the left-hand margin. When quoting poetry, use a slash mark (/) to show the shift from one line to the other in the original: "A honey tongue, a heart of gall,/ Is fancy's spring, but sorrow's fall." Pages 301–304 provide added information on handling quotes.

Documentation.   Document ideas and quotations from outside sources by following the guidelines on pages 296–300.

If your instructor wants you to document quotations from the work you're writing about, include the information within parentheses following the quotations. Use page numbers ("page 7") for fiction, line numbers ("line 27") for poetry; and give act, scene, and line numbers ("II, 3, 18–19") for plays. When discussing a work of fiction not in your textbook, identify the book you used as your source. Your instructor can then easily check your information. With short works, internal documentation is often omitted.

Tense.   Write your essay in the present rather than the past tense. Say "In *The Sound and the Fury*, William Faulkner uses four narrators, each of whom provides a different perspective on the events that take place," not ". . . William Faulkner used four narrators, each of whom provided a different perspective on the events that took place."

Instructors have different views on making assignments. Some tell you,

"Write on this topic." Others say, "Pick one of the following for your paper." Still others allow free choice. Let's assume you have free choice. Here's how you might approach a 750-word writing assignment on "The Bride Comes to Yellow Sky." You begin by rereading the story and thinking about it. As a result, you rule out a paper centering on plot, setting, irony, narrator and point of view, or theme. Because your class has discussed the first three so thoroughly, you doubt you can offer anything more. The matter of the narrator stumps you; you can understand why Crane uses a third-person narrator who airs Potter's thoughts, but you can't see what's accomplished by the brief looks into other character's minds. Regarding theme, you doubt you can do justice to the topic in 750 words. As you mentally mine the remaining elements for possible topics, your thoughts turn to the many gunfighters you've watched in the movies and read about in western fiction. Because gunfighters have always fascinated you and Scratchy Wilson seems an intriguing example of the breed, you decide to analyze his character.

You briefly consider going to the library to read what the critics have said, but since your instructor hasn't recommended this approach, you decide to handle Scratchy by drawing on what's in the story. At this point, you draft a thesis statement:

> A close look at Scratchy shows that he has much more depth than his pulp fiction counterparts.

You brainstorm by listing details that will help develop your thesis, and the rest is like doing any other paper: organizing, writing a rough draft, and revising.

THE FINISHED PRODUCT

Scratchy Wilson: No Cardboard Character
WENDELL STONE

Stephen Crane's "The Bride Comes to Yellow Sky" is artful on several counts. For one thing, the story is rich in irony. It makes use of an elaborate set of symbols to get its point across. It is filled with vivid language, and in Jack Potter and Scratchy Wilson it offers its readers two very unusual characters. Potter's actions and thoughts clearly show that he is a complex person. In fact, his complexity is so conspicuous that it becomes easy to regard Scratchy as nothing more than a one-dimensional badman. But this judgment is mistaken. A close look at Scratchy shows that he, like Potter, has much more depth than his pulp fiction counterparts.

Nothing in what the bartender says about Scratchy hints that there is anything unusual about the old outlaw. We learn that Scratchy is "a wonder with a gun," that he is "about the last one of the old gang that used to hang out along the river here," and that "He's a terror when he's drunk" but mild-mannered and pleasant at other times. One thing may strike the careful reader as a little odd, though. Although Potter "goes out and fights Scratchy when he gets on one of these tears," he has wounded Scratchy just once, and then only in the leg. Apparently, Potter has been able to talk the supposed terror out of a shootout each of the other times. Nor has Potter apparently tried doing anything to stop Scratchy's "tears."

As he steps onto the main street of Yellow Sky, Scratchy seems every bit as menacing as the bartender has described him. His face flames "in a rage begot of whisky," the cords in his neck throb and bulge with anger, and he hurls "cries of ferocious challenge" at the barricaded buildings. Scratchy is clearly no stranger to either weapons or shootouts. He walks with "the creeping movement of the midnight cat," moves his revolvers with "an electric swiftness," and keeps constantly on the alert for an ambush.

Nevertheless, Scratchy comes across as less than totally menacing. For one thing, his maroon shirt and gilded, red-topped boots make him look not like a westerner but like some child's notion of one. When he sees the dog, he deliberately shoots to frighten rather than to kill it. And in spite of all his bluster, he makes no real attempt to break down any doors and get at the people hiding behind them. Scratchy's clothing shows that eastern ways have touched even this "child of the earlier plains." But one could easily argue that eastern gentleness has had some slight softening influence on him, too. Be that as it may, it seems evident that Scratchy, perhaps without quite realizing it himself, is mainly playacting when he goes on his rampages and that Potter knows this.

During the whole final confrontation, Scratchy seems more of an actor than a gunman wanting revenge against his "ancient antagonist." Instead of shooting when Potter makes a slight movement, Scratchy warns him not to go for a gun and says that he intends to take his time settling accounts, to "loaf along with no interferin'." Significantly, he threatens to hit Potter with a gun, not shoot him, if the marshal does not "mind what I tell you." Even when Potter, recovered from his brief fright, calls Scratchy a "damn fool" and says "If you're goin' to shoot me up, you better begin now; you'll never get a chance like this again," Scratchy does nothing except sneer. This confrontation, like all but one of the others, ends with no shots fired. But one thing is different. Potter's marriage has forced Scratchy to realize that something unstoppable is changing the Old West forever. When he drops his revolver to his side, stands silent for awhile, and then says, "I s'pose it's all off now," we sense that he means not just this episode but any future clashes as well.

Scratchy is not a cardboard creation. His behavior is by no means as easily explainable as it at first seems, and he is capable of some degree of insight. Nonetheless, Scratchy remains very much a creature of the past, something that time has passed by. As he leaves, his feet make funnel-shaped tracks, reminiscent of hourglasses, in the sand. Soon these tracks, along with Scratchy and his way of life, will disappear.

EXERCISE   Using the guidelines offered in this chapter, write an essay comparing and contrasting the two poems below. (You might find it helpful to review pp. 74–78 on comparison.) Limit your focus and back any general statements you make with appropriate support from the poems.

There Is a Garden in Her Face
THOMAS CAMPION (1617)

There is a garden in her face,
Where roses and white lilies grow;
A heavenly paradise is that place,
Wherein all pleasant fruits do flow.
There cherries grow which none may buy
Till "Cherry ripe" themselves do cry.

Those cherries fairly do inclose
Of orient pearl a double row,
Which when her lovely laughter shows,
They look like rosebuds filled with snow;
Yet them nor peer nor prince can buy,
Till "Cherry ripe" themselves do cry.

Her eyes like angels watch them still;
Her brows like bended bows do stand,
Threat'ning with piercing frowns to kill
All that attempt with eye or hand
Those sacred cherries to come nigh,
Till "Cherry ripe" themselves do cry.

Sonnet 130
WILLIAM SHAKESPEARE (1609)

My mistress' eyes are nothing like the sun;
Coral is far more red than her lips red;
If snow be white, why then her breasts are dun;
If hairs be wires, black wires grow on her head.
I have seen roses damask'd, red and white,
But no such roses see I in her cheeks;
And in some perfumes there is more delight

Than in the breath that from my mistress reeks.
I love to hear her speak, yet well I know
That music hath a far more pleasing sound;
I grant I never saw a goddess go;
My mistress, when she walks, treads on the
   ground.
And yet, by heaven, I think my love as rare
As any she belied with false compare.

CHAPTER THIRTEEN

The Library Research Paper

SCENE: A dark, sinister-looking laboratory. In the center of the stage stands a large laboratory bench crowded with an array of mysterious chemistry apparatus. Tall, cadaverous, and foreboding, Dr. Frankenslime leers as he pours the contents of a tube through a funnel and into a bubbling flask. A short, hunchbacked figure looks on with interest. Suddenly the doctor spreads his arms wide and flashes a sardonic smile.

FRANKENSLIME: Igor! At last! At last I've got it! With this fluid, I can control. . . .

Research yes. But not all researchers are mad scientists, or scientists, or even mad. You aren't any of these things, but no doubt you'll be asked to prepare a *library research paper* for your composition class. This assignment calls for you to gather information and ideas from a variety of sources and then to focus, organize, and present them in a formal paper that documents these sources and the use you make of them. From such research you gain experience in locating, evaluating, and using sources—experience that will carry over and help you meet the research demands of other courses and perhaps your job. You'll become familiar with the mechanics of documentation. And when you finish the project, you'll have a good grasp of your topic and can point with pride to your accomplishment.

LEARNING ABOUT YOUR LIBRARY

Long before you start a library research topic, take time to familiarize yourself with your library. Many college libraries offer guided tours to acquaint students with their resources, and almost all libraries display floor plans that show where and how the books are grouped. If your library doesn't have tours, explore it on your own by browsing through it and scanning its contents. As you do, note the following features:

Stacks: These are the bookshelves that hold books and bound periodicals (magazines and newspapers). Stacks are either open or closed. Open stacks allow you to go directly to the books you want, take them off the shelf, and check them out. Closed stacks do not allow you direct access to shelved material. Instead, someone on the library staff brings you what you want.

Circulation Desk: Here's where you check materials in and out, renew books you want to keep longer, and pay overdue fines. If you can't find something you want, the desk clerk will tell you whether it's missing, on reserve, or checked out to someone else. If it's out, fill out a hold card, and the library will notify you when the other borrower returns it.

Reserve Area: This area contains books that instructors have asked the library to remove from general circulation so students can use them for particular courses. Ordinarily you can keep these books for only a few hours or overnight.

Reference Area: This area houses the library's collection of encyclopedias, periodical indexes, almanacs, handbooks, dictionaries, and other research tools that you'll use as you investigate your topic. You'll also find here one or more reference guides—Eugene P. Sheehy's *Guide to Reference Books* (1979) is an example—that direct you to useful reference tools. To ensure that these books are always available, they must be used in the library. Someone is always on duty to answer questions.

Periodical Area: Here you'll find current and recent issues of magazines and newspapers. If your topic calls for articles that have appeared within the last few months, you're likely to find them in this area.

Microfilm and Microfiche Files: Microfilm is a filmstrip bearing a series of photographically reduced printed pages. Microfiche is a small card with a set of photographically reduced pages mounted on it. Often, most of a library's magazine and newspaper collection is on film. Ask a librarian how to work the viewing machines. Once you can run them, you'll have access to many library resources.

Card Catalog: The card catalog, located close to the circulation desk, indexes all the library's books and often most of the other holdings as well. Libraries classify and arrange books by either the Library of Congress system or the Dewey Decimal system. Each labels the cards with call numbers that enable you or a librarian to locate items quickly. Pages 270 to 274 discuss the card catalog in detail.

CHOOSING A TOPIC

Instructors take different approaches in assigning library research papers. Some want explanatory papers, others want papers that address a two-sided question, and still others allow students a free choice. An explanatory paper lays out, in noncommittal fashion, various facts, opinions, statistics, and experimental findings that give the reader a better grasp of the topic. For example, it may explain key advantages and disadvantages of solar heating, thereby clearing up popular misconceptions. An argument paper, on the other hand, uses the same types of evidence to sway the reader toward one point of view—for instance, that solar heat is commercially feasible. Some instructors specify not only the type of paper but also the topic. Others restrict students to a general subject area, ask them to pick topics from lists, or give them free choice. If you have little to say in the selection, look at the bright side: at least you won't have to fret and fume over discovering a topic.

TOPICS TO AVOID

Let's suppose that your instructor has given you free rein in picking your topic. How to proceed? To begin, rule out certain types of topics:

- Those based entirely on personal experience or opinion, such as "The Thrills I Have Enjoyed Waterskiing" or "Colorado Has More [or Less] Scenic Beauty than New Mexico." Such topics can't be supported by library research. Don't hesitate, however, to include personal judgments and conclusions that emerge from your reading.
- Those fully explained in a single source. An explanation of a process, such as cardiopulmonary resuscitation, or the description of a place, such as the Gobi Desert, does not require coordination of materials from various sources. Although you may find several articles on such topics, basically they will repeat the same information.
- Those that are brand new. Often it's impossible to find sufficient source material about such topics.
- Those that are overly broad. Don't try to tackle such elephant-sized topics as "The Causes of World War II" or "Recent Medical Advances." Instead, slim them down to something like "The Advent of Jet Fighters" or "Eye Surgery with Laser Beams." The techniques discussed on pages 15–20 can help you to reduce a topic to manageable size.

Using the advice on topics to avoid, explain why each of the following would or would not be suitable for a library research topic.   **EXERCISE**

1. Genetic counseling
2. Communism
3. The home computer revolution
4. How last night's riot got started
5. Building a solar oven
6. A third world hot spot as described on the evening news
7. Reforming the financing of presidential election campaigns

DRAWING ON YOUR INTERESTS

Let your interests guide your choice. Ask yourself what topic really intrigues you. Which one offers rewards beyond a good grade? A long-standing interest in baseball might lead you to a paper on the Black Sox Scandal of 1919. An instructor's lecture might spark your interest in a historical event or person, an economic crisis, a scientific development, a sociological trend, a medical milestone, a political scandal, or the influences on an author. An argument with a friend might spur you to investigate no-fault divorce. A television documentary might arouse your curiosity about a group of primitive people. A recent article or novel might inspire you to explore the occult or some taboo.

Be practical when you are trying to decide on a topic. If you know that you will eventually have to delve into a particular aspect of your major field, why not get a head start by researching it now? It might be some management, marketing, or advertising strategy; the beginnings of current contract law; medical ethics. All these topics—and many others—qualify. Think about your audience, the availability of information on your subject, and whether or not you can fit it into the specified length of your paper and the time you have to complete it.

CASE
HISTORY

Christine Harding was a freshman composition student when she wrote the library research paper at the end of this chapter. Christine's instructor had limited the class to writing on some recent technological development. After watching a TV rerun of the movie *Star Wars*, she decided to explore some aspect of robots. Because her focus was fuzzy, she decided to sharpen it by doing a little background reading. For starters, she turned to two general encyclopedias: the *Encyclopedia Americana* and the *Encyclopaedia Britannica,* where she skimmed the articles on robots. Often, encyclopedia articles contain bibliographies that can help launch a list of sources. Next, she decided to search out a couple of other articles in more specialized publications. Not knowing how to proceed, she consulted a reference room librarian who acquainted her with the *McGraw-Hill Encyclopedia of Science and Technology* and *Van Nostrand's Scientific Encyclopedia.*

This reading suggested to Christine several areas of focus: the history of robots, the factors involved in designing them, and their possible impact on industry. After a little thought, she elected the third possibility. Unlike the first one, it interested her greatly, and she felt it would also interest her target audience—fellow students at the vocationally oriented school she attended. Unlike the second focus, it would not require highly technical source material, which she might not understand. *(To be continued in next section.)*

This same general procedure—skimming encyclopedia articles and other background material—is helpful in approaching almost any research topic. Other background material depends on your topic: for a historical figure, there are the *Dictionary of American Biography,* the *Dictionary of National Biography* (for deceased British figures), and the *McGraw-Hill Encyclopedia of World Biography.* Librarians can suggest appropriate background books.

ASSEMBLING A WORKING BIBLIOGRAPHY

Once you have a topic, you're ready to verify whether the library has sufficient resources for you to carry the project through. At this point, then, you'll need to check additional reference tools and compile a working bibliography—a set of cards that list promising sources of information. This section explains these reference tools and how to use them.

ENCYCLOPEDIAS

What They Are.   Encyclopedias fall into two categories, general and specialized. General encyclopedias, the *Encyclopedia Americana* and the *Encyclopaedia Britannica,* for instance, offer general articles on a wide range of subjects. Specialized encyclopedias restrict their offerings to a particular field, such as advertising or human behavior. Here's a sampling of specialized encyclopedias:

> *Encyclopedia of Advertising*
> *Encyclopedia of Education*
> *Encyclopedia of Environmental Science*
> *Encyclopedia of Human Behavior: Psychology, Psychiatry, and Mental Health*
> *Encyclopedia of Social Work*
> *Encyclopedia of World Art*
> *Harper's Encyclopedia of Science*
> *International Encyclopedia of the Social Sciences*
> *McGraw-Hill Encyclopedia of Science and Technology*

How to Use Them.   Encyclopedias are a convenient launching pad for your investigation because they provide an overview of the broad field your topic fits into. If you've selected a nonspecialized topic, like the impact of commercial television during the 1950s, check the articles on television in one or more general encyclopedias. If you've opted for a specialized aspect of television, say the development of the picture tube, consult one or more specialized encyclopedias, such as *Harper's Encyclopedia of Science* and the *McGraw-Hill Encyclopedia of Science and Technology,* in addition to general encyclopedias. During this search you'll encounter for a second time material you scanned while trying to focus on a topic.

Some instructors allow you to acknowledge encyclopedias as a source, others prohibit their use, and still others allow material from specialized, but not general, encyclopedias. As always, follow your instructor's wishes.

If you will be using an encyclopedia source in your paper, jot down the following information for each note you take:

Title of article
Author(s) of article (Not always available. Sometimes only initials at the end of an
    article identify an author. In that case, check the list of contributors at the front
    of the first volume for the full name.)
Name of encyclopedia
Year of publication

Furthermore, check for bibliographies at the ends of articles and copy down any reference that looks promising.

When you've finished your exploratory reading in encyclopedias, turn to the card catalog and periodical indexes—the prime sources of information for library research papers.

THE CARD CATALOG

What It Is.   The card catalog, a file of 3×5-inch cards, indexes all of the books in the library. In some libraries, it also lists magazines, newspapers, government documents, college catalogs, records, and tape recordings. In others, these materials are cataloged separately. Your librarian will help you locate any other listings.

The card catalog contains three kinds of cards—author, title, and subject—for each nonfiction item cataloged. Fiction has author and title cards only. Except for the top line, which differs for the different types of cards, all cards for the same book are identical. The cards are arranged alphabetically, and the three kinds may be filed together, separately, or in some other manner; for example, title and author cards together, subject cards elsewhere. In alphabetizing the cards, librarians follow certain standard practices.

1. Title and subject cards are filed alphabetically according to the first word that is not an article *(a, an, the)*.
2. Cards are filed word-by-word rather than strictly letter-by-letter. To illustrate, note the following series:
    Chicken and Turkey Tapeworms
    Chicken Beacon
    Chicken Every Sunday
    Chicken Raising Made Easy
    The Chickenbone Special
    Chickens, Chickens, Chickens
    Chickens Come Home to Roost

3. "Mc" names are filed under "Mac."
4. Numbers and abbreviations are filed alphabetically as if they were spelled out. For example, the title card for the novel *Mr. Bridge* is filed under "Mister."
5. Names of people precede identical names of places and things. Thus, "Snow, C.P., *The Masters*" comes before "*Snow at Evening.*"

Knowing these conventions will lessen tedious thumbing through the cards.

The card catalog allows you to gauge your library's holdings on a subject or by an author. The cards themselves also provide helpful information, as Figure 13.1 on page 272 illustrates.

How to Use It.   Start your search for useful books by looking up any book titles gleaned from encyclopedia bibliographies. Next, draw up a list of subject headings that seem likely to yield useful material; then check the headings in the card catalog. If you're exploring the recent upsurge in satanic cults, for example, your headings might include *devil worship, satanism, diabolism,* and *cult.*

Sometimes a check of your subject headings yields nothing. If this happens, don't give up. Perhaps the list of headings you've drawn up doesn't include any that are actually used. To find the right headings, turn to the published listing that your library uses in cataloging new books. Libraries that use Library of Congress call numbers follow the *Library of Congress Subject Heading Guide.* Those that catalog by the Dewey Decimal System use the Sears' *List of Subject Headings.* Say you're researching the impact of America's entry into World War I on citizens with German roots. You've come up with the subject headings "World War I" and "First World War" but have not found catalog entries for either of them. Your library uses Dewey Decimal call numbers. Check "World War I" in Sears' *List of Subject Headings* and you'll discover that the books you want are catalogued under "European War, 1914–1918."

For each promising title you turn up, record the following information on a 3 × 5-inch card:

Author(s)
Title
Editor(s) and translator(s), as well as author(s) of any supplementary material
Total number of volumes (if more than one) and the number of the specific volume that you want to use
City of publication
Name of publisher
Date of publication

Also, copy the book's call number in the upper left-hand corner of the card.

Next, scan the books themselves. If your library stacks are closed, give the librarian a list of your call numbers and ask to see the books. If you can

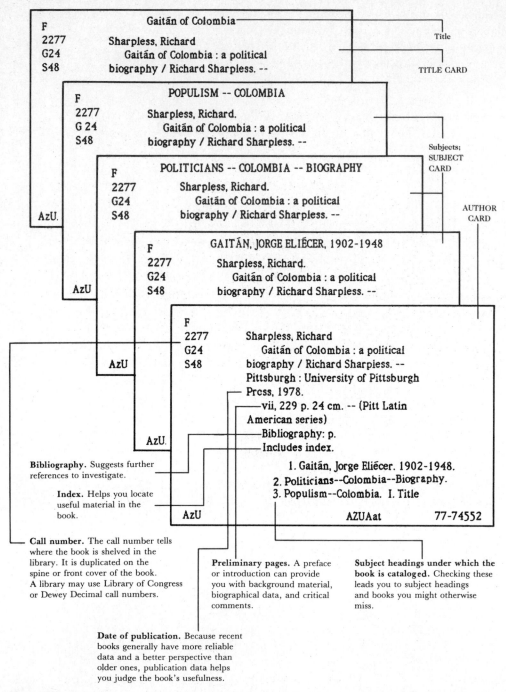

Call number. The call number tells where the book is shelved in the library. It is duplicated on the spine or front cover of the book. A library may use Library of Congress or Dewey Decimal call numbers.

Bibliography. Suggests further references to investigate.

Index. Helps you locate useful material in the book.

Preliminary pages. A preface or introduction can provide you with background material, biographical data, and critical comments.

Subject headings under which the book is cataloged. Checking these leads you to subject headings and books you might otherwise miss.

Date of publication. Because recent books generally have more reliable data and a better perspective than older ones, publication data helps you judge the book's usefulness.

Figure 13.1

enter the stacks, locate the general areas where your books are shelved. Once you find a number range that includes one of your call numbers, follow the trail of figures on the book spines until you find your book. Spend a few extra minutes browsing in the general area of each book; you may discover useful sources that you overlooked in the card catalog.

Examine each book by skimming its table of contents and any introductory material, such as a preface or introduction, to determine scope and approach. Also check the index and note the pages with discussions that relate to your topic. Finally, skim any portions that look promising. If the book won't help you, throw away the card.

Sometimes you may not be able to find in the stacks a book you're searching for. Don't assume that it's lost or not available. Ask the librarian whether it's been checked out or placed on reserve by some instructor. If it's on reserve, go to the reserve section and examine it there. If someone has checked it out, find out when it's due back. When that date is some time away, ask the librarian to identify the borrower, so that you can try to speed the return.

COMPUTERIZED CARD CATALOGS

Some libraries are now using computerized card catalogs. A terminal consists of a viewing screen and a keyboard on which the user enters requests for information. To determine what the library has on William Faulkner, for example, the user types Faulkner's name or its coded equivalent. Likewise, entering a subject heading produces a screen display of all the titles cataloged under that heading. In some systems, the screen also provides additional information, such as whether a book has been checked out and if so, the return date.

Instead of computerized catalogs, other libraries have their card catalogs on microfiche cards or microfilm, which are read with a special viewing device.

EXERCISE

1. **Select five of the following topics. Go to the card catalog and find one book about each. List each book's call number, author, title, publisher, and date of publication. Because subject headings may vary, investigate related categories, if necessary, to find an entry. To illustrate, if you find nothing under *mountaineering*, check *mountain climbing* or *backpacking*.**

   1. Adolescence
   2. Balkan Peninsula
   3. Child abuse
   4. Flying saucers
   5. Mohandas Gandhi
   6. Heraldry
   7. Doris Lessing
   8. Mass transit
   9. Mountaineering
   10. Origami

11. Pearl Harbor	16. Taxidermy
12. Parapsychological research	17. Telecommunication
13. Regional planning	18. Underwater exploration
14. Bertrand Russell	19. Volcanoes
15. Spin fishing	20. Zen Buddhism

2. Provide your instructor with a list of the books you found that appear useful for developing your topic. For each book, furnish the information specified in Part 1 above, along with a brief note indicating why you think the book will be useful.

PERIODICAL INDEXES

What They Are. Periodical indexes catalog articles appearing in magazines and newspapers. Most indexes list entries by subject and author; some also list by title. Paperback issues of the indexes appear at regular intervals, often biweekly or monthly. Each year the publisher combines the material in the paperback issues and publishes it in one or two hardback volumes.

Periodical indexes provide access to material that will not find its way into books for several years, if ever. Their listings allow you to delve into newer topics or keep your reader abreast of the latest developments in older topics. Furthermore, with articles you can explore different facets of your topic in greater depth than you could by using books alone. In short, articles help you avoid a superficial paper.

The *Readers' Guide to Periodical Literature* (1900–date) has long been the standard periodical index for locating articles that have appeared in widely circulated magazines: *Farmer's Journal, Harper's, Newsweek, Scientific American, Vital Speeches,* and the like. The *Guide* indexes over 150 magazines, listing nonfiction articles by subject and author, and other categories by title and author. It is especially useful for locating material on historical events (say the Korean War or the Iran hostage crisis) and on current social, political, and economic developments (the designer jean craze, the nuclear freeze movement). It doesn't, however, index many scientific, technical, or literary articles.

The first pages of the *Guide* identify the abbreviations used for the magazines indexed. Figure 13.2 shows the arrangement of the index and the "see also" cross-references that direct you to related subject headings.

Several periodical indexes are cataloged on microfilms or microfiche cards. *The Magazine Index,* on microfilm, deserves special mention. Indexing 400 popular publications by subject, author, and title, each monthly issue covers the past five years and includes coded references to articles no more than two weeks old. The viewing machines that hold the film resemble small television sets and have motorized controls that allow you to move rapidly through the filmstrip and arrive at your subject. Accompanying the viewer are coded

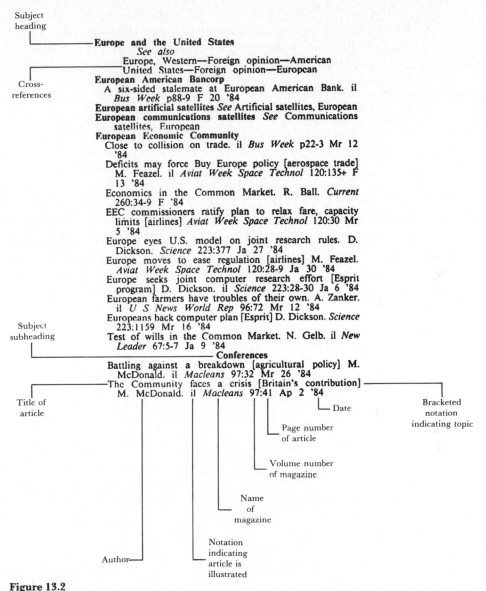

Figure 13.2

From *Readers' Guide to Periodical Literature*, May, 1984. Copyright © 1984 by the H. W. Wilson Company. Reproduced by permission.

reels of microfilm containing the indexed articles, together with a reader/
printer that allows you to read them and to obtain printed copies. Your librarian will demonstrate how these machines work. The producers of the index also publish a listing of recent articles on twenty to thirty topics of current
interest.

The *National Newspaper Index* covers five national papers: the *Christian
Science Monitor,* the *Los Angeles Times, The New York Times, The Wall Street Journal,*
and the *Washington Post.* Each monthly microfilm issue includes three years of
references and is read on the same kind of viewer as *The Magazine Index.*

Two newspaper indexes, *The New York Times Index* and *News Bank,* come
in printed form and refer readers to photographically reduced materials. *The
New York Times Index* (1913–date) lists news articles, book reviews, commentar-
ies, and features that have appeared in the *Times,* a paper with an international
reputation for comprehensive coverage of events. The index entries refer to
the "Late City Edition" of the paper, the one most libraries have on microfilm.
If your library subscribes to a regional edition, an article may appear on another page or not at all. Figure 13.3 is a sample entry from this index.

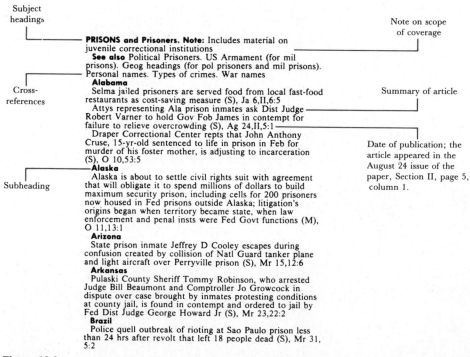

Figure 13.3
Copyright © 1969/1982 by the New York Times Company. Reprinted by permission.

For a topic of local, state, or regional interest (say the Great Lakes fishing rights of Michigan Indians), *News Bank* may be your best bet. This publication indexes articles from over 150 papers in all fifty states. It appears monthly in looseleaf notebook form; the articles themselves are supplied on microfiche cards.

Specialized indexes are also available. Here is a brief sampling of some of them. They list articles appearing in scholarly journals rather than popular magazines.

> *Applied Science and Technology Index,* 1958–date (indexed by subject)
> *Education Index,* 1929–date (indexed by subject and author)
> *Humanities Index,* 1974–date (indexed by subject and author)
> *International Index to Periodicals,* 1907–1964 (indexed by subject and author; entitled *Social Sciences and Humanities Index,* 1965–1974, and then separated into the *Humanities Index* and the *Social Science Index)*
> *Social Sciences and Humanities Index,* 1965–1974 (indexed by subject and author)
> *Social Sciences Index,* 1975–date (indexed by subject and author)

Figure 13.4 typifies the contents of the *Applied Science and Technology Index.*

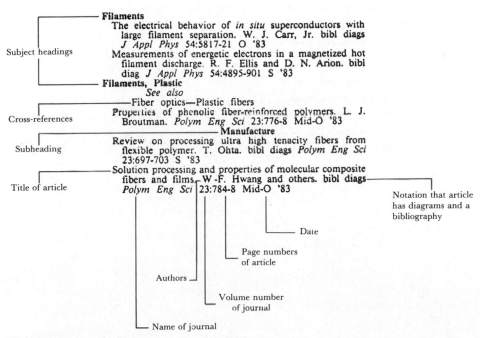

Figure 13.4

From *Applied Science and Technology Index,* March, 1984. Copyright © 1984 by the H. W. Wilson Company. Reproduced by permission.

How to Use Them.   Start your search for articles by checking general indexes; then move to appropriate specialized indexes. Each time you unearth a promising reference, copy the following information on a 3 × 5-inch note card:

> Author(s), if identified
> Title of article
> Name of periodical
> Volume or issue number (for professional and scholarly journals only)
> Date of periodical
> The page range of the entire article

Next, look at any articles referenced in *The Magazine Index* by using the coded microfilms and the machines for viewing them. Check topic sentences of the paragraphs for a rundown of the article's essential points, or scan the abstract or summary, if one is included. If the article looks promising, keep the card; otherwise, throw it away.

Take the remaining cards—and any periodical references that you found in encyclopedia bibliographies—to whatever catalog your library uses for periodicals. There you can determine whether the library subscribes to what you want and, if it does, where the periodicals are shelved. Libraries frequently keep current issues in a periodical room or some other special section. Back issues of magazines are often kept on microfilm or bound into hardcover volumes and shelved. Most newspapers are on microfilm. Check these articles in the same manner that you checked the others.

EXERCISE   **Select five of the following topics and find one magazine article about each. Use at least three different periodical indexes to locate the articles. List the author, if given, the title of the article, the name of the magazine, its date, the page range, and the name of the index used.**

1. Acting Schools	11. Investment trusts
2. Aeronautical research	12. Lasers
3. Julian Bond	13. Nuclear fusion
4. Campaign funds	14. Oral history
5. Collective bargaining	15. Sculpture
6. Dow Chemical Company	16. Television industry
7. Dwight David Eisenhower	17. Unemployment
8. Fiber optics	18. Vegetarianism
9. Fundamentalism	19. X-ray astronomy
10. Holography	20. Yale University

OTHER REFERENCE TOOLS
AND SOURCES OF INFORMATION

To beef up your preliminary bibliography, take a look at one or more of these reference tools or sources of information.

Essay and General Literature Index.   Some articles appear in edited collections that come out in book form. One or more of these articles might serve your needs. To run them down, consult the *Essay and General Literature Index* (1900–date), an annual publication that indexes, by author, title, and subject, articles appearing in several hundred anthologies. Check far enough back to root out everything useful. Then go to the card catalog and see whether the library owns the books.

Interlibrary Loans.   Sometimes you'll uncover sources your library doesn't own. Ordinarily you've reached a dead end. But if the source appears promising, check nearby libraries. If you strike out there, think about an interlibrary loan. Two special reference books can help you locate libraries that have your source. The first, the *Union List of Serials in Libraries in the United States and Canada* indexes, by periodical, the magazine and newspaper holdings of major libraries. The second, the *National Union Catalog*, provides similar information about book holdings.

Many libraries also subscribe to computerized union list services that provide the same information. These services are particularly useful for locating information in the fields of medicine, engineering, business, education, physical science, and social science, as well as for finding government documents and statistics. Using a computer keyboard to call up information on a topic, the librarian operator types a series of key words and phrases associated with that topic, and the unit produces a printout of pertinent sources. When you have your listing, the librarian can arrange to borrow whatever material you want or to obtain photographic copies of it. Because this procedure can take several weeks and may cost you money, think carefully before using it.

ADJUSTING YOUR TOPIC

After finishing your search for sources, you may need to adjust the scope and emphasis of your topic. If you start with "America's First Nuclear-Powered Submarine" but fail to turn up enough sources, you might expand your emphasis to "America's First Nuclear-Powered Warships." On the other hand, if you're working with "America's First Nuclear-Powered Warships" and find yourself floundering in an ocean of sources, you might zero in on one type of vessel. Gathering evidence helps to develop your judgment about how many sources you need to do the job.

CASE
HISTORY
(continued)

Once Christine Harding targeted a focus for her paper on robots, she began compiling her working bibliography. First, she reread the encyclopedia articles she had already skimmed, but found them uninformative.

Next, Christine turned to the card catalog and checked the listings under the headings "Robots" and "Robots, Industrial." The first heading yielded a cross-reference directing her to the headings "Androids," "Automata," and "Automation"; the second revealed a listing of seven books. A check of all four headings turned up fourteen books, four of which proved upon examination to contain material that looked useful.

Her search for periodical articles took Christine to four indexes: the *Readers' Guide to Periodical Literature,* the *Magazine Index,* the *Applied Science and Technology Index,* and the *National Newspaper Index.* The result: twenty-five articles with promising titles. Of these, sixteen were available in the college library, and eleven proved useful for her purpose.

Suspecting that the library might have helpful government documents, Christine checked the library's document catalog after having a librarian explain how to use it. Her search led to a single promising publication.

One good way to approach a topic is to pose a question about it and then draft a *tentative* answer. Here's how Christine proceeded.

Q: What impact are robots likely to have on industry?

A: Despite the misgivings of some people, robots will probably have a beneficial effect on industry and its work force.

Her answer provided Christine with a *tentative thesis,* an informed opinion that guided her later note taking, giving her a sense of direction and indicating what information would likely prove useful and what useless. Tentative theses are just that—tentative—and can be altered slightly or changed completely if necessary. If later reading indicated that robots would likely prove a mixed blessing, Christine could alter her tentative thesis accordingly. (*To be continued in next section.*)

TAKING NOTES

To take notes, read your references carefully and record significant information. Notes are the raw materials for your finished product, so develop them accurately.

EVALUATING YOUR SOURCES

Evaluate your sources by considering these factors.

The Expertise of the Author.   Judge an author's expertise by examining his or her professional status. Say you're searching for information on some new cancer-treating drug. An article by the director of a national cancer research center would be a better bet than one by a staff writer for a magazine. Similarly, a historian's account of a national figure will probably have more balance and depth than a novelist's popularized account of that person's life. Gauging a writer's credentials poses no serious difficulties. Articles in periodicals often note authors' job titles along with their names. Some even supply thumbnail biographies. For a book, check its title page, preface, or introduction, and—if it's been left on—the dust jacket. Finally, notice whether the writer has other publications on this general subject. If your sources contain two or more items by one person, or if that person's name keeps cropping up as you take notes, you're probably dealing with an expert in that field.

The Credibility of the Publication.   A book's credibility hinges on its approach and its reception by reviewers. Cast a cautious eye on books that take a popular rather than a scholarly approach. For research papers, scholarly treatments provide more solid fare. Weigh what reviewers said when a book first appeared. Two publications excerpt selected reviews and provide references to others. The *Book Review Digest* (1905–date) deals mainly with nontechnical works, while the *Technical Book Review Index* (1935–date) covers technical and scientific books. Turn first to the volume for the year the book came out. If you don't find any reviews, scan the next year's index. Often books published in the fall are not reviewed until the following year.

Periodical articles can also take a scholarly or popular tack. Editors of journals in specialized fields and of some wide-circulation magazines—for example, *Scientific American* and *The New Yorker*—publish only in-depth, accurate articles. Most newsstand publications, however, popularize to some extent, and some deliberately strive for sensationalism. Popularizing may result in broad, general statements, skimpy details, and a sensational tone.

Don't assume that you should reject a source because the writer lacks expertise or offers a popularized treatment. Often, especially when writing about some matter of current interest, you'll need to use material that falls short in some way. By recognizing and taking into account the shortcomings, you can make it serve your purpose nicely.

MECHANICS OF NOTE TAKING

Copy each note on a 4 × 6-inch card. That way you won't confuse the cards with the smaller bibliography cards. Record only one note per card, even when you take several notes from a single page: you may use the notes at different points. If you can't fit a note on a single card, continue the note on a second card and use a paper clip or staple to keep the two together. Cards allow you to test different arrangements of notes and use the best one. Copying notes in a notebook will prevent you from shuffling them into the proper order.

Before you take a note, indicate its source at the bottom of the card. You will then have all the details necessary for documenting the information if you use it in your paper. Usually, the author's last name and the page number suffice, since the bibliography card contains all other details. To distinguish between two authors with the same last name or between two works by the same author, add initials or partial titles. *Don't forget to include the page number or numbers for each note.* Otherwise, you'll have to waste time looking them up when you cite your sources in the paper.

Summarize briefly the contents of the note at the top of the card. Later, when you construct an outline, these notations will help you sort your cards into categories and subcategories.

TYPES OF NOTES

A note can be a summary, paraphrase, or quotation. *Whenever you use any kind of note in your paper, give proper credit to your source. Failure to do so results in plagiarism—that is, literary theft—a serious offense even when committed unintentionally.* Pages 304–305 discuss plagiarism, and pages 292–301 explain proper documentation of sources.

Summary.   A summary condenses original material, presenting its core ideas in your own words. You may include brief quotations if you enclose them in quotation marks. A properly written summary presents points in their original order without distorting their emphasis or meaning, and it omits supporting details and repetition. Summaries serve up the heart of the matter and help you write a shorter paper.

Begin the summarizing process by asking yourself, "What points does the author make that have an important bearing on my topic and purpose?" To answer, note especially the topic sentences in the original. Often, though not always, they provide essential information. Copy the points, following the order in the original. That done, condense and rewrite them in your own words. Figure 13.5 on page 284 is a summary of the Bertrand Russell passage that precedes it. We have underscored key points in the original.

Under the influence of the romantic movement, a process began about a hundred and fifty years ago, which has continued ever since—a process of revaluing the traditional virtues, placing some higher on the scale than before, and others lower. The tendency has been to exalt impulse at the expense of deliberation. The virtues that spring from the heart have come to be thought superior to those that are based upon reflection: a generous man is preferred to a man who is punctual in paying his debts. *Per contra*, deliberate sins are thought worse than impulsive sins: a hypocrite is more harshly condemned than a murderer. The upshot is that we tend to estimate virtues, not by their capacity for providing human happiness, but by their power of inspiring a personal liking for the possessors, and we are not apt to include among the qualities for which we like people, a habit of reflecting before making an important decision.

The men who started this movement were, in the main, gentle sentimentalists who imagined that, when the fetters of custom and law were removed, the heart would be free to display its natural goodness. Human nature, they thought, is good, but institutions have corrupted it; remove the institutions and we shall all become angels. Unfortunately, the matter is not so simple as they thought. Men who follow their impulses establish governments based on pogroms, clamour for war with foreign countries, and murder pacifists and Negroes. Human nature unrestrained by law is violent and cruel. In the London Zoo, the male baboons fought over the females until all the females were torn to pieces; human beings, left to the ungoverned impulse, would be no better. In ages that have had recent experience of anarchy, this has been obvious. All the great writers of the middle ages were passionate in their admiration of the law; it was the Thirty Years' War that led Grotius to become the first advocate of international law. Law, respected and enforced, is in the long run the only alternative to violent and predatory anarchy; and it is just as necessary to realize this now as it was in the time of Dante and Grotius.

What is the essence of law? On the one hand, it takes away from private citizens the right of revenge, which it confers upon the government. If a man steals your money, you must not steal it back, or thrash him, or shoot him; you must establish the facts before a neutral tribunal, which inflicts upon him such punishment as has seemed just to the disinterested legislators. On the other hand, when two men have a dispute, the law provides a machinery for settling it, again on principles laid down in advance by neutrals. The advantages of law are many. It diminishes the amount of private violence, and settles disagreements in a manner more nearly just than that which would result if the disputants fought it out by private war. It makes it possible for men to work without being perpetually on the watch against bandits. When a crime has been committed it provides a skilled machine for discovering the criminal.

Without law, the existence of civilized communities is impossible. In international law, there is as yet no effective law, for lack of an international police force capable of overpowering national armies, and it is daily becoming more evident that this defect must be remedied if civilization is to survive. Within single nations there is a dangerous tendency to think that moral indignation excuses the extra-legal punishment of criminals. In Germany an era of private murder (on the loftiest grounds) preceded and followed the victory of the Nazis. In fact, nine-tenths of what appeared as just indignation was sheer lust for cruelty; and this is equally true in other countries where mobs rob the law of its functions. In any civilized community, toleration of mob rule is the first step towards barbarism.

Bertrand Russell, "Respect for Law,"
San Francisco Review, Winter 1958, 63–65.

Necessity for law

About a century and a half ago, there began a still-existing preference for impulsive actions over deliberate ones. Those responsible for this development believed that people are naturally good but institutions have perverted them. Actually, unfettered human nature breeds violence and brutality, and law is our only protection against anarchy. The law assumes the responsibility for revenge and settles disputes equitably. It frees people from the fear of being victimized by criminals and provides a means of catching them. Without it, civilization could not endure.

Russell, pp. 63-65

Figure 13.5

EXERCISE   **A. Prepare a summary note card for the following passages.**

1.   This is a report about islands, but it's not about calypso or Mai Tais or hula dancers or hot dogs. The islands I'm interested in are off the coasts of Georgia and South Carolina, and their names are Hilton Head, Seabrook, Sea Island, St. Simons, Fripp and Kiawah—not the sort of names you're ever going to hear on an afternoon game show.

The islands, different as they are individually, share any number of common virtues. All have great beaches—large, romantic beaches free, for the most part, of high-rises and free of anything suggesting honky-tonk. All of the islands, moreover, have been developed in a manner that has preserved the basic environmental character of the land, has kept the trees standing where possible and has left unspoiled the nesting groups of the many types of wild birds that breed there. A 10-minute walk from any of the lodgings on just about any of the islands puts you in the middle of a wilderness.

But what is most appealing about these islands, I think, is that they generate much the same low-keyed atmosphere that prevails at vacation retreats populated by only the very rich, while, at the same time, offering leisure opportunities—tennis in particular—on a scale, a variety, and a quality simply not found at most vacation home retreats.

> Barry Tarshis, "Islands of Tennis:
> Where to Vacation in the Southeast"

2.   There are currents of change on the public scene which I believe will have profound implications for education. This is a time in which the expectations for schools are at an all-time high and support is, at best, confused. This confusion threatens to destroy our system of public education.

What's more, it is my belief that there's a good deal more at stake than a simple concept of education. For just as surely as the loss of free speech would destroy our ability to maintain our freedom and democracy, the loss of public education would destroy our ability to preserve that freedom and to regenerate it across the years.

Furthermore, loss of universal, public education would tend to stimulate the kind of class divisions which have torn apart so many other nations throughout the world.

Why are our public schools being threatened? Because our economy has become sick. Costs of all things continue to rise, and inflation puts every citizen under the economic gun. So, whatever way a wage earner can find to save money in such trying times becomes much more attractive than it does at other times. And being what we are, all too often we become penny-wise and pound-foolish, willing to risk long-term disaster in exchange for short-term relief.

Today, unfortunately, too many Americans seem willing to risk sacrificing the very foundation of our future as a free people—our public schools—in order to achieve financial relief. But we all know the problem does not lie with the schools; the problem lies with our system for financing them.

The facts are that property taxes are inequitable and that inflation has robbed our salaries of much of their value. But teachers are taxpayers too—and property owners as well. We share in these problems just like everyone else. We have no desire whatever to bleed the taxpayers of our nation. Nor, on the other hand, do we intend to subsidize the increased costs of education by absorbing the effects of inflation in already inadequate salaries. We do want for education a fair share of funding in order that we can bring to all Americans the full opportunities that only universal, public education can bring. To achieve that, there must be a transfusion of federal funds into locally controlled public school systems. For many years, NEA has called for one-third federal funding of education. That proposal has taken on greater importance in this day of inflation and taxpayer revolt.

John Ryor, "Save Our Schools"

B. Submit summaries of three pieces of information that you plan to use in writing your paper; also submit photocopies of the original information.

Paraphrase.   To paraphrase is to restate material in your own words without attempting to condense it. Unlike a summary, a paraphrase allows you to present an essentially complete version of the original material in your own words. Here is a sample passage, and Fig. 13.6 is its paraphrase.

Over time, more and more of life has become subject to the controls of knowledge. However, this is never a one-way process. Scientific investigation is continually increasing our knowledge. But if we are to make good use of this knowledge, we must not only rid our minds of old, superseded beliefs and fragments of magic, but also recognize new superstitions for what they are. Both are generated by our wishes, our fears, and our feelings of helplessness in difficult situations.

Margaret Mead, "New Superstitions for Old,"
A Way of Seeing. New York: McCall, 1970. 266.

Combatting Superstitions

As time has passed, knowledge has asserted its sway over larger and larger segments of human life. But the process cuts two ways. Science is forever adding to the storehouse of human knowledge. Before we can take proper advantage of its gifts, however, we must purge our minds of old and outmoded convictions, while recognizing the true nature of modern superstitions. Both stem from our desires, our apprehensions, and our sense of impotence under difficult circumstances.

Mead, p. 266

Figure 13.6

Paraphrase a short passage from one of your textbooks.   **EXERCISE**

Quotation.   A quotation is a copy of original material. Since your paper should demonstrate that you've mastered your sources, don't rely extensively on quotations. You need practice in expressing yourself. As a general rule, avoid quotations except when

- the original displays special elegance or force
- you really need support from an authority
- you need to back up your interpretation of a passage from a literary work

Paraphrasing a passage as well-written as the one below would rob it of much of its force.

> Man is himself, like the universe he inhabits, like the demoniacal stirring of the ooze from which he sprang, a tale of desolation. He walks in his mind from birth to death the long resounding shores of endless disillusionment. Finally, the commitment to life departs or turns to bitterness. But out of such desolation emerges the awful freedom to choose beyond the narrowly circumscribed circle that delimits the rational being.
>
> Loren Eiseley, *The Unexpected Universe*

Special rules govern the use of quotations. If, for clarity, you need to add an explanation or substitute a proper name for a personal pronoun, enclose the addition in *brackets* (see p. 415).

> The Declaration of Independence asserts that "the history of the present King of Great Britain [George III] is a history of repeated injuries and usurpations. . . ."

If your typewriter cannot type brackets, insert them neatly with a dark pen.

Reproduce any grammatical or spelling errors in a source exactly as they appear in the original. To let your reader know that the original author, not you, made the mistake, insert the Latin word *sic* (meaning "thus") within brackets immediately after the error.

> As Wabash notes, "The threat to our enviroment [sic] comes from many directions."

If you exclude an unneeded part of a quotation, show the omission with an ellipsis—three spaced periods. Indicate omissions *within sentences* in the following way:

Writing in *Step by Step, 1936–1939,* Winston Churchill observed, "To France and Belgium the avalanche of fire and steel which fell upon them twenty years ago . . . [was] an overpowering memory and obsession."

When an omission comes *at the end of a sentence* and what is actually quoted can also stand as a complete sentence, use an unspaced period followed by an ellipsis.

In his second inaugural address, Lincoln voiced his hopes for the nation: "With malice toward none, with charity for all, with firmness in the right as God gives us to see the right, let us strive on to finish the work we are in. . . ."

Do the same when you drop *a whole sentence* within a quoted passage.

According to newspaper columnist Grace Dunn, "Williamson's campaign will undoubtedly focus primarily on the legalized gambling issue because he hopes to capitalize on the strong opposition to it in his district. . . . Nonetheless, commentators all agree he faces an uphill fight in his attempt to unseat the incumbent."

Don't change or distort when you delete. Tampering like the following violates ethical standards:

Original passage   This film is poorly directed, and the acting uninspired; only the cameo appearance by Laurence Olivier makes it truly worth seeing.

Distorted version   This film is . . . truly worth seeing.

You can summarize or paraphrase original material but retain a few words or phrases to add vividness or keep a precise shade of meaning. Simply use quotation marks but no ellipsis.

Because of the "passionate advocacy" of its supporters, the push to roll back property taxes has been gaining momentum across the country.

When you copy a quotation onto a note card, put quotation marks at the beginning and the end, so you won't mistake it for a paraphrase or a summary when you write the paper. If the quoted material starts on one page and ends on the next, use a slash mark (/) to show exactly where the shift comes. Then if you use only part of the quotation in your paper, you'll know whether to use one page number or two.

Don't expect to find a gold mine of information on every page you read. Sometimes one page will yield several notes, at other times nothing. If you can't immediately gauge the value of some material, take it down. Useless information can be discarded later. Place a rubber band around your growing stack of note cards. Store them in a large envelope closed with a snap or string and labeled with your name and address. Submit them with your completed paper if your instructor requests.

Working bibliography in hand, Christine Harding began taking notes for her paper. Most were in summary form, but in a few cases she chose quotations because of the importance of the source, the significance of the material, or the force with which it was presented. One quotation offered the Robot Institute of America's definition of the term *robot*. Several spoke optimistically of the impact of robots, while yet another related a landmark agreement between General Motors and the United Auto Workers on the retraining of displaced workers.

As she read, Christine realized that she should focus on (1) the benefits that robots promise and (2) the steps being taken to lessen their harmful effects, while giving passing attention to (3) the history of robots and (4) the fears they have caused. A plan started to emerge: the paper would begin with a historical overview, touch lightly on the fears aroused by robots, and then deal in depth with the other two matters. (*To be continued in next section.*)

CASE
HISTORY
(*continued*)

ORGANIZING AND OUTLINING

Next comes your formal outline, the blueprint that shows the divisions and subdivisions of your paper, the order of your ideas, and the relationships between ideas and supporting details. An outline is a tool that benefits both writer and reader.

A formal outline follows the pattern shown below:

    I.
        A.
        B.
            1.
            2.
                a.
                b.
    II.

You can see the significance of an item by its numeral, letter, or number designation and by its distance from the left-hand margin: the farther it's indented, the less important it is. All items with the same designation have roughly the same importance.

DEVELOPING YOUR OUTLINE

Developing an outline is no easy job. It involves arranging material from various sources in an appropriate manner. Sorting and re-sorting your note cards is a good way to proceed. First, determine the main divisions of your paper by checking the summarized notations at the tops of your cards, and then make one stack of cards for each division. Next, review each stack carefully to determine further subdivisions and sort it into smaller stacks. Finally, use the stacks to prepare your outline.

There are two types of formal outlines: *topic* and *sentence*. A topic outline presents all entries as words, short phrases, or short clauses. A sentence outline presents them as complete sentences. For easy reading and to emphasize the relationships among elements, items of equal importance have parallel phrasing. Although neither is *the* preferred form, a sentence outline includes more details and also your attitude toward each idea. The following segments of a topic and a sentence outline for a paper on tranquilizer dependence illustrate the difference between the two.

Topic Outline

II. The abuse problem
    A. Reasons for the problem
        1. Over-promotion
        2. Over-prescription
        3. Patients' misuse
            a. Dosage
            b. Length of usage
    B. Growth of the problem

Sentence Outline

II. Tranquilizers are widely abused.
    A. Several factors account for the abuse of tranquilizers.
        1. Drug companies over-promote their product.
        2. Doctors often unnecessarily prescribe tranquilizers.
        3. Patients often do not follow their doctors' instructions.
            a. Some patients take more than prescribed doses.
            b. Some continue to use tranquilizers beyond the prescribed time.
    B. The problem of tranquilizer abuse appears to be growing.

Note that the items in the sentence outline are followed by periods, but those in the topic outline are not.

KEYING YOUR NOTE CARDS
TO YOUR OUTLINE

When your outline is finished, key your note cards to it by writing at the top of each card the letters and numbers—such as IIA or IIIB2—for the appropriate outline category. Now arrange the cards into one stack, so that their designations follow the order shown in the outline. Finally, start with the top card in the stack and number all of them consecutively. If they later fall off the table or slide out of place, you can easily put them in order again. You might have a few stragglers left over when you complete this keying. Some of these may be worked into your paper as you write or revise it.

Sorting and re-sorting was challenging and at times frustrating for Christine. Since some of her material could be arranged in different ways, she found herself experimenting, evaluating, and rearranging as she tested various options. After much thought and some trial and error, the following *initial draft* of her outline evolved.

CASE
HISTORY
(continued)

   I.   Introduction
  II.   History of robots
      A.   Origin of the term *robot*
      B.   Who started the robot revolution?
      C.   Who were the first purchasers of robots?
      D.   Present status of robots and their future prospects
 III.   Fears about robots
      A.   Company managers' fears
      B.   Fears of people not working for companies
 IV.   What benefits will robots bring?
      A.   Past benefits of automation
      B.   Company benefits
      C.   What workers can expect
          1.   More interesting jobs
          2.   Shorter workweek
          3.   There will be fewer workers being injured
  V.   The unemployment threat
      A.   Reassignment of displaced workers to other jobs
      B.   Where displaced workers will be retrained
          1.   By industry
          2.   By colleges
          3.   By others
 VI.   Conclusion

Since Christine did not yet know what she would include in her introduction and conclusion, she merely mentioned them in her initial outline. This version is marked by nonparallelism, poor phrasing, and inadequate attention to some points. Despite these weaknesses, her tentative outline provided an adequate blueprint for the first draft of Christine's paper. *(To be continued.)*

ACKNOWLEDGING AND HANDLING YOUR SOURCES PROPERLY

Before starting to write your first draft, it's helpful to know how to (1) prepare bibliographic references, (2) document sources within your text, (3) handle quotations, and (4) avoid plagiarism.

PREPARING PROPER BIBLIOGRAPHIC REFERENCES

The bibliography, prepared from your bibliography cards, lists all the sources you actually used in writing your paper. Type it on a separate page, headed "Works Cited," and place it immediately after the last page of the paper. List each entry alphabetically according to the author's last name or, if no author is given, the first significant word in the title. For a work with more than one author, alphabetize according to the name that appears first. Begin the first line of each entry at the margin; indent the next lines in each reference five spaces. Double-space every line, within and between entries. The entries below, based on the *MLA Handbook for Writers of Research Papers,* 2nd ed. (1984) illustrate conventions. If you need additional information, consult this handbook.

Bibliographic References for Books.   The basic biblographic reference for a book includes:

> Author of the book, last name first
> Title of the book, underlined
> Place of publication
> Publisher (shortened to the essential name)
> Date of publication

If your bibliography includes two or more works by the same author, give the author's name for the first entry only. For subsequent entries, type three hyphens and a period in place of the author's name; then cite the titles. Add the other facts of publication as necessary. Examine the following sample bibliography entries, particularly noting punctuation.

A BOOK WITH ONE AUTHOR:

Wilk, Max. Every Day's a Matinee. New York: Norton, 1975.

A BOOK WITH TWO AUTHORS:

Bolt, A. B., and M. E. Wardle. Communicating with a Computer. Cambridge, Eng.:
    Cambridge UP, 1970.

Don't reverse the second author's name, since it's not used in alphabetizing.

A BOOK WITH THREE OR MORE AUTHORS:

Alder, Roger William, et al. Mechanisms in Organic Chemistry. New York: Wiley,
    1971.

A BOOK WITH CORPORATE AUTHORSHIP:

United Nations, Public Administration Division. Local Government Training.
    New York: 1968.

AN EDITION OTHER THAN THE FIRST:

Turabian, Kate L. A Manual for Writers of Term Papers, Theses, and
    Dissertations. 4th ed. Chicago: U of Chicago P, 1973.

A BOOK IN TWO OR MORE VOLUMES:

Hicks, John D., et al. History of American Democracy. 2 vols. Boston: Houghton,
    1970.

A REPRINT OF AN OLDER WORK:

Matthiessen, F. O. American Renaissance: Art and Expression in the Age of
    Emerson and Whitman. 1941. New York: Oxford UP, 1970.

A BOOK WITH AN EDITOR RATHER THAN AN AUTHOR:

Deetz, James, ed. Man's Imprint from the Past: Readings in the Methods of
    Archaeology. Boston: Little, 1971.

A BOOK WITH BOTH AN AUTHOR AND AN EDITOR:

Melville, Herman. The Confidence Man. Ed. Hershel Parker. New York: Norton,
    1971.

When the editor has also prepared an introduction, the entry is as follows:

Austen, Jane. Sense and Sensibility. Ed. and intro. Helen Wills. Chicago: Classic

P, 1976.

A TRANSLATION:

Beauvoir, Simone de. All Said and Done. Trans. Patrick O'Brian. New York:

Putnam, 1974.

AN ESSAY OR CHAPTER IN A COLLECTION OF WORKS BY ONE AUTHOR:

Woolf, Virginia. "The Lives of the Obscure." The Common Reader, First Series.

New York: Harcourt, 1925. 111–18.

AN ESSAY OR CHAPTER IN A COLLECTION CONTAINING SEVERAL AUTHORS'
CONTRIBUTIONS COMPILED BY AN EDITOR:

Angell, Roger. "On the Ball." Subject and Strategy. Ed. Paul Eschholz and Alfred

Rosa. 2nd ed. New York: St. Martin's, 1981. 34–41.

Bibliographic References for Periodicals.   The basic bibliographical reference
for a periodical includes:

> Name of the author, last name first
> Title of the article, in quotation marks
> Name of the periodical, underlined
> Volume number of the periodical
> Year of publication, in parentheses
> Page range of the entire article

For periodicals published weekly, monthly, or seasonally, in which each issue
is paged separately, specify the full date of publication. For popular periodicals, omit the volume number and parentheses.

AN ARTICLE IN A JOURNAL CONSECUTIVELY PAGED THROUGH THE ENTIRE VOLUME:

Alvord, John A. "Literature and Law in Medieval England." PMLA 92 (1977):

941–51.

AN ARTICLE IN A JOURNAL THAT PAGES EACH ISSUE SEPARATELY:

Block, Joel W. "Sodom and Gomorrah: A Volcanic Disaster." Journal of

Geological Education 23 (May 1975): 74–77.

AN ARTICLE IN A POPULAR MAGAZINE:

Kraft, Joseph. "Letter from Saudi Arabia." New Yorker 20 Oct. 1975: 111–39.

A SIGNED ARTICLE IN A DAILY NEWSPAPER:

Walker-Lynn, Joyce. "The Marine Corps Now Is Building Women, Too." Chicago

    Tribune 30 Oct. 1977: 15.

AN UNSIGNED ARTICLE IN A DAILY NEWSPAPER:

"Lawmakers Unite on Mileage Rules." Detroit Free Press 21 Oct. 1975: B3.

Bibliographic References for Encyclopedia Articles.   The basic bibliographical
reference for an encyclopedia article includes:

> Author's name, in reverse order
> Title of the article, in quotation marks
> Name of the encyclopedia, underlined
> Year of publication

Davis, Harold S. "Team Teaching." The Encyclopedia of Education. 1974 ed.

For an unsigned article, the reference begins with the title of the article:

"Hydrography." The American People's Encyclopedia. 1965 ed.

**A. Write a proper "Works Cited" reference for each of the following sets of infor-
mation.**

    EXERCISE

1. A book titled Gas Conditioning Fact Book. The book was published in 1962 by
   Dow Chemical Company in Midland, Michigan. No author is named.
2. An unsigned article titled Justices Restrict Action by Courts in Nuclear Cases. The
   article was published in the April 5, 1982, issue of the Wall Street Journal. It appears on page 2.
3. An essay written by C. Wright Mills and titled The Competitive Personality. The
   essay appeared in a collection of Mill's writings entitled Power, Politics, and People. The collection was published in 1963 by Ballantine Books in New York. The
   book is edited and introduced by Irving Louis Horowitz. The essay appears on
   pages 263 through 273.

4. An unsigned article titled Inflation: Where Do We Go From Here? The article was published in the October 4, 1982, issue of U.S. News and World Report. It appears on pages 30 to 33.

5. A book written by Paul Theroux and titled The Kingdom by the Sea. The book was published in 1983 by the Houghton Mifflin Company in Boston.

6. A book written by Kate Chopin and titled The Awakening. The book, edited by Margaret Culley, was published in 1976 by W. W. Norton and Company in New York.

7. An article written by Gertrude R. Schmerdler and titled Parapsychology. The article appears in volume 11 of International Encyclopedia of the Social Sciences, published in 1968. It appears on pages 386 through 398.

8. An article written by Christopher Willcox and titled Right-to-Die Bill Sparks Hot Debate. The article was published in the February 28, 1983, issue of the Detroit News. It appears on page 2 of section B.

9. A book written by Carol R. Ember and Melvin Ember and titled Anthropology. The book was published in 1973 by Appleton-Century-Crofts in New York.

10. A book written by Jean Descola and titled A History of Spain. The book, translated by Elaine P. Halperin, was published in 1962 by Alfred A. Knopf in New York.

11. An article written by John T. Flanagan and Raymond L. Grimer and titled Mexico in American Fiction to 1850. The article was published in 1940 in a journal called Hispania. It appears on pages 307 through 318. The volume number is 23.

12. A book written by Babette Deutsch and titled Poetry in Our Time. The second edition of the book was published in 1956 by Columbia University Press in New York.

13. A book written by Joseph Blotner and titled Faulkner: A Biography. The book was published in two volumes in 1974 by Random House in New York.

14. An article written by Jerome L. Singer and titled Fantasy: The Foundation of Serenity. The article was published in the July 1983 issue of Psychology Today. It appears on pages 32 through 37.

15. A book written by Thomas Beer and titled Stephen Crane: A Study in American Letters. The book was published in 1923 and reprinted in 1972 by Octagon Books in New York.

B. Prepare a proper "Works Cited" entry for each of the works you plan to use in writing your paper.

HANDLING IN-TEXT CITATIONS

Up until 1984, the sources used in writing a library research paper were indicated either at the bottom of each page or immediately after the last page. Then the Modern Language Association introduced a simplified system of notations that appear within the text and are set off by parentheses. This system is explained below. In each case, documentation is identical, regardless of whether the material came from a book, periodical, encyclopedia, or government document. If your instructor prefers the endnote or footnote system, follow the guidelines in the Appendix to this book.

Basic Citation Form. The citation consists of the last name of the author and the page numbers of the publication in which the material originally appeared. Here are two documented passages, one from a source with a single author, the other from a source with two. Unless you introduce borrowed material by citing the names of its authors, follow this form. Note the lack of a comma between the author's name and the page number, as well as the position of the period.

BIBLIOGRAPHIC REFERENCE

Bryan, Christopher. "Big Steel's Winter of Woes." Time 24 Jan. 1983: 58.

PASSAGE AND CITATION

Steel workers in this country make an average of twenty-four

dollars an hour, including benefits, whereas Japanese workers

make just over eleven dollars an hour (Bryan 58).

BIBLIOGRAPHIC REFERENCE

Weider, Benjamin, and David Hapgood. The Murder of Napoleon. New York:

Congdon, 1982.

PASSAGE AND CITATION

Four different autopsy reports were filed. All the reports agreed

that there was a cancerous ulcer in Napoleon's stomach, but none

of them declared that the cancer was the cause of death.

Nevertheless, cancer has become accepted as the cause (Weider

and Hapgood 72).

If a source has more than three authors, use et al., meaning "and others," for all but the first-named one.

BIBLIOGRAPHIC REFERENCE

Baugh, Albert C., et al. A Literary History of England. New York: Appleton, 1948.

PASSAGE AND CITATION

> Although no one knows for certain just when Francis Beaumont
> and John Fletcher started collaborating, by 1610 they were
> writing plays together (Baugh et al. 573).

Authors with the Same Last Name.   If your notes include authors with the same last name, use the initials of their first names to distinguish them.

BIBLIOGRAPHIC REFERENCE

Adler, Jerry. "Search for an Orange Thread." Newsweek 16 June 1980: 32–34.

Adler, William L. "The Agent Orange Controversy." Detroit Free Press 18 Dec.
    1979: B2.

PASSAGE AND CITATION

> As early as 1966, government studies showed that dioxin-
> contaminated 2,4,5-T caused birth defects in laboratory animals.
> Later studies also found that this herbicide was to blame for
> miscarriages, liver abscesses, and nerve damage (J. Adler 32).

Separate Works by Same Author.   If your references include two or more works by the same author, add shortened forms of the titles to your in-text citation. Underline shortened book titles and use quotation marks around article and essay titles.

BIBLIOGRAPHIC REFERENCE

Mullin, Dennis. "After U.S. Troops Pull Out of Grenada." U.S. News & World
    Report 14 Nov. 1983: 22–25.

------. "Why the Surprise Move in Grenada—and What Next." U.S. News & World
    Report 7 Nov. 1983: 31–34.

PASSAGE AND CITATION

As the rangers evacuated students, the marines launched another

offensive at Grand Mal Bay, then moved south to seize the capital

and free the governor (Mullin "Why the Surprise" 33).

Unsigned References.   When you use a source for which no author is given, the in-text citation consists of all or part of the title and the appropriate page numbers.

BIBLIOGRAPHIC REFERENCE

"Reform in Sight for People's Right to Know." American Libraries 4 (1975): 540.

PASSAGE AND CITATION

In 1974, Congress proposed several amendments to the Freedom

of Information Act, only to have President Ford reject them on the

grounds that they were "unconstitutional and unworkable." But

while Ford was out of the country in early 1975, Congress voted

overwhelmingly to enact them into law ("Reform in Sight" 540).

Citing Quotations.   When the quotation is run into the text, position the citation as shown below.

BIBLIOGRAPHIC REFERENCE

Verney, Thomas, M.D., and John Kelly. The Secret Life of the Unborn Child. New
    York: Simon, 1981.

PASSAGE AND CITATION

Investigators who have studied mother-child bonding have found

that "women who bond become better mothers, and their babies

almost always are physically healthier, emotionally more stable

and intellectually more acute than infants taken from their

mothers right after birth" (Verney and Kelly 146).

With longer, indented quotations, skip two horizontal spaces after the end punctuation and type the reference in parentheses.

BIBLIOGRAPHIC REFERENCE

Newhouse, John. "The Diplomatic Round: A Freemasonry of Terrorism." New Yorker 8 July 1985: 46–63.

PASSAGE AND CITATION

One commentator offers this assessment of why foreign terrorist groups don't operate in this country:

> The reason that America has been spared so far, apparently, is that it is less vulnerable than Europe, especially to Middle Eastern extremists. Moving in and out of most European countries isn't difficult for non-Europeans; border controls are negligible. But American customs and immigration authorities, being hyper-alert to drug traffic, tend to pay attention to even marginally doubtful people, and a would-be terrorist ... could come under surveillance for the wrong reason   (Newhouse 63).

Authors Identified in Text.   Sometimes you'll want to introduce a paraphrase, summary, or quotation with the name of its author. When you do, include only the page numbers of the source in your citation. The citation may come immediately after the name or follow the material cited.

BIBLIOGRAPHIC REFERENCE

Jacoby, Susan. "Waiting for the End: On Nursing Homes." New York Times Magazine 31 March 1974: 80.

PASSAGE AND CITATION

Susan Jacoby (80) sums up the grim outlook of patients in bad nursing homes by noting that they are merely waiting to die.

Susan Jacoby sums up the grim outlook of patients in bad nursing homes by noting that they are merely waiting to die (80).

HANDLING QUOTATIONS

Set off quotations less than five lines long with quotation marks and run
them into the text of the paper. For longer quotes, omit the quotation marks
and indent the material ten spaces from the left margin. Double-space the typing. If you quote part or all of one paragraph, don't further indent the first
line. If you quote two or more consecutive paragraphs, indent each one's first
line three additional spaces. Use single quotation marks for a quotation within
a shorter quotation and double marks for a quotation within a longer, indented
quotation. The following examples illustrate the handling of quotations.

SHORT QUOTATION

> Ellen Goodman offers this further observation about writers who
>
> peddle formulas for achieving success through selfishness: "They
>
> are all Doctor Feelgoods, offering placebo prescriptions instead of
>
> strong medicine. They give us a way to live with ourselves,
>
> perhaps, but not a way to live with each other" (16).

QUOTATION WITHIN SHORT QUOTATION

> The report further stated, "All great writing styles have their
>
> wellsprings in the personality of the writer. As Buffon said, 'The
>
> style is the man' " (Duncan 49).

QUOTATION WITHIN LONGER, INDENTED QUOTATION

> Barbara Tuchman's The Proud Tower presents a somewhat different view
>
> of the new conservative leaders:
>
>> Besides riches, rank, broad acres, and ancient lineage, the new
>>
>> government also possessed, to the regret of the liberal
>>
>> opposition, and in the words of one of them, "an almost
>>
>> embarrassing wealth of talent and capacity." Secure in
>>
>> authority, resting comfortably on their electoral majority in

> the House of Commons and on a permanent majority in the
> House of Lords, of whom four-fifths were conservatives, they
> were in a position, admitted the same opponent, "of
> unassailable strength" (4).

Always provide some context for material that you quote. Various options exist. When you quote from a source for the first time, you might provide the author's full name and the source of the quotation, perhaps indicating the author's expertise as well. The passage just above omits the author's expertise; the passage below includes it.

> Writing in Newsweek magazine, Riena Gross, chief psychiatric
> social worker at Illinois Medical Center in Chicago, said, "Kids
> have no real sense that they belong anywhere or to anyone as
> they did ten or fifteen years ago. Parents have loosened the reins,
> and kids are kind of floundering" (74).

Or you might note the event prompting the quotation and then the author's name.

> Addressing a seminar at the University of Toronto, Dr. Joseph
> Pomeranz speculated that "acupuncture may work by activating a
> neural pain suppression mechanism in the brain" (324).

On other occasions you might note only the author's full name and expertise.

> Economist Richard M. Cybert, President of Carnegie-Mellon
> University, offers the following gloomy prediction of the steel
> industry's future: "It will never be as large an industry as it has
> been. There are a lot of plants that will never come back and a lot
> of labor that will never be rehired" (43).

When quoting from a source with no author given, introduce the quotation with the name of the source.

> Commenting upon the problems that law enforcement personnel
> have in coping with computer crime, Credit and Financial
> Management magazine pointed out that "A computer crime can be
> committed in three hundredths of a second, and the criminal can
> be thousands of miles from the 'scene,' using a telephone"
> ("Computer Crime" 43).

After first citing an author's full name, use only the last name for subsequent references.

> In answering the objections of governmental agencies to the
> Freedom of Information Act, Wellford commented, "Increased
> citizen access should help citizens learn of governmental
> activities that weaken our First Amendment freedoms. Some
> administrative inconvenience isn't too large a price to pay for
> that" (137).

Page numbers are not helpful when you cite passages from plays and poems, since these literary forms are available in many editions. When you quote from a play, identify the act, scene, and line numbers. Use Arabic numbers separated by periods. Here's how to cite Act 2, Scene 1, lines 258–263 of Shakespeare's *Othello:*

> That Cassio loves her, I do well believe it;
> That she loves him, 'tis apt, and of great credit:
> The Moor, how be it that I endure him not,
> Is of a constant, loving, noble nature;
> And I dare think he'll prove to Desdemona
> A most dear husband (Othello. 2.1. 258–63).

When quoting from a short poem, use "line" or "lines" and the line number(s):

> In "Dover Beach," Matthew Arnold offers this melancholy assessment of
> the state of religion:

> The Sea of Faith
>
> Was once, too, at the full, and round earth's shore
>
> Lay like the folds of a bright girdle furl'd.
>
> But now I only hear
>
> Its melancholy, long, withdrawing roar (lines 21–26).

In quoting poetry that has been run into the text, use a slash mark (/) to indicate the shift from one line to another in the original:

> In his ode "To Autumn," Keats says that Autumn is the "Season of
>
> mists and mellow fruitfulness, / Close bosom-friend of the
>
> maturing sun" (lines 1–2).

AVOIDING PLAGIARISM

Plagiarism occurs when a writer uses another person's information without properly acknowledging the debt. *Any summary, paraphrase, idea, or quotation borrowed from another must be documented.* Only a fact widely available in many sources, such as the year of Shakespeare's death, the size of the 1980 national budget deficit, or the location of the Taj Mahal escapes this requirement.

Any piece of information not set off with quotation marks must be in your own words. Otherwise, even though you name your source, you plagiarize by stealing the original phrasing.

The following passages illustrate the improper and proper use of source material.

Original Passage

One might contend, of course, that our country's biological diversity is so great and the land is so developed—so criss-crossed with the works of man—that it will soon be hard to build a dam anywhere without endangering some species. But as we develop a national inventory of endangered species, we certainly can plan our *necessary* development so as to exterminate the smallest number possible . . .

> James L. Buckley, "Three Cheers for the
> Snail Darter," *National Review*, September
> 14, 1979: 1144–45.

Plagiarism

Our country's biological diversity is so great and the land is so developed that it will soon be hard to build a dam anywhere without endangering some species.

But as we develop a national inventory of endangered species, we certainly can plan our necessary development so as to exterminate the smallest number possible.

This writer deliberately plagiarizes. The absence of Buckley's name and the failure to enclose his words in quotation marks create the impression that this passage is the student's own work.

Plagiarism

Our country's biological diversity is so great and the land so developed that in the near future we may pose a threat to some creature whenever we construct a dam. By developing a national inventory of endangered species, however, we can plan necessary development so as to preserve as many species as possible (Buckley 1144).

This version acknowledges that the ideas are Buckley's, not the student's. But the student has plagiarized by failing to put quotation marks around the phrasing (underlined above) that was copied from the original. As a result, readers will think that the passage represents the student's own wording.

Proper Use of Original

America has so many kinds of plants and animals, and it is so built up, that in the near future we may pose a threat to some living thing whenever we construct a dam. If, however, we knew which of our nation's plants and animals were threatened, we could use this information to preserve as many species as possible (Buckley 1144).

This student has identified the author and used her own words. As a result, no plagiarism occurs.

Plagiarism is a serious offense because it robs the original writer of recognition. Students caught plagiarizing risk failure in the course or perhaps suspension from school. Whenever you are unsure whether material requires documentation, supply a reference. And always indent, or use quotation marks around, the words of others.

WRITING YOUR PAPER

You already know the general procedure for writing a paper that is entirely your own. With this assignment you'll be working other people's material into your writing. Some students think of a library research paper as a series of quotations, paraphrases, and summaries, one following the other throughout the paper. Not so. Without question, you use the material of others, but *you* select and organize it according to *your purpose*. *You* develop insights, and *you* draw conclusions about what you've read.

WRITING THE FIRST DRAFT

Your final research results will be expressed in a thesis. You've already drafted a tentative thesis (see p. 280), and now you'll probably refine or revise it, accounting for any change in perspective. Position the thesis in your introduction unless you're analyzing a problem or recommending a solution; then you might hold the thesis back until the conclusion. If you do hold it back, state the problem clearly at the outset. Because of the paper's length, it's a good idea to reveal your organizational plan for the paper in the introduction.

Write the paper section by section, following the divisions of your outline. Link the material on your note cards with transitional elements and your own assessments. Don't fret if the style bumps along or connections aren't always clear. These problems can be smoothed out when you revise.

On occasion you may want to include supplementary information that would interrupt the flow of thought if you placed it in the paper. When this happens, use an *explanatory note*.[1] A typical explanatory note might clarify or elaborate upon a point, discuss some side issue, or define a term used in a specialized way.

When you finish writing, let this version sit for a day or two. Then revise it, just as you would with a shorter essay. Keep track of all sources, so that preparing the bibliography will go smoothly.

REVISING YOUR DRAFT

Follow the general revision procedure presented on pages 31–35. Check to verify that you have

- ✔ clearly organized your material
- ✔ included all key information
- ✔ not overloaded your paper with quotations
- ✔ provided contexts for quotations
- ✔ worked in your own observations
- ✔ put in-text documentation and bibliographic references in proper form

---

[1]This is an explanatory note. Position it at the bottom of the page, spaced four lines away from the main text. If more than one note occurs on a page, double-space between them. If the note carries over to the next page, separate it from your text with a solid, full-length line. Put two spaces above the line and two spaces below it.

   V. Robots and the unemployment threat

      A. Reassignment of displaced workers to other jobs

      B. Retraining of displaced workers

         1. By industry

         2. By colleges

            a. In Michigan

            b. Nationwide

         3. By government and other organizations

 VI. Conclusion: possible future nonindustrial applications

Sentence Outline

I. Introduction: The introduction places robots in a historical context, defines the term "robot," and presents the thesis statement.

II. Robots have had a short but highly successful history.

    A. Karl Capek, a Czech writer, coined the term "robot."

    B. George C. Devol and Joseph F. Engelberger launched the robot revolution.

    C. The first robots were sold to automakers.

    D. Robots are now firmly established in American industry.

    E. Robots will continue to become more sophisticated and important to American industry.

III. Many people fear the impact that robots will have.

    A. Corporate management often looks with disfavor on robots.

        1. Some managers fear their financial impact.

        2. Some worry about unemployment.

    B. Some people outside of corporations also worry about unemployment.

IV. Robots are another form of mechanization, and mechanization is beneficial, not harmful.

    A. Historical evidence points up the benefits of automation.

        1. The introduction of the assembly line into the auto industry caused manufacturing costs and car prices to plummet and sales and employment to leap.

       2. The invention of the Hargreaves spinning jenny

          benofitod omployment in Dritain's textile industry.

   B. Robots offer corporate managers a number of advantages.

       1. They are more efficient than human workers.

       2. They are more economical than human workers.

   C. Robots offer advantages to workers as well as managers.

       1. Jobs become more interesting and challenging.

       2. Workers will spend less time on the job.

       3. Workers will face fewer health and safety risks.

V. Robots do not pose a serious unemployment threat.

   A. Most displaced workers will move into jobs directly or

      indirectly associated with robots.

   B. Efforts are now underway to provide the specialized

      training these workers will need.

       1. Industry is initiating training programs.

       2. Colleges are also rising to the challenge.

          a. Twelve Michigan colleges are offering or considering

            programs.

          b. Nationwide, over 30 colleges have programs.

       3. Government and private organizations may also play a

          role in training workers.

VI. The conclusion points out possible future nonindustrial

   applications for robots.

Robots in Industry

In the beginning, industry relied upon the muscle power of workers, using a few hand tools, to perform its tasks. As time passed, these hand tools gave way to complicated machines. Today, robots have entered the picture and will replace many present machines.

The Robot Institute of America says that a robot is "a reprogrammable multifunctional manipulator designed to move material, parts, tools, or specialized devices through variable programmed motions for the performance of a variety of tasks" (Rosenblatt 349). Despite the misgivings of some people, robots will probably have beneficial effects on industry and its workforce.

The term "robot" was coined by Karel Capek, a Czech writer. He was writing a play and needed a name for the machine in the script, which resembled people but worked twice as hard (Rosenblatt 348). It was George C. Devol who developed the basic technology that made the robot industry possible. In 1956, Devol met Joseph Engelberger, a physics student. He (Devol) shared his dream of when robots would be widely used in industry. Engelberger founded and became president of a company that produced the first robots that industry bought (Feder 6F).

Christine Harding

Professor Roinking

English 113

May 6, 1985

Robots in Industry: A Boon for Everyone

Historically, industry has relied on humans to perform its
tasks. In the beginning, productivity depended upon the sheer
muscle power of workers, augmented by a few hand-operated
devices. With the Industrial Revolution, these devices gave way to
ever-larger, ever-more-complicated machines that made modern
factories possible and multiplied enormously the production
capacity of their workers. Now technological advances have
ushered in a new Industrial Revolution, one in which robots will
take over many of the operations now carried out by conventional
machines and their human attendants.

What is a robot anyhow? The Robot Institute of America
defines it as "a reprogrammable multifunctional manipulator
designed to move material, parts, tools, or specialized devices
through variable programmed motions for the performance of a
variety of tasks" (Rosenblatt 349). A robot consists essentially of
a manipulator arm, a pair of grippers, an electrical control unit,
and a power pack to move the mechanical arm (McElroy 43).
Currently, efforts are underway to develop robots that can "see"
and "feel" so that they can respond to changes in the environment

Title reflects main thrust
of paper

New information
smoothes writing, points
to robots' impact

Context provided for
short, run-in quote within
quotation marks

More about robots, future
capabilities

ROUGH
DRAFT

General Motors bought the first robots. It used them to weld 1969 Vega automobiles. The factory where they were produced was in Lordstown, Ohio. By 1975, Ford was using robots for many welding operations in Kansas City. This facility was recognized as the world's most technically advanced auto assembly plant (Weisel 19).

Robots have now become firmly established in many industries, where they do welding, machine tool loading and unloading, forging, shot blasting, and painting (Weisel 18). Future prospects for robots seem good. By 1990, many robots will be able to see and feel and be controlled by computers (McElroy 43). Robots will do a considerable share of all welding, material handling, and assembly (Rosenblatt 360).

2

without expensive human assistance (Rosenblatt 350, 352).

Although the rapid growth in robot technology has aroused some

fears of its consequences, robots will actually benefit everyone,

and efforts are being made to lessen any harmful impact upon the

work force.

> Thesis statement truer to content and organization

  As Rosenblatt notes, the term "robot" was coined in 1921 by

Karel Capek, a Czech writer, who used it to designate the

humanoid factory workers in his satirical play R.U.R., or Rosson's

Universal Robots (348). George C. Devol, an engineer, developed

the basic technology that made the robot industry possible. In

1956, Devol met Joseph F. Engelberger, a physics student at

Columbia University, and shared with him his dream of a day

when robots would be used for a broad spectrum of industrial

tasks. Engelberger, an avid disciple of Devol, went on to become

the founder and president of Unimation, Inc., which produced the

first robots industry was to buy (Feder 6F).

> Cites play, corrects grammar, adds history, improves writing

  These first robots were sold to auto makers. The pioneer

purchaser, General Motors, installed a robot welding line in its

Lordstown, Ohio, auto plant, where it was used in respot welding

on the 1969 Vega automobile. By 1975, Ford was using robots for

a whole range of welding operations, and its Kansas City facility

was recognized as the world's most technically advanced auto

assembly plant (Weisel 19).

> Corrects phrasing, describes use at GM and Ford

  Robots have become firmly established in many industries. By

1982, 29 percent of all automated factories were using robots, 19

percent were planning to install them very soon, and 44 percent

were considering them for a later time ("Robot Productivity" 53).

> One paragraph now two; statistics, forecasts of functions and sales add interest, depth

ROUGH
DRAFT

Many people fear the effects that robots will have. Many corporate managers are afraid to invest in them. They reason that workers are plentiful, and the high cost of robots as well as the long payback period could hurt the company (Rosenblatt 360). Other people outside the corporate fold worry about robots too. They include Harley Shaiken, a labor analyst at the Massachusetts Institute of Technology (Skrzycki 25), and William Wimpisinger, of the International Association of Machinists (Cromie 16). Both have made strongly worded negative statements about the impact of robots. Shaiken said, "What of the worker in Flint, Mich.? He's being asked to commit economic suicide so GM can return to profitability" (Skrzycki 25). Wimpisinger went so far as to declare that "The union worker is the endangered species in the robot revolution" (Cromie 16).

3

Specific functions now performed by robots in automobile plants
and elsewhere include die casting, arc and spot welding, machine
tool loading and unloading, forging, shot blasting, and spray
painting (Weisel 18).

As time passes, robots will become more sophisticated and
their industrial role will continue to enlarge. The Robot Institute
of America forecasts that by 1990, 25 percent of all robots will
have "vision," 20 percent will be able to "feel," and 88 percent will
be controlled by computers (McElroy 43). At that time, the
Institute says, the nation's robot population will number between
75,000 and 100,000 (Hunt and Hunt 3). Robots will do 15 to 20
percent of all arc welding, 30 to 35 percent of all materials
handling, and 35 to 40 percent of all assembly work in our
factories (Rosenblatt 360). Annual sales of robots in the United
States will be as much as $2.5 billion, as compared to 1984 sales
of $190 million (Stepanek 4B).

The swift industrial inroads made by robots have led many
people to fear their impact on industry as well as on the overall
economy. Corporate management is often reluctant to invest in
robots, reasoning that workers are plentiful and that the high
initial cost and long payback period could jeopardize the financial
position of their companies. Many managers also fear that robots
may bring about massive unemployment (Rosenblatt 360). Others
outside the corporate fold have criticized the impact of robots
upon the employment picture. Thus Harley Shaiken, a labor
analyst at the Massachusetts Institute of Technology, wonders,
"What of the worker in Flint, Mich.? He's being asked to commit

Corrects strung-out
phrasing; reinforces
thrust with views of
management and labor on
cost and job loss; cites
figures

ROUGH
DRAFT

These fears would shrink or disappear if people realized that robots are merely another form of automation or mechanization. History shows that automation is good for employment. Henry Ford proved this when he started using assembly lines and mass production. By so doing, he increased the productivity of his workers and reduced the number of hours needed to produce each car. The increase amounted to 8.5 percent per year and the decrease to 56 percent. The average price of a car dropped over 62 percent, ten times as many cars were sold, and the number of workers in the Ford factory jumped from 37,000 to 206,000. All of this took place in just one decade (Vedder 26). Some 140 years earlier, the invention of the Hargreaves spinning jenny helped the British textile industry too (Deane 90-91).

4

Short quotations put in
context, enclosed in
quotation marks

economic suicide so GM can return to profitability" (Skrzycki 25).

William Wimpisinger, of the International Association of

Machinists, goes so far as to declare that "The union worker is the

endangered species in the robot revolution" (Cromie 16). At first

glance, this gloomy assessment of the impact of robotics on the

work force seems only too well-founded since, Skrzycki notes,

robots may eliminate 1.3 million jobs by the year 2000 (25).

These fears would shrink or disappear if the people holding

them would only stop to realize that robots are merely another

form of automation or mechanization. Historical evidence shows

that automation leads to more, not less, employment. Consider, for

example, Henry Ford's introduction of the assembly line and mass

production into the automobile industry. This innovation proved

spectacularly successful, boosting the productivity of the work

force by 8.5 percent a year and reducing by 56 percent the number

of hours needed to build each vehicle. As a result, the average

price of a Ford car dropped by more than 62 percent, sales

increased tenfold, and the employment of assembly workers in the

Ford factory jumped from 37,000 to 206,000 in just one decade

(Vedder 26).

Some 140 years earlier, the invention of the Hargreaves

spinning jenny brought about much the same happy outcome in

Britain's textile industry. This invention made it possible for one

spinner to do as much in a day as 200 could have done previously.

But instead of creating mass unemployment, the jenny led to a

sharp jump in the work force--from approximately 100,000 in

Expansion to two
paragraphs likens benefits
of robots to those of
assembly line and
spinning jenny; writing
tightened and honed

ROUGH
DRAFT

Robots offer corporate managers a number of advantages over human workers. Robots require less instruction and can outperform people. They can be reassigned and reprogrammed instantly, too (Cromie 13). A survey found that over 30 percent of the average workday is lost because of human frailty (Weisel 18). Sickness, vacations, physical disabilities, injuries, carelessness, and boredom also cut into productivity. Robots surpass human capabilities by working in hot, dirty, noisy, dangerous, and fume filled areas without any type of safety equipment (Chamberlin 32).

Robots cost a lot but are much more economical than human workers. The Robot Institute of America says that an average human assembly-line worker costs management around $17 an hour. In contrast, a robot costs around $5-6 (Cromie 13). Often the cost of a robot can be recovered in two years, a small fraction of its working life ("Robots are Coming" 75).

5

1770 to 350,000 in 1800 (Deane 90-91). As more and more
industries become highly robotized, we can expect this pattern of
falling prices and surging sales to repeat itself.

Robots offer corporate managers a number of advantages over
human workers. To begin, robots require much less instruction
and can outperform even the best humans by working around the
clock with precision and high speed. Furthermore, robots, unlike
humans, can be reassigned and reprogrammed for new jobs
instantly (Cromie 13). Adopting robots also allows management
to avoid production losses that stem from human frailty. A survey
cited by Walter Weisel found that 30 percent of the workday is lost
because of scheduling problems, misunderstood assignments,
improper staffing, and poor discipline (18). Other sources have
pointed out the extent to which sickness, vacations, physical
disabilities, injuries, carelessness, and boredom cut into
productivity. Robots have none of these shortcomings. In fact,
they surpass human capabilities by working in hot, dirty, noisy,
dangerous, fume-filled areas without any type of safety equipment
(Chamberlin 32).

Not surprisingly, robots, despite their high initial cost, are
much more economical than human workers. According to the
Robot Institute of America, an average human assembly-line
worker costs management around $17 per hour in wages, fringe
benefits, and the expenses associated with absenteeism, work
stoppages, and so on. In contrast, the cost of a robot--including
maintenance charges, indirect labor support costs, depreciation,
and property tax liabilities--works out to be $5 to $6 per hour

Independent conclusion;
no reference necessary

Clarifies robots'
advantages, immunity to
specific human frailties;
writing level raised

More sophisticated topic
sentence; compares costs
of humans and robots

ROUGH
DRAFT

Robots offer important advantages to workers as well as
management. The introduction of robots into a plant makes it
necessary for workers to tend them more carefully. The workers
must also show more ability to plan, besides exercising good
judgment. The result is more interesting and challenging work
(Mueller et al. 14-15).

Most of the skilled workers doing 4-7% of
American jobs that could be taken over by robots by
1990 should welcome their incursion. Robots will have
to be taught to do their jobs and be supervised while
they work. American companies are discovering that
few people can teach or supervise a robot better than
the man who did the job before. Although fewer people
are needed in the trade as a whole ... the skilled people
in factories where robots are welcomed generally get
more interesting jobs. ... Joblessness is created in
firms that fail to welcome robots ("Robots are
Coming" 75)

Besides having more interesting jobs, employees in plants
with robots will have to work fewer hours--possibly only a four-
day-week--and will earn more money (McElroy 43). A significant
number of workers may well use the extra time creatively and
usefully. This could lead to an improvement in the quality of
American life.

6

(Cromie 13). Often the costs of a robot can be recovered in two years, a small fraction of its working life ("Robots are Coming" 75).

Robots offer important advantages to workers as well as to corporate management. The introduction of robots into a plant makes it necessary for workers to tend their charges more carefully as well as to show more ability to plan and to exercise good judgment. The result: more interesting and mentally challenging work (Mueller et al. 14-15). Here's what The Economist of London says about this matter:

> Most of the skilled workers doing 4-7% of American jobs that could be taken over by robots by 1990 should welcome their incursion. Robots will have to be taught to do their jobs and be supervised while they work. American companies are discovering that few people can teach or supervise a robot better than the man who did the job before. Although fewer people are needed in the trade as a whole . . . the skilled people in factories where robots are welcomed generally get more interesting jobs. . . . Joblessness is created in firms that fail to welcome robots ("Robots are Coming" 75)

Besides having more interesting jobs, employees in plants with robots will have to work fewer hours--possibly only a four-day week--and will earn more money (McElroy 43). When this happens, a significant number of workers may well use the extra time in creative and socially useful ways--painting, carpentry,

Writing has been polished and context provided for quotation

Extended quotation, indented ten spaces, without quotation marks, double-spaced

Omission within sentence, ellipsis

Omission at end of sentence, period and ellipsis

Specific, not general, comments on leisure

Workers will face fewer health and safety risks. In many factories, robots are now doing welding, spray painting and other hazardous tasks. Efforts are also being made to develop robots that will perform other dangerous tasks. The mining industry is developing robots to excavate and haul coal and bolt mine roofs. The electrical industry is developing robots that walk up poles and search out flaws in power plants. The construction industry is developing robots that dig around natural gas lines and install tunnel liners (Armstrong 6). By 1995, the Society of Manufacturing Engineers says, robots should bring about a 41 percent decrease in factory injuries (McElroy 44).

Robots have not created an unemployment problem, nor should they have a significant impact on future employment. Government studies show that by 1990 robots will reduce the overall employment level by less than 1 percent. Many displaced workers will move into robot-related jobs (Hunt and Hunt 82, 139).

7

restoring antiques, and becoming involved in public issues such as conservation, for example. If enough of them do so, the result could be a noticeable improvement in the quality of American life.

Thanks to robots, workers will face fewer on-the-job health and safety risks. In many factories robots have already taken over welding, spray painting, and other heavy or hazardous work, and efforts are now underway to develop robots that will take over other dangerous tasks. Several robots are on the drawing board for the mining industry, including those that excavate, haul coal, and bolt mine roofs. The nuclear power industry is developing robots that walk up poles and search out flaws in power plants. For the construction industry, robots that dig around natural gas lines and install tunnel liners are in the offing (Armstrong 6). By 1995, the Society of Manufacturing Engineers says, robots should bring about a 41 percent decrease in factory injuries (McElroy 44).

Despite predictions to the contrary, robots have not created an unemployment problem, nor should they have a significant direct impact on the nation's employment level in the future. Government studies show that by 1990 robots will reduce the overall employment level by less than 1 percent. Many displaced workers will move into jobs building, installing, programming, and serving robots. Still others will become involved in designing and engineering them, while some will provide a backup cadre of clerical workers and managers (Hunt and Hunt 82, 139).

To handle these jobs, workers will have to be more highly trained than in the past. Over one half of the jobs created by robot

Independent conclusion;
no reference needed

No new information but
rewriting is subtler

Transitional phrase added
to topic sentence;
examples of jobs that will
open up to displaced
workers

Topic sentence added;
writing refined

ROUGH
DRAFT

Over half of the jobs created by robot technology will require two or more years of college. Other jobs will require extensive on-the-job training. Industry has set up a number of training programs. General Motors and the United Auto Workers have agreed that "In view of the corporation's interest in affording maximum opportunity for employes to progress with advancing technology, the Corporation shall make available short-range, specialized training programs for those employees who have the qualifications to perform the new and changed work, where such programs are reasonable and practicable." The company has agreed to provide $80 million annually (Hunt and Hunt 156-57).

A number of colleges are putting in programs to train robot technicians. In 1983, Hunt and Hunt report, four Michigan colleges were offering such programs and eight more were considering them. At one school, 600 students enrolled for the first semester. Over 800 students enrolled for the second semester (159-160). Nationwide, over 30 colleges and universities have robotics programs. Some of these are such famous institutions as the Massachusetts Institute of Technology and Pittsburgh's Carnegie-Mellon University. The salaries obtained by graduates are $30,000 or more (Rosenblatt 360).

FINAL
DRAFT

8

technology will require two or more years of college, while others will require extensive on-the-job training. Industry has risen to the challenge by initiating training programs to provide the needed technical and scientific know-how. In this connection, General Motors and the United Auto Workers have endorsed a "Statement on Technological Progress," which states that

> In view of the corporation's interest in affording maximum opportunity for employes [sic] to progress with advancing technology, the Corporation shall make available short-range, specialized training programs for those employees who have the qualifications to perform the new or changed work, where such programs are reasonable and practicable.

To implement employee training, GM has agreed to provide $80 million annually (Hunt and Hunt 156-57). This development clearly points up industry's awareness of the problems its workers face from robots and its willingness to help cope with them.

A number of colleges are now instituting programs to train robot technicians. In 1983, Hunt and Hunt report, four Michigan junior colleges were offering such programs and eight others were considering them. These programs have proved extremely popular; at one school, 600 students enrolled in the semester that the program began, and over 900 enrolled the second semester (159–60). Nationwide, over 30 colleges and universities have robotics programs, including such prestigious institutions as the Massachusetts Institute of Technology and Pittsburgh's Carnegie-Mellon University. Graduates can expect salaries ranging

Context provided for quotation

Bracketed "sic" marks misspelling

Extended quotation now indented ten spaces, without quotation marks

Independent conclusion; no reference needed

Authors' names in summary, only page numbers in citation

Improved phrasing

Government may also play a role in helping workers displaced by robots by helping pay the costs of retraining workers. It could also distribute labor market information, not to mention reshaping vocational education programs with the aim of having them meet the needs of industry (Vedder 20). In time, help may come from other sources too.

Robots are entrenched in industry. They have greatly altered the manufacture of many products. In the future their impact will continue to grow. Robots will also have an effect on the world outside the factory. They will perform many household tasks and may do such jobs as fire fighting and ditch digging. Because of robots, the world will never be the same.

9

upward from $30,000 (Rosenblatt 360).

Government can also play a role in retraining the victims of

robotization for different jobs. Help could, for example, be provided

in the form of vouchers to cover the costs of retraining in private

or public schools. In addition, government could distribute labor

market information and help reshape vocational educational

programs to meet the needs of industry (Vedder 20). As time

passes, help may come from other sources. Labor unions, for

instance, might establish their own retraining programs. Other

organizations--churches, service clubs, charitable groups--might

also offer some retraining or help displaced workers find jobs

unconnected with robots.

Robots are firmly and irreversibly entrenched in industry.

Already they have greatly altered the manufacture of many

products, and in the coming years they could transform the world

of work as greatly as did the first Industrial Revolution in the

18th century. But that's not the whole story. As technology

advances, we can expect robots to move out of the factory and into

the wider world. Someday, household robots may vacuum our

floors, feed our dog, cook our meals, take out our trash, balance

our checkbook, and then, for relaxation, challenge us to checkers

or chess. Out-of-the-home mechanical servants may include robot

security officers, fire fighters, ditch diggers, trash collectors, and

salesclerks, to name just a few possibilities. Whatever the future of

robots, we can be sure of one thing: the world will never be the

same as before they arrived on the scene.

Right margin annotations:

Improved phrasing explains government's and other sources' aid in retraining

Independent conclusion; no reference needed

Stresses future of robots: reinforces revolutionary aspect

10

Works Cited

Armstrong, Scott. "Hard-Hat Robots May Take Risk Out of
    Dangerous Jobs." Christian Science Monitor 30 Aug. 1983: 6.

Chamberlin, Leslie J. "Facing up to Robotation." USA Today Nov.
    1982: 31-33.

Cromie, William J. "Robots: A Growing, Maturing Population."
    Sciquest Mar. 1981: 12-16.

Deane, Phyllis. The First Industrial Revolution. Cambridge, Eng.:
    Cambridge UP, 1979.

Feder, Barnaby J. "He Brought the Robot to Life." New York Times
    21 Mar. 1982: F6.

Hunt, H. Allan, and Timothy L. Hunt. Human Resource
    Implications of Robotics. Kalamazoo, MI: The W. E. Upjohn
    Institute for Employment Research, 1983.

McElroy, John. "Industrial Robot Growth: How Experts See It."
    Automotive Industries 162 (Sept. 1982): 43-45.

Mueller, Eva, et al. Technological Advance in an Expanding
    Economy. Ann Arbor: U of Mich P, 1969.

"Robot Productivity." Production Engineering 29 (May 1982): 52-
    55.

"Robots are Coming to Industry's Service." The Economist 280 (29
    Aug. 1981): 71-75.

Rosenblatt, Jean. "The Robot Revolution." Editorial Research
    Reports 1 (14 May 1982): 347-62.

Skrzycki, Cindy. "Will Robots Bring More Jobs--Or Less?" U.S.
    News & World Report 5 Sept. 1983: 25.

Entry for newspaper
article

Entry for book with one
author

Entry for book with two
authors

Entry for specialized
journal article

Entry for book with
multiple authors

Entry for specialized
journal article with no
author given

Entry for popular
magazine article

11

Stepanek, Marcia. "Automotive Leader Directs Invasion of a

Cutthroat Industry." Detroit Free Press 28 May 1984: B1, 4.

Vedder, Richard K. Robotics and the Economy. Subcommittee on

Monetary and Fiscal Policy, Joint Economic Committee, U.S.

97th Cong. 26 Mar. 1982.

Weisel, Walker K. "The Robot's Role in Productivity." Production

Engineering 28 (Dec. 1981): 18-19.

Entry for government
document

CHAPTER FOURTEEN

Business Letters and Résumés

Business people aren't the only ones who write business letters. You write quite a few yourself, or soon will, especially to request information, place orders, register complaints, and apply for jobs. There's nothing mysterious or difficult about business correspondence. True, it follows its own special format, but otherwise it breaks no new writing ground. As always, deciding what to say and how to say it is vital to your success.

LETTER LANGUAGE

Effective letter language weaves conciseness, informality, and courtesy into a three-strand finished fabric. Concise writing avoids word clutter and gets directly to the point, saving the reader time and enlivening the message. As you write and revise, guard against two kinds of wordiness: deadwood and gobbledygook. *Deadwood* repeats the same thing or uses excess words to deliver its message. Here are some examples of deadwood and ways of correcting them.

Deadwood	*Correction*
in view of the fact that, due to the fact that	because
had the effect of causing	caused
would you be kind enough to	would you please
I want to take this opportunity to thank you	thank you
in the event that	if
personally, I believe	I believe
I want to make it clear that	[simply state what you want known]

Gobbledygook uses inflated, elaborately polite expressions that make writing stiff, stuffy, and distant. Note how the corrections soften the stand-offish tone.

Gobbledygook	Correction
enclosed please find	I am enclosing
pursuant to the purchase of your	after buying your
in accordance with the terms of your warranty	your warranty provides
reference is made herewith	I am referring to
the said lawnmower	this lawnmower

Informal language is everyday language. Friendly and relaxed, it has the air of face-to-face conversation between writer and reader. To achieve it, use simple words and sentence structures; personal pronouns like *I, me, you,* and *your* are appropriate. At the same time, though, don't go overboard and resort to slang or overly casual expressions. Saying "When you guys packed my radio, you must have goofed; when I got it, it was busted" raises questions about your seriousness.

In your business letters, as in direct dealings with others, courtesy plays a key part in helping you gain your ends. Here are some tips to help you avoid antagonizing the reader:

1. Avoid insults and sarcasm.

   Sarcastic   Do you think you could possibly send me the correct size this time?

   Courteous   Would you please replace the dress with one of the correct size?

2. Avoid curt demands.

   Blunt   I want you to send me . . . , I need a copy of . . .

   Courteous   Would you please send me . . .

3. Avoid negative implications. The first example below suggests that the reader will automatically disagree.

   Negative   I take the position that . . .

   Courteous   I think you'll find that . . .

As you prepare your letter, try changing places with your reader. How would you react to the message? If you're pleased with what you see, courtesy should be no problem.

PARTS OF THE BUSINESS LETTER

The letter in Figure 14.1 on page 336, labeled to show the parts of a business letter, is set up in modified block format, a very common one for business correspondence.

Heading.   Except for the two-letter state abbreviations used by the postal service, spell out every word.

Inside Address.   *Ms.* is an acceptable personal title for both married and single women. If you don't know the name of the person you want to reach, begin the inside address with the job title or the name of the department; for example, *Vice-president for Research* or *Sales Department.* Use abbreviations only if they are part of the company name. Begin the inside address two spaces below the heading in long letters and three to eight spaces in shorter letters. The shorter the letter, the more space should be left.

Salutation.   Address an individual by title and name. If the inside address begins with a job title or the name of a department, use that title or department name for the salutation, for instance *Vice-president for Research* or *Sales Department.* The letters on pages 340 and 342 show this kind of salutation. The salutation comes two spaces below the inside address.

Body.   Most letters are one page or less. Try to keep your paragraphs short—about seven lines at most. Begin the body two spaces below the salutation. If the letter contains only one brief paragraph, double-space the typing. Otherwise use single spacing with double-spacing between paragraphs.

Complimentary Close.   Acceptable closings are *Sincerely yours, Sincerely,* and *Yours truly.* Type the complimentary close two spaces below the last line of the body.

Signature.   Both typewritten and handwritten signatures are necessary. Leave four spaces between the complimentary close and the typed signature.

Enclosure Notation.   The abbreviation *Enc.,* used in several of our sample letters, indicates that a brochure, drawing, check, money order, or other document accompanies the letter. Important documents are often specifically named:

Enc: Bill of Lading (duplicate)

Figure 14.1
Modified Block Form

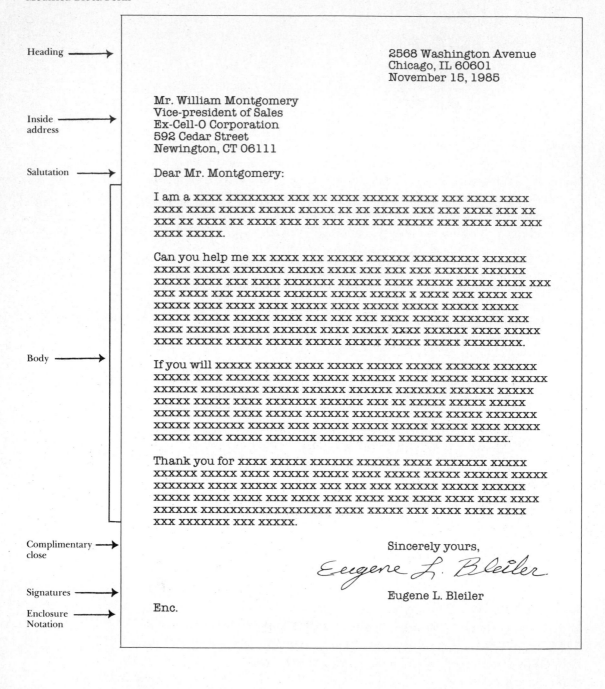

Heading

2568 Washington Avenue
Chicago, IL 60601
November 15, 1985

Inside address

Mr. William Montgomery
Vice-president of Sales
Ex-Cell-O Corporation
592 Cedar Street
Newington, CT 06111

Salutation

Dear Mr. Montgomery:

Body

I am a xxxx xxxxxxxx xxx xx xxxx xxxxx xxxxx xxx xxxx xxxx
xxxx xxxx xxxxx xxxxx xxxxx xx xx xxxxx xxx xxx xxxx xxx xx
xxx xx xxxxx xx xxxxx xxx xx xxx xxx xxx xxxxx xxx xxxx xxx xxx
xxxx xxxxx.

Can you help me xx xxxx xxx xxxxx xxxxxx xxxxxxxxx xxxxxx
xxxxx xxxxx xxxxxxx xxxxx xxxx xxx xxx xxx xxxxxx xxxxxx
xxxxx xxxx xxx xxxx xxxxxxx xxxxxx xxxx xxxxx xxxxx xxxx xxx
xxx xxxx xxx xxxxxx xxxxxx xxxxx xxxxx xxxxx x xxxx xxx xxxx xxx
xxxxx xxxxx xxxx xxxxx xxxxx xxxx xxxxx xxxxx xxxxx xxxxx
xxxx xxxxx xxxxx xxxxxx xxxx xxx xxx xxx xxxx xxxxx xxxxxxx xxx
xxxx xxxxx xxxxx xxxxxx xxxx xxxxx xxx xxxxxx xxxx xxxxx
xxxx xxxxx xxxxx xxxxx xxxxx xxxxx xxxxx xxxxx xxxxxxxx.

If you will xxxxx xxxxx xxxx xxxxx xxxxx xxxxx xxxxxx xxxxxx
xxxxx xxxx xxxxxx xxxxx xxxxx xxxxx xxxxxx xxxx xxxxx xxxxx xxxxx
xxxxx xxxxxxxx xxxxx xxxxx xxxxx xxxxxx xxxxx xxxxx xxxxx
xxxxx xxxxx xxxx xxxxx xxxxx xxxx xxx xxxx xxxxx xxxxx xxxxx
xxxxx xxxxx xxxx xxxx xxxxx xxxxxx xxxxxxx xxxx xxxxx xxxxxxx
xxxxx xxxxxx xxxxx xxxxx xxxxx xxxxx xxxxx xxxxx xxxx xxxxx
xxxxx xxxx xxxxx xxxxxx xxxxxx xxxxx xxxx xxxxxx xxxx xxxx.

Thank you for xxxx xxxxx xxxxxx xxxxxx xxxx xxxxxxx xxxxx
xxxxx xxxxx xxxxx xxxxx xxxxx xxxxx xxxxx xxxxx xxxxx xxxxx
xxxxxxx xxxx xxxxx xxxxx xxxxx xxx xxx xxx xxxxxx xxxxx xxxxxx
xxxxx xxxxx xxxx xxx xxxx xxxx xxxx xxxx xxx xxxxx xxxx xxxx xxxx
xxxxxx xxxxxxxxxxxxxxxx xxxx xxxxx xxx xxxx xxxx xxxx
xxx xxxxxxx xxx xxxxx.

Complimentary close

Sincerely yours,

Eugene L. Bleiler

Signatures

Eugene L. Bleiler

Enclosure Notation

Enc.

Type business letters on $8^{1}/_{2} \times 11$-inch unlined white paper and center them on the page. For full-page letters, make the side margins one inch wide; for shorter letters, make wider margins. In all cases, establish top and bottom margins of roughly equal width.

PREPARATION FOR MAILING

Use the form shown below for both the address and return address. The Post Office can supply you with a list of standard state abbreviations and zip codes.

2568 Washington Avenue
Chicago, IL 60601

Mr. William Montgomery
Vice-president of Sales
Ex-Cell-O Corporation
592 Cedar Street
Newington, CT 06111

Proofread your letter carefully, sign it, and then fold it neatly in thirds (Figure 14.2) so that it will fit into a number 10 size business envelope.

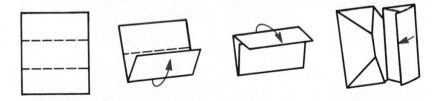

Figure 14.2

TYPES OF LETTERS

Of the many kinds of business letters, the ones you'll most likely write are inquiries, orders, complaints, and job applications. Here are guidelines and models.

Figure 14.3
The Pointers Applied: Sample Inquiry Letter

325 Darrin Hall
Prentice College
Barstow, ME 04611
December 3, 1985

Mr. John Antwerp
Antrim Industries, Inc.
6431 Honeysuckle Avenue
Modesto, CA 95355

Dear. Mr. Antwerp:

Your article in the December issue of <u>Modern Health</u>, in which you describe the features of your company's new comprehensive medical program, is a stimulating report.

I am an environmental health student investigating the benefits that small companies have obtained by instituting such programs. Can you help me by answering the following questions?

1. Has the number of employees calling in sick increased or decreased since your program began?

2. How has the program affected worker productivity and efficiency?

3. How do the costs of the program compare with those of the medical insurance you used to provide through a private insurance company?

Thank you for any information you can supply. If you wish, I will be happy to send you a copy of my finished report.

Sincerely,

René M. Hewitt

René M. Hewitt

LETTERS OF INQUIRY

Your letters of inquiry may be written to request information about a vacation spot, a hobby, or a project that you are working on; or you may write for data to be used in a term paper. (See Figure 14.3.) Here's how to proceed:

1. Identify yourself, indicate the kind of information you're after, and explain why you need it.
2. To avoid inconveniencing your reader, keep your questions to a minimum, make them clear, and word them so they can be answered briefly.
3. If you have three or more questions, set them up in a numbered list, so the reader is less likely to miss answering one.
4. If you're using the information for a paper, and it's appropriate to do so, offer to supply a copy of your paper. Acknowledge the source of information when you write the paper.
5. Close by expressing appreciation for any help the reader can give.

Write a letter of inquiry that requests one of the following kinds of information.   **EXERCISE**

1. More details about a project reported in a magazine or newspaper article
2. Performance data for something you might buy
3. Detailed information about the credit policies of a company
4. Information for a research project or term paper
5. Your congressional representative's, mayor's, or other public official's position on an issue you're concerned about
6. Membership information for a club or professional organization

---

ORDER LETTERS

Order letters, used to order sports equipment, hobby supplies, appliances, furniture, clothing, and the like, must be brief and to the point. (See Figure 14.4.) Write the letter as follows:

1. Identify the merchandise by name, model, or catalog number, size, weight, color, finish, or whatever else is needed.
2. To order a single item, write the letter in paragraph form. Otherwise set up a numbered list.
3. Specify how many items of each sort you want, the cost of a single item, and the total cost of the order.
4. Indicate when you wish to pay and how: by check, money order, or credit card. If you are enclosing payment, say so.
5. If you're ordering a gift to be shipped to someone at another address, be sure to include that address in the body of your letter.

Figure 14.4
The Pointers Applied: Sample Order Letter

420 Bayshore Drive
Durham, NC 27701
October 18, 1985

Order Department
Fitzpatrick Manufacturing Company
123 Getty Street
Philadelphia, PA 19141

Order Department:

Please ship the following merchandise as advertised in the
October 1985 issue of Better Homes and Gardens:

1	Model 979-14/ES Luxury Lady Kitchen Center. Unit price: $121.77.	$121.77
1	Model 5109/WN Whippet five-quart Automatic Oriental Wok. Unit price: $28.67.	28.67
	TOTAL	$150.44

Please send the order at your earliest convenience to the above
address. I have enclosed a check for the total amount.

Sincerely yours,

Cheryl A. Forrest

Cheryl A. Forrest

Enc. Check

Write one of the following letters.

1. Order one or more pieces of furniture, household appliances, garden implements, or automobile accessories.
2. Order a gift to be shipped to a friend or relative.

COMPLAINT LETTERS

Writing a complaint (claim) letter is unpleasant but sometimes necessary. (See Figure 14.5.) An improperly filled order, damaged or shoddy merchandise, a misunderstanding over prices—these and many other situations can trigger complaints. The letter points out the problem and asks that it be corrected. When writing your letter, don't let anger make you discourteous. Remember, you're trying to settle a problem, not antagonize your reader. These guidelines will help:

1. Begin by identifying the problem precisely. Tell exactly what happened and when, giving size, colors, model numbers, prices—whatever the reader needs to investigate and make an adjustment.
2. If you've suffered serious inconvenience, mentioning it may speed the settlement.
3. Clearly state the adjustment you want.
4. Back your position with supporting evidence or arguments, positioned at whatever point in the letter seems most appropriate.
5. End courteously by expressing hope for a speedy settlement or offering any further information needed to reach that settlement.

Write a complaint letter calling attention to one of the following.

1. An improperly or incompletely filled order
2. An order that was delivered late
3. Merchandise damaged in transit because of improper packing
4. Improper billing by a credit card company or utility

JOB APPLICATION LETTERS

Once you've finished your academic preparation and started looking for a permanent job, you'll have to write one or more job application letters. (See Figure 14.6.) In the meantime, you may need to write one to apply for summer work.

Figure 14.5
The Pointers Applied: Sample Complaint Letter

815 Buckaroo Lane
Dallas, TX 75226
July 10, 1985

Customer Relations Department
Carlson Craft
P. O. Box 87
Mankato, MN 56001

Customer Relations Department:

On June 12, I sent a check for $10.19 and an order for 150 imprinted white luncheon napkins, style 7219. These napkins were intended for my wedding reception.

The napkins came today, but instead of saying "Kathleen and Ward" they have the wrong imprint--"Kathleen and Lard." I am enclosing one of them to show you the mistake.

My wedding is less than five weeks off, and I'd like to settle the details of the reception well before then. Therefore, I'd appreciate a replacement order as soon as possible.

My beanpole fiancé and I both hope you'll take care of this matter promptly.

Yours truly,

Kathleen M. Van Meer

Kathleen M. Van Meer

Enc.

Figure 14.6
The Pointers Applied: Sample Job Application Letter

1407 East Elm Street
Big Rapids, MI 49307
February 24, 1986

Ms. Helen Thompson
Medical Records Administrator
St. Luke's Hospital
411 West Cooper Street
Saginaw, MI 48602

Dear Ms. Thompson:

Ms. Leslie Goldstein, director of your nursing department, has informed me that you intend to hire an assistant administrator. I believe that my formal training in medical records administration and my hospital experience qualify me for this position. Please regard this letter as my formal application.

Attracts interest

On May 24, 1986, I shall receive a Bachelor of Science degree in medical records administration from Ferris State College. This program offers a thorough background in medical terminology, health science, technical skills, and personnel management, and emphasizes health administration.

As an intern, I served three months in the medical records department of a large hospital, learning the day-to-day operations of such a department and the managerial skills necessary to hold a supervisory position. To help pay for my education, I have worked three summers as a waitress. This job has provided experience in meeting and dealing with people on a one-to-one basis.

Establishes superiority

While in college, I have been social chairman of the Ferris Medical Records Association and a member of the American Medical Records Association. The enclosed résumé provides further information about my experience and background.

May I arrange an interview to discuss my qualifications in greater detail? You can reach me by writing to the above address or by calling (616) 796-7791.

Requests interview

Sincerely,

Karen K. Auernhamer

Karen K. Auernhamer

Enc.

343

Take great care to do a first-rate job. Companies scan applications carefully and immediately discard those that fail to measure up. Grammatical or punctuation errors, misspellings, strikeovers, obvious erasures, smudge marks, beverage stains—all can earn your letter a quick trip to the reject pile. Be sure to include enough information for the employer to evaluate your qualifications. Here are some guidelines.

1. If you know an opening exists, begin by naming the position and how you heard about it. If you're writing to ask whether an opening exists, specify exactly what position you're after. Use the opening to attract the reader's interest. Name one or more of your qualifications or mention some service you can provide.
2. Establish your superiority over other candidates. Elaborate on the qualifications mentioned at the outset, stressing features that qualify you for the position. Keep the letter brief by directing the reader to your data sheet for additional information. Don't take a hard-sell approach. Asserting that "I'm just the person you're looking for" would probably backfire. If the statement is true and you present yourself well, the employer will know.
3. End by asking for an interview.

PERSONAL DATA SHEET

The personal data sheet, sent with the application letter as a supplement, outlines your job qualifications. (See Figure 14.7.) Since it, like the letter, helps sell you as a candidate, spare no effort to ensure that it's attractive, well-organized, and easy to read. Here are some tips:

1. Capitalize the captions to make them stand out on the page.
2. To condense information, use phrases and clauses rather than complete sentences.
3. List your most recent education and employment experience first and then work backward so the employer can quickly gauge what you've done recently.
4. Don't try to cram too much material onto a page. Ample white space is important.
5. Center the heading at the top of the page.

Typically, information in the data sheet is grouped under the six captions below. If you are a recent graduate with little or no full-time work experience, list education before work experience. If you've worked for a number of years, however, reverse the order.

1. *Personal Information.* This section is optional. If you include it, give your date of birth, marital status, and general condition of health. Avoid race, religion, national origin, or sex, since this information can't be used as a basis for hiring.
2. *Employment Objective.* State your immediate work goals and the direction you hope your career will take.

Figure 14.7
The Pointers Applied: Sample Data Sheet

Karen K. Auernhamer
1407 East Elm Street
Big Rapids, MI 49307
Telephone: (616) 796-7791

PERSONAL DATA

Date of Birth: August 3, 1965
Marital Status: Single
Health: Excellent

EMPLOYMENT OBJECTIVE

To work in a technical or an assistant managerial position in a
medical records department, gain experience, and eventually
assume an administrative position.

EDUCATION

May 1986, Bachelor of Science degree, medical records
administration, Ferris State College, Big Rapids, MI 49307

Academic Honors:
    3.85/4.0 G.P.A., medical records courses

Extracurricular Activities:

    Chairman, Ferris Medical Records Association

June 1982, graduated from Reese High School, Reese, MI 48757,
college preparatory program.

EMPLOYMENT EXPERIENCE

June 1985 to August 1985	Technical trainee (internship program) Saginaw Osteopathic Hospital, Saginaw, MI 48602 Assisted with technical duties in the medical records department.
Summers of 1982, 1983, 1984	Waitress, Zehnder's of Frankenmuth, 215 South Main Street, Frankenmuth, MI 48734

PERSONAL AND PROFESSIONAL INTERESTS

Member, American Medical Records Association. Enjoy tennis, reading, biking, skiing, ice skating, and arts and crafts.

REFERENCES

Mr. Jeffrey Zielinski
Manager, Zehnder's of Frankenmuth
215 South Main Street
Frankenmuth, MI 48734
Telephone: (517) 652-9925

Ms. Brenda Pretzer
Director, Medical Records Department
Saginaw Osteopathic Hospital
515 North Michigan Avenue
Saginaw, MI 48602
Telephone: (517) 776-2682

Ms. Paula Rehfus
Instructor, School of Allied Health
Ferris State College
Big Rapids, MI 49307
Telephone: (616) 796-0416 Extension 3483

3. *Education.* List pertinent facts of your college and high school education, in that order.
4. *Employment Experience.* Highlight your full-time work experience, or if this is limited, your part-time or temporary jobs. Mention any promotions or raises you received or any supervisory experience you gained. Don't mention job duties unless they are similar to the job you're after.
5. *Personal and Professional Interests.* Cite memberships in professional societies and indicate any hobbies you enjoy.
6. *References.* You can list references or indicate that they will be furnished on request. Either way, don't give a person's name without first asking permission. Typical references include teachers, supervisors, and prominent people in the community.

1. Write a letter applying for an advertised job or one that someone has told you about. **EXERCISE**
2. Write a letter applying for a position for which there may or may not be a vacancy.
3. Prepare a data sheet to accompany your letter.

SENTENCE ELEMENTS, SENTENCE ERRORS, PUNCTUATION AND MECHANICS, SPELLING, GLOSSARIES

SENTENCE ELEMENTS

Learning the parts of English sentences won't in itself improve your writing, but it will equip you to handle errors at the sentence level. Before you can identify and correct unwarranted shifts from past to present time, for example, you need to know about verbs and their tenses. Similarly, recognizing and correcting pronoun case errors requires a knowledge of what pronouns are and how they are used. In this section we first cover subjects and predicates, then complements, appositives, the parts of speech, and finally phrases and clauses.

SUBJECTS AND PREDICATES

The subject of a sentence tells who or what it is about. A *simple subject* consists of a noun (that is, a naming word) or a noun substitute. A *complete subject* consists of a simple subject plus any words that limit or describe it.

The predicate tells something about the subject and completes the thought of the sentence. A *simple predicate* consists of one or more verbs (words that show action or existence); a *complete predicate* includes any associated words also. In the following examples the simple subjects are underlined once and the simple predicates twice. The subjects and predicates are separated with slash marks.

William / laughed.
Mary / has moved.
Sarah / painted the kitchen.
The student over there in the corner / is majoring in art.

A sentence can have a compound subject (two or more separate subjects), a compound predicate (two or more separate predicates), or both.

The elephants and their trainer / bowed to the audience and left the ring.

Sentences that ask questions don't follow the usual simple subject–simple predicate order. Instead, the order may be reversed; or if the simple predicate consists of two verbs, the simple subject may come between them.

> When is your theme due? (Simple subject follows simple predicate.)
>
> Has / Joan / walked her pygmy goat yet? (Simple subject comes between verbs.)

EXERCISE   **Place a slash mark between the complete subject and the complete predicate; then underline the simple subject once and the verb(s) twice. If a subject comes between two verbs, set it off with two slash marks.**

1. The new recruits were exhausted by the strenuous exercise.
2. My favorite color is red.
3. Myron and his sister shouted and laughed at the good news.
4. Where are the minutes of last month's meeting?
5. The cruisers and destroyers wheeled and fired their guns.
6. This new sports car has won several awards for its design.
7. The glowering bouncer stood menacingly near the door.
8. A small statue sat on the mantel.
9. Have you heard about Silvana's accident?
10. A good slogan can contribute to the success of a new product.

COMPLEMENTS

A complement is a word or word group that forms part of the predicate and helps complete the meaning of the sentence. Complements fall into four categories: direct objects, indirect objects, subject complements, and object complements.

A *direct object* names whatever receives, or results from, the action of a verb.

> The millwright repaired the *lathe*. (Direct object receives action of verb *repaired*.)
>
> Hilary painted a *picture*. (Direct object results from action of verb *painted*.)
>
> They took *coffee* and *sandwiches* to the picnic. (Direct objects receive action of verb *took*.)

As the last sentence shows, a sentence may have a compound direct object— two or more separate direct objects.

An *indirect object* identifies someone or something that receives whatever is named by the direct object. It always precedes the direct object.

Doris lent *me* her calculator. (Indirect object *me* receives *calculator*, the direct object.)

Will and Al bought their *boat* new sails. (Indirect object *boat* receives *sails*, the direct object.)

An indirect object can be converted to a prepositional phrase that begins with *to* or *for* and follows the direct object.

Doris lent her calculator *to me*.

Will and Al bought new sails *for their boat*.

A *subject complement* follows a linking verb—one that indicates existence rather than action. It renames or describes the subject.

Desmond is a *carpenter*. (Complement *carpenter* renames subject *Desmond*.)

The lights are too *bright* for Percy. (Complement *bright* describes subject *lights*.)

An *object complement* follows a direct object and renames or describes it.

The council named Rosamond *treasurer*. (Object complement *treasurer* renames direct object *Rosamond*.)

The audience thought the play *silly*. (Object complement *silly* describes direct object *play*.)

APPOSITIVES

An appositive is a noun or word group serving as a noun that follows another noun or noun substitute and expands its meaning. Appositives may be restrictive or nonrestrictive. Restrictive appositives distinguish whatever they modify from other items in the same class. They are written without commas.

My sister *Heidi* is a professional golfer. (Appositive *Heidi* distinguishes her from other sisters.)

I have just read a book by the novelist *Henry James*. (Appositive *Henry James* distinguishes him from other novelists.)

Nonrestrictive appositives provide more information about whatever they modify. This sort of appositive is set off by a pair of commas except at the end of a sentence; then it is preceded by a single comma.

Nicolai Karpov, *the Rusitarian Consul,* was interviewed on TV last week. (Appositive names *Karpov's* occupation.)

Dierdre's job, *driving a school bus,* does not pay well. (Appositive names *job.*)

Todd plans to major in paleontology, *the study of fossils.* (Appositive defines *paleontology.*)

EXERCISE   **Identify each italicized item as a direct object (DO), an indirect object (IO), a subject complement (SC), an object complement (OC), or an appositive (AP).**

1. The players called their coach *incompetent.*
2. The small boy kicked the *can* along the sidewalk.
3. Mavis sent *Dick* a Valentine.
4. Nancy was a *nurse* for ten years.
5. Bernice Alcott, *my old chemistry teacher,* now works for Monsanto.
6. Armand's co-workers thought him a *workaholic.*
7. Mary is a *buyer* for Macy's department store.
8. The bellhop carried Ilsa's *luggage* toward the elevator.
9. Miguel's mother made *him* a sandwich.
10. My brother *Tom* spends every weekend in New York.

PARTS OF SPEECH

Traditional English grammar classifies words into eight parts of speech: *nouns, pronouns, verbs, adjectives, adverbs, prepositions, conjunctions,* and *interjections.* This section discusses these categories as well as verbals, phrases, and clauses, which also serve as parts of speech.

NOUNS

Nouns name persons, places, things, conditions, ideas, or qualities. Some nouns, called *proper nouns,* identify one-of-a-kind items like the following:

France	Christmas
Pacific Ocean	North Dakota
George Washington	Mona Lisa
Pulitzer Prize	World Series
Spirit of St. Louis	Wyandotte Corporation
Declaration of Independence	Miami–Dade Junior College

Mount Everest, on the border of *Tibet* and *Nepal,* was named for *Sir George Everest,* an Englishman.

Common nouns name general classes or categories of items and include abstract, concrete, and collective nouns.

Abstract Nouns.   An abstract noun names a condition, idea, or quality—something we can't see, feel, or otherwise experience with our five senses.

arrogance	harmony	sickness
envy	liberalism	understanding
fear	love	

His *desire* to win caused him to cheat.

Mary felt great *loyalty* to her family.

Concrete Nouns.   A concrete noun identifies something that we can experience with one or more of our senses.

man	desk	pillow	needle
bicycle	lemon	airplane	pan
building	piston	carton	smoke

The *air* was thin at the *peak* of the *mountain.*

The *hammer* had a broken *handle.*

Collective Nouns.   A collective noun is singular in form but stands for a group or collection of items.

assembly	committee	crowd	group	tribe
class	convoy	family	herd	troop

The *jury* filed into the courtroom to announce its verdict.

The *flock* of geese settled onto the lake.

EXERCISE   **Identify the nouns in the following sentences.**

1. My roommates play loud music every evening.
2. Isabel lives in Phoenix, Arizona.
3. You showed great strength and courage when disaster struck.
4. The Kiwanis Club places great stress on service to the community.
5. Mr. Fowler assigned the class twenty chemistry problems.
6. The driver collected tickets as the passengers boarded the bus.
7. For twenty years, the Christian Democrats have held power in this country.
8. Ben Franklin proved that lightning was a form of electricity.
9. A car was parked in the alley behind the building.
10. My grandmother rides a bicycle to work every day.

PRONOUNS

Pronouns, which take the place of nouns in sentences, help you avoid the awkward repetition of nouns.

If Brad doesn't like the *book*, take *it* back to the library.

There are eight categories of pronouns: *personal, relative, interrogative, demonstrative, reflexive, intensive, indefinite,* and *reciprocal.*

Personal Pronouns.   Personal pronouns refer to one or more clearly identified persons, places, or things.

Subjective	*Objective*	*Possessive*
I	me	my, mine
you	you	your, yours
he	him	his
she	her	her, hers
it	it	its
we	us	our, ours
you	you	your, yours
they	them	their, theirs

Subjective pronouns serve as the subjects of sentences or clauses; objective pronouns serve as direct and indirect objects; and possessive pronouns show possession or ownership. *My, your, her, our,* and *their* always precede nouns and thus function as possessive adjectives. *His* and *its* may or may not precede nouns.

He bought a sport shirt. (pronoun as subject)

Donald saw *them*. (pronoun as direct object)

Simon lent *her* ten dollars. (pronoun as indirect object)

That car is *theirs*. (pronoun showing ownership)

Relative Pronouns.   A relative pronoun relates a subordinate clause—a word group that has a subject and a predicate but does not express a complete idea—to the main part of its sentence. The relative pronouns include:

who	whose	what	whoever	whichever
whom	which	that	whomever	whatever

Who in its various forms refers to people, *which* to things, and *that* to either people or things.

Mary Beth Cartwright, *who* was arrested last week for fraud, was Evansville's "Model Citizen" two years ago. (The antecedent of *who* is *Mary Beth Cartwright*.)

He took the typewriter, *which* needed cleaning, to the repair shop. (The antecedent of *which* is *typewriter*.)

David Bullock is someone *that* we should definitely hire. (The antecedent of *that* is *someone*.)

Montreal is a city *that* I've always wanted to visit. (The antecedent of *that* is *city*.)

Which typically introduces clauses that provide more information about whatever they modify.

The palace, *which* was in bad condition a century ago, is finally going to be restored. (Clause adds information about palace.)

That is typically used in other situations, especially to introduce clauses that distinguish the things they modify from others in the same class.

The used car *that* I bought last week at Honest Bill's has already broken down twice. (Clause distinguishes writer's used car from others.)

Interrogative Pronouns.   Interrogative pronouns introduce questions. All of the relative pronouns except *that* also function as interrogative pronouns.

who   whose   what   whoever   whichever
whom   which   that   whomever   whatever

What is the matter?

Who asked you?

Whatever do you mean?

When *who*, *what*, and *which* are followed by nouns, they act as adjectives, not pronouns.

Which movie should we see?

Demonstrative Pronouns.   As their name suggests, demonstrative pronouns point things out. There are four such pronouns.

this   these
that   those

This and its plural *these* identify recent or nearby things:

This is the play to see.

These are the times that try men's souls.

That and its plural *those* identify less recent or more distant things:

That is Mary's house across the road.

Those were very good peaches you had for sale last week.

Reflexive and Intensive Pronouns.   A reflexive pronoun reverses the action of a verb, making the doer and the receiver of the action the same. An intensive pronoun lends emphasis to a noun or pronoun. The two sets of pronouns are identical.

myself   herself   ourselves
yourself   itself   yourselves
himself   oneself   themselves

My father cut *himself* while shaving. (reflexive pronoun)

The President *himself* has asked me to undertake this mission. (intensive pronoun)

Don't substitute a reflexive pronoun for a personal pronoun.

Faulty   Jill and *myself* are going to a movie.

Revision   Jill and *I* are going to a movie.

Faulty   Give the tickets to John and *myself*.

Revision   Give the tickets to John and *me*.

Sometimes you'll hear people say things like "He made it *hisself*," "They're only fooling *theirself*," or "They bought *theirselves* sodas." Such forms are non-standard. Say "himself" and "themselves" instead.

Indefinite Pronouns.   The pronouns in this group refer to unidentified persons, places, or things. The group includes the following:

anybody	everything	one
anyone	nobody	somebody
anything	no one	someone
everybody	nothing	something
everyone		

These words consistently act as pronouns. Other words may function either as indefinite pronouns or as adjectives:

all	any	most	few	much
another	each	either	many	neither

Here are some examples:

Everyone is welcome. (indefinite pronoun)

Many are called, but *few* are chosen. (indefinite pronouns)

Many men but only a *few* women attend the Air Force Academy. (adjectives)

Reciprocal Pronouns.   The two reciprocal pronouns show an interchange of action between two or more parties. *Each other* is used when two parties interact; *one another,* when three or more do.

Pearl and Petula accidentally gave *each other* the same thing for Christmas. (two persons)

The members of the football team joyfully embraced *one another* after their victory. (more than two persons)

EXERCISE   **Identify each pronoun in the following sentence and indicate its type.**

1. He blames himself for his poor test score.
2. If you act friendly toward whoever comes along, you will find life much more pleasant.
3. This is the best-equipped auditorium for the demonstration she is planning.
4. You yourself must bear the responsibility for the accident.
5. What are they planning to do next summer?
6. Which of you would like to talk to me next?
7. If we help one another, we will finish the job soon.
8. Of the two plans, yours is more feasible than hers.
9. These are times that anyone would find trying.
10. Everyone who wishes to take the tour can sign up for it tomorrow.

VERBS

A verb indicates action or existence: what something is, was, or will be. Verbs fall into three classes: *action verbs*, *linking verbs*, and *helping verbs*.

Action Verbs.   As its name suggests, an action verb expresses action. Some action verbs are transitive, others intransitive. A *transitive* verb has a direct object, which receives or results from the action and rounds out the meaning of the sentence.

> The photographer *took* the picture.

Without the direct object, this sentence would not express a complete thought. In contrast, an *intransitive* verb requires no direct object to complete the meaning of the sentence.

> Lee Ann *gasped.*

> Little Tommy Tucker *sings* for his supper.

Many action verbs can play both transitive or intransitive roles, depending on the sentences they are used in.

> Kari *rode* her bicycle into town. (transitive verb)

> Karl *rode* in the front seat of the car. (intransitive verb)

Linking Verbs.   A linking verb shows existence—what something is, was, or will be—rather than action. Linking verbs are intransitive and tie their subjects to subject complements. Some subject complements are nouns or noun substitutes that rename their subjects. Others are adjectives that describe their subjects.

> Ms. Davis is our new director. (Complement *director* renames subject *Ms. Davis.*)

> The soup was lukewarm. (Complement *lukewarm* describes subject *soup.*)

The most common linking verbs are forms of the verb *to be (is, are, am, was, were, been).* Some other verbs that may function as linking verbs are *seem, become, appear, remain, feel, look, smell, sound,* and *taste.*

Helping Verbs.   Helping verbs accompany action or linking verbs, allowing them to express with great precision matters such as possibility, obligation, and time. Common helping verbs include the following:

has	been	had (to)
have	do	shall
had	does	will
am	did	going (to)
is	used (to)	about (to)
are	may	would
was	might	should
were	must	ought (to)
be	have (to)	can
being	has (to)	could

> I *shall ask* him. (helping verb *shall* with action verb *ask*)

> The driver *was being lifted* onto a stretcher. (helping verbs *was* and *being* with action verb *lifted*)

> You *have been* good. (helping verb *have* with linking verb *been*)

> The patient *will feel* better soon. (helping verb *will* with linking verb *feel*)

> We *might go* to Corvallis next weekend. (helping verb *might* with action verb *go*)

Helping verbs usually appear next to the main verbs, but they don't have to:

> Ellen *will* undoubtedly *resign.*

As we noted before, combinations of two or more verbs are called verb phrases.

EXERCISE   Identify each verb in the following sentences and indicate its type.

1. Jocasta and Ismene have been arguing all afternoon.
2. Frank must be tired after his long journey.
3. I am still working at Barrett's clothing store.
4. If you will jog a mile a day, you will soon be in much better physical condition.
5. Please talk slowly when you make your speech.
6. Will you please hand those shoes to me?
7. At the time of the accident, I had been driving for twelve hours.
8. Have you read this new best-seller?
9. The car handled beautifully, but its brakes were defective.
10. These chairs and tables were made at the time of Louis XV.

Principal Parts.   Verbs change in form to show time (tense) distinction. For every verb, tenses are built from three principal parts: *present, past,* and *past participle.* The present is the principal part you would look up in the dictionary (*win, skip, go,* and so on). If the subject of a verb is a singular pronoun (*he, she, it*) or a singular noun, add an *s* or *es* to the dictionary form (*wins, skips, goes*). Most verbs have identical past and past participles.

I, you, we, they	talk	talked	talked
He, she, it, Henry	talks	talked	talked
I, you, we, they	stand	stood	stood
He, she, it, the decision	stands	stood	stood

Of the remaining verbs, most have different past and past participles.

	Present	*Past*	*Past Participle*
I, you, we, they	swim	swam	swum
He, she, it, the boy	swims	swam	swum
I, you, we, they	bite	bit	bitten
He, she, it, the dog	bites	bit	bitten

With a few verbs, the past and past participles are identical to the dictionary form.

	Present	*Past*	*Past Participle*
I, you, we, they	set	set	set
He, she, it	sets	set	set

If you're uncertain about the principal parts of a verb, check your dictionary.

Tense.   English has six basic tenses: present, past, future, present perfect, past perfect, future perfect. They are formed from the principal parts of action and linking verbs, either alone or combined with helping verbs.

The *present tense* is formed from the present principal part of the main verb and used without helping verbs. It shows present condition and general or habitual action, indicates permanent truths, tells about past events in the historical present, and sometimes denotes action at some definite future time.

> Helen *looks* beautiful in her new gown. (present condition)
>
> John *works* on the eighteenth floor. (general action)
>
> I *brush* my teeth each morning. (habitual action)
>
> The sun *rises* in the East. (permanent truth)
>
> On November 11, 1918, the guns *fall* silent, and World War I *comes* to an end. (historical present)
>
> Monday, I *begin* my new job. (future action)

The *past tense* is based on the past principal part of the verb. Like the present tense, it uses no helping verb. The past tense shows that a condition existed or an action was completed in the past. The verb tense leaves the time indefinite, but surrounding words may specify it.

> Paul *was* angry with his noisy neighbors. (past condition, time indefinite)
>
> Lucretia *received* a long letter yesterday. (past action, time specified by *yesterday*)

The *future tense* combines *shall* or *will* and the present principal part of the main verb. It indicates that a condition will exist or an action will take place in the future.

> You *will feel* better after a good night's sleep. (future condition)
>
> I *shall attend* the concert next week. (future action)

The *present perfect* tense is formed with *has* or *have* and the past participle of the main verb. It shows that a past condition or action, or its effect, continues until the present time.

> The players *have been* irritable since they lost the homecoming game. (Condition continues until present.)
>
> Juanita *has driven* a United Parcel Service truck for five years. (Action continues until present.)

William *has repaired* the snow blower. (Effect of action continues until present, although the action itself was completed in the past.)

The *past perfect* tense combines *had* and the past participle of the main verb. It refers to a past condition or action that was completed before or after another past condition or action.

He *had been* in the army two years when the war ended. (Past perfect condition occurred first.)

Two minutes after the tornado struck, it *had blown* our house down. (Past perfect action occurred last.)

Vivian moved into the house that she *had built* the summer before. (Past perfect action occurred first.)

The *future perfect* tense is formed from the verbs *shall have* or *will have* plus the past participle of the main verb. It shows that a condition or an action will have been completed at some time in the future. Surrounding words specify time.

Our sales manager *will have been* with the company ten years next July. (Condition will end.)

By the end of this year, I *shall have written* the great American novel. (Action will be completed.)

Each of these basic tenses has a *progressive tense* that indicates action in progress. The progressive tense always includes some form of the verb *to be* followed by a present participle, a verb that ends in *-ing*.

Present progressive	I *am running.*
Past progressive	I *was running.*
Future progressive	I *shall be running.*
Present perfect progressive	I *have been running.*
Past perfect progressive	I *had been running.*
Future perfect progressive	I *shall have been running.*

Voice.   Transitive verbs have two voices: active and passive. A verb is in the *active voice* when the subject carries out the action named by the verb.

Barry *planned* a picnic. (Subject *Barry* performs action.)

A verb is in the *passive voice* when the subject receives the action. The performer may be identified in an accompanying phrase or go unmentioned.

A picnic *was planned* by Barry. (The phrase *by Barry* identifies the performer.)

The picnic *was canceled*. (The performer goes unmentioned.)

A passive construction always uses a form of *to be* and the past participle of an action verb. Like other constructions, the passive may show past, present, or future time.

Amy *is paid* handsomely for her investment advice. (present tense)

I *was warned* by a sound truck that a tornado was nearby. (past tense)

I *will be sent* to Ghana soon by the Peace Corps. (future tense)

I *have been awarded* a sizeable research grant. (present perfect tense)

The city *had been shelled* heavily before the infantry moved in. (past perfect tense)

By the end of this month, the site for our second factory *will have been chosen*. (future perfect tense)

To convert a sentence from the passive to the active voice, make the performer the subject, the original subject the direct object, and drop the form of *to be*.

The treaty was signed by the general. (passive)

The general signed the treaty. (active)

Technical and scientific writing commonly use the passive voice to explain processes since its flat, impersonal tone adds an air of scientific objectivity and authority. Other kinds of writing, however, avoid the passive voice except when it is desirable to conceal the doer of the action or when the action is more significant than the actor. See pages 190–192 for more information on usage.

Identify each verb in the following sentences, indicate its tense, and note any use of the passive voice.   **EXERCISE**

1. Alan is changing his clothes for dinner.
2. I will oversee the construction of the building.
3. I shall have finished the report by Friday.
4. The instructions have been followed by Todd.

5. Drusilla kept her first car for twelve years.
6. The President was informed of the incident two hours after it took place.
7. Twenty minutes after he began the crossword puzzle, Terry had completed it.
8. I have seriously considered two majors: sociology and political science.
9. These shrubs will be pruned tomorrow.
10. Sally leaves for London on Saturday.
11. He is constantly humiliated by his supposed friends.
12. Prudence shouted angrily at the fighting children.

Mood. The mood of a verb shows whether the writer regards a statement as a

1. fact
2. command or request
3. wish, possibility, condition contrary to fact, or the like

English has three moods: the indicative, imperative, and subjunctive.

A sentence in the *indicative mood* states a real or supposed fact or asks a question.

Nancy *graduates* from high school tomorrow.

We *lived* in Oakmont when Rachel was born.

He *had been* a sailor during the war.

Has Joe *asked* anyone to the prom yet?

Most verbs are used in the indicative mood.

A sentence in the *imperative mood* delivers a command or makes a request.

Leave the room immediately! (command)

Please *turn* the phonograph down. (request)

The subject of a sentence in the imperative mood is always *you.* Although ordinarily unstated, the subject sometimes appears in the sentence.

You leave the room immediately!

The *subjunctive mood* is used

1. in *if, as if,* and *as though* clauses to express a possibility or an action or condition contrary to fact
2. in *that* clauses expressing orders, demands, requests, resolutions, proposals, or motions

3. with modal auxiliaries to express wishes, probability, possibility, permission, requirements, recommendations, suggestions, and conditions contrary to fact

To express present or future wish, possibility, condition or action in an *if, as if,* or *as though* clause, use *were* with any personal pronoun or noun serving as the subject of the clause.

> If only Stan *were* less gullible! (present wish contrary to fact)
>
> Even if Kay *were* to explain, Mary wouldn't believe her. (future possibility)
>
> Arthur is behaving as if he *were* a millionaire. (present condition contrary to fact)

To express a wish, possibility, or condition contrary to past facts, use *had been* or *had* plus the past participle of an action verb.

> If the engine *had been* lubricated, the bearing wouldn't have burned out. (past condition contrary to fact)
>
> Alice looked as if she *had lost* her best friend. (condition expressed in clause occurs before action of verb *looked*)

When writing *that* clauses expressing orders, demands, requests, resolutions, proposals, or motions, use *be* or the present form of an action verb.

> I move that they *be* rewarded for their bravery.
>
> The group proposed that Margaret *go* to the scene of the accident and *inspect* it personally.

In other *that* clauses, use the appropriate indicative form of the verb.

> I know that they *were* rewarded for their bravery.
>
> The group believed that Margaret *had gone* to the scene of the accident and *inspected* it personally.

The modal auxiliaries include the helping verbs *can, could, may, might, must, shall, will, would, should,* and *ought to.* The examples below illustrate the meanings they can express.

1. Wishes *(could, would)*

> I wish I *could* shimmy like my sister Kate.
>
> The Republicans wish the Democrats *would* go away and *vice versa.*

2. Probability *(should)*

Because I've studied diligently, I *should* do better on my next chemistry test.

3. Possibility *(may, might, can, could)*

High interest rates *could* cause our housing industry to collapse.

I *might* stay up to watch the eclipse of the moon tonight.

4. Permission *(can, may)*

The public *can* use these tennis courts every afternoon.

You *may* leave as soon as you've finished filing these folders.

5. Requirements *(must)*

The landlord has raised our rent again; we *must* find another apartment.

6. Recommendations, suggestions *(should, ought to)*

Randy *should* see a doctor about his chest pains.

The nuclear powers *ought to* reduce their stockpiles of atomic weapons.

7. Conditions contrary to fact *(could)*

If only I *could* live my life over!

EXERCISE   **For each of the following sentences, identify the mood as indicative (IND), imperative (IMP), or subjunctive (SUB).**

1. Have a good time at the party.
2. They demanded that the secretary be removed for failing to keep adequate records of the meetings.
3. Senator Conwell will seek reelection next year.
4. Can you believe that Mr. Scrooge has raised Bob Cratchet's wages?
5. Don't you dare to make this foolish mistake again.
6. I'd put a statue of myself on every street corner if I were running the world.
7. Everybody should visit our nation's capital and tour its public buildings.
8. Someday the earth may establish colonies on Mars.
9. The American public has lost its infatuation with the automobile.
10. Unless attendance drops off drastically, this movie should make more money than any other.

ADJECTIVES

An adjective *modifies* a noun or pronoun by describing it, limiting it, or otherwise making its meaning more exact.

The *brass* candlestick stood next to the *fragile* vase. (*Fragile* modifies *vase*.)

The cat is *long-haired* and *sleek*. (*Long-haired* and *sleek* modify *cat*.)

There are three general categories of adjectives: limiting, descriptive, and proper.

Limiting Adjectives. A limiting adjective identifies or points out the noun or pronoun it modifies. It may indicate number or quantity. Several categories of pronouns can serve as limiting adjectives, as can numbers and nouns.

Whose briefcase is on the table? (interrogative adjective)

The couple *whose* car was stolen called the police. (relative adjective)

This restaurant has the best reputation for gourmet food. (demonstrative adjective)

Some people have no social tact at all. (indefinite adjective)

Sally swerved *her* car suddenly to avoid an oncoming truck. (possessive adjective)

Three people entered the lecture hall late. (number as adjective)

The *schoolgirl* look is fashionable this year. (noun as adjective)

Descriptive Adjectives. A descriptive adjective name a quality, characteristic, or condition of a noun or pronoun. Two or more of these adjectives, members of the largest category of adjectives, may modify the same noun or pronoun.

The *yellow* submarine belongs to the Beatles.

He applied *clear* lacquer to the table top.

The *slim, sophisticated* model glided onto the runway.

The child wore a *thick, green, quilted* jacket.

Proper Adjectives. A proper adjective is derived from a proper noun and is always capitalized.

Harwell is a *Shakespearean* actor.

Articles as Adjectives. Articles appear immediately before nouns and can therefore be considered adjectives. There are three articles in English: *a, an,* and *the. The* points to a specific item, *a* and *an* do not. *A* precedes words beginning with consonant sounds; *an* precedes words with vowel sounds, making pronunciation easier.

> *The* right word at *the* right moment can save a friendship. (Definite articles suggest there is one right word and one right moment.)

> *A* right word can save *a* friendship. (Indefinite articles suggest there may be several right words and friendships.)

> I think I'd like *an* apple with my lunch. (No particular apple is specified.)

Sometimes the definite article refers to a class of items.

> *The* tiger is fast becoming an endangered species.

Context shows whether such a sentence refers to particular items or entire classes.

Comparison with Adjectives.   Adjectives may be used to show comparison. When two things are compared, shorter adjectives usually add *-er* and longer adjectives add *more*. When three or more things are compared, shorter adjectives usually add *-est* and longer ones add *most*.

> John is *taller* than Pete. (short adjective comparing two things)

> Sandra seems *more* cheerful than Jill today. (long adjective comparing two things)

> John is the *tallest* of the three brothers. (short adjective comparing three things)

> Sandra is the *most* cheerful girl in the class. (longer adjective comparing more than three things)

Some adjectives, like the examples below, have irregular forms for comparisons.

> good—better—best

> bad—worse—worst

Don't use the *-est* form of the shorter adjective for comparing just two things.

> *Faulty*   This is the *smallest* of the two castles.

Instead, use the *-er* form.

> *Revision*   This is the *smaller* of the two castles.

Position of Adjectives.   Most adjectives come immediately before the words they modify. In a few set expressions (for example, heir *apparent*), the adjective immediately follows the word it modifies. Similarly, adjective pairs sometimes appear in a follow-up position for added emphasis (The rapids, *swift* and *dangerous,* soon capsized the raft). Sometimes adjectives also serve as subject complements and follow their subjects (The puppy was *friendly*).

Identify the adjectives in the following sentences.
EXERCISE

1. We had three weeks of vacation.
2. A tall, cool drink is very welcome on a hot day.
3. Because of bad weather, only ten people attended the meeting.
4. The short, slight jockey wore a yellow outfit in the race.
5. The pretty girl sat quietly, her golden hair blowing in the breeze.
6. The Chinese ambassador speaks beautiful English.
7. An apple a day keeps the doctor away.
8. Lilacs may be purple, white, or pink.
9. The sharp rocks on the beach bruised my bare feet.
10. Marlena was tired after her difficult day in school.

ADVERBS

An adverb modifies a verb, an adjective, another adverb, or a whole sentence. Adverbs generally answer questions such as "how?" "when?" "where?" "how often?" and "to what extent?"

The floodwaters receded *very* slowly. (Adverb modifies adverb and answers the question "how?")

My sister will visit me *tomorrow.* (Adverb modifies verb and answers the question "when?")

The coach walked *away* from the bench. (Adverb modifies verb and answers the question "where?")

The tire is *too* worn to be safe. (Adverb modifies adjectives and answers the question "how much?")

The teller is *frequently* late for work. (Adverb modifies adjective and answers the question "how often?")

Unfortunately, the game was canceled because of rain. (The adverb modifies the whole sentence but does not answer any question.)

Formation of Adverbs.   Most adverbs are formed by adding *-ly* to adjectives.

The wind is *restless*. (*Restless* is an adjective modifying *wind*.)

He walked *restlessly* around the room. (*Restlessly* is an adverb modifying *walked*.)

Many common adverbs, however, (*almost, never, quite, soon, then, there,* and *too*) lack *-ly* endings.

I *soon* realized that pleasing my boss was impossible.

This movie is *too* gruesome for my taste.

Furthermore, some words such as *better, early, late, hard, little, near, straight,* and *wrong* do double duty either as adjectives or adverbs.

We must have taken a *wrong* turn. (*Wrong* is an adjective modifying the noun *turn*.)

Where did I go *wrong*? (*Wrong* is an adverb modifying the verb *go*.)

Comparison with Adverbs.   Like adjectives, adverbs can show comparison. When two things are compared, shorter adverbs add *more*. When three or more things are compared, *most* is used.

Harold works *more* efficiently than Don. (adverb comparing two people)

Of all the people in the shop, Harold works the *most* efficiently. (adverb comparing more than three people)

Some adverbs, like some adjectives, use irregular forms for comparisons:

well—better—best

much—more—most

Position of Adverbs.   Adverbs are more moveable than any other part of speech. Usually, adverbs that modify adjectives and other adverbs appear next to them to avoid confusion.

Her *especially* fine tact makes her a welcome guest at any party. (Adverb *especially* modifies adjective *fine*.)

The novel was *so* badly written that I couldn't finish it. (Adverb *so* modifies adverb *badly*.)

Adverbs that modify verbs, however, can often be shifted around in their sentences without causing changes in meaning.

Quickly, he slipped through the doorway.

He slipped *quickly* through the doorway.

He slipped through the doorway *quickly.*

Identify the adverbs in the following sentences.

1. Sue paddled her canoe tirelessly upstream.
2. Giovanni thought the graduation address was very inspiring.
3. Nothing can save the troops now.
4. The deer flashed by more quickly than the hunter had thought possible.
5. Pam yawned sleepily and soon went to sleep.
6. This restaurant is too expensive for us.
7. The service station attendant told us that our turnoff was ten miles south.
8. They divided the pizza evenly and ate it quickly.
9. Actually, I thought the movie was very dull.
10. I felt very energetic yesterday, but now I am totally exhausted.

PREPOSITIONS

A preposition links its object—a noun or noun substitute—to some other word in the sentence and shows a relationship between them. The relationship is often one of location, time, means, and reason or purpose. The word group containing the preposition and its object makes up a prepositional phrase.

The new insulation *in* the attic keeps my house much warmer now. (Preposition *in* links object *attic* to *insulation* and shows location.)

We have postponed the meeting *until* tomorrow. (Preposition *until* links object *tomorrow* to *postponed* and shows time.)

The tourists traveled *by* automobile. (Preposition *by* links object *automobile* to *traveled* and shows means.)

Warren swims *for* exercise. (Preposition *for* links object *exercise* to *swims* and shows reason or purpose.)

The following list includes the most common prepositions, some of which consist of two or more words.

above	at	between	except
after	because of	by	for
against	before	by reason of	from
along with	below	contrary to	in
among	beside	during	instead of

into	of	over	toward
like	on	since	under
near	onto	through	with
next to	out of	to	without

Many of these combine to form additional prepositions: *except for, in front of, by way of, on top of,* and the like.

Certain prepositions sometimes occur in close association with certain verbs, forming verb units with altered meanings. When this happens, we call the prepositions verb particles. Here is an example.

The instructor let Jeff make *up* the test.

Note the great difference between the meaning of the foregoing sentence and "The instructor let Jeff make the test."

EXERCISE   **Identify the prepositions and their objects in the following sentences.**

1. The nun sang softly as she walked through the chapel.
2. Aunt Helga will probably visit us at the end of September.
3. With a rattle, Carrie amused the fussing baby.
4. The judge sentenced the arsonist to prison for ten years.
5. The architect chose Italian marble for the walls of the lobby.
6. Because of the epidemic of flu, several schools in this town have closed for the week.
7. Over the river and through the woods to Grandmother's house we go.
8. Admittance to this sale is by special invitation only.
9. Nelson has been busy with household tasks this morning.
10. For exercise, Harriet jogs five miles each day.

CONJUNCTIONS

Conjunctions serve as connectors, linking parts of sentences or whole sentences. These connectors fall into three groups: coordinating conjunctions, subordinating conjunctions, and conjunctive adverbs.

Coordinating Conjunctions. Coordinating conjunctions connect terms of equal grammatical importance: words, word groups, and simple sentences. These conjunctions can occur singly (*and, but, or, nor, for, yet, so*) or in pairs called correlative conjunctions (*either–or, neither–nor, both–and,* and *not only–but also*). The elements that follow correlative conjunctions must be parallel; that is, have the same grammatical form.

Tom *and* his cousin are opening a video arcade. (Coordinating conjunction connects nouns.)

Shall I serve the tea in the living room *or* on the veranda? (Coordinating conjunction connects phrases.)

I am going to Europe this summer, *but* Marjorie is staying home. (Coordinating conjunction connects simple sentences.)

Kenzo *not only* teaches English *but also* writes novels. (Correlative conjunctions connect parallel verbs.)

You can study nursing *either* at Ferris State College *or* at DeWitt College. (Correlative conjunctions connect parallel phrases.)

Friendship is *both* pleasure *and* pain. (Correlative conjunctions connect parallel nouns.)

Subordinating Conjunctions.   Like relative pronouns, subordinating conjunctions link subordinate clauses to elements of higher rank; namely, independent clauses, the parts that can stand alone as complete sentences. Examples of subordinating conjunctions include *because, as if, even though, since, so that, whereas,* and *whenever* (see page 381 for a fuller list).

I enjoyed the TV program *because* it was so well acted. (Conjunction connects *because it was so well acted* to rest of sentence.)

Whenever you're ready, we can begin dinner. (Conjunction connects *whenever you're ready* to rest of sentence.)

Conjunctive Adverbs.   These connectors resemble both conjunctions and adverbs. Like conjunctions, they serve as linking devices, joining elements of equal rank. Like adverbs, they function as modifiers, showing such things as similarity, contrast, result or effect, addition, emphasis, time, and example. The following list groups the most common conjunctive adverbs according to function.

Similarity: likewise, similarly
Contrast: however, nevertheless, on the contrary, on the other hand, otherwise
Result or effect: accordingly, as a result, consequently, hence, therefore, thus
Addition: also, furthermore, in addition, in the first place, moreover
Emphasis or clarity: in fact, in other words, indeed, that is
Time: afterwards, later, meanwhile, subsequently
Example: for example, for instance, to illustrate

The job will require you to travel a great deal; *however,* the salary is excellent.

Sean cares nothing for clothes; *in fact,* all of his socks have holes in their toes.

INTERJECTIONS

An interjection is an exclamatory word used to gain attention or to express strong feeling. It has no grammatical connection to the rest of the sentence. An interjection is followed by an exclamation point or a comma.

Hey! Watch how you're driving! (strong interjection)

Oh, is the party over already? (mild interjection)

EXERCISE   **Identify the coordinating conjunctions (CC), subordinating conjunctions (SC), conjunctive adverbs (CA), and interjections (I) in the following sentences.**

1. The fish we ordered finally arrived; however, it was stone cold.
2. Sasha walked away from the panhandler, but he kept following her.
3. Can you talk to me now, or are you too busy?
4. Wow! Did you see that slam dunk?
5. Mark and Terry attended the dance even though both felt under the weather.
6. Glen had both strawberry ice cream and chocolate cake for dessert.
7. Because we have classes at the same hour, let's drive to school together.
8. Golly, it's a relief to be home again.
9. I don't want the job; in fact, I've refused it once already.
10. Gina is not only attractive but also intelligent.
11. Because I forgot to punch the time clock, I lost several hours' pay.
12. Andrea misread the instructions for carrying out the experiment; as a result, she had to repeat it.

PHRASES AND CLAUSES
PHRASES

A phrase is a group of words that lacks a subject and a predicate and serves as a single part of speech. This section discusses four basic kinds of phrases: *prepositional phrases, participial phrases, gerund phrases,* and *infinitive phrases.* The last three are based on participles, gerunds, and infinitives, verb forms known as verbals. A fifth type of phrase, the verb phrase, consists of sets of two or more verbs (*has fixed, had been sick, will have been selected,* and the like).

Prepositional Phrases. A prepositional phrase consists of a preposition, one or more objects, and any associated words. These phrases serve as adjectives or adverbs.

The picture *over the mantel* was painted by Andy Warhol. (prepositional phrase as adjective)

He bought ice skates *for himself.* (prepositional phrase as adverb modifying verb)

The toddler was afraid *of the dog.* (prepositional phrase as adverb modifying adjective)

Our visitors arrived late *in the day.* (prepositional phrase as adverb modifying another adverb)

Frequently, prepositional phrases occur in series. Sometimes they form chains in which each phrase modifies the object of the preceding phrase. At other times some or all of the phrases may modify the verb or verb phrase.

John works *in a clothing store / on Main Street / during the summer.*

Here the first and third phrases serve as adverbs modifying the verb *works* and answering the questions "where?" and "when?" while the second phrase serves as an adjective modifying *store.*

On occasion, especially in questions, a preposition may be separated from its object, making the phrase difficult to find.

This is the book *that* I've been looking *for.*

What are you shouting *about?*

Participial Phrases.   A participial phrase consists of a participle plus associated words. Participles are verb forms that, when used in participial phrases, function as adjectives. A present participle ends in *-ing* and indicates an action currently being carried out. A past participle ends in *-ed, -en, -e, -n, -d,* or *-t* and indicates some past action.

The chef *preparing dinner* trained in France. (present participial phrase)

The background, *sketched in lightly,* accented the features of the woman in the painting. (past participial phrase)

The dress uniform *worn by General McArthur* commanded a high price at the auction. (past participial phrase)

A perfect participial phrase consists of *having* or *having been* plus a past participle and any associated words. Like a past participial phrase, it indicates a past action.

Having alerted the townspeople about the tornado, the sound truck returned to the city garage. (perfect participial phrase)

Having been alerted to the tornado, the townspeople sought shelter in their basements. (perfect participial phrase)

Some participial phrases that modify persons or things distinguish them from others in the same class. These phrases are written without commas. Other phrases provide more information about the persons or things they modify and are set off with commas.

> The man *fixing my car* is a master mechanic. (Phrase distinguishes man fixing car from others.)

> Mr. Welsh, *fatigued by the tennis game,* rested in the shade. (Phrase provides more information about Mr. Welsh.)

Gerund Phrases.   A gerund phrase consists of a gerund and the words associated with it. Like present participles, gerunds are verb forms that end in *-ing*. Unlike participles, though, they function as nouns rather than as adjectives.

> Kathryn's hobby is *collecting stamps.* (gerund phrase as subject complement)

> Kathryn's hobby, *collecting stamps,* has made her many friends. (gerund phrase as appositive)

> He devoted every spare moment to *overhauling the car.* (gerund phrase as object of preposition)

Infinitive Phrases.   An infinitive phrase consists of the present principal part of a verb preceded by *to (to fix, to eat),* together with any accompanying words. These phrases serve as adjectives, adverbs, and nouns.

> This looks like a good place *to plant the shrub.* (infinitive phrase as adjective)

> Lenore worked *to earn money for college.* (infinitive phrase as adverb)

> My goal is *to have* my own business some day. (infinitive phrase as noun)

Gerunds can often be substituted for infinitives and vice versa.

> *To repair this fender* will cost two hundred dollars. (infinitive phrase as subject)

> *Repairing this fender* will cost two hundred dollars. (gerund phrase as subject)

At times the *to* in an infinitive may be omitted following verbs such as *make, dare, let,* and *help.*

> Constanzia didn't dare *(to) move* a muscle.

> The psychiatrist helped me *(to) overcome* my fear of flying.

Verbals Not in Phrases.   Participles, gerunds, and infinitives can function as nouns, adjectives, and adverbs, even when they are not parts of phrases.

That *sunbathing* woman is a well-known model. (participle)

Dancing is fine exercise. (gerund)

The children want *to play.* (infinitive as noun)

If you're looking for a job, Sally is the person *to see.* (infinitive as adjective)

I'm prepared *to resign.* (infinitive as adverb)

Identify the italicized phrases as prepositional, participial, gerund, or infinitive, and tell whether each is used as a noun, an adjective, or an adverb.   **EXERCISE**

1. *Annoyed by Sam's remarks,* Lolita closed her magazine and left the room.
2. Next summer the Whittakers plan *to buy a lakeside cottage.*
3. *Losing this game* will eliminate us from the playoffs.
4. The coffee will be ready *in about five minutes.*
5. Louis flipped *through the report* until he found the "Results" section.
6. The bluff *overlooking the rapids* is called Lover's Leap.
7. *Parched by the heat,* Roseann quickly downed two glasses of lemonade.
8. The Jeffersons are quite pleased *with their new car.*
9. Amy went to the library *to study her biology lesson.*
10. The refrigerant *used to cool our food* was ordinary ice.
11. *Burdened by mountainous debts and ill health,* Mr. Goodman shot himself.
12. My favorite spot is *fishing for salmon.*
13. This is the best spot *for our flower garden.*
14. The host shouted loudly *to get the attention of the guests.*
15. *To do well in college* has been my goal ever since I set foot on campus.

CLAUSES

A clause is a word group that includes a subject and a predicate. An *independent clause,* sometimes called a main clause, expresses a complete thought and can function as a simple sentence. A *subordinate clause,* or dependent clause, cannot stand by itself. Subordinate clauses may serve as nouns, adjectives, or adverbs.

Noun Clauses.   A noun clause can serve in any of the ways that ordinary nouns can.

What the neighbor told John proved to be incorrect. (noun clause as subject)

The woman asked *when the bus left for Spokane.* (noun clause as direct object)

I'll give a reward to *whoever returns my billfold.* (noun clause as object of preposition *to*)

Noun clauses normally begin with one of the following words:

Relative Pronouns		*Subordinating Conjunctions*
who	whoever	when
whom	whomever	why
whose	that	where
what	whatever	how
which	whichever	whether

The relative pronoun *that* is sometimes omitted from the beginning of a clause that acts as a direct object.

Dr. Kant thinks *(that) he knows everything.*

If a clause is serving as a noun, you can replace it with the word *something* or *someone,* and the sentence will still make sense.

Dr. Kant thinks *something.*

If the clause is serving as an adjective or an adverb, making the substitution turns the sentence into nonsense.

The person *who wins the lottery* will receive two million dollars.

The person *someone* will receive two million dollars.

Adjective Clauses.   Like ordinary adjectives, adjective clauses modify nouns and noun substitutes.

Give me one reason *why you feel the way you do.* (Adjective clause modifies noun.)

I'll hire anyone *that Dr. Stone recommends.* (Adjective clause modifies pronoun.)

Generally, adjective clauses begin with one of the following words:

Relative Pronouns	*Subordinating Conjunctions*
who	when
whom	where
whose	why
what	after
which	before
that	

Sometimes the word that introduces the clause can be omitted.

The chair *(that) we ordered last month* has just arrived. (pronoun *that* omitted but understood)

The man *(whom) we were talking to* is a movie producer. (pronoun *whom* omitted but understood)

Sometimes, too, a preposition comes ahead of the introductory pronoun.

The grace *with which Nelson danced* made the onlookers envious.

An adjective clause may be restrictive and distinguish whatever it modifies from others in the same class, or it may be nonrestrictive and provide more information about whatever it modifies.

Flora wiped up the cereal *that the baby had spilled.* (restrictive clause)

Harriet Thomas, *who was born in Alaska,* now lives in Hawaii. (nonrestrictive clause)

As these examples show, restrictive clauses are not set off with commas, but nonrestrictive clauses are.

Adverb Clauses. These clauses modify verbs, adjectives, adverbs, and sentences, answering the same question as ordinary adverbs do.

You may go *whenever you wish.* (Adverb clause modifies verb.)

Sandra looked paler *than I had ever seen her look before.* (Adverb clause modifies adjective.)

Darryl shouted loudly *so that the rescue party could hear him.* (Adverb clause modifies adverb.)

Unless everyone cooperates, this plan will never succeed. (Adverb clause modifies whole sentence.)

The word or word group that introduces an adverb clause is always a subordinating conjunction. Here are the most common of these conjunctions, grouped according to the questions they answer.

When? after, as, as soon as, before, since, until, when, whenever, while
Where? where, wherever
How? as if, as though
Why? as, because, now that, since, so that
Under what conditions? although, if, once, provided that, though, unless
To what extent? than

Occasionally in an adverb clause, the omission of one or more words won't hurt its meaning. Such a construction is called an *elliptical clause.*

While (he was) making a sandwich, Garth hummed softly. (*he was* omitted but understood)

Unlike noun and adjective clauses, adverb clauses can often be moved about in their sentences.

Garth hummed softly *while (he was) making a sandwich.*

EXERCISE   **Identify the italicized clauses as noun, adjective, or adverb.**

1. *That he was no friend* became apparent when he started gossiping about me.
2. We will leave *whenever everybody is ready.*
3. Anyone *who has ever heard him speak* recognizes his power to sway crowds.
4. *If the taxi doesn't arrive soon,* we will miss our flight.
5. The used car *Sam bought last week* has already broken down.
6. I don't know *what you're talking about.*
7. The committee will give *whoever has the best costume* two tickets to the theater.
8. I had to work last weekend *because I couldn't finish the job on schedule.*
9. We have found a lake *where the fishing is excellent.*
10. Sandra had an accident *while driving to Spokane.*
11. I hope *Barry solves his financial problems soon.*
12. The producer *with whom he signed a contract* proved dishonest.

SENTENCE ERRORS

Accepted usage improves the smoothness of your prose, makes your writing easier to understand, and demonstrates that you are a careful communicator. These assets, in turn, increase the likelihood that the reader will accept your ideas.

When you've completed the first draft of a piece of writing, revise with a critic's eye to ensure that your English is standard. Circle sentences or parts of them that are faulty or suspect. Then check your circled items against this section of the handbook, which deals with the most common errors in college writing.

SENTENCE FRAGMENTS

A sentence fragment is a group of words that fails to qualify as a sentence but is capitalized and punctuated as if it were a sentence. To be a sentence, a word group must (1) have a subject and a verb and (2) make sense by itself.

The first of the following examples has a subject and a verb; the second does not. Neither makes sense by itself.

> If you want to remain.

> His answer to the question.

Methods of Revision.   Eliminating a sentence fragment is not hard. Careful reading often shows that the fragment goes with the sentence that comes just before or just after it. And sometimes two successive fragments can be joined. Note how we've corrected the fragments (italicized) in the following pairs.

Faulty	*Having been warned about the storm.* We decided to stay home.
Revision	Having been warned about the storm, we decided to stay home.
Faulty	*After eating.* The dog took a nap.
Revision	After eating, the dog took a nap.
Faulty	Sally went to work. *Although she felt sick.*
Revision	Sally went to work although she felt sick.
Faulty	Dave bought a new suit. *Over at Bentley's.*
Revision	Dave bought a new suit over at Bentley's.
Faulty	*That bronze clock on the mantel. Once belonged to my grandmother.*
Revision	That bronze clock on the mantel once belonged to my grandmother.

Joining a fragment to a sentence or to another fragment works only if the problem is simply one of mispunctuation. If the fragment stems from an improperly developed thought, revise the thought into correct sentence form.

Punctuating Your Corrections.   When you join a fragment to the following sentence, you need not place a comma between the two unless the fragment has six or more words or if omitting a comma might cause a misreading. When joining a fragment to the preceding sentence, omit a comma unless there is a distinct pause between the two items. The preceding examples illustrate these points.

Intentional Fragments.   Fragments are commonly used in conversation and the writing that reproduces it. Professional writers also use fragments to gain special emphasis or create special effects. Pages 193–194 discuss these applications.

EXERCISE   **Twelve main clauses paired with fragments are shown below. In each case identify the sentence and the fragment, and then eliminate the fragment.**

1. After a short wait. I was summoned into the interviewer's office.
2. Chris ate three sandwiches and drank six root beers. While he watched the game.
3. Because the workers are fast and efficient. They receive large bonuses every year.
4. If my parents will lend me the money. I'll go to Florida during the Easter break.
5. Jack told Anne. That he was moving to another state in one month.
6. I'd like you to meet Dr. Gorbichou. Our chief chemist.
7. I crashed into a tree. To avoid hitting the car ahead of me.
8. Jill bought a dress. Where I did.
9. To make more accurate engineering drawings. Dolores sharpened her pencil frequently.
10. Suzette bought a stuffed bear. For her daughter's bed.
11. Frustrated by his lack of progress. Delbert abandoned his project.
12. Muddy and wet after a two-mile walk through sodden fields. Phil was eager for hot coffee and a shower.

RUN-ON SENTENCES
AND COMMA SPLICES

A run-on, or fused, sentence occurs when one sentence runs into another without anything to mark their junction. A comma splice occurs when only a comma marks the junction. These errors lead your readers to think that you are hasty or careless. Here are several examples.

Run-on sentence   Laura failed to set her alarm she was late for work.

Comma splice   Violets are blooming now, my lawn is covered with them.

Run-on sentence   Rick refused to attend the movie he said he hated horror shows.

Comma splice   Perry watched the road carefully, he still missed his turn.

Run-on sentence   Janet worked on her term paper her friend studied for a calculus test.

Comma splice   Janet worked on her term paper, her friend studied for a calculus test.

Methods of Revision.   You can correct run-on sentences and comma splices in several ways.

1. Create two separate sentences.

   Revision   Violets are blooming now. My lawn is covered with them.

   Revision   Rick refused to attend the movie. He said he hated horrow shows.

2. Join the sentences with a semicolon.

   Revision   Violets are blooming now; my yard is covered with them.

   Revision   Rick refused to attend the movie; he said he hated horror shows.

3. Join the sentences with a comma and a coordinating conjunction *(and, but, or, nor, for, yet, so).*

   Revision   Laura failed to set her alarm, *so* she was late for work.

   Revision   Perry watched the road carefully, *but* he still missed his turn.

4. Join the sentences with a semicolon and a conjunctive adverb (see pp. 411–412).

   Revision   Laura failed to set her alarm; *consequently,* she was late for work.

   Revision   Violets are blooming now; *in fact,* my yard is covered with them.

5. Introduce one of the sentences with a subordinating conjunction (see pp. 381–382).

   Revision   *Because* Laura failed to set her alarm, she was late for work.

   Revision   Janet worked on her term paper *while* her friend studied for a calculus test.

As our examples show, often you can correct an error in several ways.

Indicate whether each item is correct (C), is a run-on sentence (RO), or contains a comma splice (CS), and then correct the faulty items.   **EXERCISE**

1. I like your sport coat; perhaps I'll buy one like it for myself.
2. Stress often leads to heart attacks, everyone should know how to combat it.
3. Paul left the room, he was tired of being harassed.
4. Here's Jackie she'll tell us where Father and Mother went.
5. The exercises looked easy, nevertheless, they proved very difficult to do.

6. John was certain he had locked his house door, when he arrived home again he found it unlocked.
7. We were all wide awake, so we took sleeping pills before going to bed.
8. The battle was savagely fought; consequently, there were many casualties.
9. We are not accepting job applications now, try again in another two months.
10. Chieu spent just two days in Chicago she can hardly be said to know the city well.

SUBJECT–VERB AGREEMENT

A verb should agree in number with its subject. Singular verbs should have singular subjects, and plural verbs should have plural subjects.

Correct   My *boss is* a grouch. (singular subject and verb)

Correct   The *apartments have* two bedrooms. (plural subject and verb)

Ordinarily, matching subjects and verbs causes no problems. The following special situations, however, can create difficulties.

Subject and Verb Separated by a Word Group.   Sometimes a word group that includes one or more nouns comes between the subject and the verb. When this happens, match the verb with its subject, not a noun in the word group.

Correct   Our *basket* of sandwiches *is* missing.

Correct   Several *books* required for my paper *are* not in the library.

Correct   *Mr. Schmidt,* along with his daughters, *runs* a furniture store.

Correct   The old *bus,* crammed with passengers, *was* unable to reach the top of the hill.

Two Singular Subjects.   Most singular subjects joined by *and* take a plural verb.

Correct   The *couch* and *chair were* upholstered in blue velvet.

Sentences like the one above almost never cause problems. With subjects like *restoring cars* and *racing motorcycles*, however, singular verbs are often mistakenly used.

Faulty   *Restoring cars* and *racing motorcycles consumes* most of Frank's time.

Revision   *Restoring cars* and *racing motorcycles consume* most of Frank's time.

When *each* or *every* precedes the subjects, use a *singular* verb in place of a plural.

Correct Every *book* and *magazine was* badly water-stained.

Singular subjects joined by *or, either-or,* or *neither-nor* also take singular verbs.

Correct A *pear* or an *apple is* a nice afternoon snack.

Correct Neither *rain* nor *snow slows* our letter carrier.

One Singular and One Plural Subject. When one singular subject and one plural subject are joined by *or, either-or,* or *neither-nor,* match the verb with the closer of the two.

Correct Neither *John* nor his *parents were* at home.

Correct Neither his *parents* nor *John was* at home.

As these examples show, the sentences are usually smoother when the plural subject follows the singular.

Collective Nouns as Subjects. Collective nouns (*assembly, class, committee, family, herd, majority, tribe,* and the like) are singular in form but stand for groups or collections of people or things. Ordinarily, collective nouns are considered to be single and therefore take singular verbs.

Correct The *class is* writing a test.

Correct The *herd was* clustered around the water hole.

Sometimes, though, a collective noun refers to the separate individuals making up the grouping, and it requires a plural verb.

Correct A *majority* of the voters in this town *are* Republicans.

Sentences in Which the Verb Comes Ahead of the Subject. Sentences that begin with words such as *here, there, how, what,* and *where* fall into this category. With such sentences, the verb must agree with the subject that follows it.

Correct Here *is* my *house.*

Correct Where *are* my *shoes?*

Correct   There *is* just one *way* to solve this problem.

Correct   There *go* my *chances* for a promotion.

EXERCISE   **Choose the correct verb form from the pair in parentheses.**

1. Either Sonia or Sophie (owns, own) this notebook.
2. The rules governing this contest (seem, seems) terribly complicated.
3. Jane's sister, together with her two cousins, (is, are) at the hockey game.
4. Either the puppy or the kittens (is, are) responsible for this terrible mess.
5. A line of black clouds (was, were) forming on the horizon.
6. Holding a full-time job and caring for a small child (leaves, leave) Penny with no time for recreation.
7. Every car and truck (is, are) slated to be overhauled this month.
8. Neither Kevin nor his brothers (plays, play) paddleball very well.
9. There (is, are) several possible solutions to this problem.
10. Each of my classes (requires, require) me to do a great deal of homework.
11. The committee (has, have) agreed to my proposal for a research project.
12. (Has, Have) either of your children been immunized against polio?

CONSISTENCY IN SHOWING TIME

Inconsistencies occur when a writer shifts from the past tense to the present or vice versa without a corresponding shift in the time of the events being described. The following paragraph contains an uncalled-for shift from the present tense to the past.

> As *The Most Dangerous Game* opens, Sanger Rainsford, a famous hunter and author, and his old friend Whitney are standing on the deck of a yacht and discussing a mysterious island as the ship passes near it. Then, after everyone else has gone to bed, Rainsford manages to fall overboard. He swims to the island and ends up at a chateau owned by General Zaroff, a refugee from the Communist takeover in Russia. Zaroff, bored with hunting animals, has turned to hunting humans on his desert island. Inevitably, Rainsford is turned out into the jungle to be hunted down. There were [shift to past tense] actually four hunts over a three-day period, and at the end of the last one, Rainsford jumped into the sea, swam across a cove to the chateau, and killed Zaroff in the general's own bedroom. Afterward he sleeps [shift back to present tense] and decides "he had never slept in a better bed."

The sentence with the unwarranted shift in tense should read as follows:

There are actually four hunts over a three-day period, and at the end of the last one, Rainsford jumps into the sea, swims across a cove to the chateau, and kills Zaroff in the general's own bedroom.

The time shift in the quotation part of the final sentence is justified because the sleeping has occurred before Rainsford's thoughts about it.

Indicate whether each sentence is correct (C) or contains an unwarranted shift in tense. Then correct the faulty sentences.   EXERCISE

1. I am working as a gardener this summer and liked the work very much.
2. Once the sirens sounded, people start heading for air-raid shelters.
3. The buses start running at 6 A.M. and continued operating until 10 P.M.
4. Before the game started, the audience stood and sang the national anthem.
5. While the instructor lectured, the students take notes.
6. As I turned slightly to the right, I see the hazy outline of a tall building.
7. After he had rested awhile, he resumed his hike.
8. Lois laid her cards face up on the table, then swept the pot toward her.
9. When Miranda starts to play, everyone gathered around the piano.
10. Arthur waved goodbye to his friends, starts his car, and left on his vacation.

PRONOUN–ANTECEDENT AGREEMENT

The antecedent of a pronoun is the noun or pronoun to which it refers, Just as subjects should agree with their verbs, pronouns should agree with their antecedents: singular pronouns require singular antecedents, and plural pronouns require plural antecedents. Ordinarily you will have no trouble matching pronouns and antecedents. The situations discussed below, however, can cause problems.

Indefinite Pronouns as Antecedents.   Indefinite pronouns include words like *each, either, neither, any, everybody, somebody,* and *nobody.* Whenever an indefinite pronoun is used as an antecedent, the pronoun that refers to it should be singular.

> *Faulty*   *Neither* of the actors had learned *their* lines.
>
> *Revision*   *Neither* of the actors had learned *his* lines.

When the gender of the antecedent is unknown, you may follow it with *his or her;* or if this results in awkwardness, rewrite the sentence in the plural.

> *Correct*   *Anyone* who has studied *his or her* assignments properly should do well on the test.

> *Correct*   *Those* who have studied *their* assignments should do well on the test.

Occasionally, a ridiculous result occurs when a singular pronoun refers to an indefinite pronoun that is obviously plural in meaning. When this happens, rewrite the sentence to eliminate the problem.

> *Faulty*   *Everybody* complained that the graduation ceremony had lasted too long, but I didn't believe *him.*

> *Revision*   Everybody complained that the graduation ceremony had lasted too long, but I didn't think so.

Two Singular Antecedents.   Two or more antecedents joined by *and* ordinarily call for a plural pronoun.

> *Correct*   Her briefcase and umbrella were missing from *their* usual place on the hall table.

When *each* or *every* precedes the antecedent, use a singular pronoun.

> *Correct*   Every college and university must do *its* best to provide adequate student counseling.

Singular antecedents joined by *or, either–or,* or *neither–nor* call for singular pronouns.

> *Correct*   Neither Helga nor Irene had paid *her* rent for the month.

Applying this rule can sometimes yield an awkward or foolish sentence. When this happens, rewrite the sentence to avoid the problem.

> *Faulty*   Neither James nor Sally has finished *his or her* term project.

> *Revision*   James and Sally have not finished *their* term projects.

Singular and Plural Antecedents.   If one singular and one plural antecedent are joined by *or, either–or,* or *neither–nor,* the pronoun agrees with the closer one.

| *Correct* | Either Terrence James or the Parkinsons have agreed to let us use *their* lawn mower. |

| *Correct* | Either the Parkinsons or Terrence James has agreed to let us use *his* lawn mower. |

Sentences of this sort are generally smoother when the plural subject follows the singular.

Collective Nouns as Antecedents.   When a collective noun is considered a single unit, the pronoun that refers to it should be singular.

| *Correct* | The *troop* of scouts made *its* way slowly through the woods. |

When the collective noun refers to the separate individuals in the group, use a plural pronoun.

| *Correct* | The staff lost *their* jobs when the factory closed. |

Choose the right pronoun from the pair in parentheses.

1. Anyone who believes ballet is for sissies should try it for (himself, themselves).
2. Each bus and taxi must have (its, their) engine overhauled twice a year.
3. Everyone planning to attend the reunion should have (his or her, their) hotel reservations by July 15.
4. After flying for many days, the flock reached (its, their) destination in Canada.
5. Vernon and Harry made (his, their) way slowly through the packed room.
6. I understand that neither Joan nor the Benson sisters made (her, their) tuition payments on time.
7. Nobody should leave a hotel room without locking (his or her, their) door.
8. If someone wants to commit suicide badly enough, no one can stop (him, them).
9. The jury filed into the courtroom and took (its, their) seats.
10. Either the Meursaults or Pierre Chardonnay will let us use (his, their) house for the wine-tasting party.

AVOIDING FAULTY PRONOUN REFERENCE

Any definite pronoun (see p. 359) that you write should refer to just one noun or noun substitute—its antecedent. Reference problems result when the pronoun has two or more antecedents, a hidden antecedent, or no antecedent. These errors can cause mixups in meaning as well as ridiculous sentences.

More Than One Antecedent.   The following sentences lack clarity because their pronouns have two possible antecedents rather than just one.

Faulty   Take the screens off the windows and wash *them*.

Faulty   Harry told Will that he was putting on weight.

The reader can't tell whether the screens or the windows should be washed, or who is putting on weight.

Sometimes we see a sentence like this one:

Faulty   If the boys don't eat all the Popsicles, put *them* in the freezer.

In this case, we know it's the Popsicles that should be stored, but the use of *them* creates an amusing sentence.

Correct these faults by replacing the pronoun with a noun or by rephrasing the sentence.

Revision   Wash the windows after you have taken off the screens.

Revision   Take off the screens so that you can wash the windows.

Revision   Harry told Will, "I am (you are) putting on weight."

Revision   Put any uneaten Popsicles in the freezer.

Hidden Antecedent.   An antecedent is hidden if it takes the form of an adjective rather than a noun.

Faulty   The movie theater is closed today, so we can't see *one*.

Faulty   As I passed the tiger's cage, *it* lunged at me.

To correct this fault, replace the pronoun with the noun used as an adjective; or switch the positions of the pronoun and the noun and make any needed changes in their forms.

Revision   The theater is closed today, so we can't see a movie.

Revision   As I passed its cage, the tiger lunged at me.

No Antecedent.   A no-antecedent sentence lacks any noun to which the pronoun can refer. Sentences of this sort occur frequently in everyday conversation but should be avoided in formal writing. The examples below illustrate this error.

Faulty   The lecture was boring, but *they* took notes anyway.

Faulty   On the news program, *it* told about a new crisis in the Persian Gulf.

To set matters right, substitute a suitable noun for the pronoun or reword the sentence.

Revision   The lecture was boring, but the students took notes anyway.

Revision   The news program told about a new crisis in the Persian Gulf.

Sometimes a *this, that, it,* or *which* will refer to a whole idea rather than a single noun. This usage is acceptable provided the writer's meaning is obvious, as in this example.

Correct   The instructor spoke very softly, *which* meant we had difficulty hearing him.

Problems occur, however, when the reader can't figure out which of two or more ideas the pronoun refers to.

Faulty   Ginny called Sally two hours after the agreed-upon time and postponed their shopping trip one day. *This* irritated Sally very much.

What caused Sally to be irritated—the late call, the postponement of the trip, or both? Again, rewording or adding a clarifying word will correct the problem.

Revision   Ginny called Sally two hours after the agreed-upon time and postponed their shopping trip one day. This *tardiness* irritated Sally very much.

Revision   Ginny called Sally two hours after the agreed-upon time and postponed their shopping trip one day. Ginny's *change of plans* irritated Sally very much.

The first of these examples illustrates the addition of a clarifying word; the second illustrates rewriting.

Indicate whether each sentence is correct (C) or contains a faulty pronoun reference (F), and correct any faulty sentences.   **EXERCISE**

1. Remove the clothes from the trunks and give them to the Salvation Army.
2. I'm not married and don't plan on it for another two years.

3. Mary asked Cheryl whether she danced well.
4. In the Humanities department, they offer several courses in popular culture.
5. I am experienced in turfgrass management and irrigation procedures, which qualifies me for your summer job.
6. Eaton had lived among cannibals, and it led him to reject the belief that savages are noble.
7. When the children had finished playing with the bicycles, we chained them to a tree for the night.
8. As I walked toward the dog's pen, it started barking.
9. They say that the Atlas Company will hire 150 more people soon.
10. Sue told Barbara that she was getting gray hair.
11. The store was crowded with customers because it was holding a sale.
12. My father made me turn down my radio and clean my room, which annoyed me greatly.

AVOIDING UNWARRANTED SHIFTS IN PERSON

Pronouns can be in the first person, second person, or third person. *First-person* pronouns identify people who are talking or writing about themselves, *second-person* pronouns identify people being addressed directly, and *third-person* pronouns identify persons or things that are being written or spoken about. The following table sorts pronouns according to person.

First Person	*Second Person*	*Third Person*
I	you	he
me	your	she
my	yours	it
mine	yourself	his
we	yourselves	hers
us		its
our		one
ours		they
ourselves		theirs
		indefinite pronouns

All nouns are in the third person. As you revise, be alert for unwarranted shifts from one person to another.

Faulty   I liked *my* British vacation better than *my* vacation in France and Italy because *you* didn't have language problems.

Revision   I liked *my* British vacation better than *my* vacation in France and Italy because *I* didn't have language problems.

Faulty	Holidays are important to *everyone*. They boost *your* spirits and provide a break from *our* daily routine.
Revision	Holidays are important to *everyone*. They boost *one's* spirits and provide a break from *one's* daily routine.
Faulty	The taller the *golfer*, the more club speed *you will* have with a normally paced swing.
Revision	The taller the *golfer*, the more club speed *he* or *she* will have with a normally paced swing.

As these examples show, the shift can occur within a single sentence or when the writer moves from one sentence to another.

All shifts in person, however, are not unwarranted. Read the following correct sentence:

Correct	*I* want *you* to deliver these flowers to Ms. Willoughby's house by 3 o'clock. *She* needs them for a party.

Here the speaker identifies himself or herself (I) while speaking directly to a listener (you) about someone else (she). In this case, shifts are needed to get the message across.

Indicate whether the sentence is correct (C) or contains an unwarranted shift in person (S). Correct faulty sentences.   **EXERCISE**

1. Would you ask Julio to bring his guitar to my party?
2. Those people who plan to attend the potluck should bring a dish to pass and your own dishes and silverware.
3. Why should I enlist in the armed forces when a person can get a better paying civilian job?
4. Our neighborhood is very friendly; you are always being invited to get-togethers.
5. Once we have taken a position on some issue, it is difficult for people to alter their attitudes.
6. Whenever we worked late, the company provided employees with a free meal.
7. Anyone wanting to exercise your option to purchase stock must do so within three months.
8. Millions of people celebrate Mother's Day by giving gifts to our mothers.
9. We think this hotel is outstanding; it offers you spacious rooms and friendly service for a low price.
10. Unless you have an aptitude for mathematics, nobody can successfully complete an engineering program.

USING THE RIGHT
PRONOUN CASE

Case means the changes in form that a pronoun undergoes to show its function in a sentence. Unlike a noun, a personal pronoun (see pp. 356–357) has one form when it is the subject of a sentence or accompanies the subject, and it has another form when it plays a nonsubject role or accompanies a noun that is not a subject.

Subject Form	Nonsubject Form
I	me
he	him
she	her
we	us
they	them
who	whom

The following pointers will help you select the proper pronoun as you revise.

We *and* Us *Preceding Nouns.* Nouns that serve as subjects take the pronoun *we*. Other nouns take the pronoun *us*.

> *Correct*   *We* tourists will fly home tomorrow. (*We* accompanies the subject.)
>
> *Correct*   The guide showed *us* tourists through the cathedral. (*Us* accompanies a nonsubject.)

If you can't decide which pronoun is right, mentally omit the noun and read the sentence to yourself, first with one pronoun and then with the other. Your ear will indicate the correct form.

> My mother made (we, us) children vanilla pudding for dessert.

Omitting *children* shows immediately that *us* is the right choice.

> *Correct*   My mother made *us* children vanilla pudding for dessert.

Pronouns Paired with Nouns. When such a combination serves as the subject of a sentence or accompanies the subject, use the subject form of the pronoun. When the combination plays a nonsubject role, use the nonsubject form of the pronoun.

Correct   Wilhelmina and *I* plan to join the Peace Corps. (*I* is part of the compound subject.)

Correct   Two people, Mary and *I,* will represent our school at the meeting. (*I* is part of a compound element accompanying the subject.)

Correct   The superintendent told Kevin and *him* that they would be promoted soon. (*Him* is part of a compound nonsubject.)

Correct   The project was difficult for Jeffrey and *him* to complete. (*Him* is part of a compound nonsubject.)

Again, mentally omitting the noun from the combination will tell you which pronoun is correct.

Who *and* Whom *in Dependent Clauses*.   Use *who* for the subjects of dependent clauses; otherwise use *whom.*

Correct   The Mallarys prefer friends *who are interested in the theater.* (*Who* is the subject of the clause.)

Correct   Barton is a man *whom very few people like.* (*Whom* is not the subject of the clause.)

A simple test will help you decide between *who* and *whom.* First, mentally isolate the dependent clause. Next, block out the pronoun in question and then insert *he* (or *she*) and *him* (or *her*) at the appropriate spot in the remaining part of the clause. If *he* (or *she*) sounds better, *who* is right. If *him* (or *her*) sounds better, *whom* is right. Let's use this test on the sentence below.

The woman *who(m) Scott is dating* works as a mechanical engineer.

Scott is dating (she, her.)

Clearly *her* is correct; therefore, *whom* is the proper form.

Correct   The woman *whom Scott is dating* works as a mechanical engineer.

Pronouns as Subject Complements.   In formal writing, pronouns that serve as subject complements (see p. 353) always take the subject form.

Correct   It is *I.*

Correct   It was *she* who bought the old Parker mansion.

This rule, however, is often ignored in informal writing.

It's *her.*

That's *him* standing over by the door.

Comparisons Using **than** *or* **as . . . as.**   Comparisons of this kind often make no direct statement about the second item of comparison. When the second naming word is a pronoun, you may have trouble choosing the right one.

> Harriet is less outgoing than *(they, them)*.
>
> My parents' divorce saddened my sister as much as *(I, me)*.

Not to worry. Expand the sentence by mentally supplying the missing material. Then try the sentence with each pronoun in turn, and see which sounds right.

> Harriet is less outgoing than *(they, them)* are.
>
> My parents' divorce saddened my sister as much as it did *(I, me)*.

Obviously *they* is the right choice for the first sentence, and *me* is the right choice for the second one.

> *Correct*   Harriet is less outgoing than *they* are.
>
> *Correct*   My parents' divorce saddened my sister as much as it did *me*.

EXERCISE   **Choose the right form of the pronoun for each of the following sentences.**

1. Bob, Joe, and (I, me) plan to attend the Willie Nelson concert in Omaha.
2. The strong American dollar is hurting (we, us) farmers by reducing the overseas markets for our crops.
3. John is a better student than (I, me).
4. (We, us) Democrats stand a good chance of capturing the state house this year.
5. Sandra is the only person (who, whom) I think has the right background for this job.
6. The boss recommended two people, Clarissa and (I, me), for raises.
7. Two people in the class, Roberta and (I, me), were born outside the United States.
8. I don't know (who, whom) to blame for this mistake.
9. The police officer told Debra and (I, me) that we were trespassing and would have to leave.
10. The travel agent said that (we, us) fellows would enjoy Montreal.

AVOIDING MISPLACED MODIFIERS

A misplaced modifier is a word or word group that is improperly separated from the word it modifies. When separation of this type occurs, the sentence often sounds awkward, ridiculous, or confusing.

Usually you can correct this error by moving the modifier next to the word it is intended to modify. Occasionally you'll also need to alter some of the phrasing.

Faulty	There is a bicycle in the basement *with chrome fenders*. (The basement appears to have chrome fenders.)
Faulty	David received a phone call from his uncle *that infuriated him*. (The uncle appears to have infuriated David.)
Revision	There is a bicycle *with chrome fenders* in the basement.
Revision	David received an *infuriating* phone call from his uncle. (Note the change in wording.)

In shifting the modifier, don't inadvertently create another faulty sentence.

Faulty	Fritz bought a magazine with an article about Michael Jackson *at the corner newsstand*. (The article appears to tell about Jackson's visit to the corner newsstand.)
Faulty	Fritz bought a magazine *at the corner newsstand* with an article about Michael Jackson. (The corner newsstand appears to have an article about Jackson.)
Revision	*At the corner newsstand,* Fritz bought a magazine with an article about Michael Jackson.

As you revise, watch also for *squinting modifiers*—that is, modifiers positioned so that the reader doesn't know whether they are supposed to modify what comes ahead of them or what follows them.

Faulty	The man who was rowing the boat *frantically* waved toward the onlookers on the beach.

Is the man rowing frantically or waving frantically?

Correct this kind of error by repositioning the modifer so that the ambiguity disappears.

Revision	The man who was *frantically* rowing the boat waved toward the onlookers on the beach.
Revision	The man who was rowing the boat waved *frantically* toward the onlookers on the beach.

EXERCISE   **Indicate whether each sentence is correct (C) or contains a misplaced modifier (MM). Correct faulty sentences.**

1. Jane was ticketed for driving on the highway with a broken taillight.
2. The principal told the teacher after class to stop by his office.
3. Mercedes bought a mynah bird at the pet shop that could talk.
4. We heard last week he had suffered a heart attack.
5. I drove the car to the repair shop that needed an overhaul.
6. The computer error was discovered by the bank before the account was overdrawn.
7. Geologists found a coal deposit on Uncle George's abandoned farm of great value.
8. Cedric showed the steak to the waitress that was too tough to eat.
9. Eleanor found a collie that could do tricks at the local dog pound.
10. The river overflowed its banks and swept away dozens of houses swollen by heavy rains.

AVOIDING DANGLING MODIFIERS

A dangling modifier is a phrase or clause that lacks clear connection to the word or words it is intended to modify. As a result, sentences are inaccurate, often comical. Typically, the modifier leads off the sentence, although it can also come at the end.

Sometimes the error occurs because the sentence fails to specify who or what is modified. At other times, the separation is too great between the modifier and what it modifies.

Faulty   *Walking in the meadow,* wildflowers surrounded us. (The wildflowers appear to be walking in the meadow.)

Faulty   Dinner was served *after saying grace.* (The dinner appears to have said grace.)

Faulty   *Fatigued by the violent exercise,* the cool shower was very relaxing. (The cool shower appears to have been fatigued.)

The first of these sentences is faulty because the modifier is positioned too far away from *us*. The other two are faulty because they do not identify who said grace or found the shower relaxing.

You can correct dangling modifiers in two basic ways. First, leave the modifier unchanged and rewrite the main part of the sentence so that it begins with the term actually modified. Second, rewrite the modifier so that it has its own subject and verb, thereby eliminating the inaccuracy.

Revision   *Walking in the meadow,* we were surrounded by wildflowers. (The main part of the sentence has been rewritten.)

Revision   *As we walked in the meadow,* wildflowers surrounded us. (The modifier has been rewritten.)

Revision   Dinner was served *after we had said grace.* (The modifier has been rewritten.)

Revision   *Fatigued by the violent exercise,* Ted found the cool shower very relaxing. (The main part of the sentence has been rewritten.)

Revision   *Because Ted was fatigued by the violent exercise,* the cool shower was very relaxing. (The modifier has been rewritten.)

Ordinarily, either part of the sentence can be rewritten, but sometimes only one can.

Indicate whether each sentence is correct (C) or contains a dangling modifier (DM). Correct faulty sentences.   **EXERCISE**

1. After typing for two hours, a cup of coffee refreshed me.
2. At the age of sixteen, my father bought me a car.
3. While picking cherries, a bee stung me.
4. Lying in the hot sun, I got a severe sunburn.
5. Our car broke down while on a trip to Georgia.
6. In order to install this part, you will need a special tool.
7. The engine must be shut off before putting gasoline in the car's tank.
8. By making use of anecdotes and examples, Professor Yamashita's students find her lectures easy to understand.
9. Because the road was slick with ice, Vernon couldn't make it to the top of the steep hill.
10. As a child, Halloween was one of my favorite days.

AVOIDING NONPARALLELISM

Nonparallelism results when equivalent ideas follow different grammatical forms. One common kind of nonparallelism occurs with words or word groups in pairs or in a series.

Faulty   Althea enjoys *jogging, to bike,* and *to swim.*

Faulty   The superintendent praised the workers *for their productivity* and *because they had an excellent safety record.*

Faulty   The banner was *old, faded,* and *it had a rip.*

Note how rewriting the sentences in parallel form improves their smoothness.

Revision   Althea enjoys *jogging, biking,* and *swimming.*

Revision   The superintendent praised the workers for *their productivity* and *their safety record.*

Revision   The banner was *old, faded,* and *ripped.*

Nonparallelism also occurs when correlative conjunctions (*either . . . or, neither . . . nor, both . . . and,* and *not only . . . but also*) are followed by unlike elements.

Faulty   That sound *either was a thunderclap or an explosion.*

Faulty   The basement was *not only poorly lighted but also it had a foul smell.*

Ordinarily, repositioning one of the correlative conjunctions will solve the problem. Sometimes, however, one of the grammatical elements must be rewritten.

Revision   That sound was *either a thunderclap or an explosion.* (*Either* has been repositioned.)

Revision   The basement was *not only poorly lighted but also foul smelling.* (The element following *but also* has been rewritten.)

EXERCISE   **Indicate whether each sentence is correct (C) or nonparallel (NP). Correct faulty sentences.**

1. Despite having a week's preparation time, Jethroe could neither recite the Pledge of Allegiance nor the Preamble to the Constitution.
2. The room was large, sunny, and pleasant.
3. The tryouts involved not only acting, but there was singing also.
4. Playing cards is more boring than to play baseball.
5. This winter I want either to vacation in Florida or in Bermuda.
6. Sergei hates math, history, and to draw.
7. Elban is neither a good dancer nor an interesting conversationalist.

8. As the midnight countdown began, corks popped, champagne spurted, and "Happy New Years" filled the air.
9. Danielle has many virtues, including reliability, kindness and she is honest.
10. Next term Sandy will be taking beginning math and work in the library.

AVOIDING FAULTY COMPARISONS

A faulty comparison results if you (1) mention one of the items being compared but not the other, (2) omit words needed to clarify the relationship, or (3) compare different sorts of items. Advertisers often offend in the first way.

> *Faulty*   Irish tape has better adhesion.

With what other tape is Irish tape being compared? Scotch tape? All other transparent tape? Mentioning the second term of a comparison eliminates reader guesswork.

> *Revision*   Irish tape has better adhesion than any other transparent tape.

Two clarifying words, *other* and *else,* are frequently omitted from comparisons, creating illogical sentences.

> *Faulty*   Sergeant McNabb has made more arrests than any officer in his precinct.
>
> *Faulty*   Scaffold Haight is taller than anyone on his basketball team.

The first sentence is illogical because McNabb is one of the officers in his precinct and therefore cannot be more conscientious than any officer in the precinct. Similarly, because Haight is a member of his basketball team, he can't be taller than everyone on his team. Adding *other* to the first sentence and *else* to the second corrects matters.

> *Revision*   Sergeant McNabb has made more arrests than any *other* officer in his precinct.
>
> *Revision*   Scaffold Haight is taller than anyone *else* on his basketball team.

Comparing unlike items is perhaps the most common kind of comparison error. Here are two examples.

Faulty   The cities in California are larger than North Dakota.

Faulty   The cover of this book is much more durable than the other book.

The first sentence compares the cities of California with a state, while the second compares the cover of a book with a whole book. Correction consists of rewriting the sentence so that it compares like items.

Revision   The cities in California are larger than *those in* North Dakota.

Revision   The cover of this book is much more durable than *that of* the other book.

EXERCISE   **Indicate whether the sentence is correct (C) or contains a faulty comparison (FC). Correct any faulty comparison.**

1. Compared with Harry, Chad is a much less efficient worker.
2. Unlike my brother's house, I have a fireplace in mine.
3. Tests conducted on Steelgrip glue show that its bonding strength is much greater.
4. That novel was better than anything I've read.
5. The duties of a firefighter are just as hazardous as a police officer.
6. I found it hard to surf in Florida because the waves in the Gulf of Mexico weren't as big as the Pacific Ocean.
7. The relationship between Brett and Bryant is not as good as most brothers.
8. Our house is larger than any house on our block.
9. The English Department has more members than any other department on this campus.
10. The trees on the far riverbank are different from this riverbank.

PUNCTUATION AND MECHANICS

Punctuation marks replace the pauses and the changes in tone and pitch of spoken language, and they also indicate relationships among different sentence elements. As a result, punctuation marks help clarify the meaning of written material. Similarly, a knowledge of mechanics—capitalization, abbreviations, numbers, and italics—helps you avoid distracting inconsistencies.

This part of the handbook covers the fundamentals of punctuation and mechanics. Review it carefully and use it to help you when you revise your writing.

PERIODS, QUESTION MARKS, AND EXCLAMATION POINTS

Since periods, question marks, and exclamation points signal the ends of sentences, they are sometimes called *end marks*. In addition, periods and question marks function in several other ways.

Periods.   Periods (.) end sentences that state facts or opinions, give instructions, make requests that are not in the form of questions, and ask indirect questions—those that have been rephrased in the form of a statement.

Linda works as a hotel manager. (Sentence states fact.)

Dean Harris is a competent administrator. (Sentence states opinion.)

Clean off your lab bench before you leave. (Sentence gives instruction.)

Please move away from the door. (Sentence makes request.)

I wonder whether Ruthie will be at the theater tonight. (Sentence asks indirect question.)

Periods also follow common abbreviations as well as a person's initials.

Mr.	Sr.	P.M.
Mrs.	B.C.	a.s.a.p.
Ms.	A.D.	St.
Dr.	A.M.	Corp.

Mark Valentini, Jr., has consented to head the new commission on traffic safety.

Writers today often omit periods after abbreviations for the names of organizations or government agencies, as the following examples show.

ABC	FBI	IRS
ACLU	FHA	NAM
AFL-CIO	GM	USAF

An up-to-date college dictionary will indicate whether a certain abbreviation should be written without periods.

Periods also precede decimal fractions and separate numerals standing for dollars and cents.

0.81 percent	$5.29
3.79 percent	$0.88

Question Marks.   A question mark (?) ends a whole or a partial sentence that asks a direct question (one that repeats the exact words of the person who asked it).

Do you know how to operate this movie projector? (whole sentence asking a direct question)

Has Cinderella scrubbed the floor? Swept the hearth? Washed the dishes? (series of sentence parts asking direct questions)

Dr. Baker—wasn't she your boss once?—has just received a promotion to sales manager. (interrupting element asking a direct question)

The minister inquired, "Don't you take this woman to be your lawful wedded wife?" (quotation asking a direct question)

A question mark in parentheses may be used to indicate uncertainty about some piece of information.

Winfield reached America in 1721 (?) and spent the rest of his life in Philadelphia.

Exclamation Points.   Exclamation points (!) are used to express strong emotion or especially forceful commands.

Darcy! I never expected to see you again!

Sam! Turn that radio down immediately!

Help! Save me!

Use exclamation points sparingly; otherwise, they will quickly lose their force.

EXERCISE   **Supply periods, question marks, or exclamation points wherever they are necessary. If a sentence is correct, write *C*.**

1. Porterhouse steak costs $395 a pound this week.
2. What would you like for Christmas.

3. My brother asked me whether I wanted to go fishing.

4. Where would you like me to set this sack of groceries.

5. Please don't touch the exhibits.

6. For heaven's sake, stop making that damn noise.

7. Washington Square—it was once a burial ground for paupers—is a popular park in New York's Greenwich Village.

8. The play starts at 8 P M sharp, and latecomers will not be admitted until the end of the first act.

9. Last year the inflation rate was 350 percent, a very low figure indeed.

10. When you are in London, will you see Buckingham Palace Visit the Tower of London Shop at Harrod's department store.

COMMAS

Since commas (,) occur more frequently than any other mark of punctuation, it's vital that you learn to use them correctly. When you do use them correctly, your sentence structure is clearer, and your reader grasps your meaning without having to reread.

Commas separate or set off independent clauses, items in a series, coordinate adjectives, introductory elements, places and dates, nonrestrictive expressions, and parenthetical expressions.

Independent Clauses.   When you link two independent clauses with a coordinating conjunction *(and, but, or, not, for, yet,* or *so),* put a comma in front of the conjunction.

> Arthur is majoring in engineering, *but* he has decided to work for a clothing store following graduation.

> The water looked inviting, *so* Darlene decided to go for a swim.

Don't confuse a sentence that has a compound predicate (see p. 351) with a sentence that consists of two independent clauses.

> Tom watered the garden and mowed the lawn. (single sentence with compound predicate)

> Tom watered the garden, *and* Betty mowed the lawn. (sentence with two independent clauses)

Here's a simple test. Read what follows the comma. Unless that part can stand alone as a sentence, don't use a comma.

Items in a Series.   A series consists of three or more words, phrases, or clauses following on one another's heels. Whenever you write a series, separate its items with commas.

> *Sarah, Paul,* and *Mary* are earning *A*'s in advanced algebra. (words in a series)
>
> Nancy strode *across the parking lot, through the revolving door,* and *into the elevator.* (phrases in a series)
>
> The stockholders' report said *that the company had enjoyed record profits during the last year, that it had expanded its work force by 20 percent,* and *that it would soon start marketing several new products.* (clauses in a series)

Coordinate Adjectives.   Use commas to separate coordinate adjectives—those that modify the same noun or noun substitute and can be reversed without altering the meaning of the sentence.

> Andrea proved to be an efficient, cooperative employee.
>
> Andrea proved to be a cooperative, efficient employee.

When reversing the word order wrecks the meaning of the sentence, the adjectives are not coordinate and should be written without a comma.

> Many new brands of video cassette recorders have come on the market lately.

Reversing the adjectives *many* and *new* would turn this sentence into nonsense. Therefore, no comma should be used.

Introductory Elements.   Use commas to separate introductory elements—words, phrases, and clauses—from the rest of the sentence. When an introductory element is short and the sentence will not be misread, you can omit the comma.

> *Correct*   After bathing, Anton felt refreshed.
>
> *Correct*   Soon I will be changing jobs.
>
> *Correct*   Soon, I will be changing jobs.
>
> *Correct*   When Sarah smiles her ears wiggle.
>
> *Correct*   When Sarah smiles, her ears wiggle.

The first example needs a comma; otherwise, the reader might become temporarily confused.

> After bathing Anton. . . .

Always use commas after introductory elements of six or more words.

> *Correct*   Whenever I hear the opening measure of Beethoven's *Fifth Symphony*, I get goose bumps.

Places and Dates.   Places include mailing addresses and geographical locations. The following sentences show where commas are used.

> Sherry Delaney lives at 651 Daniel Street, Memphis, Tennessee 38118.
>
> I shall go to Calais, France, next week.
>
> Morristown, Oklahoma, is my birthplace.

Note that commas appear after the street designation and the names of cities, countries, and states, except when the name of the state is followed by a zip code.

Dates are punctuated as shown in the following example.

> On Sunday, June 9, 1985, Elaine received a degree in environmental science.

Here, commas follow the date of the week, the day of the month, and the year.

With dates that include only the month and the year, commas are optional.

> *Correct*   In July 1979 James visited Scotland for the first time.
>
> *Correct*   In July, 1979, James visited Scotland for the first time.

Nonrestrictive Expressions.   A nonrestrictive expression supplies added information about whatever it modifies. This information, however, does not affect the basic meaning of the sentence. The two sentences below include nonrestrictive expressions.

> Senator Conwell, *the senior senator from this state*, faces a tough campaign for reelection.
>
> My dog, *frightened by the thunder*, hid under my bed while the storm raged.

If we delete the phrase *the senior senator from this state* from the first sentence, we still know that Senator Conwell faces a tough reelection battle. Likewise, if we delete *frightened by the thunder* from the second sentence, we still know that the dog hid during the storm.

Restrictive expressions, which are written *without commas*, distinguish whatever they modify from other persons, places, or things in the same category. Unlike nonrestrictive expressions, they are almost always essential sentence elements. Omitting a restrictive expression alters the meaning of the sentence, and the result is often nonsense.

Any person *caught stealing from this store* will be prosecuted.

Dropping the italicized part of this sentence leaves us with the absurd statement that any person, not just those caught stealing, faces prosecution.

Parenthetical Expressions.   A parenthetical expression is a word or word group that links one sentence to another, provides emphasis, or makes an idea clearer. Parenthetical expressions include the following:

> Interrupting and clarifying phrases
> Names and titles of people being addressed directly
> Abbreviations of degree titles and of *junior* and *senior* following people's names
> Echo questions
> "Not" phrases
> Adjectives that come after, rather than before, the words they modify

The examples that follow show the uses of commas.

All of Joe's spare time seems to center around reading. Kevin, *on the other hand,* enjoys a variety of activities. (phrase linking two sentences together)

I think, *Jill,* that you'd make a wonderful teacher. (name of person addressed directly)

Tell me, *Captain,* when the cruise ship is scheduled to sail. (title of person addressed directly)

Harley Kendall, *Ph.D.,* will be this year's commencement speaker. (degree title following name)

Peter Bradley, *Jr.,* has just taken over his father's plumbing business. (personal abbreviation following name)

Alvin realizes, *doesn't he,* that he stands almost no chance of being accepted at West Point? (echo question)

Mathematics, *not home economics,* was Tammy's favorite high school subject. ("not" phrase)

The road, *muddy and rutted,* proved impassable. (adjectives following word they modify)

Supply commas as necessary to correct the following sentences.

1. The solenoid valve is faulty so we'll have to replace it.
2. His suit which he had tailor-made in England cost him over seven hundred dollars.
3. The rewards of hard work include financial security peace of mind and self-respect.
4. Annette Dorian 341 Plainfield Avenue Augsburg Maine has won the Pulitzer Prize for literature.
5. After eating the lion licked his paws and rested.
6. Norton Hillburg my closest friend in college now works for the State Department.
7. Pete is a dedicated skillful fisherman.
8. You realize don't you that you must write an *A* final to pass this course?
9. When I have graduated from college I plan to spend a summer in Europe.
10. On Saturday June 4 1975 a train derailment near my home town took six lives.

SEMICOLONS

The semicolon (;) marks pronounced pauses in the flow of sentences. Its main use is to separate independent clauses, which may or may not be connected with a conjunctive adverb (see page 375). Other uses include separating

two or more series of items
items containing commas in a single series
independent clauses that contain commas and are connected with a coordinating conjunction

Independent Clauses.   The examples that follow show the use of semicolons to separate independent clauses.

The fabric in this dress is terrible; its designer must have been asleep at the swatch. (no conjunctive adverb)

Steve refused to write a term paper; *therefore,* he failed the course. (conjunctive adverb *therefore* joining independent clauses)

Conjunctive adverbs can occur within, rather than between, independent clauses. When they do, set them off with commas.

Marsha felt very confident. Jane, *on the other hand,* was nervous and uncertain. (conjunctive adverb within independent clause)

To determine whether a pair of commas or a semicolon and comma are required, read what comes before and after the conjunctive adverb. Unless both sets of words can stand alone as sentences, use commas.

Two or More Series of Items.   With sentences that have two or more series of items, writers often separate the series with semicolons in order to lessen the chances of misreading.

> My duties as secretary include typing letters, memos, and purchase orders; sorting, opening, and delivering mail; and making plane and hotel reservations for traveling executives.

The semicolons provide greater clarity than commas would.

Comma-Containing Items within a Series.   When commas accompany one or more of the items in a series, it's often better to separate the items with semicolons instead of commas.

> The meal included veal, which was cooked to perfection; asparagus, my favorite vegetable; and brown rice, prepared with a touch of curry.

Once again, semicolons provide greater clarity than additional commas.

Independent Clauses with Commas and a Coordinating Conjunction.
Ordinarily, a comma is used to separate independent clauses joined by a coordinating conjunction. When one or more of the clauses have commas, however, a semicolon provides clearer separation.

> The long, black limousine pulled up to the curb; and Jerry, shaking with excitement, watched the President alight from it.

The semicolon makes it easier to see the two main divisions.

EXERCISE   **Supply semicolons wherever they are necessary or desirable in the following sentences. If a sentence is correct, write *C*.**

1. I don't want the job, as a matter of fact, I'll turn it down if it's offered to me.
2. Worthington plays golf, tennis, and handball, collects china, Tiffany lamps, and art prints, and attends, plays, concerts, and operas.

3. Victoria wanted a house that was large, well-constructed, and in an established neighborhood, and finally, after many months of looking, she found one that suited her perfectly.

4. The ship, battered by the furious storm, finally made port, and the sailors, exhausted by their dangerous ordeal, received permission to spend the weekend ashore.

5. The heat in this office is unbearable; therefore, I think I'll take the afternoon off.

6. So far I've been a very unlucky investor; all my stocks are now worth less than I paid for them.

7. Remove yourself from my presence posthaste, in other words, get lost immediately.

8. It's OK for you to be here, I crashed this party myself.

9. Mildred forgot to put a stamp on the letter, as a result, the Post Office returned it to her.

10. The photograph showed Donald McAndrews, president of the college, Barth James, the registrar, and Amelia Conklin, dean of women.

COLONS, DASHES, PARENTHESES, AND BRACKETS

Colons, dashes, parentheses, and brackets separate and enclose, thereby clarifying relationships among the various parts of a sentence.

Colons.   Colons (:) introduce appositives, formal lists, and explanations following materials that could stand alone as a complete sentence.

His aim in life is grandiose: to corner the market in wheat. (appositive)

Three students have been selected to attend the conference: Lucille Perkins, Dan Blakely, and Frank Napolis. (list)

Three factors account for the financial problems of most farmers: (1) high interest rates, (2) falling land values, and (3) the strong dollar, which makes it difficult to sell crops abroad. (explanation)

The first of the following sentences is incorrect because the words preceding the colon can't stand alone as a sentence.

Faulty   The tools needed for this job include: a hacksaw, a file, and a drill.

Revision   The tools needed for this job include a hacksaw, a file, and a drill.

Colons are frequently used to introduce formal quotations that extend beyond a single sentence.

The speaker stepped to the lectern and said: "I am here to ask for your assistance. Today several African nations face a food crisis because drought has ruined their harvests. Unless we provide help quickly, thousands of people will die of starvation."

In such situations, the material preceding the quotation need not be a complete sentence.

Colons also separate hours from minutes (8:20 A.M.), salutations of business letters from the body of the letters (Dear Ms. Stanley:), titles of publications from subtitles (*The Careful Writer: A Guide to English Usage*), numbers indicating ratios (a 3:2:2 ratio), and chapter from verse in Biblical references (Luke 6:20–49).

Dashes.   Like colons, dashes (—) set off appositives, lists, and explanations but are used in less formal writing. A dash emphasizes the material it sets off.

> Only one candidate showed up at the political rally—Jerry Manders. (appositive)
>
> The closet held only three garments—an out-at-the-elbows sportscoat, a pair of blue jeans, and a tattered shirt. (list)
>
> I know why little Billy is fussing—he needs changing. (explanation)

Dashes set off material that interrupts the flow of thought within a sentence.

> Her new car—didn't she get it just three months ago?—has broken down twice.

Similarly , dashes are used to mark an interrupted segment of dialogue.

> "I'd like to live in England when I retire."
> "In England? But what will your wife—?"
> "My wife likes the idea and can hardly wait for us to make the move."

Dashes set off parenthetical elements containing commas, and a dash can set off comments that follow a list.

> The comedian—short, fat, and squeaky-voiced—soon had everyone roaring with laughter. (parenthetical element with commas)
>
> A brag, a blow, a tank of air—that's what Senator Conwell is. (comment following a list)

Type a dash as two unspaced hyphens and leave no space between it **and the words on either side of it.**

Parentheses.   Parentheses ( ) are used to enclose numbers or letters that designate the items in a formal list and to set off incidental material within sentences. Except in the kind of list shown in the first example below, a comma does not usually precede a parenthesis.

> Each paper should contain (1) an introduction, (2) several paragraphs developing the thesis statement, and (3) a conclusion.

> Some occupations (computer programming, for example) may be overcrowded in ten years.

If the material in parentheses appears within a sentence, don't use a capital letter or period, even if the material is itself a complete sentence.

> The use of industrial robots (one cannot foresee their consequences) worries some people today.

If the material in parentheses is written as a separate sentence, however, then punctuate it as you would a separate sentence.

> Millicent's angry outburst surprised everyone. (She had seemed such a placid person.)

If the material in parentheses comes at the end of a sentence, put the final punctuation after the closing parentheses.

> This company was founded by Willard Manley (1876–1951).

In contrast to dashes, parentheses deemphasize the material they enclose.

Brackets.   In quoted material, brackets [ ] enclose words or phrases that have been added to make the message clearer. They are also used with the word *sic* (Latin for "thus") to point out errors in quoted material.

> "This particular company [Zorn Enterprises, Inc.] pioneered in the safe disposal of toxic wastes," the report noted. (The bracketed name is added to the original.)

> "[Carl Sagan's] expertise in science has made him a popular figure on the lecture circuit," his friend stated. (The bracketed name replaces *his* in the original.)

> "The principle [sic] cause of lung cancer is cigarette smoking," the article declared. (The word *principal* is misspelled "principle" in the original.)

To call attention to an error, follow it immediately with the bracketed *sic*. The reader will then know that the blame rests with the original writer, not with you.

EXERCISE   **Supply colons, dashes, parentheses, and brackets wherever they are necessary.**

1. The fire was reported at 235 A.M.
2. Four pieces of equipment are required for downhill skiing 1 skis, 2 boots, 3 bindings, and 4 ski poles.
3. Lucy told Santa she wanted two things for Christmas a doll and a picture book.
4. The results of van Groot's investigation see Chapter 4 supports earlier findings concerning the harmful effects of cocaine.
5. All that week Andreas had his mind on just one thing hitting the mountain trails for a weekend of backpacking.
6. The newspaper story noted that "Any rock star who captures the public's attention can expect to recieve sic several thousand fan letters each week."
7. The havoc wreaked by the hurricane two thousand people killed and five thousand buildings destroyed or damaged led the President to declare the city a disaster area.
8. To begin the experiment, combine water and glycerin in a 31 ratio.
9. Love, good health, an adequate income, a pleasant home what sensible person would trade them for wealth alone?
10. Remember this rule smoking is prohibited in the respiratory care unit.
11. Three corporals Nimms, Kravitz, and Steiner have been promoted to sergeant.
12. "His Senator William Proxmire's crusade against waste in the federal government has occupied him for many years," the columnist noted.

QUOTATION MARKS

Quotation marks (" ") set off direct quotations, titles of short pieces of writing, subdivisions of books, and expressions singled out for special attention.

Direct Quotations.   A direct quotation repeats a speaker or writer's exact words.

> The placement director said, "The recruiter for Procter and Gamble will be on campus next Thursday to interview students for marketing jobs." (spoken comment)

> "The U.S. trade deficit is expected to reach record levels this year," *The Wall Street Journal* noted. (written comment)

> Jackie said the party was "a total flop."

As these sentences show, a comma that precedes a direct quotation goes outside the quotation marks, and one that follows a direct quotation goes inside the marks. When a quotation is a sentence fragment, commas are omitted.

When an expression like "he said" interrupts a quoted sentence, use commas to set off the expression. When the expression comes between two complete quoted sentences, use a period after the expression and capitalize the first word of the second sentence.

> "Hop in," said Jim. "I'll give you a ride to school."
> "Thank you," replied Kelly, opening the car door and sliding into the front seat.
>
> "I can't remember," said Jim, "when we've had a worse winter."

Titles of Short Works and Subdivisions of Books.   These short works include magazine articles, essays, short stories, chapters of books, one-act plays, short poems, songs, and television and radio programs.

> The article was titled "The Real Conservatism." (article)
>
> Last night I read John Cheever's "The Enormous Radio," "Torch Song," and "The Swimmer." (short stories)
>
> Many John Denver fans consider "Take Me Home, Country Roads" to be his greatest piece of music. (song)

Here, as with direct quotations, commas that introduce titles go outside the quotation marks, and follow-up commas and periods go inside the marks.

Expressions Singled Out for Special Attention.   Writers who wish to call the reader's attention to a word or symbol sometimes put it within quotation marks.

> The algebraic formula included a "π" and a "Δ."
> "Bonnets" and "lifts" are British terms for car hoods and elevators.

More frequently, however, these expressions are printed in italics (p. 431). Again, the follow-up commas and periods precede the quotation marks.

Quotation Marks Within Quotation Marks.   When a direct quotation or the title of a shorter work appears within a direct quotation, use single quotation marks (' ').

> The instructor told the class, "For tomorrow, read Ernest Hemingway's 'The Killers.' "

Note that the period comes ahead of both the single and the double quotation marks.

Positioning of Semicolons, Colons, and Question Marks. Position semicolons and colons that come at the end of quoted material after, not before, the quotation marks.

> Marcia calls Francine "that greasy grind"; however, I think Marcia is simply jealous of Francine's abilities.

> There are two reasons why I like "Dallas": the plot is interesting, and the acting is good.

When a question mark accompanies a quotation, put it outside the quotation marks if the whole sentence rather than the quotation asks the question.

> Why did Cedric suddenly shout, "This party is a big bore"?

Put the question mark inside the quotation marks if the quotation, but not the whole sentence, asks a question or if the quotation asks one question and the whole sentence asks another.

> Marie asked, "What college is your brother planning to attend?" (The quoted material, not the whole sentence, asks the question.)

> Whatever possessed him to ask, "What is the most shameful thing you ever did?" (The whole sentence and the quoted material ask separate questions.)

EXERCISE   **Supply properly positioned quotation marks wherever they are necessary.**

1. Euphilia called the following my favorite flowers: roses, peonies, and carnations.
2. What poem has the lines, And malt does more than Milton can/To justify God's ways to man?
3. I have strong objections to such jargon expressions as sibling rivalry, meaningful relationships, and parenting.
4. Orlando, said the boss, I'd like you to step into my office for a moment.
5. Hand me the dictionary; I want to look up macerate.
6. What made the instructor say, Whoever told you that you should major in chemistry?
7. Herbert told his friends, I care little for TV; nevertheless, he owns two expensive sets.
8. Patrick said the party had been one super bash.
9. Larry asked Sally, Would you like to have dinner with me tonight?
10. This weather is terrible, sighed John. I think I'll stay inside all day.

11. Quit saying you know so many times, the instructor told the student.
12. The word fractious, according to *Webster's New World Dictionary*, means hard to manage, unruly, rebellious.

APOSTROPHES

Apostrophes (') show possession, mark contractions, and indicate plurals that are singled out for special attention.

Possession. Possessive apostrophes usually show ownership (*Mary's cat*). Sometimes, though, they identify the works of creative people (*Hemingway's novels*) or indicate an extent of time or distance (*one hour's time, one mile's distance*).

Possessive apostrophes are used with nouns and with pronouns like *someone, no one, everybody, each other,* and *one another.* The possessive form is easily recognized because it can be converted to a prepositional phrase beginning with *of.*

The collar of the dog

The whistle of the wind

The intention of the corporation

The birthday of Scott

To show possession with pronouns, singular nouns, and plural nouns that do not end in an *s,* add an apostrophe followed by an *s.*

Someone's car is blocking our drive. (possessive of pronoun *someone*)

The *manager's* reorganization plan will take effect next week. (possessive of singular noun *manager*)

The *women's* lounge is being redecorated. (possessive of plural noun *women*)

The boss's orders must be obeyed. (possessive of singular noun *boss*)

With singular nouns that end in *s,* the possessive is sometimes formed by merely adding an apostrophe at the end (James' helmet). The preferred usage, however, is *'s* (James's helmet).

Plural nouns ending in *s* form the possessive by adding only an apostrophe at the end.

All the *ladies'* coats are on sale today. (possessive of plural noun *ladies*)

The *workers'* lockers were moved. (possessive of plural noun *workers*)

To show joint ownership by two or more persons, use the possessive form for the last-named person only. To show individual ownership, use the possessive form for each person's name.

> Ronald and *Joan's* boat badly needed overhauling. (joint ownership)
>
> *Laura's* and *Alice's* term projects are almost completed. (individual ownership)

Hyphenated nouns form the possessive by adding *'s* to the last word.

> My *mother-in-law's* house is next to mine.

Never use an apostrophe with the possessive pronouns *his, hers, whose, its, ours, yours, theirs.*

> This desk is *his;* the other one is *hers.* (no apostrophes needed)

Contractions.   Contractions of words or numbers omit one or more letters or numerals. An apostrophe shows exactly where the omission occurs.

> *Wasn't* that a disappointing concert? (contraction of *was not*)
>
> Around here, people still talk about the blizzard of *'79.* (contraction of 1979)

Don't confuse the contraction *it's,* meaning *it is* or *it has,* with the possessive pronoun *its,* which should never have an apostrophe. If you're puzzled by an *its* that you've written, try this test. Expand the *its* to *it is* or *it has* and see whether the sentence still makes sense. If it does, the *its* is a contraction and needs the apostrophe. If the result is nonsense, the *its* is a possessive pronoun and does not get an apostrophe. Here are some examples.

> *Its* awfully muggy today.
>
> *Its* been an exciting trip.
>
> Every dog has *its* day.

The first example makes sense when the *its* is expanded to *it is.*

> *It is* awfully muggy today.

The second also makes sense when the *its* is expanded to *it has.*

> *It has* been an exciting trip.

Both of these sentences therefore require apostrophes.

It's awfully muggy today.

It's been an exciting trip.

The last sentence, however, turns into nonsense when the *its* is expanded.

Every dog has *it is* day.
Every dog has *it has* day.

It this case, the *its* is a possessive pronoun and requires no apostrophe.

Every dog has *its* day.

Plurals. To improve clarity, the plurals of letters, numbers, symbols, and words being singled out for special attention are written with apostrophes.

Mind your *p*'s and *q*'s. (plurals of letters)
Your *5*'s and *6*'s are hard to tell apart. (plurals of numbers)
The formula was sprinked with Π's and Σ's. (plurals of symbols)
Don't use so many *however*'s and *therefore*'s in your writing. (plurals of words)

Apostrophes are often used to form the plurals of abbreviations.

How many rpm's does this shaft turn at? (plural of abbreviation for revolutions per minute)

When no danger of confusion exists, an *s* alone will suffice.

During the late 1960s, many university students demanded changes in academic life.

Supply apostrophes where necessary to correct the following sentences.

EXERCISE

1. The automobile accident happened in front of Tom and Margarets house.
2. Too many *and*s weaken a persons writing.
3. Dan mowed two neighbors lawns and weeded one neighbors garden.
4. When everyones going on a trip, somebodys got to take responsibility for the arrangements.
5. Lets leave the gifts in the childrens room.
6. Kens embarrassment was due to his borrowing his teachers pen and losing its cap.
7. How many *t*s are in your history teachers name?
8. Its clear that this book is on its way to becoming a best-seller.
9. For Petes sake, havent you heard the news about Julie?
10. Eloises costume outshone all her companions costumes.

HYPHENS

Hyphens (-) are used to join compound adjectives and nouns, compound numbers and word-number combinations, and certain prefixes and suffixes to the words with which they appear. In addition, hyphens help prevent mis-readings and awkward combinations of letters or syllables.

Compound Adjectives and Nouns. Hyphens are often used to join separate words that function as single adjectives and come before nouns. Typical examples follow.

> Howard is a very *self-contained* person.
>
> The *greenish-yellow* cloud of chlorine gas drifted toward the village.
>
> Betty's *devil-may-care* attitude will land her in trouble someday.

When the first word of the compound is an adverb ending in *-ly* or when the compound adjective follows the noun it modifies, no hyphen is used.

> The *badly* burned crash victim was rushed to the hospital.
>
> The color of the chlorine gas was *greenish yellow.*

When two or more compound adjectives modify the same last term, the sentence will flow more smoothly if that term appears just once, after the last item in the series. The hyphens accompanying the earlier items in the series are kept, however.

> Many seventeenth-, eighteenth-, and nineteenth-century costumes are on display in this museum.

Hyphenated nouns include such expressions as the following:

secretary-treasurer	good-for-nothing
sister-in-law	man-about-town

Here is a sentence with hyphenated nouns.

> Denton is *editor-in-chief* of the largest newspaper in this state.

Compound Numbers and Word–Number Combinations. Hyphens are used to separate two-word numbers from twenty-one to ninety-nine and fractions that have been written out.

> Marcy has worked twenty-one years for this company.
>
> One-fourth of my income goes for rent.

Similarly, hyphens are used to separate numerals followed by units of measurement.

> This chemical is shipped in 50-gallon drums.

Prefixes and Suffixes.   A prefix is a word or set of letters that precedes a word and alters its meaning. A suffix is similar but comes at the end of the word. Although most prefixes are not hyphenated, the prefixes *self-* and *all-* do get hyphens, as does the suffix *-elect* and the prefix *ex-* when it accompanies a noun.

> This stove has a *self-cleaning* oven.
>
> Let Claire Voyant, the *all-knowing* soothsayer, read your future in her crystal ball.
>
> Ethel is the *chairperson-elect* of the club.
>
> Several *ex-teachers* work in this department.

A prefix used before a capitalized term is always hyphenated.

> The *ex-FBI* agent gave an interesting talk on the operations of that agency.

Preventing Misreadings and Awkward Combinations of Letters and Syllables. Hyphens help prevent misreadings of certain words and also break up awkward combinations of letters and syllables between certain prefixes and suffixes and their core words.

> The doctor *re-treated* the wound with a new antibiotic. (The hyphen prevents the misreading *retreated*.)
>
> The company plans to *de-emphasize* sales of agricultural chemicals. (The hyphen prevents the awkward repetition of the letter *e* in *de-emphasize*.)

Between Syllables.   Whenever you have to split a word between two lines, place a hyphen at the end of the first line to show the division. The word is always broken, and the hyphen inserted, between syllables. (Any good dictionary shows the syllable divisions of each word it includes.) Never divide a one-syllable word or leave two letters to be placed on the second line, even if those two letters constitute a syllable.

Supply hyphens wherever they are necessary. If the sentence is correct, write *C*.   **EXERCISE**

1. The signal had a deep belllike tone.
2. The hostess said there would be a ten to twenty minute wait before we could be seated for dinner.

3. About three fourths of the students who begin our electrical engineering program complete it.
4. Silvano Columbo is the presidentelect of our fraternity.
5. The antidemocratic measures of the new regime soon led to its overthrow.
6. The canary yellow walls of the room provided a sharp contrast to the dark green of the curtains.
7. I plan to take a 60 day cruise to the Far East this summer.
8. At the age of twenty nine, I became a father for the first time.
9. The upholsterer recovered the Victorian sofa in sky blue plush.
10. Many selfemployed people make no financial preparations for their retirement.
11. Mr. Perez is an exstockbroker.
12. Langley has always been a ne'er do well.

CAPITALIZATION

Capitalize the first word in any sentence, the pronoun *I*, proper nouns and adjectives, titles used with—or in place of—names, and the significant words in literary and artistic titles.

Proper Nouns.   A proper noun names one particular person, group of persons, place, or thing. Such nouns include names of the following:

Persons
Organizations
Racial, political, and religious groups
Countries, states, cities, and streets
Companies and buildings
Geographical locations and features
Days, months, and holidays
Trademarks
Languages
Ships and aircraft
Names of academic degrees and the abbreviations for them
Sacred writings and pronouns standing for God and Jesus

The sentences below show the capitalization of proper nouns.

Sigmund works for the *National Psychoanalytical Institute,* an organization which has done much to advance the science of psychiatry.

How much does this roll of *Saran Wrap* cost?

Gwen Greene moved to *Paris, France,* when her father became the *American* consul there.

On *Tuesday, June* 12, 1985, *President Reagan* visited our city.

Larry has a *Master of Arts* degree, and his sister has a *Ph.D.*

My father works for the *Ford Motor Company,* but I work for *Chrysler.*

Do not capitalize words like *institute, college, company,* or *avenue* unless they form part of a proper name. Likewise, do not capitalize the names of non-language courses unless they start a sentence or are accompanied by a course number.

I have a 95 average in *English* 112 but only a 73 average in sociology.

Do you plan to attend *Drew College* or some other college?

Proper Adjectives.   Adjectives created from proper nouns are called proper adjectives. Like the nouns themselves, they should be capitalized.

Lolita Martinez, our class valedictorian, is of *Mexican* ancestry. (*Mexican* is derived from the proper noun *Mexico.*)

Abbreviations.   As a general rule, capitalize abbreviations only if the words they stand for are capitalized.

Milton DeWitt works for the *IRS*. (*IRS* is capitalized because "Internal Revenue Service" would be.)

The flask holds 1500 *cc* of liquid. (The abbreviation *cc* is not capitalized because "cubic centimeters" would not be.)

A few abbreviations are capitalized even though all or some of the words they stand for aren't. Examples include TV (television) and VCR (video cassette recorder). Others are shown on page 427.

Personal Titles.   Capitalize a personal title if it precedes a name or is used in place of a name. Otherwise, do not capitalize.

The division is under the command of *General* Arnold Schafer.

Tell me, *Doctor,* do I need an operation?

The *dean* of our Engineering Division is Dr. Alma Haskins.

Many writers capitalize titles of high rank when they are used in place of names.

The *President* will sign this bill tomorrow.

The president will sign this bill tomorrow.

Either usage is acceptable.

Titles of Literary and Artistic Works. When citing the title of publications, pieces of writing, movies, television programs, paintings, sculptures, and the like, capitalize the first and last words and all other words except *a, an, the,* coordinating conjunctions, and one-syllable prepositions.

> Last week I played *Gone with the Wind* on my VCR and read Christopher Isherwood's *Goodbye to Berlin.* (The preposition *with,* the article *the,* and the preposition *to* are not capitalized.)

> John is reading a book called *The Movies of Abbott and Costello.* (The preposition *of* and the coordinating conjunction *and* are not capitalized.)

> My favorite TV show is "Hill Street Blues." (All the words in the title are capitalized.)

Note that the titles of literary and artistic works are italicized and that the titles of TV programs are set off by quotation marks.

EXERCISE   **Identify any word or abbreviation that should be capitalized in the following sentences.**

1. Jennifer works for the federal housing administration (fha).
2. Let's ask professor Jablonski about this problem.
3. It looks as if the dispute between clarkson university and the nea will have to go to arbitration.
4. The edwardian period of english history (1901–1910) takes its name from king Edward VII, the son of queen Victoria.
5. Tell me, senator, how you'd go about cutting the federal deficit.
6. What is the price of this swingline stapler?
7. When I took english 321, I did my term paper on robert browning's poem *the ring and the book.*
8. The article "japanese and american industry: a comparison" appeared in *the wall street journal.*
9. The present governor of our state is governor helen markus.
10. The brandt corporation has just announced a two-for-one stock split.

ABBREVIATIONS

Items that are abbreviated include certain personal titles, names of organizations and agencies, Latin terms, and scientific and technical terms.

Personal Titles.   Abbreviate *Mister, Doctor,* and similar titles when they come just ahead of a name, and *Junior, Senior,* and degree titles when they follow names.

> Will *Mr.* Harry Babbitt please come to the front desk?

> Arthur Compton, *Sr.,* is a well-known historian; his son, Arthur Compton, *Jr.,* is a television producer.

> This article on marital discord was written by Irma Quarles, *Ph.D.*

Names of Organizations and Agencies.   Many organizations and agencies are known primarily by their initials rather than their full names. Several examples follow.

> AAA   FBI   NBC
> CARE   FHA   NATO
> CIA   IBM   UNESCO

Latin Terms.   Certain Latin terms are always abbreviated; others are abbreviated when used with dates or times.

> e.g. (*exempli gratia:* for example)
> i.e. (*id est:* that is)
> etc. (*et cetera:* and [the] others)
> vs. (*versus:* against)
> A.D. (*anno Domini:* in the year of our Lord)
> A.M. or a.m. (*ante meridiem:* before noon)
> P.M. or p.m. (*post meridiem:* after noon)

> The play starts at 8 *P.M.*

> Many writers (*e.g.,* Dylan Thomas and Truman Capote) have had serious problems with alcohol.

For consistency with A.D., the term "before Christ" is abbreviated as B.C.

Scientific and Technical Terms.   For brevity's sake, scientists and technicians abbreviate terms of measurement that repeatedly occur. Terms that the reader would not know are written out the first time they are used, and they are accompanied by their abbreviation in parentheses. Unfamiliar organizations and agencies that are mentioned repeatedly are handled in like manner.

> The viscosity of the fluid measured 15 centistokes (cks) at room temperature.

Common practice calls for writing such abbreviations without periods unless they duplicate the spelling of some word.

Standard dictionaries list common abbreviations. When you don't recognize one, look it up. Use abbreviations sparingly in essays. If you're unsure about what is appropriate, don't abbreviate.

EXERCISE   **Supply abbreviations wherever they are necessary or are customarily used.**

1. The train is scheduled to pull out at 2:35 *post meridiem.*
2. If you'll remove your shirt, Mister Franklin, I'll check your heart and lungs.
3. The Central Intelligence Agency and the Federal Bureau of Investigation will be getting larger budgets during the next fiscal year.
4. The experiment requires a 500-milliliter flask.
5. My stock in International Business Machines has jumped nine points in the last two days.
6. Doctor Pierre Coeur, Junior, will do the heart transplant.
7. Water freezes at 32° Fahrenheit and 0° Celsius.
8. The Food and Drug Administration is expected to approve a new artificial sweetener soon.
9. Jeremy didn't realize that *exempli gratia* means "for example."
10. The book is coauthored by Sally Westfall, Master of Science, and Amy Gonson, Doctor of Philosophy.

NUMBERS

Some instructors ask their students to use figures for numbers larger than ninety-nine and spell out numbers smaller than one hundred; others prefer that students switch to figures beginning with the number ten. In either case, several exceptions are discussed below.

Numbers in a Series.   Write all numbers in a series the same way regardless of their size.

Gatsby has *64* suits, *110* shirts, and *214* ties.

In just one hour the emergency room personnel handled *two* stabbings, *five* shootings, and *sixteen* fractures.

We have *150* salespeople, *51* engineers, and *7* laboratory technicians.

Dates.   Use figures for dates that include the year.

February 14, 1985 (not February 14th, 1985)

When the date includes the day but not the year, you may use figures or spell out the number.

> June 9
> June ninth
> the ninth of June

Page Numbers and Addresses.   Use figures for page numbers and street numbers in addresses.

> Check the graph on page *415*.
>
> I live at *111* Cornelia Street, and my office is at *620* Fifth Avenue.

Numbers Beginning Sentences.   Spell out any number that begins a sentence. If this requires three or more words, rephrase the sentence so that the number comes after the opening and numerals can be used.

> The year *1980* was a good one for this wine.
>
> *Sixty thousand* fans jammed the stadium.
>
> An army of *265,000* troops assaulted the city. (If this number began the sentence, five words—an excessive number—would be needed to write it out.)

Decimals, Percentages, Times.   Use figures for decimals and percentages as well as for expressions of time that are accompanied by A.M. or P.M.

> The shaft is *0.37-inch* in diameter.
>
> Last year the value of my house jumped *25* percent.
>
> The plane leaves here at *9:50* A.M. and reaches New Orleans at *2:30* P.M.

Identify any miswriting of numbers in the following sentences and rewrite these numbers correctly.   **EXERCISE**

1. During the last two years, Frank has worked 8 months as a checkout clerk in a supermarket, 5 months as a busboy, and six months as a plumber's helper.
2. The *Small Publishers' Directory*, page seventeen, lists the address of the Phoenix Publishing Company as two hundred twenty-three, Fuego Street, Phoenix, Arizona.
3. On June twenty-nine, 1971, I began work for the General Tool and Die Company.
4. The movie begins at eight P.M. on channel 13.
5. For tomorrow, do the exercise on page nineteen of your text.

6. My newest IRA account is earning eight and one half percent interest.
7. On November eleven, 1918, at eleven A.M., the guns fell silent, and World War I came to an end.
8. The outer wall should have a thickness of seventy-five hundredths inch.
9. 500 of our employees face indefinite layoffs within the next month.
10. Nineteen eighty-five did not go at all well for me.

ITALICS

Italics are used for the titles of longer publications, the names of vehicles and vessels, foreign words and phrases, and expressions singled out for special attention. When writing or typing papers, use underlining to represent italics.

Titles of Longer Publications and Artistic Works.   These items may include the following:

books	record albums	long musical works and poems
magazines	paintings	plays
newspapers	movies	sculptures

As noted on p. 417, quotation marks are used for the titles of articles, short stories, short poems, one-act plays, and other brief pieces of writing.

Last night I finished F. Scott Fitzgerald's *The Great Gatsby* and read two articles in *The New Yorker*. (book, magazine)

Michelangelo's *David* is surely one of the world's greatest sculptures. (sculpture)

The *Detroit Free Press* had praise for the revival of Tennessee Williams's play *The Glass Menagerie*. (newspaper, play)

Stephen Vincent Benét's poem *John Brown's Body* won a Pulitzer Prize in 1929. (book-length poem)

Do not use italics when naming the Bible or its parts.

Joanna's favorite book of the Bible is the Book of Ecclesiastes, part of the Old Testament.

Names of Vehicles and Vessels.   Names of particular airplanes, ships, trains, and spacecraft are italicized.

The plane in which Charles Lindbergh flew over the Atlantic Ocean was named *The Spirit of St. Louis*.

Foreign Expressions.   Use italics to identify foreign words and phrases that have not yet made their way into the English language.

> The writer has a terribly pessimistic *weltanschauung*. (philosophy of life)
>
> This season, long skirts are the *dernier cri*. (the latest thing)

When such expressions become completely assimilated, the italics are dropped. Most dictionaries use an asterisk (*), a dagger (†), or other symbol to identify expressions that need italicizing.

Expressions Singled Out for Special Attention.   These include words, letters, numerals, and symbols.

> The Greek letter *pi* is written II.
>
> I can't tell whether this letter is meant to be an *a* or an *o* or this number a *7* or a *9*.
>
> In England, the word *lorry* means truck.

As noted on p. 417, quotation marks sometimes replace italics for this purpose.

Supply italics wherever they are necessary.   EXERCISE

1. His carpe diem philosophy led him to make no financial provision for his future.
2. I subscribe to two publications: the Chicago Tribune and Business Week.
3. When John leaves London for Venice, he'll travel on a famous train, the Orient Express.
4. Yesterday, Althea bought a copy of Miro's painting Fishes.
5. The column As I See Things is the most popular feature of this newspaper.
6. Is this letter supposed to be a q or a g?
7. Tonight, I plan to play a tape of High Noon, my favorite Gary Cooper movie.
8. In a sudden coup d'etat, the army seized control of Gorgistan and ousted the president.
9. When you're at the library, will you please check out a copy of Pride and Prejudice for me?
10. The ship Tropic Seafarer offers several different Caribbean cruises each winter.

"Deer Mom, Wud you belive I lost my job at the offise today? I gess sumwun thair doesnt like me."

From *Recess Time,* The Best Cartoons from *The Kappan,* edited by Kristin Herzog, 1983.

SPELLING

"Why the big deal about accurate spelling?"
"Does it really make that much difference if I have an *i* and an *e* turned around or if I omit a letter when spelling a word?"

Students frequently question the importance of proper spelling. Perhaps the answer is suggested by the following sentence, taken from a student essay:

I spent over seven hours studing one day last week.

The omission of a *y* changes the person from one who is studious to one who is a dreamer. Not only does inaccurate spelling smack of carelessness, but also it sometimes drastically alters meaning.

Although there is no sure-fire way of becoming a good speller, you can minimize the difficulties by learning basic spelling rules, applying helpful spelling tips, and memorizing the proper spelling of troublesome words.

SPELLING RULES

The following four rules should ease spelling pains.

Rule 1.   If a word has the double vowels* *ie* or *ei* and the combination has a long *e* sound (as in *me*), use *ie* except after *c*. If the combination has an *a* sound, use *ei*.

ie (*as long* e)	ei *after* c	ei *as* a
achieve	deceive	freight
belief	receive	neighbor
grieve	receipt	reign
piece	perceive	weigh

The main exceptions to this rule include *either, financier, leisure, neither, seize, species,* and *weird.*

Rule 2.   If a one-syllable word (example: *sin*) ends in a single consonant preceded by a single vowel, double the consonant before adding a suffix (see p. 434) that starts with a vowel. Apply the same rule with a word of two or more syllables (example: *admit*) if the final syllable is accented and ends with a single consonant preceded by a vowel.

Words with Single Syllables	*Words with Two or More Syllables*
rig — rigged	admit — admittance
sin — sinned	control — controller
stop — stopping	equip — equipped

If the accent does not fall on the last syllable, do not double the final consonant.

audit — audited	chatter — chattered
counsel — counselor	simmer — simmering

Rule 3.   If a word ends in *y* preceded by a single consonant, change the *y* to an *i* unless you are adding the suffix *-ing.*

y *changed to* i	y *retained*
beauty — beautiful	busy — busying
busy — business	defy — defying
easy — easily	dry — drying
vary — various	vary — varying

*The vowels are *a, e, i, o,* and *u.* The consonants are the remaining letters of the alphabet.

Rule 4.   If a word ends in a silent *e*, the *e* is usually dropped when a suffix starting with a vowel is added.

blue — bluish   fame — famous
dense — density   grieve — grievous

In a few cases, the *e* is retained to avoid pronunciation difficulties or confusion with other words.

dye — dyeing (not dying)   singe — singeing (not singing)
shoe — shoeing (not shoing)

The *e* is also retained when it is preceded by a soft *c* sound (pronounced like the letter *s*) or a soft *g* sound (pronounced like the letter *j*) and the suffix being added starts with an *a* or an *o*.

peace — peaceable   courage — courageous
change — changeable   manage — manageable

HELPFUL SPELLING TIPS

Here are some tips that can further improve your spelling.

1. Examine each problem word carefully, especially prefixes (*au*dience, *au*dible), suffixes (superintend*ent*, descend*ant*), and double consonants (sate*ll*ite, room*m*ate, and co*ll*apsible).
2. Sound out each syllable carefully, noting its pronunciation. Words like *height, governor,* and *candidate* are often misspelled because of improper pronunciation.
3. Make a list of your problem words and review them periodically. Concentrate on each syllable and any unusual features (ar*c*tic, ambig*uous*).
4. Use any crutches that will help: there is *gain* in *bargain*; to *breakfast* is to *break a fast*; a disease causes *dis-ease*).
5. When you copy anything from the blackboard or a textbook, copy it carefully. Writing a word correctly helps you to spell it correctly the next time.
6. Buy a good collegiate dictionary and look up the words you don't know how to spell. (See pp. 202-204 for more information on dictionaries.)

LIST OF TROUBLESOME WORDS

Students frequently misspell the words in the following list. Study these words carefully until the correct spelling becomes automatic. Then have a friend read them to you while you write them down. Tag the ones you misspell, and whenever you revise a paper check especially for these words.

abbreviate
absence
absorb
absorption
absurd
academy
accelerate
accept
access
accessible
accident
accidentally
accommodate
accomplish
accumulate
accustom
achieve
achievement
acknowledge
acknowledgment
acquaintance
acquire
acquit
acquitted
address
advice
advise
aerial
aggravate
aggravated
aggression
aggressive
aging
alcohol
allege
alleviate
alley(s)
allot
allotted
allowed
all right
already
although
altogether
always
amateur

ambiguous
among
analysis (analyses)
analyze
anonymous
anxiety
apartment
apparent
appearance
appreciate
appropriate
architecture
arctic
argue
arguing
argument
arithmetic
ascent
assassin
assent
assistance
assistant
athlete
athletics
attempt
attendance
average
bachelor
balance
balloon
barbarous
barbiturate
beautiful
beggar
believe
beneficial
benefit
benefited
biscuit
boundary
bourgeois
breathe
Britain
bulletin
bureau
bureaucracy

business
cafeteria
calendar
camouflage
campaign
candidate
carburetor
carriage
carrying
casual
category
causal
ceiling
cellar
cemetery
changeable
changing
characteristic
chauffeur
chief
colloquial
colonel
column
commission
commit
commitment
committed
committee
committing
comparatively
competent
competition
concede
conceive
condemn
condescend
confident
connoisseur
conqueror
conscience
conscientious
conscious
consistency
consistent
conspicuous
contemptible

continuous	dissatisfied	forward
controversy	dissipate	friend
convenience	dominant	fulfill
convenient	drunkenness	gaiety
cooperate	echoes	gases
coolly	ecstasy	gauge
corollary	efficiency	genius
corps	efficient	genuine
corpse	eighth	government
correlate	eligible	grammar
counterfeit	eliminate	guarantee
courteous	embarrass	guard
criticism	emphasis	handkerchief
criticize	employee	harass
cruelty	engineer	height
curiosity	enthusiastic	heroes
curriculum	environment	hindrance
dealt	equal	hygiene
deceit	equip	hypocrisy
deceive	equipment	hysterical
decent	equipped	illiterate
decision	equivalent	illogical
defendant	especially	illusion
defense	exaggerate	immediate
definite	exceed	implement
definitely	excellent	impromptu
dependent	except	inadequate
descent	excerpt	incident
describe	excess	incidentally
description	excitement	independent
desert	exercise	indict
desirable	existence	indispensable
despair	experience	individual
desperate	extremely	inevitable
dessert	extraordinary	infinitely
develop	fallacy	ingenious
development	familiar	ingenuous
difference	fascinate	innocent
dilemma	fascist	intelligent
disappear	February	interest
disastrous	fiery	interfere
discernible	finally	irresistible
disciple	financier	irresponsible
discipline	foreign	jeopardy
discussion	foreword	judgment
disease	forfeit	judicial

knowledge
knowledgeable
laboratory
legitimate
leisure
library
license
lightning
loneliness
loose
lose
magnificent
maintain
maintenance
maneuver
manual
marriage
mathematics
mattress
meant
medicine
medieval
mediocre
melancholy
miniature
minute
miscellaneous
mischievous
misspell
modifies
modify
modifying
moral
morale
mortgage
mosquitoes
muscle
mysterious
necessary
neither
nevertheless
niece
noticeable
obedience
occasion
occasionally

occur
occurred
occurrence
occurring
official
omission
omit
omitted
omitting
opinion
opponent
opportunity
optimistic
original
outrageous
pamphlet
parallel
paralysis
parliament
particularly
pastime
patent
peaceable
perceive
perfectible
perform
permanent
permissible
perseverance
persuade
physical
physician
picnic
picnicked
playwright
pleasant
pleasurable
politician
possess
possession
possible
potatoes
practice
precede
precedent
precious

predominant
preference
preferred
prejudice
preparation
procedure
proceed
privilege
probably
propaganda
procedure
professor
prominent
pronounce
pronunciation
propagate
propeller
prophecy
prophesy
prostate
prostrate
protein
psychiatry
psychology
pursue
pursuit
quantity
questionnaire
quiet
quite
quiz
quizzes
realize
receipt
receive
recipe
recognizable
recommend
refer
reference
referring
reign
relevant
relieve
religious
remembrance

reminisce
reminiscence
reminiscent
rendezvous
repellent
repentance
repetition
representative
resemblance
resistance
restaurant
rhetoric
rhyme
rhythm
roommate
sacrifice
sacrilege
sacrilegious
safety
salary
sandwich
scarcely
scene
scenic
schedule
science
secretary
seize
sensible
separate
sergeant
severely
siege
similar
simultaneous
sincerely
skeptical
skillful
skiing
skis
society
sophomore
source
specifically
specimen
sponsor

spontaneous
statistics
steely
strategy
studying
subtle
subtlety
subtly
succeed
success
successful
succinct
suffrage
superintendent
supersede
suppose
suppress
surprise
syllable
symmetry
sympathize
synonym
synonymous
tangible
tariff
technical
technique
temperament
temperature
temporary
tenant
tendency
thorough
thought
through
traffic
trafficking
tragedy
tranquillity
transcendent
transcendental
transfer
transferred
transferring
translate
tries

truly
twelfth
typical
tyrannical
tyranny
unanimous
unconscious
undoubtedly
unmistakable
unnecessary
until
unwieldy
urban
urbane
usage
useful
using
usual
usually
vacancy
vacillate
vacuum
valuable
vegetable
vengeance
victorious
village
villain
waive
warrant
warring
weather
Wednesday
weird
whether
whole
wholly
wield
wintry
wiry
worshiped
wreak
wreck
writing
written
yield

GLOSSARY OF WORD USAGE

The English language has many words and expressions that confuse writers and thereby lessen the precision and effectiveness of their writing. These troublesome items include:

Word pairs that sound alike or almost alike but are spelled differently and have different meanings

Word pairs that do not sound alike but still are often confused

Words or phrases that are unacceptable in formal writing

The following glossary identifies the most common of these troublemakers. Familiarize yourself with its contents. Then consult it as you revise your writing if you have even the slightest doubt about the proper use of a word, phrase, or expression.

a, an   Use *a* with words beginning with a consonant sound (even if the first written letter is a vowel); use *an* with words beginning with a vowel or a vowel sound.

> *a* brush, *a* student, *a* wheel, *a* risky situation, *a* once-in-a-lifetime oppportunity

> *an* architect, *an* apple, *an* unworthy participant, *an* interesting proposal, *an* honest politician

accept, except   *Accept* is a verb meaning "to receive" or "to approve." *Except* is used as a verb or a preposition. As a verb, *except* means "to take out, exclude, or omit." As a preposition, it means "excluding" or "other than."

> She *accepted* the bouquet of flowers.

> Linda *excepted* Sally from the list of guests. (verb)

> All of Linda's friends *except* Sally came to the party. (preposition)

access, excess   *Access* is a noun meaning "means or right to enter, approach, or use." *Excess* is an adjective meaning "too much; more than needed; lack of moderation."

> I have *access* to a summer cottage this weekend.

> The airline booked an *excess* number of passengers on that flight.

adapt, adopt   To *adapt* is "to adjust," often by modification. To *adopt* is to "take as one's own."

He *adapted* to the higher elevations of the Rocky Mountains.

She *adopted* the new doctrine expounded by the prophet.

adverse, averse   *Adverse* is an adjective meaning "against one's interests." *Averse* is an adjective meaning "disinclined" or "feeling distaste for."

Adverse circumstances caused the ceremony to be postponed.

Martha was *averse* to naming all the guilty children.

advice, advise   *Advice* is a noun meaning "a recommendation about how to deal with a situation or problem." *Advise* is a verb meaning "to recommend or warn."

The young man followed his sister's *advice*.

Mr. Smith *advised* John to buy 10,000 shares of the stock.

affect, effect   Although both words may function as nouns and verbs, usually *affect* is a verb and *effect* is a noun. The verb *affect* means "to influence, cause a change in, or arouse the emotions of." The noun *affect* is a technical term in psychology and refers to feeling. The noun *effect* means "result or outcome." The verb *effect* means "to bring about or achieve."

His speech *affected* me greatly. (verb)

The *effect* of the announcement was felt immediately. (noun)

The doctor was soon able to *effect* a cure. (verb)

aggravate   *Aggravate* is a verb meaning "to intensify or make worse" an existing situation. The use of *aggravate* to mean "annoy' or "anger" is colloquial.

Colloquial: Susan's behavior at the dance really *aggravated* me.

Standard English: Marcy's interference only *aggravated* the conflict between Bill and Nadine.

ain't   This nonstandard term for *isn't* or *aren't* is unacceptable in college writing.

all ready, already   *All ready* means "completely prepared" or "everyone is ready." *Already* means "previously, even now, even then."

The scouts are *all ready* for the camp out.

When we arrived we found he had *already* gone.

The report is *already* a week overdue.

all right, alright   *Alright* is a nonstandard spelling of *all right* and is not acceptable in college writing.

all together, altogether   *All together* means "all in one place." *Altogether* is an adverb meaning "completely, entirely."

> The family was *all together* at the wedding.

> Mr. Doe is *altogether* at fault for writing the letter.

allusion, delusion, illusion   An *allusion* is an indirect reference. A *delusion* is a mistaken belief, often part of a psychological condition. An *illusion* is a deceptive appearance presented to the sight or created by the imagination.

> In his sermon, the minister made many *allusions* to the New Testament.

> He suffers from the *delusion* that he is a millionaire.

> They wore makeup to give the *illusion* of beauty.

a lot, alot   *Alot* is an erroneous spelling of the two words *a lot*. The phrase *a lot* is usually colloquial; avoid it in formal writing.

already   See *all ready, already.*

alright   See *all right, alright.*

altogether   See *all together, altogether.*

among, between   Use *between* when referring to two things and *among* when referring to more than two.

> He divided the candy *between* Allan and Stephanie.

> He divided the candy *among* the five children.

amoral, immoral   *Amoral* means "outside or beyond the moral order or code." *Immoral* simply means "not moral."

> The movie, which takes no clear position on the behavior it depicts, seems curiously *amoral.*

> Murder is an *immoral* act.

amount, number   *Amount* refers to total quantities, things in bulk, or weight. *Number* refers to countable things. Never use *amount* when referring to people.

> Cassandra inherited a large *amount* of money.

> Cassandra now has a large *number* of friends.

an, a   See *a, an.*

and/or   Although often used in commercial and legal documents, this combination should be avoided in other writing.

angry, mad   *Mad* means "insane," although it is often used colloquially to mean "annoyed" or "angry." To be precise, use *mad* only to mean insane.

Colloquial:	I was *mad* at Debbie.
Standard English:	I was *angry* with Debbie.

any, any other   Do not use *any* when you mean *any other*. Using *any* in the following example would mean that Theresa is more qualified than herself.

Theresa is more qualified than *any other* candidate.

appraise, apprise   *Appraise* means "to determine the value of something." *Apprise* means "to notify" or "to tell."

The jeweler *appraised* the gold brooch at $1500.

Having been *apprised* of the situation, the family priest was able to reconcile the parents and the children.

apt, liable, likely   Both *apt* and *liable* express a tendency or inclination. *Liable* suggests something unpleasant or likely to result in legal action. It should be used only when the event may have unpleasant consequences.

We are *liable* to miss the train.

My lawyer said that I was *liable* for the damage my car had caused.

If the probable consequences are not unpleasant, *apt* is the better word.

I am *apt* to buy books if we go to the shopping center.

Likely merely implies strong probability.

Sandra is *likely* to pass this course without any difficulty.

around   *Around* is colloquial use for "approximately" or "about."

Colloquial:	She arrived *around* 10:00 P.M.
	The blouse cost *around* $15.
Standard English:	She arrived at *approximately* 10:00 P.M.
	The blouse cost *about* $15

as   *As* is frequently used as a weak substitute for *because, since, when,* and *while*.

Weak: She ran out of the house *as* it was on fire.

Better: She ran out of the house *because* it was on fire.

As should not be used in place of *whether* or *that*.

Nonstandard:	I don't know *as* I like her.
Standard English	I don't know *that* I like her.
	I don't know *whether* I like her.

as, like   *As* may be used as a conjunction that introduces an adverb clause, but *like* should not be used this way.

Unacceptable:	*Like* my father always said, "You can fool some of the people all of the time."
Standard English:	*As* my father always said, "You can fool some of the people all of the time."

Like may, however, be used as a preposition.

In times *like* this, it's hard not to despair.

Any woman *like* Sally can expect a successful career in business.

assure, ensure, insure   To *assure* is "to make safe from risk, to guarantee" or "to convince." *Ensure* and *insure* can be variant spellings meaning "to make certain." *Insure,* however, is now generally associated with the business of insurance.

The counselor tried to *assure* the students that they had made a wise choice.

The captain *assured* them that they would be rescued.

The father, wanting to *ensure* his son's college education, applied for a federally *insured* loan.

averse   See *adverse, averse.*

awful, awfully   In everyday speech, *awful* is used to describe things disagreeable or objectionable: "an *awful* movie," "an *awful* character." *Awfully* is used colloquially as an intensifier: "*awfully* nice," "*awfully* bad." Unless they are used to mean "solemnly impressive," however, both words should be avoided in formal writing.

The *awful* majesty of the cathedral silenced the chattering tourists.

awhile, a while   *A while,* consisting of the noun *while* and the article *a,* means "a period of time." *Awhile* is an adverb meaning "for a short time."

Dinner will be served in *a while.*

Sit *awhile* and tell me the latest gossip.

bad, badly   *Bad* is an adjective. *Badly* is an adverb. *Badly* is colloquial when used to mean "very much."

Unacceptable:	She feels *badly* about her mistake. Tom behaved *bad* at the circus. I want a new car *badly.*
Standard English:	She feels *bad* about her mistake. (predicate adjective) Tom behaved *badly* at the circus. (adverb) I want a new car *very much.*

being as, being that   When used as substitutes for *because* or *since,* these expressions are nonstandard.

Nonstandard: *Being that* I was the first in line, I was able to purchase choice tickets.

Standard English: *Because* I was first in line, I was able to purchase choice tickets.

beside, besides   Both words are prepositions, but they have different meanings. *Beside* means "at the side of" and *besides* means "in addition to."

Sheila and Bill sat *beside* the trailer to eat their lunch.

Besides Harvey, Seymour is coming to dinner.

between   See *among, between.*

broke   *Broke,* when used to mean "without money," is colloquial.

Colloquial: Because Shelley was *broke,* she had to miss the movie.

Standard English: Because Shelley *had no money,* she had to miss the movie.

can, may   *Can* refers both to permission and to the ability to do something, while *may* refers to permission only.

I think I *can* pass the exam on Friday. (ability)

My mother says I *can* go to the movies. (permission)

May I take the test next Monday? (permission)

When used to denote permission, *can* lends a less formal air to writing than does *may.*

cannot, can not   The use of *cannot* is preferred unless the writer wishes to italicize the *not* for emphasis.

You *cannot* expect a raise this year.

No, you can *not* expect a raise this year.

can't hardly   This nonstandard form for *cannot, can't,* or *can hardly* is unacceptable in college writing.

can't help but   In college writing, this colloquial phrase should be revised to the simpler *I can't help* or *I cannot help.*

Colloquial: I *can't help but* wish that I were going to the concert.

Standard English: I *can't help* wishing that I were going to the concert.

capital, capitol   *Capital* means "a city that serves as a seat of government." *Capitol* means "a building in which a state legislature meets" or "the building in which Congress meets."

Dover is the *capital* of Delaware.

The *capitol* in Dover is popular with visitors.

censor, censure   To *censor* is "to judge"—literature, movies, letters and the like—and to decide what material is unfit to be read or seen. To *censure* is "to judge harshly" or "find fault with."

The warden *censored* all the prisoners' mail.

The judge *censured* Clyde's criminal behavior.

childish, childlike   Both of these terms mean "like a child." *Childish*, however, has a negative connotation.

He is fifty-two years old, but he behaves in a *childish* manner.

Jon's face has a *childlike* quality that everyone likes immediately.

cite, sight, site   *Cite* means "to mention or quote as an example," *sight* means "to see" or "a view," and *site* means "a location."

Cheryl *cited* Abraham Lincoln's Emancipation Proclamation in her talk.

He was able to *sight* the enemy destroyers through the periscope.

The building *site* is a woody area south of town.

climactic, climatic   *Climactic* is an adjective that means "of, being, or relating to a climax." *Climatic* is an adjective meaning "of or relating to a climate."

Riding the roller coaster was the *climactic* event of Alice's day.

The *climatic* features of Arizona are desirable to many people.

complement, compliment   Both words can act as nouns or verbs. As a noun, *complement* means "something that completes or makes up the whole." As a verb, it means "to complete or perfect." As a noun, *compliment* means "a flattering or praising remark." As a verb, it means "to flatter or praise."

A *complement* of navy personnel boarded the foreign freighter. (noun)

This fruit will *complement* the meal nicely. (verb)

Scott paid Sara Jane a lovely *compliment* at the time of her graduation. (noun)

Mother *complimented* me for cleaning my room. (verb)

conscience, conscious   *Conscience* refers to the sense of moral right or wrong. *Conscious* refers to the awareness of one's feelings or thoughts.

Whether or not to have extramarital sex is a matter for the *conscience*.

Basil was not *conscious* of his angry feelings.

Do not confuse *conscious* with *aware;* although these words are similar in meaning, one is *conscious* of feelings or actions but *aware* of events.

contemptible, contemptuous   *Contemptible* means "deserving of contempt." *Contemptuous* means "displaying contempt."

Peter's drunkenness is *contemptible*.

Mary is *contemptuous* of Peter's drunkenness.

continual, continuous   *Continual* means "frequently or regularly repeated." *Continuous* means "uninterrupted."

His telephone seems to ring *continually*.

The flame at the Tomb of the Unknown Soldier burns *continuously*.

could have, could of   *Could of* is an unacceptable substitute for *could have* because a preposition cannot substitute for a verb.

Nonstandard: I *could of* gone with my parents to Portugal.

Standard English: I *could have* gone with my parents to Portugal.

council, counsel   A *council* is a group of people that governs or advises. *Counsel* can be used as both a noun and a verb. The noun means "advice," and the verb means "to advise."

The city *council* meets on the second Tuesday of every month.

The lawyer's *counsel* was sound. (noun)

The psychologist *counsels* many abused children. (verb)

couple   *Couple* denotes two things and should not be used to refer to more than that number.

criteria, criterion   *Criterion* is always singular, *criteria* always plural.

The primary *criterion* for performing this job is manual dexterity.

Manual dexterity is but one of many *criteria* on which you will be judged.

cute   *Cute*, an overused colloquialism, should be avoided; it has too many connotations to be used precisely in writing.

data   *Data* is the plural of *datum*. Therefore use *data* only in the plural.

These *data* are incorrect.

definite, very definite   Since *definite* means "precise" or "unmistakable," *very definite* is repetitive. One really cannot be more definite than *definite*.

delusion   See *allusion, delusion, illusion*.

desert, deserts, dessert   *Desert* is land that is arid. With the accent on the last syllable, it is a verb meaning "to abandon." *Deserts* means "that which is deserved." *Dessert* is food served after dinner.

The Sonoran *desert* is full of plant life.

You'll get your just *deserts* if you *desert* me now.

They had cheesecake for *dessert* every Thursday night.

device, devise   *Device* is a noun meaning "a mechanical contrivance, gadget, or tool." *Devise* is a verb meaning "to plan or invent."

This new *device* gives us better gas mileage.

We must *devise* a new approach to our problem.

different from, different than   *Different from* is preferred over *different than*.

His ideas on marriage were *different from* those of his wife.

Different than is accepted, however, when a clause follows and the *from* construction would be wordy.

Acceptable: Susan looks *different than* she did last summer.

Wordy: Susan looks *different from* the way she looked last summer.

discreet, discrete   To be *discreet* means to be "prudent, tactful, or careful of one's actions." *Discrete* means "distinct or separate."

Jack was always *discreet* when he talked to his grandparents.

When two atoms of hydrogen are combined with one atom of oxygen, they are no longer *discrete* entities.

disinterested, uninterested   A person who is *disinterested* is impartial or unbiased. A person who is *uninterested* is indifferent or not interested.

We need a *disinterested* judge to settle the dispute.

Joe is completely *uninterested* in sports.

don't   This contraction for *do not* should never be used with singular subjects such as *he*, *she*, or *it*. Instead use *doesn't*, the contraction for *does not*, with singular subjects.

Nonstandard: *Don't* he know how to spell?
She *don't* think of anyone except herself.
That mistake *don't* help your image.

Standard English: *Doesn't* he know how to spell?
She *doesn't* think of anyone except herself.
That mistake *doesn't* help your image.

due to   *Due to* has always been acceptable following a linking verb.

Her success was *due to* hard work.

Purists, however, object to *due to* when it is used in other situations, especially in introductory phrases.

> *Due to* the many requests we have had, not everyone who wishes tickets will receive them.

In such cases, it's best to recast the sentence.

> *Because* we have had so many requests, not everyone who wishes tickets will receive them.

effect   See *affect, effect.*

e.g.   This abbreviation, from the Latin *exempli gratia,* means "for example." Avoid using it except in comments in parentheses and in footnotes.

elicit, illicit   *Elicit* is a verb that means "to draw forth." *Illicit* is an adjective meaning "not permitted."

> A good professor can always *elicit* responses from students.

> He was engaged in many types of *illicit* activities.

emigrate, immigrate   When people *emigrate,* they move out of a country. When people *immigrate,* they move into a country.

> The family *emigrated* from Poland.

> Many Russians *immigrated* to America.

eminent, imminent   *Eminent* means "prominent," whereas *imminent* means "about to happen."

> Niels Bohr was an *eminent* physicist.

> Our instruments show that an earthquake is *imminent.*

ensure   See *assure, ensure, insure.*

enthuse, enthusiastic   *Enthuse* is a colloquial word and should not be used in place of *enthusiastic.*

> *Colloquial:*   John was *enthused* about the prospects for jobs in his home town.

> *Standard
> English:*   John was *enthusiastic* about the prospects for jobs in his home town.

especially, specially   The term *especially* means "particularly, notably." *Specially* means "for a specific purpose."

> He is an *especially* talented pianist.

> He was *specially* chosen to represent his group.

et al.   This expression, from the Latin *et alii,* means "and others," referring to people. Ordinarily the abbreviation should be used only in footnotes and bibliographic entries.

etc.   This abbreviation, from the Latin *et cetera*, means "and other things" and is used in reference to objects rather than people. It should be avoided except in comments in parentheses or in footnotes. It should never be preceded by *and*.

except   See *accept, except*.

excess   See *access, excess*

explicit, implicit   *Explicit* means "clearly expressed" or "straightforward." *Implicit* means "implied" or "understood without direct statement."

> You must state your needs *explicitly* if you want them fulfilled.

> When I took on the project, I made an *implicit* commitment to see it through.

extant, extent   *Extant* is an adjective meaning "still existing." *Extent* is a noun meaning "scope, size, range, limit."

> The dodo bird is no longer *extant*.

> From Nevada to Colorado is the *extent* of my travels.

farther, further   The traditional distinction is that *farther* refers to physical distance and *further* to distance in time. *Further* is now generally accepted in either context. Only *further* should be used to mean "additional."

> In the race for the Muscular Dystrophy Association, Janet ran *farther* than Cindy.

> If you think *further* on the matter, I am certain we can reach an agreement.

> Let me make one *further* point.

fewer, less   *Fewer* refers to countable items. *Less* refers to quantity or degree.

> Mrs. Smith has *fewer* dogs than cats.

> There is *less* money in Joan's checking account than in Stanley's.

> Jack was *less* ambitious in his later years.

Never use *less* to refer to people.

> *Nonstandard:*   *Less* people were there than I expected.

> *Standard:*   *Fewer* people were there than I expected.

flaunt, flout   To *flaunt* is "to display in a showy way." To *flout* is "to express contempt" or "to show scorn."

> Jay *flaunted* his handsome physique before all his friends.

> Jerrold *flouted* the convention of dressing for dinner by arriving in tennis shoes.

formally, formerly   *Formally* means "according to established forms, conventions, and rules; ceremoniously." *Formerly* means "in the past."

The ambassador *formally* greeted his dinner guests.

Formerly, smallpox was one of our most serious diseases.

funny   *Funny* refers to something that is amusing. It should not be used to mean "odd" or "unusual" in college writing.

Colloquial: I felt *funny* visiting my old fourth-grade classroom.

Standard English: I felt *odd* visiting my old fourth-grade classroom.

further   See *farther, further.*

get   *Get,* in any of its many colloquial senses, should not be used in writing.

Colloquial: Her way of looking at a man really *gets* me.
I'll *get* him if it's the last thing I do.

Standard English: Beth will *get* at least a *B* in this course.

good and   Replace this colloquial phrase with *very.*

Colloquial: She is *good and* tired of the cafeteria food.

Standard English: She is *very* tired of the cafeteria food.

good, well   *Good* should always be used as an adjective, never as an adverb.

Unacceptable: John did *good* on his first test.

Standard English: John is making *good* progress on his report.
John is a *good* student.

Well can be used as an adjective meaning "in good health." Otherwise it should always be used as an adverb.

Last week I had a bad cold, but now I am *well.* (adjective)

John did *well* on his first test. (adverb)

got, gotten   Both are acceptable past-participle forms of the verb *to get.*

had ought, hadn't ought   Both are incorrect in formal writing. The correct forms are *ought* and *ought not.*

I *ought* to start studying.

You *ought not* to cut class again.

hanged, hung   People may be *hanged*. Objects may be *hung*.

> The prisoner was *hanged* at noon.

> Mavis *hung* the picture in the dining room.

hisself, theirself, theirselves   These are nonstandard forms of *himself* and *themselves*.

hopefully   *Hopefully* means "in a hopeful manner." In informal speaking, it is used to mean "it is hoped" or "I hope," but this usage is not correct in formal writing. (Compare this with *carefully*, which means "in a careful manner"; no one uses *carefully* to mean "it is cared.")

> *Colloquial:*   *Hopefully,* it will not rain during the class picnic.

> *Standard*
> *English:*   *Hopefully* I bought a lottery ticket.

hung   See *hanged, hung*.

i.e.   This abbreviation meaning "that is" comes from the Latin *id est*. Avoid using it except in comments in parentheses or footnotes.

if, whether   *If* is used to introduce adverb clauses, where it means "assuming that."

> *If* I finish my report on time, I'll attend the concert with you.

If and *whether* are often used interchangeably to introduce noun clauses that follow verbs such as *ask, say, doubt, know,* and *wonder*.

In formal writing, however, *whether* is preferred.

> *Less Desirable:*   I don't know *if* we'll be able to see the North Star tonight.

> *More Desirable:*   I don't know *whether* we'll be able to see the North Star tonight.

illicit   See *elicit, illicit*.

illusion   See *allusion, delusion, illusion*.

immigrate   See *emigrate, immigrate*.

imminent   See *eminent, imminent*.

immoral   See *amoral, immoral*.

implicit   See *explicit, implicit*.

imply, infer   To *imply* is "to indicate indirectly or give implication." To *infer* is "to conclude from facts, evidence, or indirect suggestions."

> Jack *implied* that he wanted a divorce.

> Doris *inferred* that Jack wanted a divorce.

incidence, incidents   *Incidents* are separate, countable experiences. *Incidence* refers to the rate at which something occurs.

> Two *incidents* during childhood led to her reclusiveness.

> The *incidence* of cancer in Japan is less than in the United States.

incredible, incredulous   *Incredible* means "fantastic, unbelievable." *Incredulous* means "skeptical, disbelieving."

> That she could run so fast seemed *incredible*.

> He was *incredulous* that she could run so fast.

infer   See *imply, infer*.

in regards to   This is an incorrect use of *in regard to*.

insure   See *assure, ensure, insure*.

in terms of   Avoid this vague, overused expression.

> *Vague:*   *In terms of* the price he is asking, I would not recommend purchasing Tom's car.

> *Preferred:*   *Because* of the price he is asking, I would not recommend purchasing Tom's car.

irregardless   This nonstandard form of *regardless* includes the repetitive elements of *ir* and *less*, both of which mean "without."

is when, is where   *Is when* properly refers only to time.

> April *is when* our lilac bush blooms.

Is where properly refers only to place.

> Athens *is where* I met him.

The following sentences are faulty because muckraking is not a place, and an abscess is not a time.

> Muckraking *is where* someone investigates corporate or governmental abuses of power.

> An abscess *is when* some spot in body tissue fills with pus.

These sentences should be rephrased to eliminate the faulty assertion.

> Muckraking is the investigation of corporate or governmental abuses of power.

> An abscess occurs when some spot in body tissue fills with pus.

its, it's   *Its* is a possessive pronoun. *It's* is a contraction of *it is* or *it has*.

> The gold chair was ruined, for someone had torn *its* seat.

> *It's* all I have to offer. (It is all I have to offer.)

> *It's* been a difficult day. (It has been a difficult day.)

There is no correct use for *its'*.

kind of, sort of   In college writing, these are unacceptable substitutes for *somewhat*, *rather*, or *slightly*.

Colloquial:	She is *sort of* angry.
	I am *kind of* glad she went away.
Standard	She is *somewhat* angry.
English:	I am *rather* glad she went away.

When *kind* and *sort* refer to a type, use them with singular nouns and verbs. With their plural forms, *kinds* and *sorts*, use plural nouns and verbs.

Unacceptable:	These *kind* of exams are difficult.
Standard	This *kind* of exam is difficult.
English:	These *kinds* of exams are difficult.

In such constructions, be certain that *kind of* or *sort of* is essential to your meaning. Otherwise, these phrases are unnecessary.

later, latter   *Later* refers to time; *latter* points out the second of two items. If more than two items are listed, use *last* to refer to the final one.

> He arrived at the party *later* than he was expected.

> Although Professors Stein and Patterson both lectured during the course, only the *latter* graded the final exam.

> Of my three cats, Sheba, Tiger, and Spot, only the *last* still needs the vaccination.

lay, lie   *Lie* means "to recline" or "to remain in a particular position." It never takes a direct object. *Lay* means "to place" and always takes a direct object. These verbs are often confused, in part because the past tense of *lie* is *lay*. (The past tense of *lay* is *laid*.)

> If I *lie* here a minute, I shall feel better.

> *Lay* the book on the table, please.

As I *lay* asleep, a robber entered my apartment and stole my stereo.

He *laid* a hand on her shoulder.

leave, let   *Leave* means "to depart," and *let* means "to allow." Never use *leave* when *let* is meant.

Nonstandard: Leave him figure it out alone.

*Standard
English:*   Let him figure it out alone.

lend, loan   Traditionally, *loan* has been classed as a noun and *lend* as a verb. Today, the use of *loan* as a verb is so commonplace that it is accepted as Standard English.

I have applied for a *loan* so that I can buy a car. (noun)

Please *lend* me your class notes. (verb)

Please *loan* me your class notes. (verb)

less   See *fewer, less.*

let   See *leave, let.*

liable   See *apt, liable, likely.*

lie   See *lay, lie.*

like   See *as, like.*

likely   See *apt, liable, likely.*

literally   The word *literally* means "restricted to the exact, stated meaning." In formal writing, use *literally* only with factual statements.

Colloquial: It was 65°, but I was *literally* freezing.

*Standard
English:*   It was 65°, but I was *very cold.*

loan   See *lend, loan.*

loose, loosen, lose   *Loose* can be used as both a verb and an adjective. As a verb, it means "untie or unfasten"; as an adjective, it means "unattached, unrestrained, or not confined." *Loosen* is a verb meaning "undo or ease." *Lose* can be used only as a verb meaning "mislay, fail to win, or unable to maintain."

He *loosed* the restraints on the tiger. (verb)

One should wear *loose* clothing when bowling. (adjective)

When will Mrs. Brady *loosen* control of young Tom?

You would *lose* your nose if it were not attached to your face.

lots, lots of   *Lots* and *lots of* colloquially mean "many, much, a large amount, or a great amount." Avoid these expressions in college writing.

> *Colloquial:*   I've spent *lots of* money in my life.
>
> *Standard English:*   I have spent *much* money in my life.

mad   See *angry, mad.*

many, much   *Many* is used when referring to a certain quantity; *much* is used when referring to an indefinite amount or to abstract concepts.

> There are *many* students in the biology class.
>
> How did Betty learn so *much* in so little time?

may   See *can, may.*

may be, maybe   *May be* is always used as a verb phrase. *Maybe* is an adverb meaning "perhaps."

> I *may be* chairman of the board by next June.
>
> *Maybe* we will see Jim at home.

medium, media   *Medium* is the singular form of this word; *media* is the plural.

> Television is the *medium* I use most to get the news.
>
> The *media* gave extensive coverage to the brain transplant story.

much   See *many, much.*

myself   *Myself* is a reflexive pronoun and cannot substitute for a personal pronoun such as *I* or *me.*

> *Unacceptable:*   Four other students and *myself* founded the club.
>
> *Standard English:*   Four other students and *I* founded the club.

nice   Avoid this trite, ambiguous word in formal writing.

number   See *amount, number.*

of between, of from, off of   Eliminate the unnecessary *of* from these colloquial phrases.

> *Colloquial:*   There was a crowd *of between* three and four thousand people at the contest.
> Get *off of* my property!
>
> *Standard English:*   The crowd at the contest numbered *between* three and four thousand people.
> Get *off* my property!

on account of   This is a nonstandard substitute for *because*.

Nonstandard:	The team was unable to practice *on account of* everyone was still upset over Tuesday's loss.
Standard English:	The team was unable to practice *because* everyone was still upset over Tuesday's loss.

persecute, prosecute   *Persecute* means "to harass persistently because of race, religion, or belief." *Prosecute* means "to bring legal suit against."

Ethnic groups are often *persecuted*.

The company will *prosecute* anyone caught stealing.

personal, personnel   *Personal* is an adjective meaning "private, individual." *Personnel* are the people working in an organization.

Religious preference is a *personal* matter that you do not have to reveal during a job interview.

The *personnel* of the sanitation department will not be involved in the city workers' strike.

plenty   When used as an adverb, *plenty* should be replaced by *very*.

Colloquial:	That geology exam was *plenty* hard.
Standard English:	That geology exam was *very* hard.

precede, proceed   *Precede* means "to go before or ahead of." *Proceed* means "to go on" or "to go forward."

The ritual of sharpening his pencils always *preceded* doing his homework.

The guide then said, "If you will *proceed*, I will show you the paintings by da Vinci."

predominant, predominate   *Predominant* is an adjective meaning "chief, main, most frequent." *Predominate* is a verb meaning "to have authority over others."

The *predominant* European influence on South American culture was Spanish.

In America, the will of the people *predominates*.

presently   *Presently* means "soon" rather than "at the present time." *Currently* is preferred for the second meaning.

I will be there *presently*.

Currently, I am otherwise engaged.

principal, principle   *Principal*, which means "chief," "most important," or "the amount of money on which interest is computed," is used as both a noun and an adjective. *Principle* is used only as a noun and means "truths, beliefs, or rules generally dealing with moral conduct."

> The *principal* suspect in the case was arrested last Friday by the police.

> The *principal* of Lewiston High School is Alison Cooperstein.

> At this interest rate, your *principal* will double in ten years.

> His *principles* are unconventional.

proceed   See *precede, proceed.*

prosecute   See *persecute, prosecute.*

quiet, quite   *Quiet* is an adjective meaning "silent, motionless, calm." *Quite* is an adverb meaning "entirely; to a considerable extent or degree."

> The class grew *quiet* when the teacher walked in.

> He is *quite* wrong.

> The movie was *quite* good.

real, really   *Real* is an adjective; *really* is an adverb.

> She had *real* plants decorating the bedroom.

When used as an adverb, *real* is a colloquialism and should be replaced with *really.*

> *Colloquial:*   We had a *real* good time at the party.

> *Standard English:*   We had a *really* good time at the party.

reason is because, reason is that   The *reason is because* is colloquial and unacceptable in formal writing; the *reason is that* is the preferred usage.

> *Colloquial:*   The *reason is because* I love her.

> *Standard English:*   The *reason is that* I love her.

respectfully, respectively   *Respectfully* means "with respect." *Respectively* indicates that the items in one series are related to those in a second series in the order given.

> Joseph should treat his parents *respectfully.*

> Tom, Anna, and Susan were assigned *Bleak House, Great Expectations,* and *Dombey and Son, respectively,* for their reports.

sensual, sensuous   *Sensual* refers to bodily or sexual sensations. *Sensuous* refers to impressions or experiences through the five senses.

Singles bars offer *sensual* pleasures without emotional commitments.

The Tivoli Garden provides many *sensuous* delights for visitors.

set, sit   Generally, *set* means "to place" and takes a direct object. *Sit* means "to be seated" and does not take a direct object.

Alice *set* her glass on the mantel.

May I *sit* in this chair?

When it refers to the sun or a hen, however, *set* is used without a direct object.

As the sun *set,* we turned homeward.

Hens *set* on eggs to hatch them. (*Sit* may also be used here.)

should have, should of   *Should of* is an unacceptable substitute for *should have* because a preposition cannot substitute for a verb.

Nonstandard: I *should of* gone to the lake.

Standard
English: I *should have* gone to the lake.

[sic]   This Latin word, always enclosed in brackets, follows quoted errors in grammar, spelling, or information. Inclusion of [sic] indicates that the error appeared in the original, which is being quoted exactly.

sight   See *cite, sight, site.*

sit   See *set, sit.*

site   See *cite, sight, site.*

so   *So* is an acceptable coordinating conjunction but tends to add an informal effect to writing and should therefore be used sparingly. For example, "Tom said he was divorcing me, *so* I began to cry" would be more effective if restated as follows: "When Tom said he was divorcing me, I began to cry." Do not use *so* as a substitute for *extremely* or *very.*

Colloquial: You are *so* careless in what you say.
The discussion was *so* informative.

Standard   You are *very* careless in what you say.
English: The discussion was *extremely* informative.

some   *Some* is colloquial and unacceptable in writing when used as an intensifier (We had *some* time of it!) or an adverb (He'll probably pout *some* after you leave).

sometime, some time, sometimes   *Sometime* means "at a future unspecified time," *some time* means "a span of time," and *sometimes* means "occasionally."

We should get together *sometime* and play bridge.

The weather has been hot for *some time*.

Sometimes I go to dinner with Ethel.

sort of   See *kind of, sort of*.

specially   See *especially, specially*.

stationary, stationery   *Stationary* means "not moving" or "fixed." *Stationery* means "paper for writing letters."

> The circular part in the center must remain *stationary,* or the machine will not function.

> Sue always writes on scented *stationery*.

such, such . . . that   The use of *such* when it means "very" or "extremely" is unacceptable unless it is followed by a *that* clause completing the thought.

> *Colloquial:*   They were *such* good cookies.
>
> *Standard
> English:*   They were *such* good cookies *that* I asked Steve for his recipe.

sure, surely   *Sure* is colloquial for the adverb *surely*.

> *Colloquial:*   You *sure* know how to make good coffee, Mrs. Olsen.
>
> *Standard
> English:*   You *surely* know how to make good coffee, Mrs. Olsen.

Although *surely* is correct, it may sound too formal and insincere. Therefore *certainly* is often a better word to use.

take and, try and   Avoid these expressions. Simply eliminate them from the sentence, or substitute *try to* for *try and*.

> *Unacceptable:*   If you *take and* cover the tomato plants, they probably won't freeze.
> I think you should *try and* settle your differences.
>
> *Standard
> English:*   If you cover the tomato plants, they probably won't freeze.
> I think you should *try to* settle your differences.

than, then   *Than* is used to make comparisons; *then* means "at that time, in that case."

> Jill is taller *than* her brother.

> First we will eat, and *then* we will discuss business.

that, which   These two words have the same meaning. *That* may refer to both persons and things; *which,* only to things. When referring to things, *that* is generally used with clauses that distinguish the things they modify from others in the same class (restrictive clauses). *Which* is generally used with clauses that add information about the things they modify (nonrestrictive clauses).

Any book *that* she likes is certain to be trashy. (restrictive clause)

The Winthrop Building, *which* cost two million dollars to construct, could not now be duplicated for ten times that much. (nonrestrictive clause)

See pages 409–410 of the Handbook for a fuller explanation of restrictive and nonrestrictive expressions.

their, there, they're   These three separate words are often confused because they sound alike. *Their* is the possessive form of *they*. *There* is an expletive that appears at the beginning of a sentence and introduces the real subject, or it is an adverb meaning "in or at that place, at that point." *They're* is a contraction of *they are*.

It is *their* basketball.

There are many reasons why I cannot come.

Put the sofa down *there*.

They're going to be here soon.

theirself, theirselves   See *hisself, theirself, theirselves*.

then   See *than, then*.

there   See *their, there, they're*.

they're   See *their, there, they're*.

thorough, through   *Thorough* means "careful, complete, exact, painstaking." *Through* means "in one side and out the other, from end to end, from start to finish, over the whole extent of, finished."

Brenda has done a *thorough* job.

Let's run *through* the plan again.

thusly   *Thusly* is a nonstandard form of *thus*.

to, too, two   *To* is a preposition meaning "as far as, toward, until, onto." *Too* is an adverb meaning "excessively" or "also." *Two* is a number.

I'm going *to* the store.

Are you going *too*?

This car is *too* expensive for me.

There are *two* characters in the play.

toward, towards   Both forms are correct. *Toward* generally is used in the United States and *towards* in England.

try and   See *take and, try and.*

two   See *to, too, two.*

uninterested   See *disinterested, uninterested.*

unique   *Unique* means "without an equal" or "extremely unusual" and thus should not be modified by an adverb such as *very.*

use to, used to   *Use to* is the nonstandard form of *used to.* In speech it is difficult to hear the *d* on *used,* and one may say *use to* without being detected; however, the written form is always *used to.*

used to could   This phrase is nonstandard for *used to be able to.*

> *Nonstandard:*   I *used to could* run ten miles.
>
> *Standard*
> *English:*   I *used to be able to* run ten miles.

very definite   See *definite, very definite.*

way, ways   *Ways* may be used to refer to two or more means or methods but not to time or distance.

> *Unacceptable:*   Final examination week is a long *ways* off.
> Timbuktu is a long *ways* from the United States.
>
> *Standard*   There are two *ways* of thinking about that issue.
> *English:*   Final examination week is a long *way* off.
> Timbuktu is a long *way* from the United States.

well   See *good, well.*

were, where   *Were* is the past form of the verb *to be* and is used with *we, you,* and *they. Where* is an adverb or a pronoun meaning "in, at, to, or from a particular place or situation" or "which or what place."

> I'm sorry that you *were* ill yesterday.
>
> Mr. Morris will show you *where* to register.

where . . . at, to   *At* and *to* are unnecessary after *where.*

> *Wordy:*   *Where* are you taking the car *to?*
> *Where* does she live *at?*
>
> *Standard*   *Where* are you taking the car?
> *English:*   *Where* does she live?

whether   See *if, whether.*

which   See *that, which*.

who, whom   In formal writing, *who* should be used only as a subject in clauses and sentences and *whom* only as an object.

Unacceptable:	*Who* are you taking to dinner on Friday?
	I know *who* the boss will promote.
	John is the candidate *whom* I think will be elected.
Standard	*Whom* are you taking to dinner on Friday?
English:	I know *whom* the boss will promote.
	John is the candidate *who* I think will be elected.

See page 397 of the Handbook for a fuller discussion of *who* and *whom*.

who's, whose   *Who's* is a contraction of *who is* or *who has*, and *whose* is the possessive form of *who*.

Who's coming to see us tonight?

I would like to know *who's* been dumping trash in my yard.

Whose book is that?

wise   Do not randomly add *wise* to the ends of nouns. Such word coinings are ineffective.

Ineffective:	Personality*wise*, Sheila is ideal for the job.
Standard	
English:	Sheila has *an ideal personality* for the job.

without   See *unless, without*.

would have, would of   *Would of* is an unacceptable substitute for *would have*. (A preposition cannot substitute for a verb.)

Nonstandard:	I *would of* enjoyed seeing the Picasso exhibit.
Standard	
English:	I *would have* enjoyed seeing the Picasso exhibit.

would have been, had been   When *would* occurs in the main part of a sentence, use *had been* (not *would have been*) in an "if" clause.

Nonstandard:	If the engine *would have been* lubricated, the bearing *would not* have burned out.
Standard	If the engine *had been* lubricated, the bearing *would not* have
English:	burned out.

your, you're   *Your* is a possessive form of *you*; *you're* is a contraction of *you are*.

Where is *your* history book?

Tell me when *you're* ready to leave.

GLOSSARY OF GRAMMATICAL TERMS

This glossary provides a convenient checklist of the grammatical terms used in the Handbook and elsewhere in this text. For a more detailed discussion of each entry, consult the page reference in the parentheses following the entry.

abstract noun   The name of something we can't experience with our five senses. (p. 355)

action verb   Expresses action carried out by the subject of a sentence or a clause. (p. 360)

active voice   The form of a verb indicating that the subject of the sentence performs the action. (pp. 364–365)

adjective   A word that modifies a noun or a pronoun by describing it, limiting it, or otherwise making its meaning more exact. (pp. 369–371)

adjective clause   A subordinate clause that functions as an adjective. (pp. 380–381)

adverb   A word that modifies a verb, an adjective, another adverb, or a whole sentence and generally answers questions such as "how?" "when?" "where?" "how often?" and "to what extent?" (pp. 371–373)

adverb clause   A subordinate clause that functions as an adverb. (pp. 381–382)

antecedent   A word or word group to which a pronoun refers. (p. 389)

appositive   A noun or word group serving as a noun and expanding the meaning of a preceding noun or noun substitute. (pp. 353–354)

article   The words *a, an,* and *the,* which modify nouns and can therefore be considered adjectives. (pp. 369–370)

case   The form of a pronoun that shows whether it is serving as, or accompanying, the subject or some other part of the sentence or is showing possession. (pp. 396–398)

clause   A word group that includes a subject and a predicate. It may or may not express a complete thought. (pp. 379–382)

collective noun   Singular in form but stands for a group or collection of items. (p. 355)

comma splice   The error of using only a comma to join two sentences. (pp. 384–385)

complement   A word or word group that forms part of the predicate and helps complete the thought of the sentence. (pp. 352–353)

concrete noun   Identifies something we can experience with one or more of our five senses. (p. 355)

conjunction   A connecting word that links parts of sentences or whole sentences. (pp. 374–375)

conjunctive adverb   A word or phrase that links elements of equal grammatical rank and shows some relationship—for example, similarity, contrast, or result—between them. (p. 375)

coordinating conjunction   A word that links terms of equal grammatical importance—words, word groups, and simple sentences. (pp. 374–375)

dangling modifier   A word group that lacks clear connection to what it is intended to modify, either because the sentence does not specify what is modified or because the separation between the modifier and what is modified is too great. (pp. 400–401)

demonstrative pronoun   A pronoun that points out things. (p. 358)

dependent clause   See *subordinate clause*. (p. 379)

descriptive adjective   An adjective that names a quality, characteristic, or condition of a noun or pronoun. (p. 369)

direct object   A noun or noun substitute that names whatever receives, or results from, the action of a verb. (p. 352)

faulty comparison   A fault that occurs when a writer or speaker fails to mention one of the items being compared, omits words needed to clarify the relationship between the items, or compares different sorts of items. (pp. 403–404)

first-person   The form of a pronoun that indicates the writer or speaker is talking about himself or herself. (p. 394)

future perfect tense   Shows that an action or a condition will have been completed at some time in the future. (p. 364)

future tense   Indicates that an action will occur or a condition will exist in the future. (p. 363)

gerund   A verb form ending in *-ing* and serving as a noun. (p. 378)

gerund phrase   A phrase that consists of a gerund plus associated words. Like a gerund, it serves as a noun. (p. 378)

helping verb   Accompanies an action or linking verb, giving it a high degree of precision in expressing matters such as time, possibility, and obligation. (p. 361)

hidden antecedent   Takes the form of an adjective rather than a noun. (p. 392)

imperative mood   The form of a verb indicating that the sentence is delivering a command or making a request. (p. 366)

indefinite pronoun   Refers to an unidentified person, place or thing. (p. 359)

independent clause   Expresses a complete thought and can function as a simple sentence. (p. 379)

indicative mood   The form of a verb indicating that the writer regards the statement as a fact. (p. 366)

indirect object   A noun or noun substitute identifying someone or something that receives whatever is named by the direct object. (p. 353)

infinitive   The word *to* plus the base form of a verb *(to hit, to swim)*. Infinitives serve as nouns, adjectives, and adverbs. (p. 378)

infinitive phrase   An infinitive plus associated words. Like an infinitive, it can serve as a noun, adjective, or adverb. (p. 378)

intensive pronoun   Lends emphasis to a noun or pronoun. (pp. 358–359)

interjection   A word used to gain attention or to express strong feeling. (p. 376)

interrogative pronoun   Introduces a question. (pp. 357–358)

intransitive verb   An action verb that has no direct object. (p. 360)

limiting adjective   Identifies or points out the noun it modifies. (p. 369)

linking verb   Shows existence—what someone or something is, was, or will be—rather than action. (p. 361)

main clause   See *independent clause*. (p. 379)

misplaced modifier   A word group that is improperly separated from the word it modifies. (pp. 398–400)

modal auxiliary   A helping verb that is used to express a wish, probability, possibility, requirement, recommendation, suggestion, or condition contrary to fact. (pp. 367–368)

mood   The form of a verb that indicates whether the writer regards a statement as a fact; a command or request; or a wish, possibility, condition contrary to fact, or the like. (pp. 366–368)

nonparallelism   A fault that results from the use of different grammatical forms to express equivalent ideas. (pp. 401–403)

noun   A word that names a person, place, thing, condition, idea, or quality. (pp. 354–356)

noun clause   A subordinate clause that functions as a noun. (pp. 379–380)

object complement   A noun or an adjective that follows a direct object and renames or describes it. (p. 353)

participle   A verb that is used to form the perfect (pp. 363–364) and progressive (p. 364) tenses and that can serve as an adjective. (p. 377)

participal phrase   A participle plus associated words. Like a participle, it serves as an adjective. (p. 377–378)

passive voice   The form of a verb indicating that the subject of the sentence is acted upon. (p. 365)

past perfect tense   Indicates that a past action was completed or a past condition ended before or after another past action or condition. (p. 364)

past tense   Shows that an action was completed or a condition existed in the past. (p. 363)

person   The form of a pronoun that reveals whether the speaker or writer is referring to himself or herself, addressing someone directly, or referring to one or more other persons. (p. 394)

personal pronoun   Refers to one or more clearly identified persons, places, and things. (pp. 356–357)

phrase   A group of words that lacks a subject and a predicate and that serves as a single part of speech. (pp. 376–379)

predicate   The part of a sentence that tells something about the subject and completes the thought of the sentence. (p. 351)

preposition   A word that links its object, a noun or noun substitute, to some other word in the sentence and shows a relationship between them. (pp. 373–374)

prepositional phrase   A preposition with one or more objects and associated words, serving as an adjective or an adverb. (pp. 376–377)

present perfect tense   Shows that a past action or condition, or its effects, continues until the present. (pp. 363–364)

present tense   Denotes present condition, present action, permanent truths, and sometimes action at some definite future time. (p. 363)

progressive tense   Shows action in progress. There is a progressive tense for each of the six basic tenses. (p. 364)

pronoun   A word that takes the place of a noun in a sentence. (pp. 356–360)

reciprocal pronoun   Establishes an interchange of action between two or more parties. (p. 359)

reflexive pronoun   Reverses the action of a verb, making the doer and receiver of the action the same. (p. 359)

relative pronoun   Relates a subordinate clause to the main part of its sentence. (p. 357)

run-on sentence   Two (or more) sentences that are run together with nothing to mark their junction. (pp. 384–385)

second-person   The form of a pronoun indicating that the writer or speaker is addressing someone directly. (p. 394)

sentence fragment   A group of words that fails to qualify as a sentence, but is capitalized and punctuated like one. (pp. 382–384)

subject   The part of a sentence that tells who or what the sentence is about. (p. 351)

subject complement   A noun or an adjective that follows a linking verb and renames or describes the subject. (p. 353)

subjunctive mood   The form of a verb indicating that the sentence is expressing a wish, possibility, condition contrary to fact, or the like. (p. 366–368)

subordinate clause   Does not express a complete thought and cannot stand alone. (p. 379)

subordinating conjunction   A word that links a subordinate clause to an independent clause (simple sentence). (p. 375)

tense   The form of a verb that indicates the time of an action. (pp. 363–366)

third-person   The form of a pronoun revealing that the writer or speaker is referring to someone else rather than writing about himself or herself or addressing someone directly. (p. 394)

transitive verb   An action verb having a direct object that receives or results from the action. (p. 360)

verb   A word that shows action or existence—what something is, was, or will be. (pp. 360–368)

voice   The form of a verb that indicates whether the subject of the sentence performs or receives the action. (pp. 364–366)

Appendix

USING FOOTNOTES OR ENDNOTES
FOR DOCUMENTATION

Some instructors prefer to have their students use footnotes or endnotes for library research papers instead of the 1984 MLA documentation system. This appendix supplies a guide.

HANDLING FOOTNOTES
AND ENDNOTES

Footnotes and endnotes come in two forms—primary and secondary. Use the *primary* form when you first cite a source. Use the *secondary* form for any later citations of that source.

Indicate citations in the text by placing a number, raised one-half space above the line, at the end of the borrowed material. (Some instructors prefer the number on the line, enclosed in parentheses.) Place the same number before the note itself. Number all notes consecutively throughout the entire paper.

Some instructors prefer footnotes at the bottom of the page. If yours does, separate the notes from the text by double-spacing twice before typing the first note. Type the notes single-spaced, and double-space between notes. More commonly, the notes are grouped immediately following the text of the paper and referred to as endnotes. In this case, type the heading *Notes* two inches from the top of the page, so that the reader will not confuse it with your bibliography. Allow four single spaces below the heading *Notes*. Indent the first line of each note five spaces, type its number one-half space above the line, skip a horizontal space, and then begin the note. Double-space each line within and between entries.

HANDLING PRIMARY NOTES

Primary Notes for Books.   The basic note for a book includes:

Name of the author, in normal order
Title of the book, underlined
Place of publication, the publisher (shortened to the essential name), and the date
   of publication, all in parentheses
Page or pages on which cited material appears

A *p.* precedes a citation from one page, and *pp.* precedes one from two or more pages. Add other facts of publication to the basic form as necessary. Use the following examples as models for your own notes, observing punctuation as well as content.

A BOOK WITH ONE AUTHOR:

[1] Max Wilk, Every Day's a Matinee (New York: Norton, 1975), pp. 124-25.

A BOOK WITH TWO AUTHORS:

[2] A. B. Bolt and M. E. Wardle, Communicating with a Computer
(Cambridge, Eng.: Cambridge Univ. Press, 1970), pp. 97-98.

List the authors' names in the order of their appearance on the title page. Indicating the country distinguishes the place of publication from Cambridge, Massachusetts.

A BOOK WITH THREE OR MORE AUTHORS:

[3] Roger William Alder et al., Mechanisms in Organic Chemistry (New
York: Wiley, 1971), p. 159.

A BOOK WITH A CORPORATE AUTHORSHIP:

[4] United Nations, Public Administration Division, Local Government
Training (New York: United Nations, 1968), p. 57.

If no individual author is identified, the name of the group or organization goes in the author slot.

AN EDITION OTHER THAN THE FIRST:

[5] Kate L. Turabian, A Manual for Writers of Term Papers, Theses, and
Dissertations, 4th ed. (Chicago: Univ. of Chicago Press, 1973), p. 74.

A BOOK IN TWO OR MORE VOLUMES:

[6] John D. Hicks et al., <u>History of American Democracy</u> (Boston: Houghton, 1970), II, 73.

Omit the *p.* or *pp.* when the volume number is cited. Use capital Roman numerals for the volume, Arabic for the page.

A REPRINT OF AN OLDER BOOK:

[7] F. O. Matthiessen, <u>American Renaissance: Art and Expression in the Age of Emerson and Whitman</u> (1941; rpt. New York: Oxford Univ. Press, 1970), p. 339.

Detail the particulars of the reprint after citing the original date of publication.

A BOOK WITH AN EDITOR RATHER THAN AN AUTHOR:

[8] James Deetz, ed., <u>Man's Imprint from the Past: Readings in the Methods of Archaeology</u> (Boston: Little, 1971), p. 58.

A BOOK WITH BOTH AN AUTHOR AND AN EDITOR:

[9] Herman Melville, <u>The Confidence Man,</u> ed. Hershel Parker (New York: Norton, 1971), p. 38.

A TRANSLATION:

[10] Simone de Beauvoir, <u>All Said and Done,</u> trans. Patrick O'Brian (New York: Putnam, 1974), p. 88.

AN ESSAY OR CHAPTER IN A COLLECTION OF WORKS BY ONE AUTHOR:

[11] Virginia Woolf, "The Lives of the Obscure," in <u>The Common Reader, First Series</u> (New York: Harcourt, 1925), p. 115.

AN ESSAY OR CHAPTER IN A COLLECTION CONTAINING SEVERAL AUTHORS' CONTRIBUTIONS COMPILED BY AN EDITOR:

[12] Roger Angell, "On the Ball," in <u>Subject and Strategy,</u> ed. Paul Eschholz and Alfred Rosa, 2nd ed. (New York: St. Martin's, 1981), p. 38.

Primary Notes for Periodicals.   The basic note for a periodical includes:

> Name of the author, in normal order
> Title of the article, in quotation marks

Name of the periodical, underlined
Volume number of the periodical
Date of publication, within parentheses
Page or pages on which cited material appears

For periodicals published weekly, monthly, or seasonally in which each issue is paged separately, specify the full date of publication in parentheses. For popular periodicals—those sold on newsstands to the general public—omit the volume number and parentheses and include just the full date. Note these distinctions in the following sample notes.

AN ARTICLE IN A JOURNAL CONSECUTIVELY PAGED THROUGH THE ENTIRE VOLUME:

[1] John A. Alvord, "Literature and Law in Medieval England," PMLA, 92 (1977), 943.

When a volume number is given, omit the *p.* or *pp.*

AN ARTICLE IN A JOURNAL THAT PAGES EACH ISSUE SEPARATELY:

[2] Joel W. Block, "Sodom and Gomorrah: A Volcanic Disaster," Journal of Geological Education, 23 (May 1975), 75.

AN ARTICLE IN A POPULAR MAGAZINE:

[3] Joseph Kraft, "Letter from Saudi Arabia," The New Yorker, 20 Oct. 1975, p. 123.

A SIGNED ARTICLE IN A DAILY NEWSPAPER:

[4] Joyce Walker-Lynn, "The Marine Corps Now Is Building Women, Too," Chicago Tribune, 30 Oct. 1977, Sec. I, p. 5.

If sections are paginated separately, identify the section. Underline the city if it is part of the newspaper's title.

AN UNSIGNED ARTICLE IN A DAILY NEWSPAPER:

[5] "Lawmakers Unite on Mileage Rules," Detroit Free Press, 21 Oct. 1975, Sec. B. p. 3.

Primary Notes for Encyclopedia Articles.   The basic note for an encyclopedia article includes:

Author's name, in normal order
Title of the article, in quotation marks

Name of the encyclopedia, underlined
Year of publication

[1] Harold S. Davis, "Team Teaching," The Encyclopedia of Education, 1974 ed.

For an unsigned article, the citation begins with the title of the article.

[2] "Hydrography," The American People's Encyclopedia, 1965 ed., 479.

Cite the page number following the year if your reference is to a single page of an article covering several pages. If your source is a single-page article, no page number is needed.

HANDLING SECONDARY NOTES

Use secondary notes for second and subsequent citations of a source. Indicating the source with a Latin abbreviation, such as *ibid., loc. cit.,* and *op. cit.,* is no longer recommended. Instead, the note ordinarily consists of the author's last name and the page or pages on which cited material appears. Part of a typical set of primary and secondary notes appears below.

[1] Peter Stansky and William Abrahams, The Unknown Orwell (New York: Knopf, 1972), pp. 31-32.

[2] Robert A. Lee, Orwell's Fiction (Notre Dame, Ind.: Univ. of Notre Dame Press, 1969), p. 5.

[3] Lee, pp. 89-90.

[4] Stansky and Abrahams, p. 123.

[5] Stansky and Abrahams, p. 123.

If your notes include authors with the same last name, use the initials of their first names to distinguish them. Say your sources include a book by Margaret Thornton and a magazine article by William Thornton. Secondary notes for each would be:

[3] W. Thornton, p. 349.

[7] M. Thornton, pp. 47-48.

Similarly, if your notes include several works by the same author, add shortened forms of the titles to secondary notes for that author. Underline shortened book titles and use quotation marks around article and essay titles.

[2] Woolf, "Lives," p. 115.

[4] Woolf, Lighthouse, p. 22.

EXAMPLE PAGE SHOWING CITATION NUMBERS AND FOOTNOTES

5

Traditional medical science has held that, prior to the age of two, children cannot remember anything because of the incomplete development of their nervous systems. A process in which nerve cells are covered by a myelin membrane which protects them and helps messages move along the nerve more quickly has not been completed, and the most crucial physiological development, the growth of connections between brain cells, will require several years.[14] However, new research has found that the absence of myelin slows down conduction of nerve impulses, but it does not prevent them from passing.[15] The importance of the brain's ability to send and receive messages is beyond doubt; and because the unborn child reacts to stimuli, we can conclude that he has the ability to respond and think; therefore, he is conscious and is able to develop a personality.

In contrast to the limited knowledge about the growth of the self and intelligence in the unborn child, much is known about fetal physiological development. We can follow the physical growth of the child from conception to the birth of a fully-formed infant. The development of a baby from an implanted fertilized ovum "occurs at an incredibly fast rate and with bewildering diversity when one remembers its origins as a single cell."[16]

[14]   Edward Tronick and Lauren Adamson, Babies as People (New York: Macmillan, 1980), p. 15.

[15]   Verny, Secret Life, p. 184.

[16]   John T. Queenan, ed. A New Life (New York: Van Nostrand, 1979), p. 46.

EXAMPLE PAGE SHOWING CITATION NUMBERS FOR ENDNOTES

8

Ample evidence exists that Rasputin had very real powers of healing. This power first surfaced when, as a youth, he successfully healed sick animals on his father's farm. His reputation soon spread, and he became the community's faith-healing veterinarian.[22] During his pilgrimages, people were attracted to him because of his ability to heal, and Rasputin obliged the petitioners by praying for them and by offering reassurances that all would be well. Later, people flocked to St. Petersburg to be cured of their ailments. Reports compiled by the Tsar's secret police include long lists of such people. Some had seemingly incurable defects, some were confined to wheel chairs, and others were brought on stretchers. One by one they went in to see Rasputin, and one by one they emerged excited and healed.[23] Finally, there are Rasputin's repeated successes in saving the life of Russia's crown prince.

Rasputin's powers of prophecy and clairvoyance also seem genuine. Like his feats of healing, they first showed themselves during his boyhood. Once, for instance, a villager had his horse stolen, and the men met at the Elfimovich house to discuss the matter. Rasputin, who was sick with a fever, got up and accused one of those present of being the thief. Because the man was well respected, the villagers refused to believe the charge. However, the very next day, the accusation was proved true.[24]

EXAMPLE ENDNOTE PAGES

19

Notes

[1] Walter Terry, "Dance," <u>Saturday Review</u>, 8 July 1978, p. 26.

[2] "Mad Monk's End," <u>Newsweek</u>, 25 June 1962, p. 37.

[3] R. J. Minney, <u>Rasputin</u> (New York: McKay, 1973), p. 134.

[4] Maria Rasputin and Patte Barham, <u>Rasputin: The Man Behind the Myth</u> (Englewood Cliffs, N.J.: Prentice-Hall, 1977), p. 258.

[5] Andrew Ewart, <u>The World's Wickedest Men</u> (New York: Taplinger, 1965), p. 11.

Secondary form of note → [6] Rasputin and Barham, p. 173.

[7] Minney, pp. 3, 11, 12-13, 173.

[8] Robert Massie, <u>Nicholas and Alexandra</u> (New York: Dell, 1967), p. 195.

[9] Heinz Liepman, <u>Rasputin and The Fall of Imperial Russia</u> (New York: Rolton House, 1959), pp. 60-61, 188-89.

[10] Colin Wilson, <u>Rasputin and The Fall of the Romanovs</u> (New York: Farrar, 1964), pp. 39-40.

[11] Liepman, p. 56.

[12] Minney, p. 11.

[13] Wilson, p. 89.

[14] Ewart, p. 193.

[15] Liepman, p. 180.

HANDLING THE BIBLIOGRAPHY

The 1984 guidelines for preparing bibliographical references differ only slightly from the earlier guidelines. Here are the significant changes. See pages 292-296 for full information on constructing a bibliography.

For periodical references, the old system requires a comma after the name of the periodical and another between the date and the page number. The new system omits the first of these commas and replaces the second with a colon. If the first word in the title of a periodical is an article, it is omitted.

OLD SYSTEM

Alvord, John A. "Literature and Law in Medieval England." PMLA, 92 (1977),

941-51.

Kraft, Joseph. "Letter from Saudi Arabia." The New Yorker, 20 Oct. 1975, pp.

111-39.

Walker-Lynn, Joyce. "The Marine Corps Now Is Building Women, Too." Chicago

Tribune, 30 Oct. 1977, Sec. I, p. 5.

NEW SYSTEM

Alvord, John A. "Literature and Law in Medieval England." PMLA 92 (1977):

941-51.

Kraft, Joseph. "Letter from Saudi Arabia." New Yorker 20 Oct. 1975: 111-39.

Walker-Lynn, Joyce. "The Marine Corps Now Is Building Women, Too." Chicago

Tribune 30 Oct. 1977: sec. I 5.

Note that the new system omits the *p.* and *pp.* (page designations) in references to popular magazines and newspapers. These abbreviations have, in fact, been dropped from all citations.

When two or more works by the same author are cited, the author's name is given in only the first entry. This style is common to both systems, but in the old system ten hyphens replace the author's name. In the new system, only three hyphens are typed, followed by a comma instead of a period.

OLD SYSTEM

Barnes, Harry. The Microchip Revolution. New York: Harper, 1979.

----------. The Layman's Guide to Computers. New York: Harper, 1983.

NEW SYSTEM

Barnes, Harry. The Microchip Revolution. New York: Harper, 1979.

---, The Layman's Guide to Computers. New York: Harper, 1983.

Some abbreviations are new. *University* has been shortened from *Univ.* to *U* (no period). *Press* is now abbreviated *P* (without a period). *University Press* is therefore *UP* (no periods).

Index

ACKNOWLEDGMENTS (*continued from p. ii*)

Ray Allen Billington, "The Frontier Disappears," *The American Story*, ed. Earl Schenck Miers (Great Neck, N.Y.: Channel, 1956).

Ray Bradbury, "Scent of Sarsaparilla," from *A Medicine for Melancholy* (Garden City, N.Y.: Doubleday, 1959).

David W. Breneman, "The Outlook for Student Finance," *Change*, Oct. 1978, p. 2.

"The Brink of a Disaster," *America*, March 31, 1979, p. 247.

Claude Brown, *Manchild in the Promised Land* (N.Y.: Macmillan, 1965), p. 304.

James L. Buckley, "Three Cheers for the Snail Darter," *National Review*, September 14, 1979, pp. 1144–45.

The Bureaucrat (Citicorp Publications Unit, 399 Park Avenue, New York, N.Y. 10022). Reprinted by permission. All rights reserved.

Gladys Hasty Carroll, *Sing Out the Glory* (Boston: Little, Brown, and Co., 1958).

John Ciardi, "What Is Happiness?" in *Manner of Speaking* (New Brunswick, N.J.: Rutgers University Press, 1972).

Robert Claiborne, "Future Schlock," *The Nation*, January 25, 1971, p. 117.

Cecil Clutton and John Stanford, *The Vintage Motor-car* (N.Y.: Charles Scribner's Sons, 1955), p. 135.

Judith Coburn, "Dolores Huerta: La Pasionaria of the Farm Workers," *Ms.*, Nov. 1976, pp. 12–13.

Barry Commoner, from *The Politics of Energy*. Copyright © 1979 by Barry Commoner. Reprinted by permission of Alfred A. Knopf, Inc.

Joseph Conrad, *Lord Jim* (N.Y.: Holt, Rinehart and Winston, 1957), p. 13.

"Controlling Phobias Through Behavior Modification," *USA Today*, August 1978.

Kelly Davis, "Health and High Voltage: 765 KV Lines," *Sierra*, July–August 1978.

Vine Deloria, Jr., "Custer Died for Your Sins," *Playboy*, Aug. 1969.

Lester del Ray, *The Mysterious Sky* (N.Y.: Chilton Book Company, 1964).

Magda Denes, *In Necessity and Sorrow: Life and Death in an Abortion Hospital* (N.Y.: Basic Books, 1976), p. xiv.

Robert Dick-Read, *Sanamu: Adventures in Search of African Art* (N.Y.: E. P. Dutton, 1964), pp. 228–29.

Joan Didion, "On Self-Respect," in *Slouching Toward Bethlehem*" (N.Y.: Farrar, Straus and Giroux, 1968), pp. 143–44.

Leo Durocher, *Nice Guys Finish Last* (N.Y.: Simon & Schuster, 1975), p. 54.

Loren Eiseley, "The Judgment of the Birds," in *The Immense Journey* (N.Y.: Random House, 1956), pp. 174–75.

Loren Eiseley, *The Unexpected Universe* (N.Y.: Harcourt Brace Jovanovich, 1969), p. 88.

Marian Engle, review of *The Goddess and Other Women*, by Joyce Carol Oates, *New York Times Book Review*, Nov. 24, 1974, p. 7.

Howard Ensign Evans, *Life on a Little-Known Planet* (N.Y.: E. P. Dutton, 1968), pp. 107–8.

Henry Fairlie, "A Victim Fights Back," *The Washington Post*, April 30, 1978.

Jerry Farber, "The Student as Nigger," in *The Student as Nigger* (N.Y.: Pocket Books, Simon & Schuster, 1970), p. 80.

David Finkelstein, "When the Snow Thaws," *The New Yorker*, Sept. 10, 1979, p. 127.

James F. Fixx, "What Running Can't Do For You," *Newsweek*, Dec. 18, 1978, p. 21. Copyright © 1978, Newsweek, Inc.

Otto Friedrich, "There are 00 Trees in Russia," *Harper's Magazine*, Oct. 1964.

L. D. Hamilton, "Antibodies and Antigens," *The New Book of Knowledge* 1967, I, 317.

S. I. Hayakawa, *Language in Thought and Action*, 3rd ed. (N.Y.: Harcourt Brace Jovanovich, 1972), p. 50.

John Hersey, *Hiroshima* (N.Y.: Modern Library, 1946), p. 4.

Nancy K. Hill, "Scaling the Heights: The Teacher as Mountaineer," *The Chronicle of Higher Education*, June 16, 1980, p. 48.

Thomas Henry Huxley, "A Liberal Education and Where to Find It," *Macmillan's Magazine*, March 17, 1868.

Dina Ingber, "Computer Addicts," *Science Digest*, July 1981.

Washington Irving, "The Spectre Bridegroom," in *Selected Writings of Washington Irving*, ed. Saxe Commins (N.Y.: Modern Library, 1945), p. 53.

Bruce Jackson, "Who Goes to Prison: Caste and Careerism in Crime," *Atlantic Monthly*, Jan. 1966, p. 52.

Robert Jastrow, *Until the Sun Dies* (N.Y.: Norton, 1977).

Samuel Johnson, "Preface to the Plays of William Shakespeare," in *Johnson on Shakespeare*, ed. Arthur Sherbo (New Haven: Yale University Press, 1968), p. 74.

Suzanne Britt Jordan, "That Lean and Hungry Look," *Newsweek*, Oct. 9, 1977, p. 32. Copyright © 1977, Newsweek, Inc.

Vernon E. Jordan, Jr., "The New Negativism," *Newsweek*, Aug. 14, 1978, p. 13. Copyright © 1978, Newsweek, Inc.

Alfred Kazin, excerpt from *A Walker in the City*. Copyright 1951, 1979 by Alfred Kazin. Reprinted by permission of Harcourt Brace Jovanovich, Inc.

Doris Kearns, "Who Was Lyndon Baines Johnson?", from *Lyndon Johnson and the American Dream* (N.Y.: Harper & Row, 1976).

Helen Keller, "Three Days to See," *Atlantic Monthly*, Jan. 1933, p. 35.

John F. Kennedy, "Inaugural Address," Washington, D.C., Jan. 20, 1961.

Martin Luther King, Jr., "I Have a Dream," an address at the Lincoln Memorial, Aug. 28, 1963.

Martin Luther King, Jr., four extracts passim from pp. 83-84, 81, 78, and 85 in "Letter from Birmingham Jail, April 16, 1963" in *Why We Can't Wait* by Martin Luther King, Jr. Copyright © 1963 by Martin Luther King, Jr.

Martin Luther King, Jr., "Pilgrimage to Nonviolence," in *Stride Toward Freedom* (N.Y.: Harper & Row, 1958), p. 84

Marilyn Kluger, "A Time of Plenty," *Gourmet*, Nov. 1976, p. 22.

Pär Lagerkvist, "Father and I," from *The Marriage Feast* (N.Y.: Hill & Wang, 1954). © 1954 by Albert Bonniers Vörlag.

Charles A. Lave, "The Costs of Going 55," *Newsweek*, October 23, 1978, p. 37. Copyright © 1978, Newsweek, Inc.

Robert Lipsyte, *Sports World* (N.Y.: Quadrangle Books, 1975), p. ix.

John Lovesey, "A Myth is as Good as a Mile," *Sports Illustrated*, Nov. 9, 1964.

Marilyn Machlowitz, "Workaholism: What's Wrong with Being Married to Your Work?", *Working Woman*, May 1978, p. 51.

Malcolm X, *The Autobiography of Malcolm X* (N.Y.: Ballantine Books, 1964), p. 171.

Marshall Mandell, "Are You Allergic to Your House?", *Prevention*, Sept. 1979, p. 101.

Marya Mannes, "Wasteland," in *More in Anger* (Philadelphia: J.B. Lippincott, 1958), p. 40.

Margaret Mead, "New Superstitions for Old," from *A Way of Seeing* by Margaret Mead and Rhoda Metraux. Copyright © 1966 by Margaret Mead and Rhoda Metraux.

L. David Mech, "Where Can The Wolves Survive?", *National Geographic*, Oct. 1977, p. 536.

H. L. Mencken, "The Libido for the Ugly." Copyright 1927 by Alfred A. Knopf, Inc., and renewed 1955 by H. L. Mencken. Reprinted from *A Mencken Chrestomathy*, edited and annotated by H. L. Mencken, by permission of the publisher.

Thomas H. Middleton, "The Magic Power of Words," *Saturday Review*, Dec. 11, 1976, p. 90.

Don Ethan Miller, "A State of Grace: Understanding the Martial Arts," *Atlantic Monthly*, Sept., 1980. Reprinted by permission of Candida Donadio & Associates. Copyright © 1980 by Don Ethan Miller.

George Orwell, excerpt from "Shooting an Elephant," in *Shooting an Elephant and Other Essays*, copyright 1950 by Sonia Brownell Orwell; renewed 1978 by Sonia Pitt-Rivers. Reprinted by permission of Harcourt Brace Jovanovich, Inc., and Martin Secker & Warburg, Ltd.

Jo Goodwin Parker, "What Is Poverty?" in George Henderson, *America's Other Children: Public Schools Outside Suburbia* (University of Oklahoma Press, 1971).

Lord Richie-Calder, "The Doctor's Dilemma," *The Center Magazine*, Sept/Oct. 1971.

Bertrand Russell, *The ABC of Relativity* (London: Allen and Unwin, 1965), p. 46–47.

Bertrand Russell, "Respect for Law," *San Francisco Review*, Winter, 1958, pp. 63–65. Reprinted by permission of June Oppen Degnan.

John Ryor, "Save Our Schools," *Today's Education: Journal of the National Education Association*, Sept./Oct. 1978. Used by permission.

Gideon Sjöberg, "The Origin and Development of Cities," *Scientific American*, Sept. 1965, p. 55.

Bernard Sloan, "Old Folks at Home," *Newsweek*, Feb. 12, 1979, pp. 14–15. Copyright © 1979, Newsweek, Inc.

Elliott L. Smith and Andrew W. Hart, *The Short Story: A Contemporary Looking Glass* (N.Y.: Random House, 1981).

C. P. Snow in *The Two Cultures, A Second Look* (Cambridge, England: Cambridge University Press, 1964), pp. 17–18.

Joyce Susskind, "Surprises in a Woman's Life," *Vogue*, Feb. 1979, p. 252.

Barry Tarshis, "Islands of Tennis: Where to Vacation in the Southeast," *Tennis*, April 1977.

Deems Taylor, "The Monster," in *Of Men and Music* (N.Y.: Simon & Schuster, 1965).

Lewis Thomas, *Lives of a Cell: Notes of a Biology-Watcher* (N.Y.: Viking Penguin, 1974).

Mark Twain, *Autobiography* (N.Y.: Harper and Brothers, 1919), pp. 12–13.

Eudora Welty, "A Visit of Charity," from *A Curtain of Green and Other Stories* (N.Y.: Harcourt, 1941, 1969).

Stephen White, "The New Sophistication: Defining the Terms," *Esquire*, July 1961, p. 42.

Tom Wolfe, *The Pump House Gang* (N.Y.: World Journal Tribune, 1966), p. 293.

Orville Wyss and Curtis Eklund *Microorganisms and Man* (New York: John Wiley and Sons, 1971), pp. 232–33.

John V. Young, "When the Full Moon Shines Its Magic over Monument Valley," *New York Times*, March 16, 1969, Section 10, p. 1. Copyright © 1969/1982 by the New York Times Company. Reprinted by permission.

David Zimmerman, "Are Test-Tube Babies the Answer for the Childless?", *Woman's Day*, May 1979, p. 26.

REVISION SYMBOLS

Symbol	Problem	Page
ab	improper abbreviation	426–428
pa agr	faulty agreement of pronoun and antecedent	389–391
sv agr	faulty agreement of subject and verb	386–388
˅ *or apos*	missing or misused apostrophe	419–421
awk	awkward phrasing	
bib	faulty bibliographic form	292–295
cap	capital letter needed	424–426
case	wrong case	396–398
cl	cliché	222–223
⋀ *or com*	missing or misused comma	407–410
cs	comma splice	384–385
comp	faulty comparison	403–404
dm	dangling modifier	400–401
⊙⋅⋅⋅ *or ellip*	missing or misused ellipsis	287–288
frag	sentence fragment	382–383
ital	missing or misused italics	430–431
lc	lowercase (small) letter needed	424–426
ll or lev	wrong level of usage	206–211
log	faulty logic	
mm	misplaced modifier	398–400
num	use numerals	428–429

Symbol	Problem	Page
nsu	nonstandard usage	
¶	new paragraph needed	
no ¶	new paragraph not needed	
⊙	period needed	405–406
‖ *or para*	nonparallelism	401–402
? *or ques*	missing or misused question mark	406
"/" *or quot*	missing or misused quotation marks	416–418
ref	unclear reference of pronoun to antecedent	391–393
ro	run-on sentence	384–385
; *or sem*	missing or misused semicolon	411–412
sp	spelling error	432–438
p shift	shift in person	394–395
t shift	shift in tense	388–389
sq	squinting modifier	399
t or tense	wrong tense	363–364
trans	poor transition	
vb	wrong verb form	
wdy	wordiness	221–222
ww	wrong word	
∽	delete (omit)	
⋀	material omitted	
⟨?⟩	meaning unclear or word illegible	